AF682264

CHINA'S DEVELOPMENT AND REGULATION OF CROSS-BORDER LISTINGS

This book is the first of its kind to provide a comprehensive, contextualized and current account of China's development and regulation of cross-border listings. As the world's second-largest economy, it is crucial to understand how China regulates the overseas listing of its companies and the opening up of its capital market to foreign companies, particularly at a time of ongoing and escalating geopolitical tensions.

Offering an up-to-date account of the subject, Professor Huang enables readers to gain a holistic and accurate understanding in this area. Providing a contextualized and practical analysis of the subject from a Chinese perspective, he explains not only what the law is but also why the law is the way that it is fundamentally. The book also examines the political, economic and social factors shaping the institutional context in which the law operates, assisting readers in understanding the reasons behind past regulatory actions and predicting future regulatory developments.

ROBIN HUI HUANG is Chair Professor at the Faculty of Law and Courtesy Joint Professor at the Finance Department of the Business School, Chinese University of Hong Kong. As a leading expert on Chinese corporate and financial law, he has held visiting or guest posts at prestigious institutions in China and overseas. He has also served as an expert consultant to international organizations, Chinese courts, regulators of various jurisdictions and the private sector. He has won numerous awards for his scholarship, including the Humanities and Social Sciences Prestigious Fellowship from the HK Research Grants Council and the Outstanding Scientific Research Output Award from the Ministry of Education of the PRC.

"The international financing of Chinese enterprises is an increasingly salient topic for lawyers. This book provides a comprehensive account of the legal issues relating to cross-border listings by Chinese enterprises. Robin Hui Huang is a globally recognized expert on these topics and the book will be essential reading for academics and practitioners whose work engages with these issues."

John Armor, Dean and Professor of Law and Finance,
Faculty of Law, University of Oxford

"With this book, Professor Robin Hui Huang begins to blaze a trail that many scholars are destined to follow. Many Chinese companies have chosen to list abroad, either in the US or Hong Kong. What motivates this? What realistically can this strategy achieve? Professor Huang examines both sides of this policy issue with fairness and objectivity. What most distinguishes Professor Huang's book is that it is not written from a predominantly US perspective, but rather is China-centric. He poses and debates the questions facing Chinese regulators: How should they use the new extraterritorial jurisdiction they have been recently given? How should they cooperate with Hong Kong on enforcement and other issues? What should they do when a scandal such as the Luckin Coffee episode threatens to undermine the credibility of Chinese issuers? Should China attempt more strenuously to attract foreign issuers to its market? Professor Huang may be the first to examine these questions at length, but he will not be the last, as many will follow the trail he is opening."

John C. Coffee, Jr., Adolf A. Berle Professor of Law, Columbia Law School

"The book is an invaluable resource for anyone looking for a comprehensive and insightful exploration of the complex world of cross-border listings of Chinese companies. It deftly balances legal analysis with a keen understanding of the institutional framework surrounding these listings."

Eilis Ferran, Professor of Company and Securities Law, Faculty of Law,
University of Cambridge; Provost, Gates Cambridge Trust

"The book combines Professor Robin Hui Huang's deep expertise on the Chinese capital markets, his knowledge of cross-border securities regulation and his sophisticated integration of both empirical and theoretical academic scholarship. It offers a rare English-language window into the complex, continually evolving and economically critical Chinese legal regime. The book will be of great value to investors, policymakers and scholars who will benefit both from the insights about the Chinese markets and the broader application of those insights to capital market regulation in an increasingly global environment."

Jill E. Fisch, Saul A. Fox Distinguished Professor of Business Law,
University of Pennsylvania Law School

"In this book, Professor Robin Hui Huang – one of the world's leading experts on Chinese corporate and financial law – provides a comprehensive and up-to-date account of why and how Chinese firms list overseas, and both Chinese and American attempts to regulate these cross-listed firms. The book is essential reading for academics, policymakers and investors seeking to understand the evolving landscape of overseas listings by Chinese companies. I highly recommend it."

Jesse M. Fried, William Nelson Cromwell Professor of Law,
Harvard Law School

"*China's Development and Regulation of Cross-border Listings* skillfully illuminates how Chinese firms navigate global capital markets. Huang's comprehensive analysis of Chinese regulation of cross-border listings situates evolving legal developments within their distinctive institutional and political economy contexts. The book offers valuable insights for scholars and practitioners engaged in the study, development or enforcement of international securities regulation."

Curtis J. Milhaupt, William F. Baxter–Visa International
Professor of Law, Stanford Law School

CHINA'S DEVELOPMENT AND REGULATION OF CROSS-BORDER LISTINGS

Policies, Practices and Prospects

ROBIN HUI HUANG

The Chinese University of Hong Kong

CAMBRIDGE
UNIVERSITY PRESS

CAMBRIDGE UNIVERSITY PRESS

Shaftesbury Road, Cambridge CB2 8EA, United Kingdom

One Liberty Plaza, 20th Floor, New York, NY 10006, USA

477 Williamstown Road, Port Melbourne, VIC 3207, Australia

314–321, 3rd Floor, Plot 3, Splendor Forum, Jasola District Centre, New Delhi – 110025, India

103 Penang Road, #05–06/07, Visioncrest Commercial, Singapore 238467

Cambridge University Press is part of Cambridge University Press & Assessment, a department of the University of Cambridge.

We share the University's mission to contribute to society through the pursuit of education, learning and research at the highest international levels of excellence.

www.cambridge.org
Information on this title: www.cambridge.org/9781009495974

DOI: 10.1017/9781009495950

© Robin Hui Huang 2026

This publication is in copyright. Subject to statutory exception and to the provisions of relevant collective licensing agreements, no reproduction of any part may take place without the written permission of Cambridge University Press & Assessment.

When citing this work, please include a reference to the DOI 10.1017/9781009495950

First published 2026

Cover image: Shanghai from above. Image by Kla Karava / Moment Open via Getty Images.

A catalogue record for this publication is available from the British Library

Library of Congress Cataloging-in-Publication Data
Names: Huang, Robin Hui, 1976- author
Title: China's development and regulation of cross-border listings : Policies, Practices and Prospects / Robin Hui Huang, The Chinese University of Hong Kong.
Description: Cambridge, United Kingdom ; New York, NY : Cambridge University Press, 2026. | Includes index.
Identifiers: LCCN 2025040868 (print) | LCCN 2025040869 (ebook) | ISBN 9781009495974 hardback | ISBN 9781009495943 paperback | ISBN 9781009495950 epub
Subjects: LCSH: Securities–Listing–China | Going public (Securities)–Law and legislation–China | Corporations, Foreign–Finance–Law and legislation–China | Capital investments–Law and legislation–China | Stock exchanges–Law and legislation–China | Venture capital–Law and legislation–China | Investments, Foreign–Law and legislation–China | Corporations–Investor relations–China
Classification: LCC KNQ1064 .H83 2026 (print) | LCC KNQ1064 (ebook) | DDC 346.51/0922–dc23/eng/20250903
LC record available at https://lccn.loc.gov/2025040868
LC ebook record available at https://lccn.loc.gov/2025040869

ISBN 978-1-009-49597-4 Hardback

Cambridge University Press & Assessment has no responsibility for the persistence or accuracy of URLs for external or third-party internet websites referred to in this publication and does not guarantee that any content on such websites is, or will remain, accurate or appropriate.

For EU product safety concerns, contact us at Calle de José Abascal, 56, 1°, 28003 Madrid, Spain, or email eugpsr@cambridge.org

To my parents

CONTENTS

FIGURES AND TABLES

Figure

Tables

FOREWORD

ANTHONY NEOH, SC
Member of the Hong Kong Bar
Chairman of the Hong Kong Securities and Futures Commission (1995–1998)
Chief Adviser to the China Securities Regulatory Commission (1999–2004)
Architect of the H-Share Legal Framework for Cross-Border Listings (1992)

When I first embarked on designing the legal structure for mainland Chinese enterprises to list in Hong Kong in 1992, the task seemed as daunting as it was historic. China's economic reforms were accelerating, yet its capital markets were at its initial stages of development. The notion of state-owned enterprises (SOEs) accessing international capital markets through Hong Kong – a global financial hub operating under common law – required not just regulatory innovation but a fundamental reimagining of corporate governance, disclosure standards and cross-jurisdictional accountability. Three decades later, Professor Robin Hui Huang's *China's Development and Regulation of Cross-border Listings* arrives as a seminal work that contextualizes this journey, dissects its complexities and illuminates its enduring relevance for global finance as we go forward in the uncharted waters of the current-day world.

The Genesis of Cross-border Listings: A Personal Reflection

The 1993 listing of Tsingtao Brewery as the first H-share company marked a watershed moment. My role in crafting this framework demanded reconciling two distinct paradigms: China's socialist system with its ideology still being articulated was taking its first hesitant steps into the development of a market-driven economy within a closed capital account, and Hong Kong's open economy and internationally aligned regulatory regime underpinned by the common law developed over centuries of international commerce and investment. Key challenges included establishing investor protections for minority shareholders, ensuring SOEs met rigorous disclosure requirements and aligning accounting practices with international norms.

That was the daunting task that faced me and my colleagues from Hong Kong and the Mainland. It was accomplished in six months of meetings, some lasting weeks at a time with some lasting into the early hours of the morning, when concepts of the common law were explained, dissected and then adapted into a system of corporate constitutional documents, listing rules, dispute resolution machinery and regulatory cooperation agreements. It was a herculean task made possible only by a shared deep conviction behind the common goal before us and by the hard work, open-mindedness and talent of those involved. I was the leader on the Hong Kong side. Mr. Sun Shuyi who later became the Head of the Party's Central Finance Group (a position normally held by a Vice-Premier of the State Council) was the leader on the Mainland side. As leaders we had to rely on the people with the talent to make the enterprise work. The key person in this enterprise on the Hong Kong side was Professor Betty Ho, who later became a Chair Professor in the Tsinghua University Law School. Professor Ho was my draftsman of the many documents that had to be hammered out. On the Mainland side, it was Mr. Li Xiao Xue who had to take the drafts discussed and agreed through the vast bureaucracy in the State Council. He later became Vice Chairman of the China Securities Regulatory Commission (CSRC). Both sides were supported by other talented people, among whom was Mrs. Laura Cha, who later became Vice Chairman of the Hong Kong Securities and Futures Commission (HK SFC) and later Vice Chairman also of the CSRC, and still later Chair of the Hong Kong Stock Exchange. On the Mainland side, we had a legal talent recently returned from the United States, Mr. Gao Xiqing, who also later became a Vice Chairman of the CSRC.

As the saying goes, the rest is history. The "legal bridge" that was created facilitated not only capital flows but also a transfer of regulatory wisdom, laying the groundwork for China's subsequent integration into global markets.

As of March 2025, the success of the listings of Mainland enterprises in Hong Kong – numbering about 1,500 companies with a combined market cap exceeding HKD 32 trillion – validated this hybrid model. Yet, as Professor Huang astutely observes, cross-border listings have never been static. They evolved through phases: from SOE privatization in the 1990s to the rise of tech giants such as Tencent and Alibaba, and now to navigating geopolitical tensions and sustainability mandates.

Why This Book Matters

Professor Huang's work stands out for its threefold contributions:

1. **Historical and Analytical Rigor**
   The book meticulously traces the regulatory arc from the H-share framework to today's "Stock Connect" programs and offshore initial

public offerings (IPOs). Huang's analysis reveals how China's regulatory philosophy balances market liberalization with strategic control. His comparative critique of US and EU approaches to extraterritorial jurisdiction (e.g., the Holding Foreign Companies Accountable Act) underscores the fragility of cross-border cooperation in an era of geopolitical strife.

2. **Policy–Practice Nexus**
   Drawing on his dual expertise as a scholar and advisor to regulators, Huang bridges theory with actionable insights. His proposal for a "co-regulatory" model – where home and host jurisdictions share oversight responsibilities – resonates deeply with my own experiences as Chair of the Technical Committee of International Organization of Securities Commissions (IOSCO) and at the CSRC. During my tenure, we grappled with harmonizing China's securities laws with IOSCO and the Organisation for Economic Co-operation and Development (OECD) principles while preserving macroeconomic stability. Huang's framework offers a blueprint for mitigating conflicts in areas such as audit inspections and data localization.
3. **Future-Proofing Regulation**
   Emerging challenges – fintech disruption, environmental, social and governance data (ESG) reporting and cybersecurity risks – demand agile governance. Huang's earlier work on robo-advisors and crypto-assets informs his forward-looking analysis here, particularly on regulating AI-driven disclosures and blockchain-based listings. His call for a "dynamic equivalence" standard, rather than rigid harmonization, reflects lessons from the 2008 financial crisis and recent market volatilities.

A Scholarly Work: A Practitioner's Guide

I have long admired Professor Huang's ability to distill complex regulatory concepts into principled yet pragmatic solutions. This book exemplifies that talent. For instance, his empirical study of shareholder inspection rights in China versus the US (published in the *Vanderbilt Journal of Transnational Law*) is repurposed here to advocate for enhanced minority investor safeguards – a priority I championed during the CSRC's 2002 governance reforms.

Equally compelling is Huang's critique of the "variable interest entity" (VIE) structure, which he argues has outlived its utility amid tightening data security laws. His proposal for a multilateral VIE oversight mechanism – involving CSRC, Hong Kong Exchanges and Clearing Limited (HKEX) and the US Public Company Accounting Oversight Board (PCAOB) – could redefine how emerging markets manage jurisdictional overlaps.

Conclusion: A Prism for Understanding China's Regulatory Odyssey

As China's capital markets mature, their global interconnectedness grows irreversible. Professor Huang's book arrives at a pivotal juncture, offering not just a retrospective but a roadmap. To policymakers, it provides evidence-based strategies for balancing innovation with stability. To practitioners, it demystifies the "black box" of China's regulatory logic. To academics, it sets a new benchmark for interdisciplinary scholarship.

In endorsing this work, I am reminded of Premier Zhu Rongji's admonition during my CSRC tenure: "Reform is a perpetual experiment." Huang's analysis proves that experimentation, when grounded in rigorous scholarship and cross-border dialogue, can yield enduring institutions. This book is more than a legal treatise – it is a testament to the power of regulatory foresight.

FOREWORD

XIQING GAO

Retired Professor, Tsinghua University Law School

Vice Chairman, China Securities Regulatory Commission (1999–2002)

General Counsel, China Securities Regulatory Commission (1992–1995)

Establishing a Market in a Nascent Market Environment

Capital market is a relatively new phenomenon in China, even though there were quite a few stock exchanges in Tianjin and Shanghai over a hundred years ago. Those earlier exchanges were closed down one after another within a few years after the founding of the People's Republic in 1949. The present stock market saw its nascent development in various adventurous cities from the mid-1980s and was formally established in the form of two officially sanctioned stock exchanges in 1990. What has happened in the following thirty-five years is a manifestation of a uniquely omnipotent social system exerting itself to bring a much-needed, utilitarian market mechanism into its ideological framework, or at least have the two mesh with each other. That is a constantly evolving process which often defies the logic observed in the history of most capital markets in the world. The reason is simple: Most capital markets grow organically from the grassroot level of the markets and gradually find regulations coming down on them, due to the excesses of the self-dealing insiders, market manipulators and wild risk-takers. The name of the game in a bottom-up market here is: That which is not prohibited is allowed. The Chinese market, however, is allowed to exist only at the mercy of the government, and in this case, the central government, which, up until now, prohibits everything that is not specifically allowed. It is only by this realization that one can understand the intricacies of the myriads of constantly changing rules that are so elaborately described by Professor Huang.

Cross-border listing, by definition, requires the joint functioning of capital markets in different jurisdictions. It has become a much more common phenomenon over the past half-century, with the rapid development of the post–World War II manufacturing industries and the accompanying growth of capital markets in the developed countries.

China, likewise, despite its relatively new stage of the market, has found insatiable demand for its capital expansion into the global market. This is only natural if one looks at, on the one hand, the tremendous growth of its manufacturing capacity and, on the other hand, the unpredictable regulatory environment and often draconian obstacles for the business enterprises, especially private companies, to overcome for a domestic listing. In the early days (early-and-mid-1990s) of cross-border listings, back-door listings, as those cases were referred to, became a favored channel for the bolder entrepreneurs to get foreign funding without going through the domestic regulatory approval process that was viewed as an impossibility anyways. The central government took a practical approach, namely, choosing some of the biggest SOEs to get listed in the Hong Kong and, tangentially, US markets, thus getting the much-needed funds from international capital markets, while largely ignoring the back-door routes taken by smaller private enterprises. As time goes on and the "back door" seemed to have become an increasingly popular route, which defies bureaucratic authority and dignity, the regulators started to pay more and more attention to this "unacceptable" behavior.

It was relatively easier in the case of Hong Kong, as its government then genuinely wanted to attract Mainland companies for listing in order to change the composition of Hong Kong's capital market. The Memorandum of Understanding (MOU) signed among the two government regulatory agencies and three stock exchanges (Hong Kong, Shanghai and Shenzhen Stock Exchanges) has since become a model document of regulatory cooperation between the CSRC and various foreign regulatory agencies.

Professor Huang invites the reader to pay adequate attention to the broader issue of the institutional environment in which the relevant regulation has been made and enforced. It is worthwhile to look back today at the creation of a joint legal regime acceptable to both the Hong Kong regulators and the Mainland government. It was no small feat to try to bridge some fundamental differences in the interpretation of some legal concepts deeply rooted in common law and the Chinese law that had inherited much of the Civil Law traditions.

Take, for example, the common law concept of fiduciary duty. At the time of negotiations between Hong Kong and Mainland regulators regarding the listing of H-share companies in Hong Kong, there was no formal company law in China. The normative legal document that purported to regulate joint stock companies had just been promulgated a few months before. That document (the "Standard Opinion") required the corporate board members and top executives to bear the duty of 诚信 "honesty and trust," as the term was translated into English. When our counterparties on the Hong Kong side raised one of their greatest concerns in the Chinese law that there was no requirement for the fiduciary duty to be imposed on the corporate boards, I comforted them by saying that there was such a stipulation in the Standard Opinion, because I personally persuaded the drafters of the Standard Opinion to insert that term into the final draft. The problem was only the translation, but not the acceptance of the concept. Then we hit the biggest stonewall by then: how to interpret that term. Our Hong Kong colleagues demanded that a clause be put into the directive document for the Hong Kong listing of Mainland companies that the Chinese term 诚信 "will bear the same meaning as the term *fiduciary duty* under the common law." When I told them that even the Western/Arabic numerals were not allowed to appear in any of the Chinese legal documents, much less any foreign words, they realized how big a gap we were facing then. It is to be commended that our Hong Kong colleagues (Tony Neoh, Laura Cha, Betty Ho, Ken Koo, etc.) made tireless efforts during the following months to have finally come out with a written paragraph distilling the essence of this concept, making it ready to be enacted into the black letter law. That paragraph was included in the laws on both sides, enabling Mainland companies to list in Hong Kong, and Hong Kong investors holding those controlling the listed companies accountable for their fiduciary duties.

This was viewed not only as a technical success bridging the legal gaps, but also a contribution to the common law system, which had never attempted to reduce the voluminous case law concepts into statutory form. It was also hugely significant to me that this concept eventually found its way into the Chinese domestic legal realm, adopted by the corporation law and the CSRC in its regulatory requirements of the listed companies.

Professor Huang's book is an excellent contribution to the understanding of this long and winding journey. It helps the reader not only to see the relevant laws and regulations in their present form, but also to better understand how these rules evolve in a less predictable socio-legal environment unfamiliar to them.

PREFACE

This book is a scholarly exploration of the regulation of Chinese companies' cross-border listings, an issue that has gained increasing significance in recent years.

As the world's second-largest economy, China is the origin of numerous companies aiming for overseas listings. A profound understanding of the regulation of these overseas-listed Chinese companies and its implications for international financial markets is crucial. This has become especially so given that, against the backdrop of the ongoing (and escalating) competition (or confrontation) between China and the United States (US), China has recently made remarkable and substantial changes to its regulatory policies and enforcement approaches regarding overseas-listed companies.

Although there have been some studies on cross-border listings, further research is evidently required. First, existing research on international cross-listings mainly focuses on the US as the host market for cross-listed companies. More attention should be directed toward alternative markets, such as Hong Kong, which has attracted the largest number of overseas-listed Chinese companies. Second, while a small number of studies have begun to examine the cross-border listings of Chinese companies, they have largely become outdated due to recent market and regulatory developments. Finally, existing legal studies are mostly doctrinal, with insufficient consideration given to the broader context of the institutional environment in which relevant regulations are formulated and enforced.

This research gap is more pronounced in the case of books. Despite the obvious importance of the subject matter, there are surprisingly few English-language books in this field. This is likely due to the complexity of the subject, the rapid development of the underlying markets and the inherent difficulty in accessing relevant Chinese materials.

Therefore, this book represents a serious attempt to fill the abovementioned research gap, with several key features that I hope will benefit readers. First, it offers a comprehensive and up-to-date account of the cross-border listings of Chinese companies, enabling readers to gain a holistic and accurate understanding of this important area of law. Second, it provides a context-based and practical analysis of the subject from a Chinese perspective. To this end, the book not only expounds on what the law is but also explains why it is the way it is in the specific context of China. Last, but not least, it goes beyond the letter of the law to examine the political, economic and social factors shaping the institutional context in which the law operates. This can assist readers in understanding the reasons behind past regulatory actions and predicting future regulatory developments.

Certainly, there are numerous issues involved in the cross-border listings of Chinese companies. As a research project, this book will concentrate on controversial and unresolved issues. For example, it will discuss issues such as: why Chinese companies seek cross-border listings, under what circumstances Chinese courts may exercise extraterritorial jurisdiction of securities law to handle issues related to the cross-border listings of Chinese companies, how national security may affect the cross-border listings of Chinese companies, how to address the legality of the variable interest entity (VIE) structure, how the China–US audit oversight disputes may evolve in the future, how to regulate cross-border securities misconduct, whether foreign securities judgments can be recognized and enforced in China and whether China will open its capital markets to allow foreign companies to list.

This book will be of both theoretical and practical value. Theoretically, by examining the unique characteristics of China's legal regime for cross-border listings, it will make a significant contribution to international discussions and debates on this subject. Practically, it will offer policy suggestions to relevant government agencies, regulators and stock exchanges. It will also provide useful information for industry associations and private entities that conduct business with or invest in overseas-listed Chinese companies.

I welcome all comments that may help me improve the book in future editions.

ACKNOWLEDGMENTS

This book represents a significant research achievement of my project (Project No.: CUHK 34000322, titled "Cross-border Listings and Regulatory Responses: Chinese Experiences and International Implications"), which is funded by the Hong Kong Research Grants Council's Humanities and Social Sciences Prestigious Fellowship Scheme. Some parts of this book draw on several articles I have published previously. I am thankful for the permissions granted by the relevant journals, which have enabled me to incorporate these valuable insights into this comprehensive work.

I have greatly profited from the constructive input and comments on the earlier drafts from participants at various conferences held in Hong Kong, Mainland China and the United States. These conferences include, but are not limited to: the 2020 Conference on Securities Regulatory Cooperation for Cross-border Listings and Transactions (hosted online by the Faculty of Law, Chinese University of Hong Kong); the 2021 China Securities Law Society Annual Conference; the 2022 Shenzhen Securities Law Society Inauguration Lecture; the 2024 Shanghai Lu Jia Zui Forum; and the 2025 Conference on Geopolitics and International Finance at the University of Virginia School of Law. Additionally, the earlier drafts were presented and discussed at numerous workshops, such as those at the Tsinghua University Commercial Law Center, the East China University of Political Science and Law Distinguished Scholar Forum, the Shanghai Jiao Tong University Faculty of Law, the Fudan University Faculty of Law, the Distinguished Scholar Forum of the Law School of Shanghai University of Business and Economics, the Distinguished Scholar Forum of Jiangxi University of Finance and Economics and the internal workshop series of the Shanghai Financial Court. These exchanges have been instrumental in refining the content of this book.

I would like to express my sincere gratitude to the editors at Cambridge University Press. Their intelligent and efficient editing has significantly enhanced the quality of the manuscript, ensuring that the ideas are presented in a more polished and accessible manner. I also acknowledge the anonymous reviewers who provided extensive and incisive comments on my book proposal. Their feedback was invaluable in shaping the outline and writing of the text, guiding me to present a more comprehensive and in-depth analysis.

I am also indebted to Charles Chao Wang, Sunny Xiyuan Li, Paul Wai Ho Cheuk, Charles Yue Meng, Haoxi Zhang, Jenny Junyu Sun, Desmond Jiayi Yu, Sabrina Tsun Yee Wang, Cherie Lynn Chung and Christie Lam for their outstanding research assistance. Their efforts have contributed to the comprehensiveness and accuracy of the research in this book. I apologize if I have inadvertently overlooked the names of others who have provided valuable support; their contributions are equally appreciated.

Furthermore, I am deeply grateful to Mr. Anthony Neoh, SC (Chairman of the Hong Kong Securities and Futures Commission from 1995 to 1998; Chief Advisor to the China Securities Regulatory Commission from 1999 to 2004) and Mr. Xiqing Gao (General Counsel of the China Securities Regulatory Commission from 1992 to 1995; Vice Chairman of the China Securities Regulatory Commission from 1999 to 2002). Despite their extremely busy schedules, they took the time to write informative and profound Forewords for this book. In the 1990s, they were both key figures in formulating the legal framework for cross-border listings of Chinese companies. Their collaborative efforts, bringing together the perspectives of Hong Kong and Mainland China, have had a far-reaching impact on this area. It is an honor for this book to feature Forewords from both of them, as it not only enriches the narrative but also reflects the spirit of cooperation that has been crucial in the development and regulation of cross-border listings.

Moreover, I am truly appreciative of the warm and supportive endorsements bestowed by a diverse group of internationally renowned scholars. Their kind words not only validate my efforts but also serve as a great source of encouragement. They are (in alphabetical order by surname):

- John Armor, Dean, Professor of Law and Finance, Faculty of Law, University of Oxford;
- John C. Coffee, Jr., Adolf A. Berle Professor of Law, Columbia Law School;
- Eilis Ferran, Professor of Company and Securities Law, Faculty of Law, University of Cambridge; Provost, Gates Cambridge Trust;

- Jill E. Fisch, Saul A. Fox Distinguished Professor of Business Law, University of Pennsylvania Law School;
- Jesse M. Fried, William Nelson Cromwell Professor of Law, Harvard Law School; and
- Curtis J. Milhaupt, William F. Baxter–Visa International Professor of Law, Stanford Law School.

Last but by no means least, I express my heartfelt gratitude to my family members. Their unwavering love and support have been the bedrock of my journey. This book is a labor of love, and I dedicate it wholeheartedly to them, as a token of my appreciation for their constant presence and understanding.

ABBREVIATIONS

ADR	American Depositary Receipt
ADS	American Depositary Shares
ADT	Average Daily Turnover
AFRC	Accounting and Financial Reporting Council
AICPA	American Institute of Certified Public Accountants
ASEAN	Association of Southeast Asian Nations
BJSE	Beijing Stock Exchange
BRI	Belt and Road Initiative
CAC	Cyberspace Administration of China
CDR	Chinese Depositary Receipt
CEO	Chief Executive Officer
CFIUS	Committee on Foreign Investment in the United States
CIETAC	China International Economic and Trade Arbitration Commission
CII	Critical Information Infrastructure
CIIO	Critical Information Infrastructure Operator
CPA	Certified Public Accountants
CPC	Communist Party of China
CPL	Chinese Civil Procedural Law
CPMFI	Cross-border Market Fraud Initiative
CSRC	China Securities Regulatory Commission
EMMoU	Enhanced Memorandum of Understanding Concerning Consultation and Cooperation and the Exchange of Information
EU	European Union
FDI	Foreign Direct Investment
FIE	Foreign Invested Enterprises
FIRRMA	Foreign Investment Risk Review Modernization Act
FPI	Foreign Private Issuer
FRC	Financial Reporting Council
FTZ	Free Trade Zone
GAAP	US Generally Accepted Accounting Principles
GAPP	General Administration of Press and Publication
GDR	Global Depositary Receipts

GEM	Growth Enterprise Market
HDR	Hong Kong Depositary Receipt
HFCAA	Holding Foreign Companies Accountable Act
HK	Hong Kong
HKEX	Hong Kong Exchanges and Clearing Limited
HKICPA	Hong Kong Institute of Certified Public Accountants
HKSAR	Hong Kong Special Administrative Region
HK SFC	Hong Kong Securities and Futures Commission
IFIAR	International Forum of Independent Audit Regulators
IOSCO	International Organization of Securities Commissions
IPO	Initial Public Offering
JSC	Joint Stock Company
LSE	London Stock Exchange
M&A	Merger and Acquisition
MAD	Market Abuse Directive
MAD II	Second Market Abuse Directive
MII	Ministry of Information Industry
MIIT	Ministry of Industry and Information Technology
MJDS	Multi-jurisdictional Disclosure System
MMoU	Multilateral Memorandum of Understanding Concerning Consultation and Cooperation and the Exchange of Information
MMT	Market Misconduct Tribunal
MOF	Ministry of Finance
MOFCOM	Ministry of Commerce
MoU	Memorandum of Understanding
NAAC	National Archives Administration of China
NDRC	National Development and Reform Commission
NSL	National Security Law
NSR	National Security Review
NYSE	New York Stock Exchange
OECD	Organisation for Economic Co-operation and Development
OTC	Over-the-Counter
PCAOB	Public Company Accounting Oversight Board
POE	Private-Owned Enterprise
PRC	People's Republic of China
PSL	Private Securities Litigation
QDII	Qualified Domestic Institutional Investors
QFII	Qualified Foreign Institutional Investor
QIB	Qualified Institutional Buyer
R&D	Research and Development
RegTech	Regulatory Technology
RQFII	Renminbi Qualified Foreign Institutional Investor

SAFE	State Administration of Foreign Exchange
SEC	US Security and Exchange Commission
SEHK	Stock Exchange of Hong Kong
SFC	Hong Kong Securities and Futures Commission
SFO	Hong Kong's Securities and Futures Ordinance
SME	A Small- to Medium-Sized Enterprise
SOE	State-Owned Enterprise
SOP	Statement of Protocol
SPC	Supreme People's Court
SPV	Special Purpose Vehicle
STAR	Science and Technology Innovation Board
TID	Critical Technologies, Critical Infrastructure and Sensitive Personal Data
TREM	Transaction Reporting Exchange Mechanism
US	United States
UK	United Kingdom
VAM	Valuation Adjustment Mechanism
VIE	Variable Interest Entity
WFOE	Wholly Foreign-Owned Enterprise
WTO	World Trade Organization
WVR	Weighted Voting Right

1

Introduction

1.1 Research Context

Over the past several decades, capital markets have become increasingly globalized, with many companies seeking to be listed in overseas markets. There has been a longstanding debate on the causes and effects of this progressive integration of international financial markets.[1] Major international financial centers, such as the United States (US), the United Kingdom (UK), Hong Kong and Singapore, have engaged in fierce competition to attract cross-border listings of foreign companies. It is widely accepted that one of the key enablers of success in this race is regulation.

As the world's second-largest economy, China is one of the places of origin for most companies seeking overseas listing. At the same time, China has been making efforts to internationalize its capital markets with the view of attracting the listing of foreign companies. Since the early 1990s, a large number of Chinese companies have sought listings in overseas markets, notably the US and Hong Kong, and have come to be known as China Concept Stocks or Red-chip Stocks.[2] These overseas-listed Chinese companies have played a significant role in the host markets. For instance, as of November 2024, Mainland enterprises, which are based in Mainland China and listed in Hong Kong, accounted for 56.1 percent of all listed companies on the Stock Exchange of Hong Kong (SEHK), about 79.3 percent of the total market capitalization and about 90.5 percent of the total turnover value;[3] as of January 8, 2024, there were 265 Chinese companies listed on the US exchanges with a total market

[1] For more details on the debate, see Chapter 3.
[2] For more details on the terms, see Chapter 2.
[3] HKEX, "HKEx Monthly Market Highlights" (November 2024), www.hkex.com.hk/Market-Data/Statistics/Consolidated-Reports/HKEX-Monthly-Market-Highlights?sc_lang=en.

capitalization of $848 billion.[4] Hence, it is important to have a proper understanding of the regulation of these overseas-listed Chinese companies and their implications for the international securities markets.

In light of recent significant developments against the broad background of the ongoing competition (confrontation) between China and the US, the need for a deep, nuanced and contextualized understanding of the regulation of overseas-listed companies has become even greater. On the one hand, the US has adopted new regulatory policies for China-based US-listed companies in the past several years. In April 2020, the scandal of Luckin Coffee was exposed, attracting intense attention to the regulation of US-listed Chinese companies. In the second half of 2020, the US passed the "Holding Foreign Companies Accountable Act," under which US-listed Chinese companies may be delisted from the US securities markets if they fail to meet certain requirements, such as giving US regulators access to their audit working papers in China.[5] This has prompted many US-listed Chinese companies to make a "homecoming" plan to seek cross-listings in Mainland China or Hong Kong.

On the other hand, in the past few years China has also made some significant changes to its regulatory policy and enforcement style toward the overseas listing of Chinese companies. A high-profile example is the case of DiDi, which is a well-known Chinese taxi-hailing company. It was listed in the US in late June 2021, but soon thereafter it was put under a data security and national security investigation. The company ultimately announced a delisting plan in December 2021. More recently, the Chinese regulators have issued a spate of new regulations on the overseas listing of Chinese companies. For instance, on February 17, 2023, the CSRC issued the Interim Measures for the Administration of Overseas Securities Offering and Listing by Domestic Enterprises, introducing a recordation regime for all modes of overseas listing of Chinese companies.[6]

It is thus of both theoretical and practical significance to examine the regulation of cross-border listings from a Chinese perspective.

[4] The US–China Economic and Security Review Commission, "Chinese Companies Listed on Major US Stock Exchanges," January 8, 2024. Back in October 2020, US-listed Chinese companies had a total market capitalization of US$2.2 trillion.

[5] *See* Chapter 7.

[6] Jingnei Qiye Jingwai Faxing Zhengquan he Shangshi Guanli Shixing Banfa (境内企业境外发行证券和上市管理试行办法) [Interim Measures for the Administration of Overseas Securities Offering and Listing by Domestic Enterprises] (issued by the CSRC on February 17, 2023, effective from March 31, 2023).

Theoretically, examining the distinctive features of China's regime for cross-border listings will contribute greatly to international discourse and debate on the issue of cross-border listings. Practically, it will provide policy suggestions to relevant governmental bodies, regulators and stock exchanges in China. It will also assess the implications of the Chinese experiences for foreign jurisdictions, particularly Hong Kong, which has been a major destination for the cross-border listing of Chinese companies. It will also supply useful information for private parties who do business with or invest in Chinese companies listed overseas.

1.2 Research Questions

This book examines several important yet under-studied questions regarding the regulation of cross-border listings of Chinese companies, including: What are the reasons for Chinese companies to seek cross-border listings? What effects does it have on the listed companies and the development of the home and host markets? How has China gradually established and recently strengthened its regime for cross-border listings? What are the factors that have contributed to the constitution of the institutional environment in which China's regime for cross-border listings has been made and enforced? How can the regime be further improved in the future in striking a proper balance between facilitating the overseas listing of Chinese companies and protecting investors and national security interests? How should other jurisdictions, particularly the US and Hong Kong, cope with the issue of regulating cross-border listings through regulatory and judicial cooperation with China?

Although there have been some studies on the issue of cross-border listings, including some of the questions noted above, more research is clearly needed. To start with, existing studies of international cross-listings are mainly focused on the US as the host market, which is understandable due to the leading role of the US securities market. This has prompted suggestions from some commentators to focus more attention on other financial centers, particularly Hong Kong. Indeed, Hong Kong has long been a very popular destination for Chinese companies to seek cross-border listings. There are actually more Chinese companies listed in Hong Kong than those listed in the US, both in terms of the number of companies and the amount of market capitalization. In the context of the US market, a number of theories have been advanced to explain cross-listing, such as the market segmentation theory, the legal bonding theory, the reputational bonding theory and the theory of private benefits of control.[7] However, it is not clear which theory has the most explanatory power for the cross-border listings of Chinese companies, given the unique political economy context in which Chinese companies operate. Conversely, the Chinese experience can contribute to the theoretical debate on the issue of cross-listings. Hence, there is great value in examining the particular case of Chinese companies listing in alternative markets such as Hong Kong.

Second, although a small number of studies have started to examine cross-border listings of Chinese companies, they are largely outdated due to recent market and regulatory developments. As noted in Section 1.1, Chinese authorities have recently issued a string of new regulations in relation to the cross-border listing of Chinese companies. In light of the new developments, there is an urgent need to update the existing literature on the Chinese regulation of cross-border listings, make sense of how the new regulations have changed the regulatory landscape and evaluate its effects on both the local and international markets.

Finally, the existing legal studies are mostly doctrinal, with inadequate attention paid to the broader issue of the institutional environment in which the relevant regulation has been made and enforced. Indeed, apart from the significant changes made to the rules on the books, Chinese regulators have also adopted very different enforcement strategies with a never-before-seen level of vigor. For instance, China adopted stringent enforcement to effectively wipe out the afterschool tutoring industry, causing a violent shock wave to the US securities market where many China-based listed companies, such as New Oriental Education, lost as much as 80–90 percent of their value. The case of DiDi demonstrates how seriously China has now taken the issues of data security and national security. Clearly, there is a great need to examine the enforcement of the Chinese regime for cross-border listings in a systematic way. This entails an empirical study of relevant cases dealt with by the Chinese regulators and courts. At a more fundamental level, there is a need to examine the interaction between the political, economic and social factors which have contributed to the constitution of the institutional environment in which China's regime for cross-border listings has been made and enforced.

In sum, there are significant research gaps in the existing studies in the area, which this book attempts to fill to produce a number of research

[7] For a detailed discussion of these theories, see Chapter 3.

findings which have both theoretical and practical value. While those questions are not easy to answer, this book attempts to take the first step in this area of study. To this end, this research project adopts an interdisciplinary approach and utilizes a mixture of research methods, including theoretical and documentary analysis, comparative analysis and empirical study in the forms of semi-structured interviews and case statistics.

1.3 Research Structure

This book is comprised of eleven chapters as follows. Apart from the Introduction chapter and the Conclusion chapter there are nine substantive chapters which are divided into two parts: Part I (General Legal and Theoretical Framework) consists of Chapters 2–5, while Part II (Specific Regulatory and Practical Issues) is Chapters 6–10.

Chapter 1 is a general introduction to the book. It sets out the research context, key research questions, research methodologies and other relevant information about the book. This sets the stage for the discussion of substantive topics in the following chapters.

Chapter 2 provides an overview of the development and regulation of the overseas listing of Chinese companies. It defines the main modes of overseas listings of Chinese companies, divides the historical development of the overseas-listing market into several stages and discusses how China has gradually established its regulatory regime in this area. It then focuses on the current regime, particularly the uniform filing regime introduced in 2023, including the key elements and their implementation issues. It also conducts an evaluation of the new regime and makes relevant comments. It pays particular attention to the case of DiDi, which serves as a wake-up call that data security and protection have now become increasingly important to the overseas listing of Chinese companies.

Chapter 3 investigates the reasons why many Chinese companies have decided to seek cross-border listings in the past three decades. It examines a variety of relevant theories, such as legal bonding, private benefits and market fragmentation, and evaluates the extent to which they may apply to the case of Chinese companies.

Chapter 4 looks at the issue of extraterritorial jurisdiction of Chinese securities law over Chinese companies listed overseas. In 2019, Chinese securities law was revised significantly to introduce an explicit provision on extraterritorial jurisdiction, but it is not clear how the provision may be applied in practice. In 2020, Luckin Coffee, a China-based US-listed company, was found to have committed serious accounting fraud, which generated an intense discussion on the application of extraterritorial jurisdiction. This chapter will contribute to this discussion and shed light on the future direction of development in this area.

Chapter 5 is focused on the impact of national security review for cross-border listings of Chinese companies within the broader context of foreign investment regulation in China. In the past few years, China has gradually established a comprehensive and stringent regime for national security review.

Chapter 6 is devoted to the topic of Variable Interest Entity (VIE), which is widely used for overseas listings of Chinese companies. The legality of VIE has long been a subject of intense debate in China due to its alleged circumvention of China's foreign investment law. This chapter will look at the debate from a political-economy perspective and shed light on its future development.

Chapter 7 examines audit oversight issues concerning overseas-listed Chinese companies, paying particular attention to the disputes between China and the US. It also discusses how Hong Kong has managed to solve its audit dispute with Mainland China and how it has played an important role in solving the China–US dispute.

Chapter 8 discusses the regulation of market misconduct across borders, such as misstatement, insider trading and market manipulation. It looks at both substantive rules and enforcement mechanisms and then offers suggestions to improve cross-border regulatory coordination.

Chapter 9 examines the issue of whether and how foreign civil judgments against overseas-listed Chinese companies will be recognized and enforced in China. Again, the discussion was triggered by the case of Luckin Coffee because the defendant directors and the main assets of the company were all located in China, and the US court judgment could be meaningless if the defendants refused to cooperate, and Chinese courts refused to recognize and enforce the US judgments. This chapter thus provides an in-depth analysis of China's recognition and enforcement of foreign civil judgments, particularly securities civil judgments, and offers possible solutions to the issue.

Chapter 10 looks at the listing of foreign companies in China, which is the other side of the coin of cross-border listings. Due to the threat of the US Holding Foreign Companies Accountable Act, an increasing number of Red-chip Companies have considered returning to the A-share market. Since 2018, China has tried to establish a regime to accommodate the listing of Red-chip Companies, as part of its long-term plan to internationalize the Chinese capital market by attracting genuine foreign companies to get listed in China.

Chapter 11 concludes with a summarization of relevant research findings and suggestions for improvement. It also identifies a series of questions to be answered by future research.

PART I

General Legal and Theoretical Framework

2

The Evolution of Overseas Listings of Chinese Companies and Regulatory Responses

This chapter discusses the market development of Chinese companies' overseas listings and the gradual establishment of the regulatory regime for them. Particular attention will be paid to the filing system that has recently been introduced for all Chinese companies seeking to list overseas, either directly or indirectly.

2.1 Background Discussion: Terms and Markets

2.1.1 Listing Modes

In general, there are two main modes for Chinese companies to get listed overseas, namely direct listing and indirect listing.

Under the direct listing mode, Chinese companies incorporated within China under the Chinese company law directly issue shares in overseas markets. The shares that are issued overseas by Chinese companies are named after the listing places, such as H shares listed in Hong Kong, N shares in New York and S shares in Singapore. In practice, this mode of listing is mostly used to issue H shares and thus is nicknamed H-share listing. In general, H shares are shares issued by a People's Republic of China (PRC) issuer under PRC law and listed on the SEHK, the par value of which is denominated in Renminbi and which are subscribed for and traded in Hong Kong dollars.[1]

Under the mode of indirect listing, the owners of the Chinese companies will first establish a company in an offshore financial center such as the Cayman Islands and then use it as the listing vehicle to conduct an initial public offering. Alternatively, the offshore company may conduct a reverse takeover of an existing listed company in the overseas markets to achieve the goal of getting itself listed overseas, a process known as

[1] HKEX, *Fact Book 2021*, 354, www.hkex.com.hk/-/media/HKEX-market/market-data/statistics/consolidated-reports/HKEX-fact-book/HKEX-fact-book-2021/fb_2021.pdf.

backdoor listing. As these companies are ultimately owned and controlled by Chinese entities, they are often called "Red-chip Stock" or "China Concept Stock." As will be discussed below, while these two concepts are quite similar, there are also some differences between them.

2.1.2 Red-chip Stock and China Concept Stock

The term "Red-chip Stock" can be used in different senses. In the broad sense, it covers any company that is registered in offshore centers as listing vehicles but is ultimately owned or controlled by Chinese entities and that has their main business or assets inside China. The authorities of Mainland China have used the term in this way.[2] In practice, "Red-chip Stock" companies are further divided into two categories, namely, "Big Red-chip Stock Company" (*Da Hong Chou*) and "Small Red-chip Stock Company" (*Xiao Hong Chou*), depending on whether their controlling shareholders are government-related or private. Specifically, "Big Red-chip Stock Company" refers to companies that are owned or controlled by the Chinese government, while "Small Red-chip Stock Company" means companies owned and controlled by private entities.

In comparison, the Hong Kong Exchanges and Clearing Limited (HKEX) uses the term in a narrow sense. Specifically, "Red-chip Stock" companies are companies domiciled/registered in an overseas jurisdiction such as the Cayman Islands, which have more than 50 percent of total business incomes from Mainland China and which meet one of the following two criteria about controlling shareholders: (1) the company has at least 30 percent shareholding held in aggregate directly by Mainland China entities, and/or through companies which are controlled by Mainland China entities; or (2) the company has below 30 percent but 20 percent or above shareholding held in aggregate directly by Mainland China entities, and/or through companies which are controlled by Mainland China entities and, there is a strong influential presence, on a judgmental basis, on the company's board of directors.[3] Importantly, "Mainland China entities" are narrowly defined to mean state-owned organizations and entities controlled by China's state, provincial or municipal authorities. If the controlling shareholders of the companies are Chinese private entities that are outside the scope of "Mainland China entities," they would fall into the category of "Mainland Private

2 *See* Chapter 10.

3 HKEX, *Fact Book 2021*, p. 353.

Enterprises,"[4] which is sometimes referred to as "P-chip Stock" in practice. In more recent years, Red-chip companies and Mainland China entities have been collectively referred to as Non-H share Mainland enterprises.[5]

The term "China Concept Stock" is more commonly used in the US. This is not an officially defined term, and in practice, it tends to be very broad. For instance, the US–China Economic and Security Review Commission considers a company "Chinese" if (1) it has been identified as being from China by the relevant US stock exchange or (2) it lists a PRC address as its principal executive office in filings with the US Security and Exchange Commission (SEC).[6]

From a comparative perspective, there are similarities and differences among the Mainland-China concept of "Red-chip Stock," the Hong Kong concept of "Red-chip Stock" and the US concept of "China Concept Stock." In general, they are quite similar, as they all refer to companies that come from China with their main business operations located therein but get listed overseas. However, they are different in terms of the scope of companies covered. First, they are used to refer to Chinese companies listed in different markets. For instance, the term "China Concept Stock" generally refers to Chinese companies in the US market, while the Hong Kong concept of "Red-chip" is related to Chinese companies in the Hong Kong market.

Second, and more importantly, the three concepts are different in the way of defining the types of companies to be covered. The US term "China Concept Stock" is the broadest, as it is generally used to refer to any US-listed Chinese company, whether it is technically registered in China or not. In this aspect, it is similar to the Hong Kong concept of "Mainland Enterprises," which includes both H-share companies and Non-H share Mainland enterprises.

The Mainland-China concept of "Red-chip Stock" is narrower, as it excludes companies registered within China, such as H-share companies and N-share companies. However, due to the very small number of N-share companies in practice, there is no substantial difference in the

[4] HKEX, *Fact Book 2021*, p. 1.

[5] HKEX, "HKEX Monthly Market Highlights", www.hkex.com.hk/Market-Data/Statistics/Consolidated-Reports/HKEX-Monthly-Market-Highlights?sc_lang=en.

[6] US–China Economic and Security Review Commission, "Chinese Companies Listed on Major US Stock Exchanges," www.uscc.gov/research/chinese-companies-listed-major-us-stock-exchanges.

scope of companies between the US term "China Concept Stock" and the Mainland-China concept of "Red-chip Stock."

The Hong Kong concept of "Red-chip Stock" is the narrowest, in the sense that it only covers Chinese companies that meet the criteria relating to shareholding thresholds and the identity of controlling shareholders or actual controllers. Specifically, the Hong Kong concept of "Red-chip Stock" corresponds to the subcategory of "Big Red-chip Stock" in Mainland China, while the Hong Kong concept of "Mainland Private Enterprises" or "P-chip Stock" is similar to what is called "Small Red-chip Stock" in Mainland China.

2.1.3 *Market Developments: Four Stages*

The history of the overseas listing of Chinese companies dates back to the early 1990s, which can be broadly divided into four stages.

2.1.3.1 The 1990s: Overseas Listing of Large SOEs

The first stage was in the 1990s when overseas listings were mainly conducted by large state-owned enterprises (SOEs) in the US and Hong Kong. Back then, the newly established Chinese capital market was simply too small to meet the financing needs of many Chinese companies. In October 1992, Brilliance China Jinbei Automotive (*Hua Chen Jin Bei*) successfully got listed on the New York Stock Exchange, marking the first overseas listing of Chinese enterprises.[7] Hong Kong, however, seems to be a more attractive listing place, particularly for state-owned companies. In July 1993, Tsingtao Brewery issued and listed its H shares in Hong Kong, becoming the first Mainland company to get listed in Hong Kong.[8]

During this period, the main force of overseas listings was SOEs, particularly in Hong Kong, reflecting the government-dominant characteristics. The listed entities focused on government-supported infrastructure construction and other industries of SOEs, with most of the listing actions requiring approval from regulatory authorities.

[7] Chen Xilin (陈希琳) and Li Danyang (李丹阳), "Zhonggaigu, Sanshi He Li?" (中概股，三十何立？) [Where Do Chinese Stocks Listed Abroad Stand at 30? An Examination] (2022) 5 *Jingji (经济) [Economy]* 82.

[8] Enoch Yiu, "How Tsingtao's IPO in Hong Kong Turned on the Tap for 30 Years and US$1 Trillion of Chinese Offshore Listings," *South China Morning Post*, July 15, 2023, finance .yahoo.com/news/tsingtaos-ipo-hong-kong-turned-093000183.html.

2.1.3.2 2000–2010: Overseas Listing of Internet Companies

The second stage is the first decade of the new millennium. As the Chinese economic development accelerated in the 2000s, the total number of Chinese companies being listed overseas rose significantly, and non-state-owned Chinese companies started to seek overseas listings. On the one hand, state-owned companies continued to get listed overseas, including China's Big Four state-controlled commercial banks, which produced some of the largest initial public offerings (IPOs) in the world. In late 2001, the Chinese stock market entered into a four-year-long bear market and its financing function was severely affected. Hence, many companies, particularly those large state-owned companies, had to go overseas to do IPOs.

On the other hand, a rapidly growing number of private-owned companies, particularly high-tech companies, emerged into the scene. As the world's high-tech center, the US market witnessed a strong wave of listing of Chinese high-tech or new-economy companies. Due to China's restrictions on foreign investment in certain industries, such as the internet industry, the varied-interest-entity structure (VIE) was invented in the 2000 listing of Sina in the US and later was widely used to facilitate overseas listing of Chinese companies operating in those restricted industries.[9]

2.1.3.3 2010–2020: Overseas Listing of Private Enterprises

The third stage covers the decade of 2010 to 2020, witnessing the peak number of overseas listings of Chinese companies, with private-owned companies overtaking state-owned companies to become the main component of Chinese companies seeking overseas listing. There are many reasons behind this, and one major reason is that the Chinese capital markets were not able to meet the listing needs of many private-owned companies due to the outbreak of various financial crises or market clashes. Although the Chinese securities market did not suffer as seriously as other markets from the global financial crisis of 2008, it was affected in the context of the globalized economy. For instance, the Chinese market suspended all IPO deals from September 16, 2008 to July 10, 2009 and again from November 16, 2012 to December 30, 2013. Further, there was a big market crash in June 2015, and then IPOs in China were suspended from July 4 to November 6, 2015.

[9] For a more detailed discussion of the VIE structure, see Chapter 6.

Up until the fourth stage, which will be discussed below, China had long used the "merits-review regime" for securities offerings. The merits-review system, also known as the approval system (*He Zhun Zhi*), was introduced in 1999 under the first national securities law.[10] The merits-review regime required companies to obtain approval from the national securities regulator, the Chinese Securities Regulatory Commission (CSRC), to conduct IPOs in the Chinese capital markets. When IPOs were permitted to resume in November 2015, the CSRC considered and approved IPO applications at a much slower rate than it previously had, which led to the creation of a large backlog of IPO applications. For instance, there were a total of 801 IPO applications awaiting CSRC approval in the middle of 2016.[11] Under the merits-review system, the regulator would give priority to state-owned companies in assessing IPO applications, and thus, many private-owned companies could not access the Chinese capital markets and had to go overseas.

2.1.3.4 Since 2020: Homecoming of US-Listed Companies

The current fourth stage started in 2020 when the US passed the Holding Foreign Companies Accountable Act (HFCAA), significantly increasing the delisting risk of Chinese companies listed in the US.

Around 2020, some serious accounting frauds perpetuated by US-listed Chinese companies were exposed, such as the high-profile case of *Luckin Coffee*, which caused the US to take a tough stance on the regulation of US-listed Chinese companies, culminating in the passage of the HFCAA.[12] To be sure, these accounting fraud cases are just the last straw that broke the camel's back, and the US policy change is a reflection of the escalating US–China geopolitical tension. Further, those accounting scandals triggered a crisis of confidence in Chinese companies listed in the US, causing their stock prices to fall so significantly as to lose their ability to seek refinancing.

As a result, many US-listed Chinese companies have decided to or planned to return to the Greater China region. While some of them choose to return to China, others come to Hong Kong in different ways,

10 Robin Hui Huang, *Securities and Capital Markets Law in China* (Oxford University Press, 2014), pp. 54–55.

11 上海证券交易所 (Shanghai Stock Exchange), *A股IPO市场年度报告2016 (2016 Annual Report on A Share IPO Market)*, p. 12, www.sse.com.cn/aboutus/research/report/c/10056671/files/4501216951894bc4b1f8fb369cce45da.pdf.

12 For a more detailed discussion of the dispute over audit working papers, see Robin Hui Huang, "The US–China Audit Oversight Dispute: Causes, Solutions, and Implications for Hong Kong" (2021) 54(1) *The International Lawyer* 151.

including (1) delisting from the US and listing in Hong Kong, (2) dual listing in Hong Kong or (3) secondary listing in Hong Kong. At the same time, the number of Chinese companies seeking overseas listings has reduced for two main reasons. On the one hand, as discussed previously, the US has tightened regulation of US-listed Chinese companies, which caused a high level of uncertainty in the market and reduced the incentives for Chinese companies to get listed in the US. On the other hand, China has tried hard to establish the so-called multilayer capital market framework to increase the capacity to cater to the listing needs of Chinese companies, particularly the small, high-tech companies that previously could only go overseas for listing. For instance, in March 2019, China established the Science and Technology Innovation Board (STAR market) in the Shanghai Stock Exchange, introducing the registration-based reform of securities offerings. This reform was later recognized in the 2019 Securities Law, and in June 2020, it was expanded to the Growth Enterprise Market (GEM) of the Shenzhen Stock Exchange. In September 2021, the Beijing Stock Exchange (BJSE) was established as a market for technologically advanced small- and medium-sized enterprises and also implements the registration-based regime of securities offerings. In March 2023, the CSRC rolled out the so-called comprehensive registration reform, extending the reform to cover the whole of the Chinese capital markets. The above measures have enabled the Chinese capital markets to accommodate more listed companies, thus reducing the need for Chinese companies to get listed overseas.

2.2 The Legal Regime: Four Phases

2.2.1 *The 1990s: Approval Requirements for Overseas Listings of SOEs*

2.2.1.1 The 1993 Company Law

SOEs applying for overseas direct listing need approval from relevant departments. Under the 1993 Company Law, with the approval of the securities administration department under the State Council (viz., the CSRC), a joint stock company (JSC) may publicly offer its shares overseas, and the State Council shall formulate special provisions on the specific measures.[13] In June 1993, the CSRC, the Shanghai Stock

13 1993 Nian Zhonghua Renmin Gongheguo Gongsi Fa (1993年中华人民共和国公司法) [1993 Company Law of the People's Republic of China], art. 85.

Exchange, the Shenzhen Stock Exchange, the Hong Kong Securities and Futures Commission (SFC) and the Stock Exchange of Hong Kong signed the Regulatory Cooperation Memorandum in Beijing, allowing Mainland companies to list in Hong Kong.[14]

On August 4, 1994, the State Council promulgated the Special Provisions on Overseas IPO and Listing of Joint Stock Companies (hereinafter referred to as the 1994 Special Provisions), which became the first regulatory document specifying the requirements for Chinese enterprises' overseas listings.[15] The document reiterated that JSCs, approved by the CSRC, can list their stock abroad. On August 27, 1994, the Chinese authorities issued the Essential Clauses in the Articles of Association for Overseas Listed Companies.[16] The promulgation of these regulations provided a legal basis for the direct listing of JSCs in overseas markets.

2.2.1.2 The 1997 Red-chip Guidance

If SOEs apply for overseas listing indirectly through the Red-chip model, they also need approval from the relevant authorities. On June 20, 1997, the State Council promulgated the Notice on Further Strengthening the Management of Share Issues and Listings Overseas (hereinafter "Red-chip Guidance").[17] It requires that if a domestic enterprise plans to transfer assets to a holding company they established and get listed overseas, it must receive prior approval from the relevant provincial governments or the competent department under the State Council.

There were also other relevant regulations issued by the departments under the State Council. For instance, in July 1999, the CSRC issued a notice regarding issues related to Enterprise Applications for Overseas

[14] Hong Kong Securities and Futures Commission, "Annual Report 1993/94," pp. 13–14, www.sfc.hk/-/media/files/ER/Annual-Report/93-94-Eng.pdf.

[15] Guowuyuan Guanyu Gufen Youxian Gongsi Jingwai Muji Gufen ji Shangshi de Tebie Guiding (国务院关于股份有限公司境外募集股份及上市的特别规定) [Special Provisions of the State Council on Overseas Share Offerings and Listing of Joint Stock Co.] (promulgated by the State Council, and effective August 4, 1998).

[16] Dao Jingwai Shangshi Gongsi Zhangcheng Bizhubiaotiao (到境外上市公司章程必备条款) [Necessary Clauses for the Articles of Association of Companies Listed Abroad] (promulgated by the Securities Regulatory Commission of the State Council and the State Commission for Restructuring the Economic Systems, and effective September 29, 1994).

[17] Guowuyuan Guanyu Jin Yibu Jiaqiang Zai Jingwai Faxing Gupiao he Shangshi Guanli de Tongzhi (国务院关于进一步加强在境外发行股票和上市管理的通知) [Notice of the State Council on Further Strengthening the Administration of Issuing Shares and Listing Abroad] (promulgated by the State Council, and effective June 20, 1997) (hereinafter "Red-chip Guidance").

Listings ("1999 Notice").[18] The document clarified the requirements for Chinese enterprises' overseas listings and the implementation of the approval system.

In theory, the Red-chip model can be used by both SOEs and private enterprises, with the Red-chip model used by SOEs being called the "big Red-chip model" and that used by private enterprises "small Red-chip model." In practice, however, only a very small number of SOEs have used the big Red-chip model to indirectly get listed overseas, and most SOEs seek overseas listings directly under the H-share model in Hong Kong. By contrast, until recently, the Red-chip model has long been the main way for private enterprises to seek overseas listings.

2.2.2 *2000–2010: Regulation of Overseas Listings of Private Enterprises*

2.2.2.1 The CSRC No-Objection Letter Requirement

The regulatory framework for overseas listings of private enterprises is made up of several important rules issued by different authorities. Below is a brief survey on some of them.

The CSRC gradually relaxed its administrative approval processes. In 2000, the CSRC issued the Notice on Issues Related to Overseas Stock Issuance and Listing by Overseas Companies Involving Domestic Rights and Interests ("2000 Notice").[19] Under the rule, if private enterprises transfer their assets to their overseas listing vehicles, they need to obtain a no-objection letter from the CSRC. This requirement was cancelled in 2003, and as a result, the CSRC no longer regulated overseas listing of private enterprises using the Red-chip mode.

2.2.2.2 The MOFCOM Document 10

The Ministry of Commerce (MOFCOM) also plays an important role in regulating the overseas listing of Chinese companies, as overseas listings

[18] Guanyu Qiye Shenqing Jingwai Shangshi Youguan Wenti de Tongzhi (关于企业申请境外上市有关问题的通知) [Notice Concerning Issues Related to Enterprises Applying for Listing Abroad] (promulgated by the China Securities Regulatory Commission, and effective July 14, 1999) [hereinafter 1999 Notice].

[19] Guanyu Sheji Jingnei Quanyi de Jingwai Gongsi Zai Jingwai Faxing Gupiao he Shangshi Youguan Wenti de Tongzhi (关于涉及境内权益的境外公司在境外发行股票和上市有关问题的通知) [Notice on Issues Related to the Offering of Shares and Listing Abroad by Overseas Companies with Domestic Interests] (promulgated by the China Securities Regulatory Commission, and effective June 9, 2000) [hereinafter 2000 Notice].

inevitably involve foreign investors and thus give rise to foreign investment issues. It first issued the Tentative Provisions on the M&A of Domestic Enterprises by Foreign Investors in 2003, which was superseded by the Provisions on the M&A of Domestic Enterprises by Foreign Investors in 2006, famously known as Document 10.[20] Document 10 represented a substantial amendment and expansion of its 2003 predecessor, setting up a comprehensive and systematic legal framework for foreign merger and acquisition (M&A) in China.[21] It was slightly revised in 2009 to delete its antitrust provisions in favor of the Anti-monopoly Law, which came into effect in 2008.[22]

Apart from the MOFCOM, the State Administration of Foreign Exchange (SAFE) is another important regulator in this area. It generally oversees foreign exchange issues and thus has jurisdiction over the small Red-chip model, which usually involves foreign exchange issues. As a key step of the model, there is a need to establish a special purpose vehicle (SPV) overseas as the listing entity and use the SPV to own or control assets located in China. In 2005, SAFE introduced a rule to require SPVs to be registered with the SAFE ("2005 Foreign Exchange Issue").[23]

The Red-chip model usually involves the establishment of an SPV, which is an overseas entity directly or indirectly controlled by a domestic Chinese company or a natural person (PRC Founder) and specifically established for an overseas listing of the PRC Founder's interests in the

20 Guanyu Waiguo Touzizhe Binggou Jingnei Qiye de Guiding (关于外国投资者并购境内企业的规定) [Provisions on the M&A of Domestic Enterprises by Foreign Investors] (promulgated by Minister of Commerce, State-owned Assets Supervision and Administration Commission, State Administration of Taxation, State Administration for Industry and Commerce, China Securities Regulatory Commission, State Administration of Foreign Exchange and effective August 2006) [hereinafter Document 10].

21 Robin Hui Huang, "China's New Regulation on Foreign M&A: Green Light or Red Flag?" (2007) 30(3) *University of New South Wales Law Journal* 804.

22 Shangwubu Guanyu Waiguo Touzizhe Binggou Jingnei Qiye de Guiding (商务部关于外国投资并购境内企业的规定) [Ministry of Commerce's Provisions on M&A of Domestic Enterprises by Foreign Investors] (promulgated by the Ministry of Commerce and effective June 22, 2009).

23 Guanyu Jingnei Jumin Tongguo Jingwai Teshu Mudi Gongsi Rongzi ji Fancheng Touzi Waihui Guanli Youguan Wenti (关于境内居民通过境外特殊目的公司融资及返程投资外汇管理有关问题) [Issues Relating to Foreign Exchange Administration for Domestic Residents' Financing and Round-Tripping Investment via Overseas Special Purpose Vehicles] (issued and effective by the State Administration of Foreign Exchange, promulgated October 21, 2005, effective November 1, 2005) [hereinafter 2005 Foreign Exchange Issue].

domestic enterprise. The PRC Founder usually establishes an SPV and then uses the SPV as an acquiring vehicle to get the domestic Chinese enterprise listed overseas by swapping its shares in the domestic enterprise for shares in the SPV.[24]

Up to now, in order to clamp down on the phenomenon of "fake foreign investments," namely investments that appear to be foreign but are actually made by Chinese citizens using their overseas assets, the MOFCOM has approved close to zero foreign M&A cases that intended to achieve overseas listings of Chinese companies. Consequently, Chinese companies choose to adopt the VIE structure to get listed overseas.[25] As the VIE structure uses contractual instruments, rather than legal ownership, to effect the transfer of economic interests from Chinese domestic businesses to overseas firms, the MOFCOM's relevant approval requirement does not apply. This has attracted more attention to the legal status and risk of the VIE structure, an issue to be discussed in more detail elsewhere.[26]

2.2.3 *2010–2023: More Efforts on Regulating Foreign Exchange and Foreign Investments*

2.2.3.1 The 2013 CSRC Regulatory Guidelines and 2014 SAFE Document 37

In 2013, the CSRC published the Regulatory Guidelines for Overseas Stock Issuance and Listing Declaration Documents and Review Procedures of Joint Stock Companies.[27] The document simplified the review process, putting more emphasis on business information disclosure, compliance and alignment with national industrial policies.

Other relevant authorities also issued rules within the scope of their responsibilities. For example, the MOFCOM, the SAFE and the National Development and Reform Commission (NDRC) issued rules on overseas

24 Robin Hui Huang, *Securities and Capital Markets Law in China* (Oxford University Press, 2014), ch. 12.

25 Ibid.

26 *See* Chapter 6.

27 Guanyu Gufen Youxian Gongsi Jingwai Faxing Gupiao he Shangshi Shenbao Wenjian ji Shenhe Chengxu de Jianguan Zhiyin (关于股份有限公司境外发行股票和上市申报文件及审核程序的监管指引) [Regulatory Guidelines for Overseas Stock Issuance and Listing Declaration Documents and Review Procedures of Joint Stock Companies] (promulgated by CSRC, December 20, 2012, effective January 1, 2013) [hereinafter 2013 Regulatory Guidelines].

investment projects of Chinese companies, including the 2014 Measures for the Administration of Overseas Investments ("2014 Overseas Investment Measures"),[28] the 2015 Notice of the SAFE on Further Simplifying and Improving Foreign Exchange Management Policies for Direct Investment ("2015 Notice"),[29] and the 2018 Administrative Measures for Overseas Investment of Enterprises ("2018 Administrative Measures").[30]

In July 2014, SAFE issued the Notice on Foreign Exchange Management of Overseas Investment and Financing and Return Investment by Domestic Residents through Special Purpose Vehicles ("2014 Foreign Exchange Notice"), widely known as "Document 37." The 2014 Foreign Exchange Notice adjusted the registration regime for the so-called Special Purpose Companies or Special Purpose Vehicles (SPV) that are usually set up in offshore financial centers such as the Cayman Islands.[31] It significantly relaxes the definitions of "Special Purpose Company" and "Reinvestment" as compared with its predecessor issued in 2005 and also relaxes the regulatory standards to allow domestic residents to provide funds or properties to SPVs. It also cancels the requirement of repatriating foreign exchange earnings to the domestic market within a certain period and relaxes the time limit for registration of changes in the SPV arrangement.

[28] Jingwai Touzi Guanli Banfa (境外投资管理办法) [Measures for the Administration of Overseas Investment] (promulgated by the Ministry of Commerce of the People's Republic of China, September 6, 2014, effective October 6, 2014) [hereinafter 2014 Overseas Investment Measures].

[29] Guojia Waihui Guanli Ju Guanyu Jin Yibu Jianhua he Gaijin Zhijie Touzi Waihui Guanli Zhengce de Tongzhi (国家外汇管理局关于进一步简化和改进直接投资外汇管理政策的通知) [Notice of the State Administration of Foreign Exchange on Further Simplifying and Improving the Foreign Exchange Administration Policies for Direct Investment] (promulgated by the State Administration of Foreign Exchange, February 13, 2015, effective June 1, 2015).

[30] Qiye Jingwai Touzi Guanli Banfa (企业境外投资管理办法) [Measures for the Administration of Enterprises' Outbound Investment] (promulgated by the National Development and Reform Commission of the People's Republic of China, December 26, 2017, effective March 1, 2018) [hereinafter 2018 Administrative Measures].

[31] Guanyu Jingnei Jumin Tongguo Teshu Mudi Gongsi Jingwai Tourongzi ji Fancheng Touzi Waihui Guanli Youguan Wenti de Tongzhi (关于境内居民通过特殊目的公司境外投融资及返程投资外汇管理有关问题的通知) [Notice on Foreign Exchange Management of Overseas Investment and Financing and Return Investment by Domestic Residents through Special Purpose Vehicles] (promulgated by the State Administration of Foreign Exchange, and effective July 4, 2014) [hereinafter 2014 Foreign Exchange Notice].

Importantly, Document 37 specifically states that the registration of offshore SPVs does not have the effect of confirming that their investment and financing behaviors comply with the legal requirements of the competent authorities in the industry. The statement is a limitation of SAFE's responsibilities and the effectiveness of the certificate for foreign exchange registration under Document 37, that is, SAFE would no longer oversee compliance in areas other than foreign exchange registration and management. Hence, registration under Document 37 does not exempt enterprises from the need to obtain approval from or file with industry authorities.

2.2.3.2 The 2020 Foreign Investment Law

Over the years, the MOFCOM has maintained a negative list of special management measures for foreign investment access, which has been updated from time to time. According to the current 2021 MOFCOM Negative List, there are thirty-one items with special management measures that ban or restrict foreign investment.[32] If domestic enterprises are engaged in such investment projects and want to get listed overseas, they must be approved by relevant authorities.

If a domestic enterprise intending to list abroad falls into a field where foreign investment is banned, it must obtain additional approval by the regulations.[33] However, this provision does not specify whether it applies to both direct and indirect listings, and the relevant departments' roles are not clearly defined, which may cause some controversy and confusion in practice.

2.2.4 *From 2023: Filing Requirements for All Overseas Listings*

2.2.4.1 2023 CSRC Trial Measures for Overseas Listings

On February 17, 2023, the CSRC issued a very important and long-awaited rule, namely, the Trial Measures for the Administration of Overseas Issuance and Listing of Securities by Domestic Enterprises

[32] Waishang Touzi Zhunru Tebie Guanli Cuoshi Fumian Qingdan 2021 nianban (外商投资准入特别管理措施负面清单2021年版) [the 2021 Special Management Measures for Foreign Investment Access Negative List] (promulgated by National Development and Reform Commission, Ministry of Commerce, December 27, 2021, effective January 1, 2022) (hereinafter 2021 MOFCOM Negative List).

[33] 2021 MOFCOM Negative List, art. 15.

("2023 CSRC Trial Measures for Overseas Listings").[34] A key measure taken by this rule is to set up a uniform filing regime ("2023 Filing Regime"), covering all models of overseas listings of Chinese enterprises, no matter whether the overseas listing is conducted directly or indirectly.[35]

In general, the 2023 CSRC Trial Measures for Overseas Listings divides overseas listings of Chinese companies into two categories, namely, direct and indirect overseas listings.[36] Specifically, more details are provided in defining indirect overseas listings. An overseas listing will fall within the scope of indirect overseas listings if it meets the following conditions: (1) In the most recent fiscal year, the operating income, total profit, total assets or net assets of the domestic enterprises must account for more than 50 percent of the corresponding indicators in the issuer's audited consolidated financial statements; and (2) the main business activities or principal place of business must be in China, or most of the senior managers responsible for management must be Chinese citizens or have their habitual residence in the territory.[37]

Prior to the 2023 reform, Small Red-chip Companies were subject to the CSRC regulation only for the period of 2000–2003 and then stayed unregulated until the 2023 CSRC Trial Measures for Overseas Listings. As dicussed earlier (see Section 2.2.1.2), the regulatory focus of the 1998 Red-chip Guidance was on the overseas listing of SOEs, known as Big Red-chips, and did not target private enterprises which were small both in number and size at the early stage of China's policy of economic reform and opening-up. However, as time went by, there were increasingly more enterprises seeking overseas listings, known as Small Red-chips, which called for regulatory attention.

Subsequently, in 2000, recognizing the problem, the CSRC promulgated the 2000 Notice (see Section 2.2.2.1), with a view to bringing the "Small Red-chips" into the the regulatory ambit.[38] The 2000 Notice embraced the overseas listing of "Small Red-chips," accompanied by

[34] Jingnei Qiye Jingwai Faxing Zhengquan he Shangshi Guanli Shixing Banfa (境内企业境外发行证券和上市管理试行办法) [Trial Measures for the Administration of Overseas Issuance and Listing of Securities by Domestic Enterprises] (promulgated by the CSRC, February 17, 2023, effective March 31, 2023) (hereinafter 2023 CSRC Trial Measures for Overseas Listings).

[35] 2023 CSRC Trial Measures for Overseas Listings, art. 1.

[36] 2023 CSRC Trial Measures for Overseas Listings, Part II.

[37] 2023 CSRC Trial Measures for Overseas Listings, art. 15.

[38] *See* Section 2.2.2.1.

the introduction of the "No Objection Letter System." The 2000 Notice mandates Chinese law firms to furnish the CSRC with pertinent legal documentation regarding overseas offerings and listings. Specifically, law firms must submit corresponding legal opinions to the CSRC, that, upon review and approval, issues a letter of no objection. This letter enables overseas companies to proceed with their overseas issuance and listing applications.

However, in 2003, due to the impact of the false information disclosure scandal of Ouya Agriculture (欧亚农业), the CSRC eventually abolished the no-objection letter system, which put the "small Red-chip" listing mode back in an unregulated state and revived a wave of "small Red-chip" listings among private enterprises. In 2002, a counterfeiting scandal broke out in Ouya Agriculture. The CSRC was embarrassed by having issued a no-objection letter to the enterprise. Shi Meilun, then vice-chairman of the CSRC, said that the no-objection letter only meant that the company was registered in China and that the CSRC did not check the accuracy of the company's information. She believed that the responsibility belonged to the supervisory authority of the place where the company was listed. In February 2003, the no-objection letter system was cancelled, and the Ouya Agriculture forgery case was therefore considered to be the trigger for the cancellation of the no-objection letter system.[39]

2.2.4.2 Five Supporting Guidelines

To facilitate the implementation of the 2023 CSRC Trial Measures for Overseas Listings, the CSRC issued five Supporting Guidelines to provide practical guidance on relevant issues.[40] For example, the Supporting Guidelines I defines the circumstances under which overseas listing is prohibited by laws, administrative regulations and relevant state regulations.[41] The Supporting Guidelines II provides for the content and

[39] Sun Li (孙立), "Dui 'Wuyiyihan Shidai' de Fenxi Baogao" (对'无异议函时代'的分析报告) [An analysis of the "No-Objection Letter Era"] 2003 (5) *Jinrong Fayaun (金融法苑) [Financial Law Forum]* 87.

[40] Jingwai Shangshi Beian Guanli Zhidu Guize Fabu Shishi (境外上市备案管理制度规则发布实施), [The administrative system and rules for filing overseas listings were promulgated and implemented], www.csrc.gov.cn/csrc/c100028/c7124479/content.shtml.

[41] Jianguan Guize Shiyong Zhiyin——Jingwai Faxing Shangshilei di 1 hao (监管规则适用指引——境外发行上市类第1号) [Guidelines on the Application of Regulatory Rules – Offshore Issuance and Listing Category No. 1] (promulgated by the China Securities Regulatory Commission, and effective February 17, 2023) (Supporting Guidelines I).

format of filing materials.[42] The Supporting Guidelines III sets out guidelines on the content of reports.[43] The Supporting Guidelines IV allows issuers to communicate with the CSRC before submitting filing materials.[44] Supporting Guidelines V provides more details on the working of the filing and annual form system.[45]

To sum up, Table 2.1 provides an overview of the key changes brought about by the 2023 reform.

2.3 The 2023 Filing Regime: Key Elements

2.3.1 General Rules

The regulators for overseas listing of Chinese companies include the CSRC and other relevant departments of the State Council, such as the Ministry of Finance, MOFCOM, SAFE and the NDRC.[46] In order to implement the 2023 CSRC Trial Measures for Overseas Listings, the CSRC has established an online system of filing management information for overseas listings of domestic enterprises, which is accessible from the CSRC's official website.

The CSRC and other relevant authorities may conduct supervision, inspection or investigation and take measures such as ordering the

42 Jianguan Guize Shiyong Zhiyin——Jingwai Faxing Shangshilei di 2 hao: Beian Cailiao Neirong he Geshi Zhiyin (监管规则适用指引——境外发行上市类第2号：备案材料内容和格式指引) [Guidelines on the Application of Regulatory Rules – Offshore Issuance and Listing Category No. 2: Guidelines for the content and format of filing materials.] (Promulgated by the China Securities Regulatory Commission, and effective February 17, 2023) (Supporting Guidelines II).

43 Jianguan Guize Shiyong Zhiyin——Jingwai Faxing Shangshilei di 3 hao: Baogao Neirong Zhiyin (监管规则适用指引——境外发行上市类第3号：报告内容指引) [Guidelines on the Application of Regulatory Rules – Offshore Issuance and Listing Category No. 3: Guidelines for the content of reports] (promulgated by the China Securities Regulatory Commission, and effective February 17, 2023) (Supporting Guidelines III).

44 Jianguan Guize Shiyong Zhiyin——Jingwai Faxing Shangshilei di 4 hao: Beian Goutong Zhiyin (监管规则适用指引——境外发行上市类第4号：备案沟通指引) [Guidelines on the Application of Regulatory Rules–Offshore Issuance and Listing Category No. 4: Guidelines for Filing Communications] (promulgated and effective by the China Securities Regulatory Commission, February 17, 2023) (Supporting Guidelines IV).

45 Jianguan Guize Shiyong Zhiyin——Jingwai Faxing Shangshilei di 5 hao: Jingwai Zhengquan Gongsi Beian Zhiyin (监管规则适用指引——境外发行上市类第5号：境外证券公司备案指引) [Guidelines on the Application of Regulatory Rules–Offshore Issuance and Listing Category No. 5: Filing Guidelines for Offshore Securities Companies] (promulgated by the China Securities Regulatory Commission, and effective February 17, 2023) (Supporting Guidelines V).

46 2023 CSRC Trial Measures for Overseas Listings, art. 4.

Table 2.1 *An overview of the 2023 reform*

Model of listing		Applicable law		Review procedures	
Before the reform	After the reform	Before the reform	After the reform	Before the reform	After the reform
H shares	Direct overseas listing of domestic companies	The 1994 Special Provisions	The 2023 CSRC Trial Measures for Overseas Listings; The 5 Supporting Guidelines	Approved by the CSRC	Filing with the CSRC
Small Red-chip Big Red-chip	Indirect overseas listing of domestic companies	/ The 1997 Red-chip Guidance		/ Approved by the provincial government and/or the CSRC	

violators to take corrective action, conducting regulatory talks and issuing warning letters among other actions.[47] If a crime is committed by Chinese enterprises in seeking overseas listing, criminal liability shall be pursued.[48] If needed, the CSRC and other relevant authorities are empowered to cooperate with overseas securities supervision and administration institutions by the principle of reciprocity.[49]

In general, the enterprise seeking overseas listings has the duty to fulfill the filing requirement with the CSRC, submitting the filing report, legal opinion and other relevant materials such as the information of shareholders.[50] The actual body to discharge the filing duty may vary, depending on the circumstances of overseas listings. In the case of direct overseas listings, the issuer is clearly tasked with the filing duty, while for indirect overseas listings, the filing duty is to be discharged by the domestic responsible person (main domestic operating entity) designated by the issuer.[51] Where a domestic enterprise directly gets listed overseas, and the shareholders holding its domestic unlisted shares apply for the conversion of the domestic unlisted shares into overseas listed shares, they need to comply with the relevant provisions of the CSRC and entrust the domestic enterprise to file with the CSRC.[52] The issuer conducting overseas listings must undergo the filing procedure with the CSRC within three working days after its application documents for offering and listing are submitted overseas.[53]

2.3.2 *National Security*

National security is a key issue in the Chinese regulation of overseas listing. Domestic enterprises that issue and list overseas must abide by relevant laws and regulations, such as the Company Law and the Accounting Law, should not disclose state secrets or work secrets of state organs and must comply with relevant laws to protect personal information and important data.[54] Article 9 provides that in overseas offering and listing activities, domestic enterprises shall strictly comply with the

[47] Ibid., arts. 23, 24.
[48] Ibid., art. 31.
[49] Ibid., art. 5.
[50] Ibid., art. 13.
[51] Ibid., art. 14.
[52] Ibid., art. 18.
[53] Ibid., art. 16.
[54] Ibid., arts. 6, 7.

laws, administrative regulations and relevant rules of the state on national security in such aspects as foreign investment, cyberspace security and data security.[55] In cases where national security review is required, relevant review should be conducted *before* an application for overseas listing is filed with overseas securities regulators.[56]

The 2023 CSRC Trial Measures for Overseas Listings provides for several circumstances where Chinese companies are not allowed to pursue overseas listing: (1) The laws, administrative regulations or the relevant provisions of the state expressly prohibit public financing; (2) the overseas offering and listing may endanger national security as determined by the relevant competent department under the State Council; (3) a domestic enterprise or its controlling shareholder or actual controller has committed a criminal crime of corruption, bribery, embezzlement, misappropriation of property or disrupting the economic order of the socialist market in the last three years; (4) a domestic enterprise is under formal investigation according to the law for being suspected of any crime or major violation of laws and regulations, but no clear conclusions have been made; and (5) there is a major dispute over ownership of the equity held by the controlling shareholder or a shareholder controlled by the controlling shareholder or the actual controller.[57]

The Supporting Guidelines I provide more guidance on the circumstances where an overseas listing of Chinese companies may be prohibited under 2023 CSRC Trial Measures for Overseas Listings, art. 8(1).

(a) Listing and financing are prohibited in the Negative List for Market Access issued by the National Development and Reform Commission and the Ministry of Commerce;
(b) The domestic enterprise is a serious trust-breaking subject as stipulated in the Guiding Opinions of the State Council on Establishing and Improving the Joint Incentive System for Trust-Keeping and the Joint Punishment System for Trust-Breaking to Accelerate the Construction of Social Honesty; and
(c) There are laws that restrict or prohibit listing in the fields of industrial policy, production safety and industry supervision.[58]

55 Ibid., art. 9.
56 Ibid.
57 Ibid., art. 8.
58 Supporting Guidelines I, art. 1(1).

2.3.3 *Legal Liability*

If a domestic enterprise fails to undergo the filing procedure or conducts overseas listing in violation of the 2023 CSRC Trial Measures for Overseas Listings, the CSRC is empowered to order it to take corrective action, give a warning to it and impose a fine of not less than 1 million yuan nor more than 10 million yuan. A warning shall be given, and a fine of not less than 500,000 yuan nor more than 5 million yuan shall be imposed upon the directly liable person in charge and other directly liable persons. Where there are false records, misleading statements or major omissions in the filing materials of a domestic enterprise, the CSRC shall order it to take corrective action, give a warning to it and impose a fine of not less than 1 million yuan nor more than 10 million yuan upon it. A warning shall be given, and a fine of not less than 500,000 yuan nor more than 5 million yuan shall be imposed upon the directly liable person in charge and other directly liable persons.[59]

If the violation of the 2023 CSRC Trial Measures for Overseas Listings also triggers other relevant laws and regulations, such as those relating to foreign investment and data protection, the violators will be subject to punishment according to the provisions on punishment in those laws and regulations.[60] If the violation is sufficiently serious, the CSRC may impose a barring order, namely, banning relevant responsible persons from accessing the securities market, and if such violation constitutes a crime, the violator shall be held criminally liable by the law.[61]

2.4 The 2023 Filing Regime: Implementation in Practice

2.4.1 *Statistics of Filing Cases*

According to the official website of the CSRC, as of May 1, 2024, 117 enterprises have obtained filing confirmation for their overseas listings.[62] On July 6, 2023, Luyuan Group Holding (Cayman) Limited became the first company to successfully fulfill the filing requirement.[63]

[59] 2023 CSRC Trial Measures for Overseas Listings, art. 28.

[60] Ibid., art. 30.

[61] Ibid., art. 31.

[62] Zhengfu Xinxi Gongkai (政府信息公开) [Government Information Disclosure], CSRC, www.csrc.gov.cn/csrc/c101935/zfxxgk_zdgk.shtml?channelid=8f3f0d4be56b4f8aa8183b3234b88ede.

[63] Guanyu Luyuan Group Holding (Cayman) Limited Jingwai Faxing Shangshi Beian Tongzhishu (关于Luyuan Group Holding (Cayman) Limited境外发行上市备案通知书)

Table 2.2 *Number of monthly filings since July 2023*

Month	Filing cases for US listings	Filing cases for HK listings	Filing cases for listings elsewhere	Total filing cases
2023.7	1	13	0	14
2023.8	5	8	0	13
2023.9	5	7	0	12
2023.10	6	10	0	16
2023.11	4	8	0	12
2023.12	5	7	0	12
2024.1	11	13	0	24
2024.2	10	7	0	17
2024.3	2	9	0	11
2024.4	11	9	0	20
2024.5	7	3	0	10
2024.6	5	14	1	19
2024.7 (up to 24th)	3	8	0	11

Since July 2023, the monthly number of enterprises obtaining the filing confirmation has been gradually on the rise. Notably, since the fourth quarter of 2023, the number of filing cases for US listings has picked up (Table 2.2).[64]

In most cases, it took between two to four months from the company's first submission of filing materials to the CSRC to complete the filing process. The shortest period was only thirty-nine days, while the longest was 239 days.

Compared to indirect overseas listing, direct overseas listing tends to be quicker in obtaining the filing confirmation. Specifically, the average period for the filing process is about ninety-three days for direct overseas listing and about 124 days for indirect overseas listing (Table 2.3).[65]

[Notification of the filing of the listing of the offshore offering of Luyuan Group Holding (Cayman) Limited], www.csrc.gov.cn/csrc/c105984/c7418170/content.shtml.

64 Hu Jing (胡静), "Huigu yu Jiedu: Jingwai Shangshi Beian Xingui Shishi Qingkuang ji Guanzhu Yaodian" (回顾与解读：境外上市备案新规实施情况及关注要点) [Review and Interpretation: Implementation of the New Regulations on Overseas Listing Filing and Points of Concern], www.kwm.com/cn/zh/insights/latest-thinking/review-and-outlook-china-s-filing-regime-for-overseas-listing.html.

65 Ding Wenhao (丁文昊), Pang Ying (庞颖) and Zhu Yilin (朱艺琳), "Huishou Jingwai Shangshi Beian Shidai Yuannian: Xingui Luodi Shishi Qingkuang ji VIE Jiagou Beian

Table 2.3 *Filing duration*

Time duration	Quantities
1–2 months	9
2–3 months	22
3–4 months	16
4–5 months	18
5–6 months	9
Over 6 months	8

The enterprises that have obtained filing confirmation cover a wide range of industries, including the so-called new economy industries, such as autonomous driving, biomedicine, metaverse and AIGC, and also traditional industries such as manufacturing, engineering and construction, food and beverage, clothing and other consumer industries.

2.4.2 *CSRC Inquiries*

During the filing process, the CSRC usually makes inquiries with applicant companies about certain important issues such as the company's historical development, equity structure, shareholders (including employee stock ownership plans), main domestic operating entities and the independence of the issuer to decide whether the applicant company meets the relevant requirements for overseas listing. Table 2.4 shows the types of issues that are usually covered in the inquiry process.[66]

2.4.3 *Enterprises with a VIE Structure*

2.4.3.1 Low Number of Filing Applications

As of July 1, 2024, a total of forty-two VIE-structured enterprises have submitted filing applications for overseas IPOs. Among them, twemty-nine are proposed to list in Hong Kong, and thirteen are proposed to list in the US.

Guanzhu Yaodian" (回首境外上市备案时代元年：新规落地实施情况及VIE架构备案关注要点) [Looking back at the first year of the offshore listing filing era: the implementation of the new regulations and the key points of concern for VIE structure filing.], *Zhong Lun Law Firm*, February 5, 2024, www.zhonglun.com/research/articles/52634.html.

[66] Hu, above note 64.

Table 2.4 *Type of questions by the CSRC*

Type of question	Number of times inquired
Shareholding changes	115
Establishment of the structure	104
Shareholder status	98
Business operation	83
Employee motivation	72
Information protection	69

2.4.3.2 Long Filing Time

The filing periods for Cheche Technology and Jitu Express, which have completed the filing requirement, were seventy-nine and eighty days respectively (from the time when the CSRC received their filing materials to the time when they obtained filing confirmation). For other VIE-structured enterprises still in the filing process, the longest filing review time so far has been 300 days, with an average filing review time of 202.5 days, exceeding the average filing review time of 146 days for non-VIE-structured enterprises.

The long filing period of VIE-structured enterprises is due to complex compliance issues arising from the VIE structure. For overseas listings of VIE-structured enterprises, the CSRC will seek opinions from relevant competent departments in deciding whether their filing applications for overseas listings meet relevant compliance requirements. Since it takes time to communicate with multiple competent departments and obtain their opinions, the filing review period for VIE-structured enterprises has become longer than that for non-VIE-structured enterprises.

2.4.3.3 Industry Distribution and Foreign Investment Access Prohibition

The industries of VIE-structured enterprises submitting filing applications are widely distributed, including the internet and technology (eighteen companies), the medical industry (seven companies), education (two companies), media and entertainment (two companies), logistics (two companies) and others.[67]

[67] Ding, Pang and Zhu, above note 65.

In theory, Chinese enterprises may use the VIE structure to engage in restricted or prohibited types of foreign investment listed in the Special Administrative Measures for Foreign Investment Access (Negative List) (2021 Edition) ("2021 Negative List").[68] In practice, VIE structure enterprises submitting filing applications mainly fall within the second restricted type of value-added telecom business (twenty-two) and medical institution operation (three). The prohibited businesses that they are engaged in mainly include internet culture management (four), the first kind of value-added telecom business (four), radio and television program production business (three) and domestic express delivery business (two).

This shows that filing confirmation can be granted to even those enterprises that use the VIE structure to engage in prohibited businesses. Sometimes, a company applies for filing in an allowed industry but actually operates in a prohibited industry. Under this situation, it may successfully be granted filing confirmation. As discussed earlier, article 8 of 2023 CSRC Trial Measures for Overseas Listings sets out several circumstances under which Chinese enterprises are prohibited from seeking overseas listing, including, among others: (1) Financing through listing is expressly prohibited by laws, administrative regulations or relevant rules of the state; and (2) the overseas offering and listing may endanger national security as determined by the relevant competent department under the State Council after examination according to the law.[69] Among them, the core points to be noted are: (1) The Negative List of Market Access issued by the National Development and Reform Commission and the Ministry of Commerce prohibits listing and financing; and (2) there are laws, administrative regulations and relevant national regulations restricting or prohibiting listing and financing in industrial policy, production safety, industry supervision and other fields. Industries such as compulsory education discipline class training institutions, private kindergartens and profit-making kindergartens may find it difficult to pass the filing. Some commentators examined the regulatory effects of the reforms on particular industries, such as real estate and

[68] Waishang Touzi Zhunru Tebie Guanli Cuoshi Fumian Qingdan 2021 nian ban (外商投资准入特别管理措施负面清单2021年版) [Negative List of Special Administrative Measures for Foreign Investment Entry 2021 Edition] (promulgated by National Development and Reform Commission and Ministry of Commerce, December 27, 2021, effective January 1, 2022) (2021 Negative List).

[69] 2021 Negative List, art. 11.

education, pointing out that the reforms clearly outline the circumstances under which overseas listings are prohibited.[70]

2.4.3.4 Foreign Investment Security Review and Cybersecurity Review

In theory, a foreign investment security review is a potential issue in the overseas listing of Chinese companies. However, due to the sensitivity of this review, it is not a routine exercise, and even if it is conducted, it will usually be done in the disguise of other reviews, such as anti-monopoly reviews.[71] Hence, it is not surprising that none of the VIE-structured enterprises submitting filing applications mentioned foreign investment security review issues in their public disclosure documents.

However, cybersecurity review presents a quite different situation. Among the thirty-four VIE-structured enterprises that have applied for filing, thirty-one enterprises indicated that cybersecurity review requirements do not apply to them. However, the remaining enterprises are subject to cybersecurity review, mainly because they hold more than 1 million users' personal information, and in the end, they have all passed the cybersecurity review.

2.5 Evaluations and Comments

2.5.1 Overall Observations

In line with the gradualist approach China has adopted to reforming its economy and society at large, China has made continuous efforts to build and strengthen its regulatory regime for overseas listing of domestic enterprises. Over the past three decades, China has explored different models of overseas listings and designed differentiated rules for them. For instance, there are two main models of overseas listing for Chinese companies, namely, direct overseas listing and indirect overseas listing, and they are subject to different regulations to match their distinctive features and risk factors.

70 Gao ao (高奥), "Jingwai Shangshi Xingui xia de Xieyi Kongzhi Jiagou hequhecong" (境外上市新规下的协议控制架构何去何从) [Whither Agreement Control Structures under the New Rules for Offshore Listings] (2023)18 *Zhongguo Waihui (中国外汇) [China Forex]* 34, 37.

71 Robin Hui Huang, "China's National Security Review of Foreign Investment: A Comparison with the United States" (2023) 57 *Vanderbilt Journal of Transnational Law* 1263–1303.

In the process, China has also considered the political-economy environment in which it operates. While China continues to welcome foreign investment and facilitate overseas listing of Chinese companies, it has put more emphasis on national security issues, such as foreign investment security, cyber security and data security. This presents a paradox in the regulatory regime for overseas listing of Chinese companies: On the one hand, China has been working hard to streamline and simplify the regulatory regime, including the reduction of the number of industries on the negative list for foreign investment; while on the other hand, it adds more review requirements, which increases compliance costs and uncertainties.

2.5.2 The Implications of the 2023 Filing Regime

The filing regime introduced by the 2023 CSRC Trial Measures for Overseas Listings is a very important development and will have far-reaching implications. It marks a new stage of the Chinese regulatory regime for overseas listing of domestic companies. It has unified the supervision of direct and indirect overseas listing of domestic companies and strengthened relevant information disclosure. This move has been widely regarded as a positive step, as it improves transparency of overseas listing activities, enhances certainty in regulatory compliance and facilitates cross-border regulatory coordination.

However, there can be significant challenges in the implementation of the new regime. In the early stage of implementing the new regime, the various changes made to the regulatory standards and procedures may lead to uncertainties and confusion. The introduction of the filing requirement may increase the compliance cost for enterprises, especially for small- and medium-sized enterprises. It may take time for market participants to adjust to the reforms, and the challenge may be particularly acute for foreign investors who are not familiar with China's regulatory culture and environment.[72]

For instance, the tightening of approval affects the listing choice of enterprises. Before the filing regime was streamlined, there were no

[72] Liao Fan (廖凡), "Zhonggaigu Kuajing Jianguan Boyi: Pingxi yu Sikao" (中概股跨境监管博弈:评析与思考) [The Cross-border Regulatory Game for Chinese Shares: Commentary and Reflections] (2023) 30(1) *Shanghai Duiwai Jingmao Daxue Xuebao (上海对外经贸大学学报) [Journal of Shanghai University of International Business and Economics]* 65, 66.

corresponding verification requirements for small Red-chips due to the lack of explicit pre-approval requirements. The new filing regime's tightening of approval requirements for small Red-chips may affect the listing choices of some companies, especially small- and medium-sized private enterprises and innovative start-ups that originally tended to choose overseas listings.[73] Verification requirements may also make it difficult for some enterprises to go public. Before the filing regime reform, domestic lawyers were not required to provide clear opinions on VIE and other situations. Now, they need to carry out more stringent verification on issuers, especially for VIE structure enterprises. This may raise the costs of legal compliance for enterprises.

The 2023 CSRC Trial Measures for Overseas Listings also assign an important role to market intermediaries in verifying the truthfulness, accuracy and completeness of the information provided in the filing applications.[74] This would bring more businesses to the relevant intermediaries, such as securities companies, accounting firms and law firms. At the same time, however, they will be subject to legal liability if they fail to properly discharge their duties as gatekeepers.[75] Suppose an overseas securities company acts as the sponsor or lead underwriter for overseas offerings and listing by domestic enterprises. In that case, it should register with the CSRC within ten working days from the date of signing the business agreement for the first time, and submit the report on its business activities in the previous year in relation to overseas offering and listing by domestic enterprises to the CSRC before January 31 of each year.[76] From the perspective of Chinese enterprises seeking overseas listing, this may increase their compliance costs, but the costs may be well justified on the grounds that the involvement of those intermediaries can ensure the quality of information disclosure and thus improve regulatory efficacy and investor protection.

Finally, the 2023 CSRC Trial Measures for Overseas Listings have tried to strengthen cross-border regulatory cooperation between Chinese regulators and their counterparts overseas. If a domestic enterprise or an overseas securities company violates the 2023 CSRC Trial Measures for

[73] Sun Haotian (孙昊天), Li Nan (李楠) and Xiao Bin (肖斌), "Jingwai Shangshi Xingui Yingxiang Fenxi yu Lujing Xuanze" (境外上市新规影响分析与路径选择) [Impact Analysis and Path Choice of New Overseas Listing Regulations] (2023) 14 *Zhongguo Waihui (中国外汇) [China Forex]* 35, 36.

[74] 2023 CSRC Trial Measures for Overseas Listings, art. 20.

[75] Ibid., art. 29.

[76] Ibid., art. 21.

Overseas Listings, the CSRC may notify relevant overseas securities regulators through the cross-border regulatory cooperation mechanism. If overseas securities regulators want to carry out investigation and evidence collection on overseas listings of Chinese enterprises, they can make a request to the CSRC for assistance. A domestic entity or individual cannot provide relevant documents and materials to overseas securities regulators without obtaining prior consent from the CSRC and other relevant departments under the State Council.[77]

Cross-border regulatory cooperation is important and indispensable to the proper functioning of overseas listings of domestic companies. The foundation for effective local capacity building rests solidly on cooperation across borders, and the 2023 CSRC Trial Measures for Overseas Listings recognizes the importance of cross-border regulatory cooperation. However, there will be difficulties in the process of implementation, such as differences in regulatory concepts and practices between the Chinese regulators and their counterparts overseas.[78] Further, the actual implementation of cross-border regulatory cooperation may be affected by non-legal factors, such as cultural differences, technological compatibilities, market competition, political issues and international relations. It will take time to address these issues of regulatory cooperation and requires continuous and effective communication between the two sides.[79] In sum, cross-border regulatory cooperation is a key issue for an overseas listing of Chinese companies and thus will be an important aspect of this research project.

2.5.3 *The Impact of Cross-border Data Transfer*

As discussed earlier, the 2023 CSRC Trial Measures for Overseas Listings emphasizes the issue of national security, which includes, among others,

77 Ibid., art. 26.

78 Han Hongling (韩洪灵), Chen Shuaidi (陈帅弟) and Chen Hanwen (陈汉文), "Zhongmei Kuajing Kuaiji Shenji Chongtu: Genben Youyin, Jiben Biaoxian yu Yingdui Cuoshi" (中美跨境会计审计冲突:根本诱因,基本表现与应对措施) [Cross-border Accounting and Auditing Conflicts between China and the United States: Underlying Causes, Basic Manifestations and Countermeasures] (2023) 36(5) *Yantai Daxue Xuebao: Zhexue Shehui Kexue ban (烟台大学学报:哲学社会科学版) [Journal of Yantai University (Philosophy and Social Sciences Edition]* 38.

79 Tian Siyuan (田思远) and Li Changchang (李畅畅), "Lunwoguo Jingwai Jianjie Shangshi Zhong Kebian Liyi Shiti Jiagou de Rending" (论我国境外间接上市中"可变利益实体架构"的认定) [The Recognition of "Variable Interest Entity Structures" in China's Indirect Offshore Listings] (2023) 5 *Jilin Jinrong Yanjiu (吉林金融研究) [Journal of Jilin Financial Research]* 66, 67.

cyberspace security and data security. In recent years, cybersecurity and data security have become increasingly important in the regulation of overseas listings of Chinese companies. This is not surprising, as overseas listings of Chinese companies would usually involve cross-border data transfer in the listing process. Hence, the laws on cross-border data transfer warrant a separate treatment here. However, due to space constraints, this section will just provide an overview of the issue without going into details.

2.5.3.1 Regulatory Framework

In general, China's legislative regime for cross-border data transfer is made up of three pillars, namely, China's Cybersecurity Law,[80] China's Data Security Law[81] and China's Personal Information Protection Law.[82]

The first pillar is the Cybersecurity Law issued in 2016, which deals with the issue of cybersecurity. Cybersecurity has become an important aspect of national security,[83] given that cyberspace is considered the "fifth domain" after the sea, land, airspace and outer space.[84] According to Article 76 of Cybersecurity Law, "cybersecurity" means the capabilities of preventing network attacks and other network incidents, ensuring a stable and reliable operation of the network and safeguarding the integrity, confidentiality and availability of network data. Hence, cybersecurity is closely related to data protection.

In relation to the issue of cross-border data transfer, Article 37 of the Cybersecurity Law lays down a data localization requirement to regulate the so-called Critical Information Infrastructure (CII)[85] and Critical

80 Zhonghua Renming Gongheguo Wangluo Anquan Fa (中华人民共和国网络安全法) [Cybersecurity Law of the People's Republic of China] (promulgated November 7, 2016 and effective June 1, 2017) [hereinafter Cybersecurity Law].

81 Zhonghua Renming Gongheguo Shuju Anquan Fa (中华人民共和国数据安全法) [Data Security Law of the People's Republic of China] (promulgated June 10, 2021 and effective September 1, 2021) [hereinafter Data Security Law].

82 Zhonghua Renming Gongheguo Geren Xinxi Baohu Fa (中华人民共和国个人信息保护法) [Personal Information Protection Law of the People's Republic of China] (promulgated August 20, 2021 and effective November 2021) [hereinafter Personal Information Protection Law].

83 "Xi Jinping's Perspective on Cybersecurity," (2018), *Xinhuanet*, www.xinhuanet.com/zgjx/2016-09/19/c_135697024.htm.

84 "United Efforts for National Cybersecurity: A Record of President Xi Jinping's Guidance on China's Cybersecurity Efforts," September 28, 2022, *Xinhuanet*, www.xinhuanet.com/2022-09/28/c_1129038548.htm.

85 Guanjian Xinxi Jichu Sheshi (关键信息基础设施) [Critical Information Infrastructure] (hereinafter CII).

Information Infrastructure Operators (CIIO).[86] Under this Article, the CIIOs must store collected or generated personal information and key data within China, and if there is a genuine need for data to be transferred out of China due to business operations, approval must be sought from the Cyberspace Administration of China (CAC).[87]

The Data Security Law, promulgated in June 2021, focuses on the issue of data security, stipulating the establishment of a categorized and hierarchical data protection system.[88] Important data should be classified as key data or core data and should be subject to stricter regulation.[89] The National Technical Committee on Cybersecurity of Standardization Administration of China[90] is responsible for formulating national standards in the data governance realm. For instance, it issued a rule on data classification and grading in March 2024, dividing data into core data, key data and general data.[91] In addition, local governments also have issued rules to set up their hierarchical data protection systems. For instance, the Lin-gang New Region of China (Shanghai) Pilot Free Trade Zone (Lin-gang New Region)[92] has issued a rule on the formulation of catalogues and lists to classify data.[93] According to this rule, core data cannot be transferred out of China; key data can be transferred out

[86] Guanjian Xinxi Jichu Sheshi Yunying Zhe (关键信息基础设施运营者) [Critical Information Infrastructure Operators] (hereinafter CIIO).

[87] Zhonghua Renmin Gongheguo Guojia Hulianwang Xinxi Bangongshi (中华人民共和国国家互联网信息办公室) [Cyberspace Administration of China] [hereinafter CAC].

[88] Data Security Law, art. 21.

[89] Ibid.

[90] Quanguo Xinxi Anquan Biaozhunhua Jishu Weiyuanhui (全国网络安全标准化技术委员会) [National Technical Committee on Cybersecurity of Standardization Administration of China]. This committee was established in 2002 and is directly affiliated to the National Standardization Administration. *See* at: www.cac.gov.cn/2021-10/26/c_1636843228117807.htm.

[91] Shuju Anquan Jishu – Shuju Fenlei Fenji Guize (数据安全技术—数据分类分级规则) [Data security technology – Rules for data classification and grading] (issued by National Technical Committee on Cybersecurity of Standardization Administration of China, promulgated March 15, 2024 and effective October 1, 2024).

[92] Zhongguo (Shanghai) Ziyou Maoyi Shiyanqu Lingang Pianqu (中国（上海）自由贸易试验区临港片区) [Lin-gang New Area of China (Shanghai) Pilot Free Trade Zone] (hereinafter Lin-gang Special Area).

[93] Zhongguo (Shanghai) Ziyou Maoyi Shiyanqu Lingang Xinpianqu Shuju Kuajing Liudong Fenlei Fenji Guanli Banfa (Shixing) (中国(上海)自由贸易试验区临港新片区数据跨境流动分类分级管理办法(试行)) [Measures for the Classification and Hierarchical Management of Cross-border Flow of Data in Lin-gang New Area of China (Shanghai) Pilot Free Trade Zone (Trial Implementation)] (issued by government of Lin-gang Special Area, promulgated and effective February 8, 2024).

of China only when the data security assessment requirement is met and general data can be freely transferred out of China.[94] Until now, Lin-gang New Region has only issued general data lists in the fields of intelligent connected vehicles,[95] public offering of funds[96] and biomedicine.[97]

In August 2021, the Personal Information Protection Law was promulgated as the third pillar of China's legal framework for cross-border data transfer. It provides for three main channels for cross-border data transfers:[98] (1) Going through the security assessment of cross-border data transfer (security assessment), which is conducted by the CAC; (2) obtaining a personal information protection certification (certification), which is conducted by specialized institutions; (3) signing a standard contract for cross-border data transfer (standard contract) in accordance with relevant requirements set by the CAC.

There are also other ways for data to be transferred out of China. For instance, cross-border data transfer can be conducted under relevant international treaties or agreements concluded or acceded to by China.[99] Additionally, providing personal information stored within China to foreign judicial or law enforcement authorities is permissible only with approval from China's competent authorities.[100]

94 Details of data security assessment are discussed in Section 2.5.3.

95 Zhongguo (Shanghai) Ziyou Maoyi Shiyanqu Lingang Xinpianqu Zhineng Wanglian Qiche Lingyu Shuju Kuajing Changjinghua Yiban Shuju Qingdan (Shixing) (中国(上海)自由贸易试验区临港新片区智能网联汽车领域数据跨境场景化一般数据清单(试行)) [General Data List for Cross-border Data Transfer Scenarios in the Intelligent Connected Vehicle Sector of Lin-gang New Area of China (Shanghai) Pilot Free Trade Zone(Trail Implementation)], *see* at: www.lingang.gov.cn/html/website/lg/index/government/file/1791283594794135554.html.

96 Zhongguo (Shanghai) Ziyou Maoyi Shiyanqu Lingang Xinpianqu Gongmu Jijin Lingyu Shuju Kuajing Changjinghua Yiban Shuju Qingdan (Shixing) (中国(上海)自由贸易试验区临港新片区公募基金领域数据跨境场景化一般数据清单(试行)) [General Data List for Cross-border Data Transfer Scenarios in the Public Offering of Funds Sector of Lin-gang New Area of China (Shanghai) Pilot Free Trade Zone(Trail Implementation)], *see* at: www.lingang.gov.cn/html/website/lg/index/government/file/1791283590130069505.html.

97 Zhongguo (Shanghai) Ziyou Maoyi Shiyanqu Lingang Xinpianqu Shengwu Yiyao Lingyu Shuju Kuajing Changjinghua Yiban Shuju Qingdan (Shixing) (中国(上海)自由贸易试验区临港新片区生物医药领域数据跨境场景化一般数据清单(试行)) [General Data List for Cross-border Data Transfer Scenarios in the Biomedicine Sector of Lin-gang New Area of China (Shanghai) Pilot Free Trade Zone(Trail Implementation)], *see* at: www.lingang.gov.cn/html/website/lg/index/government/file/1791283592713760769.html.

98 Personal Information Protection Law, art. 38.

99 Ibid.

100 Personal Information Protection Law, art. 41.

The CAC is the Chinese authority responsible for cybersecurity, data security and personal information protection in China.[101] Since the CAC was established in 2011, its responsibilities have continuously expanded beyond the original task of online content censorship to cover general issues of data security and cybersecurity. Over the years, it has issued many administrative rules to implement the national laws noted above and provide guidance on compliance matters.

It should be noted that, unlike financial regulators such as the CSRC, the CAC has some special features. First, it is not only a state organ but also concurrently the Office of the Central Cyberspace Affairs Commission of the Communist Party of China (CPC), an arrangement dubbed as "one group of people, two sets of labels" in China, which is usually adopted to deal with important matters. Second, the director of the CAC is the deputy head of the Propaganda Department of the CPC, a high-ranking role in the Chinese political hierarchy. As a result, the CAC is a hybrid party–state institution with significant clout in China.

2.5.3.2 The DiDi Case

DiDi, a giant company dominating China's ride-hailing service market,[102] holds a large quantity of highly sensitive data. On June 30, 2021, it was listed on the New York Stock Exchange (NYSE) before the Data Security Law took effect in September 2021.

However, within days of DiDi's listing in the US, the CAC intervened to suspend DiDi's operations and initiate a cybersecurity review.[103] The intervention was based on data security and national security concerns due to DiDi's extensive collection of personal information and data.[104] Apart from the issue of cross-border transfer of relevant data such as audit data, the CAC also pointed to the issue of cybersecurity, which was said to be triggered by DiDi's illegal cross-border data transfer, the excessive collection of user data, potential technical vulnerabilities and risks of data breaches or misuse in DiDi's operations.[105] The CAC initiated a cybersecurity review, resulting in the removal of DiDi's apps

101 *See* the official website of the CAC, www.cac.gov.cn.

102 "Research Report on the Ride-Hailing Industry," (2020), www.haitouglobal.com/cn/academy/uploads/25/file/public/202006/20200615154420_wqtfkc6e17.pdf.

103 "Announcement by the CAC on the Launch of a Cybersecurity Review of 'DiDi Chuxing,'" (2021), *Official Website of CAC*, www.cac.gov.cn/2021-07/02/c_1626811521011934.htm.

104 Ibid.

105 "CAC Responds to Journalists' Questions Regarding the Decision to Impose Administrative Penalties Related to the Cybersecurity Review of DiDi Global Inc. in

from online stores, the suspension of its operations and a fine exceeding 8 billion RMB (more than 1 billion USD).[106]

This regulatory action led to a dramatic decline in DiDi's share price, and on December 3, 2021, DiDi announced its intention to delist from the NYSE. In June 2022, DiDi was formally delisted from the NYSE and traded on the Over-the-Counter (OTC) market in the US.

2.5.3.3 Comments

In recent years, the regulation of cross-border data transfer has become an increasingly important issue for overseas listings of Chinese companies. Cross-border data transfer may give rise to legal issues of cybersecurity and data protection, which are closely related to overseas listings, including the IPO process and, thereafter, continuous information disclosure obligations of listed companies. Consequently, as China's regulator primarily responsible for internet content censorship and cybersecurity, the CAC has started to play an increasingly important role in regulating overseas listings of Chinese companies. There are several points to be made here about the regulation of cross-border data transfer and its impact on overseas listings of Chinese companies.

First, despite the short history of the regulation of cross-border data transfer, it has already occupied a prominent place in the process of Chinese companies seeking overseas listings. In 2023, twenty-four Chinese companies were listed in the US, and all of them disclosed the risks and their compliance regarding cybersecurity issues and the impact of data protection on their business operations in their prospectuses.[107] Considering that the initiation of cybersecurity review largely depends on the CAC,[108] some companies, even without any warnings or notifications from regulatory authorities, also choose to consult the CAC to ensure they will not be subject to cybersecurity reviews. Similarly, seventy-three Chinese companies were listed in Hong Kong in 2023, with approximately 86 percent (sixty-three companies) disclosing their data compliance matters in their prospectuses. And for the ten companies that did

Accordance with Law," (2022), *Official Website of CAC*, www.cac.gov.cn/2022-07/21/c_1660021534364976.htm.

106 "Notification Regarding the Removal of the 'DiDi Chuxing' App," (2021), *Official Website of CAC*, www.cac.gov.cn/2021-07/04/c_1627016782176163.htm.

107 "Overview of Data Compliance in the U.S. IPOs for 2023," (2024), *Zhong Lun Law Firm*, www.zhonglun.com/research/articles/53085.html.

108 *See* Section 2.5.3.1.

not disclose their data compliance situation, their business is mostly unrelated to data processing.[109]

Second, the regulatory standard for cross-border data transfer seems to vary between Hong Kong and other destinations for overseas listings of Chinese companies, such as the US. To date, none of the companies seeking listing in Hong Kong has undergone the cybersecurity review, suggesting that cybersecurity review may not apply to them. Under a rule issued by the CAC, network platform operators who hold more than 1 million users' personal information must apply for a cybersecurity review to the CAC's Cybersecurity Review Office when listing "in a foreign country."[110] As it refers to "foreign country" rather than "foreign jurisdiction," there has been a debate on whether it is a deliberate use of wording to exclude listings in Hong Kong from the cybersecurity review regime, as Hong Kong is a special administrative region of China.

In practice, some companies seeking listings in Hong Kong indicated in their prospectus that they had consulted competent Chinese authorities on a no-name basis, obtaining confirmation that "listing in a foreign country" does not include "listing in Hong Kong."[111] Hence, companies listed in Hong Kong are not required to apply for cybersecurity review when they hold the personal information of over one million individuals. However, the cybersecurity review may still be required if the overseas listing affects or may affect China's national security.

Finally, the issue of cross-border data transfer has become a source of uncertainty and unpredictability for Chinese companies seeking overseas listings. Under the 2023 filing regime, the CSRC can ask the applicant to provide additional information on specific matters and supplementary explanations.[112] In practice, these special matters are usually related to cybersecurity and data protection. Before the promulgation of the 2023 CSRC Trial Measures for Overseas Listings, the CSRC seldom required companies to provide supplementary explanations regarding data protection issues. However, the situation has changed significantly thereafter. From April 14, 2023 to June 27, 2024 the CSRC requested

109 "Overview of Data Compliance in the HK IPOs for 2023," (2024), *Zhong Lun Law Firm*, www.zhonglun.com/research/articles/52819.html.

110 Wangluo Anquan Shencha Banfa (网络安全审查办法) [Cybersecurity Review Measures] (promulgated by the CAC and twelve other authorities on December 28, 2021, effective February 28, 2022) ("2022 Cybersecurity Measures"), art. 7.

111 *See*, for example, "IPO prospectus of Plus Group Holdings Inc.," p. 122, www1.hkexnews.hk/listedco/listconews/sehk/2023/0428/2023042800147.pdf.

112 2023 CSRC Trial Measures for Overseas Listings, art. 19.

256 companies to provide supplementary explanations in relation to overseas listings, and 45 percent of them (a total of 115 companies) were requested to explain their data protection issues.

In sum, cross-border data transfer is an integral part of the process for Chinese companies to seek overseas listings. As it may give rise to issues of cybersecurity and data protection, it has had an increasing impact on overseas listings of Chinese companies. This is a large area for study, as it may relate to different stages of overseas listings, namely the prospectus information disclosure requirement at the IPO stage and the continuous information disclosure requirement at the post-IPO stage, and it may also relate to different types of data, namely the company's financial data, its users' data and other data. Chapter 7 will be focused on the issue of financial data, particularly audit working papers.[113]

[113] *See* Chapter 7.

3

Why Do Chinese Companies Seek Overseas Listings?

Revisiting the Legal Bonding Theory

3.1 Introduction

As the economy becomes increasingly globalized, it is common to see the presence of foreign companies cross-listed in the major financial markets in the world, including the New York Stock Exchange, Nasdaq, the London Stock Exchange and the Hong Kong Stock Exchange. For these cross-listed firms, the legal systems of their home jurisdictions are usually less robust in protecting investors than those of the host jurisdictions where they are listed. Hence, the question arises as to why firms would choose to seek listing overseas, particularly in a jurisdiction where they would be subject to more stringent legal and regulatory requirements.

A wealth of academic literature examines this phenomenon of cross-listings, providing insight into why firms invite extra regulatory burdens on themselves. A strong explanation comes from the legal bonding theory initiated by Stulz[1] and Coffee,[2] under which cross-listed companies from jurisdictions with underdeveloped market regulation can bond themselves to the more robust market regulation of the overseas listing destination to enhance corporate governance and business performance.

It is thus interesting to see if the legal bonding theory can help explain the listing of Chinese companies in overseas markets, particularly Hong Kong. Indeed, even though Hong Kong is an international financial center and a favorite listing destination for many China-based companies that choose to list overseas, there is relatively little research that specifically examines the Mainland China (China)–Hong Kong scenario.

[1] René M. Stulz, "Globalization of Equity Markets and the Cost of Capital" (1999) 12 *Journal of Applied Corporate Finance* 8–25.

[2] John C. Coffee Jr., "The Future as History: The Prospects for Global Convergence in Corporate Governance and its Implications" (1999) 93 *Northwestern Law Review* 641–707.

At present, the vast majority of studies on international cross-listings are primarily focused on the US as the listing place.[3] A commentator has explicitly suggested that "newer research needs to overcome this U.S.-centered perspective" and specifically mentioned Hong Kong as one of the leading examples of "useful laboratories for the study of bonding."[4] Indeed, Chinese companies have now played a dominant role in the Stock Exchange of Hong Kong (SEHK). As of June 2024, Chinese companies accounted for 55.8 percent of all listed companies on the SEHK, about 79.0 percent of the total market capitalization and about 87.4 percent of the total turnover value.[5]

Further, despite the favorable underlying conditions for legal bonding of Chinese companies, the existence of legal bonding effects, as analysed in empirical studies, seems doubtful, or at least can be described as weak.[6] As it stands, empirical evidence from studies on the stock performance of Chinese companies does not unequivocally support the effect of legal bonding. This casts a shadow on the legal bonding theory and the understanding of the listing behavior of Chinese companies. Given the disparity in the level of investor protection between China and overseas listing places such as the US, it seems to be a conundrum that there is no finding of significant bonding effects. This calls for a closer examination of how to interpret these available empirical results and why the legal bonding is not as strong as expected.

Indeed, as China-based listed companies have undergone very rapid growth and internationalization, it is highly important to examine the case of Chinese companies listing overseas. More attention needs to be paid to the reasons behind the decision of Chinese companies to list overseas and the effect of overseas listing on them. Exploring the motives and trends of cross-listing is crucial to understanding the role of law in the development of the underlying securities markets, as well as the dynamics of the competition among stock exchanges and economies at large. If the effect of legal bonding can be positively confirmed, it will

3 For a detailed review of relevant studies, see Olga Dodd, "Why Do Firms Cross-list Their Shares on Foreign Exchanges? A Review of Cross-listing Theories and Empirical Evidence" (2013) 5(1) *Review of Behavioral Finance* 77–99.

4 G. Andrew Karolyi, "Corporate Governance, Agency Problems and International Cross-listings: A Defense of the Bonding Hypothesis" (2012) 13 *Emerging Markets Review* 516, 541–542.

5 HKEX, "HKEx Monthly Market Highlights", June 2024, www.hkex.com.hk/Market-Data/Statistics/Consolidated-Reports/HKEX-Monthly-Market-Highlights?sc_lang=en.

6 *See* Section 3.2.2.

certainly provide a strong model case for companies from other developing markets with less robust investor protection to encourage their companies to get listed in the better-regulated markets overseas.

This chapter will thus review the legal bonding theory as it applies to the overseas listing of Chinese companies. It shows that the effect of legal bonding, as shown in empirical research, is ambiguous or, at best, weak and then tries to explain why the empirical finding does not match the theoretical prediction. Three factors are identified to help explain the empirical anomaly. First, technical or methodological issues may contribute to the lower-than-expected bonding effect, such as the selection of research period and case samples. Second, the bonding effect may also be affected by competing considerations of relevant stakeholders involved in the overseas listing of Chinese companies. Third and most importantly, regulatory issues may seriously hinder the functioning of the legal bonding mechanism in several ways.

3.2 Applying the Legal Bonding Theory

3.2.1 The Conceptual Framework

When a company lists overseas, it will be put under the legal and regulatory system for securities offerings and trading at the listing destination and may be subject to extra regulatory requirements. For instance, if a company wants to be listed in the US, it will be required to register with the Security and Exchange Commission (SEC), and its auditing matters will be regulated by the Public Company Accounting Oversight Board (PCAOB). Likewise, a company listing in Hong Kong will be put under the scrutiny of the Hong Kong Securities and Futures Commission (SFC). A company would, therefore, incur extra costs when it chooses to cross-list on a foreign stock exchange. Thus, it is interesting to examine why companies choose to get listed overseas despite the extra financial costs and regulatory burdens.

According to the "legal bonding" theory, overseas listing presents a bonding mechanism whereby cross-listed companies can benefit from the more developed legal system of the cross-listing jurisdiction, particularly regarding corporate governance and investor protection.[7] Companies from jurisdictions with less developed company and

[7] John C. Coffee Jr., "Racing toward the Top: The Impact of Cross-listing and Stock Market Competition on International Corporate Governance" (2002) 102 *Columbian Law Review* 1757.

securities laws can leapfrog and raise their corporate governance standards by listing in jurisdictions with more developed laws and infusing themselves with stricter and well-tested legal environments, hence the legal bonding.[8] The effect of legal bonding is extensively researched in the US setting, and studies have suggested that a bonding premium does exist for companies cross-listed in the US, as compared with their domestic counterparts.[9] Moreover, studies have found a positive price effect for cross-listed companies after new and stricter securities regulations were implemented, and such an effect was more pronounced for companies coming from countries with less protection of investor rights.[10]

The effect of legal bonding is not just one-off at the time of listing and has two continuous elements. First, an overseas-listed company will be under the continuous monitoring of the more effective enforcement regime at the listing market. Second, the company will be required to constantly keep up with new legal and regulatory developments in the listing market in relation to corporate governance and investor protection. Cross-listing in an international market will allow Chinese companies to benefit from international standards and best practices.

Conceptually, the legal bonding theory provides an appealing explanation for the overseas cross-listing of Chinese companies. It is especially relevant because there exist large differences in corporate governance and investor protection between China and the overseas jurisdictions where Chinese companies are cross-listed. For instance, when Chinese companies first came to get listed in Hong Kong in the 1990s, the latter had been a common law jurisdiction with over 100 years of history, whereas China was in a state of economic transition, and its legal framework for modern companies and the financial markets had yet to emerge. The common law tradition of Hong Kong, as maintained after the 1997 handover, links it with the laws and customs of other common law jurisdictions. It remains the case that the listing approval mechanism, trading rules and ongoing obligations applicable in Hong Kong are all distinct from those in China, and the securities regulators in Hong Kong

8 Ibid.

9 Craig Doidge, G. Andrew Karolyi and René M. Stulz, "Why Are Foreign Firms Listed in the U.S. Worth More?" (2004) 71(2) *Journal of Financial Economics* 205–238.

10 Philip G. Berger, Feng Li and M. H. Franco Wong, "The Impact of Sarbanes–Oxley on Cross-listed Companies" (2005) Working Paper, Booth School of Business, University of Chicago.

and China remain independent of each other.[11] The same could be said of the differences in investor protection laws between China and the US. The listing of Chinese companies in Hong Kong and the US, therefore, seems to fit well with the setting of the legal bonding theory.

3.2.2 *The Lack of Strong Empirical Support*

There has been a wealth of empirical research trying to show and prove the existence and effect of legal bonding, but this is no easy task due to the large number of variables affecting stock prices or other financial metrics at any given time. Most of the literature on the legal bonding theory focuses on the US market as the listing destination, as it rightfully should, given its prominent position in the international securities markets. Professor Coffee proposed the legal bonding theory by looking at the circumstances of Mexican and Brazilian firms cross-listed in the US market.[12] Subsequent empirical studies often examined the stock price effects of firms cross-listed on foreign markets;[13] the hypothesis is that the legal bonding effect will help cross-listed firms to have better corporate governance and stronger financial performance. Studies found that foreign companies cross-listed in the US could have their price-to-book ratio increased by 16.5 percent compared with non-cross-listed peers.[14] There are also other ways of measuring the effects of cross-listings, such as looking at the CEO turnover rate after international cross-listing as an outcome of better corporate governance[15] or looking at whether the incident of malfeasance conducted by insiders is reduced after cross-listing due to their exposure to the stricter regulatory regime in the listing place.[16]

[11] Securities and Futures Commission, *Securities Regulation in Hong Kong* (Securities and Futures Commission, 2002).

[12] *See* note 7.

[13] *See*, for example, Craig Doidge, "U.S. Cross-listings and the Private Benefits of Control: Evidence from Dual Class Firms" (2004) 72(3) *Journal of Financial Economics* 519–553; Mark H. Lang, Karl V. Lins and Darius P. Miller, "ADRs, Analysts, and Accuracy: Does Cross Listing in the U.S. Improve a Firm's Information Environment and Increase Market Value?" (2003) 41 *Journal of Accounting Research* 317–345.

[14] *See* note 9.

[15] Ugur Lel and Darius P. Miller, "International Cross-listing, Firm Performance, and Top Management Turnover: A Test of the Bonding Hypothesis" (2008) 63(4) *Journal of Finance* 1897–1937.

[16] Jordan Siegel, "Can Foreign Firms Bond Themselves Effectively by Renting U.S. Securities Laws?" (2005) 75 *Journal of Financial Economics* 319–359.

However, there is a dearth of research looking at the case of Chinese companies listed overseas, and for the small number of empirical studies in this area, their results are mixed at best as to the existence of the legal bonding effects. An early paper that looked at share price data of twenty-nine Chinese companies listed in Hong Kong between 1998 and 2004[17] found that a certain price premium exists for companies listed with A+H-share (cross-listed in the Hong Kong market), as compared with companies listed with A+B-share (both domestic in China).[18] Another study that took a sample of ninety-two Chinese companies listed in Hong Kong between 1993 and 2006 found similar price premiums. However, this is far from conclusive, especially when a longer and later timer period is included.

A survey that examined Chinese companies listed by the American Depositary Receipt (ADR) method or through foreign initial public offerings (IPOs) from 1993 to 2005 found that these companies often underperformed the market in their post-listing period.[19] A similar survey capturing samples from 2006 again shows the same pattern, with earnings of foreign-listed firms decreasing within several years of listing.[20] Some more recent studies looked at the valuation premium for cross-listed Chinese firms from 2001 to 2012 and reported findings in contradiction to the legal bonding theory[21] or only holding partially.[22]

[17] Hongbo Shen, Li Liao and Guanmin Liao, "Cross-listing and Bonding Premium: Evidence from Chinese Listed Companies" (2010) 4(2) *Frontiers of Business Research in China* 171–184.

[18] The domestic shares of Chinese companies within Mainland China are divided into A-share and B-share. A-share is the class of shares of the most usual sense. The B class of shares was created shortly afterwards to attract foreign investment. They are traded in USD or HKD and they are only available to foreign investors. For a more detailed discussion, see Robin Hui Huang, *Securities and Capital Markets Law in China* (Oxford University Press, 2014), pp. 9–12.

[19] Cinder Zhang and Tao-Hsien Dolly King, "The Decision to List Abroad: The Case of ADRs and Foreign IPOs by Chinese Companies" (2010) 20(1) *Journal of Multinational Financial Management* 71–92.

[20] Shukuan Zhao (赵树宽), Zhili Zhao (赵智丽) and Ting Zhang (张婷), "Zhongguo Qiye Nixiang Kuajing Jiaocha Shangshi Fuhe Yueshu Jiashuo Ma?" (中国企业逆向跨境交叉上市符合约束假说吗?) [Does the Reverse Cross-border Listing of Chinese Enterprises Conform to the Bonding Hypothesis?] (2014) 9 *Hongguang Jingji Yanjiu (宏观经济研究) [Macro Economic Research]* 56.

[21] Li Xian Liu, Fuming Jiang and Milind Sathye, "Does Bonding Really Bond? Liability of Foreignness and Cross-listing of Chinese Firms on International Stock Exchanges" (2017) 41 *Research in International Business and Finance* 109–124.

[22] Li Xian Liu and Jun Li, "Corporate Governance and Listing Location of Chinese Firms: The Bonding Theory Revisited" (2020) 25(1) *Journal of the Asia Pacific Economy* 40–61.

Then again, a study covering the longest period from 1997 to 2015 with a sample size of 243 Chinese firms and an aim to look for potential excess returns for cross-listed companies reported no supporting evidence in favor of the legal bonding theory.[23] In the face of the mixed results in empirical studies and the practical difficulty in accessing the effect of legal bonding, the bonding effect of Chinese companies' overseas listing has been dubbed as "perhaps greater than zero, but not by much."[24]

In sum, existing empirical research shows ambiguous or, at best, weak effects of legal bonding. This is quite puzzling because, as described earlier, the setting of Chinese companies versus the common law and professional standards in Hong Kong or the US should have been an ideal testing ground for the legal bonding conjecture. The following sections will try to investigate possible reasons for the lack of strong evidence on legal bonding effects in relation to overseas listings of Chinese companies, including technical or methodological issues, competing considerations of relevant stakeholders and regulatory issues at both substantive law and law enforcement levels.

3.3 Technical Issues Affecting the Legal Bonding Effect

To start with, technical or methodological issues may contribute to the lower-than-expected bonding effect that can be found in relation to overseas listings of Chinese companies. First, due to various reasons, such as data availability, many empirical studies tend to select the more recent years as their research period, but the bonding effects tend to be much larger in the early years of the opening up of the Chinese capital market. Second, there are many state-owned enterprises (SOEs) in the case samples for empirical research, and the special features of SOEs may have distorting effects on the legal bonding mechanism. Finally, there are other methodological issues that may affect the calculation of the bonding effect.

[23] Hong Li, "Direct Overseas Listing Versus Cross-listing: A Multivalued Treatment Effects Analysis of Chinese Listed Firms" (2019) 66 *International Review of Financial Analysis* 101391.

[24] Donald Clarke, "The Bonding Effect in Chinese Cross-listed Companies: Is It Real?" in Robin Hui Huang and Nicholas Calcina Howson (eds.), *Enforcement of Corporate and Securities Law: China and The World* (Cambridge University Press, 2017), pp. 88, 94.

3.3.1 *The Selection of Research Period*

It should be pointed out that there is an important temporal dimension to the phenomenon of overseas listings of China-based companies, and the legal bonding effect may have changed significantly over time. Indeed, as discussed earlier, the history of cross-listing of Chinese companies can be divided into several stages, and their different characteristics may affect the legal bonding effect.

In the early stage of the 1990s, there was the greatest discrepancy in corporate governance between China and overseas listing destinations such as Hong Kong. Both the Shanghai Stock Exchange and the Shenzhen Stock Exchange were established around 1990. The first national company law in China did not come into being until 1993, and the first national securities law came into force even later in 1999.[25] By contrast, the securities market in Hong Kong has a much longer history and was already a well-established international financial center in the 1990s with a robust legal and regulatory regime.

According to the legal bonding theory, cross-listed issuers stand to gain the most where the difference in legal institutions is the largest between the home and host jurisdictions. The early stage of cross-listing during the 1990s would thus be the time when the legal bonding effect can be most significant. However, during this period, the least amount of price data is maintained for today's research. There are also a very limited number of Chinese domestic-listed companies that could be used for control-pairing purposes. Even if the effect of legal bonding during this period is significant, it could be averaged away over a longer study period, as the data may be disproportionately distributed in favor of later periods. Indeed, smaller surveys focusing on earlier periods are seemingly more able to produce evidence to support the legal bonding theory, as compared with the later studies that cover longer time frames.

Another point to note about studies covering the earlier period is that prelisting changes may hide significant bonding effects in empirical analysis. This phenomenon is especially pronounced for transitioning economies such as China. In preparation for listing in overseas markets, Chinese companies would have already made significant changes before

[25] For a more detailed discussion of the early development of the securities market and relevant laws in China, see Robin Hui Huang, *International Securities Markets: Insider Trading Law in China* (Kluwer Law International, 2006), pp. 7–23.

the actual listing.[26] These early pioneers had to undergo relevant prelisting structural changes in order to meet the listing requirements of overseas markets. This, in turn, helps bridge the large gap in corporate governance between the securities markets in Mainland and foreign jurisdictions. In a sense, the most significant part of the legal bonding effect for these companies may have occurred prior to their actual listing on an overseas exchange. Again, this part of the legal bonding effect would not be captured by statistical analysis of a company's *post-listing* compliance with regulatory requirements or price movements. Indeed, according to relevant research examining the Chinese companies immediately *before* getting listed in Hong Kong, they usually had more robust corporate governance than their domestic-listed counterparts in terms of the number of independent directors and the separation between ownership and management.[27]

Furthermore, the time window used to compare company performance before and after listing is often a couple of years, which is arguably too short to capture the full effect of legal bonding. It would only capture the legal bonding effect that is directly related to listing and only around the time of listing. Yet, the effect of legal bonding might well go beyond the very instance of listing. The bonding to the destination jurisdiction enables a company to keep up with any postlisting legal or regulatory development, leading to the continuous improvement of corporate governance on the part of the issuer. To empirically capture such continuous effects, an event study analysis can be conducted around significant legal changes in the listing destination's regulatory regime. For instance, subsequent to the enactment of the Sarbanes–Oxley Act in the US in 2002, cross-listed firms in the US market were found to have lowered their abnormal returns as compared with their domestic-listed counterparts.[28]

3.3.2 *The Composition of the Case Sample*

Given the historical and political setting of China, in considering the issue of overseas listing, it is important to take into account the

[26] Qian Sun, Wilson Tong and Yujun Wu, "Overseas Listing as a Policy Tool: Evidence from China's H-Shares" (2013) 37 *Journal of Banking and Finance* 1460–1474.

[27] Kung Fan-hua and Cheng Chia-ling, "The Determinants of Overseas Listing Decisions: Evidence from Chinese H-Share Companies" (2012) 11 *Asian Business & Management* 591–613.

[28] Omar A. Esqueda and Dave Jackson, "Cross-listing Performance and Insider Ownership: The Experience of U.S. Investors" (2015) 32–33 *Journal of Multinational Financial Management* 77–94.

distinctive features of SOEs in China. The transition of highly centralized SOEs into a more market-oriented form started in the earlier period of the 1990s. As SOEs were generally inefficient with problematic governances, the legal bonding effect of cross-listing tended to be larger in the early period of China's economic reform, which reinforces the point about the temporal change of the legal bonding effect made in the preceding section.

The case of Chinese SOEs may have other important impacts on the nature and extent of the legal bonding effect. The listing of an SOE could be initiated not for the economic benefits of the firm but rather out of political considerations or, sometimes, the personal decisions of government officials. It is found that the rate of firms doing IPO tends to increase when there is a window of impending political promotion of local officials.[29] This may come out for various reasons. For instance, it might be the result of the need for local officials to achieve more spectacular economic outcomes in order to compete for promotion, or some officials might have wanted to utilize their political power for personal gains before they are to be transferred out of a position.[30] Specifically, SOEs with strong political connections are more likely to list overseas than nonpolitically connected firms,[31] and a government official is more likely to be promoted after a company within the territory of his office gets an overseas listing rather than a domestic listing.[32]

To be sure, the decision to list overseas is often made for economic reasons. One of the officially stated objectives of SOE going public is to enhance corporate governance.[33] In essence, corporate governance aims to reduce various agency costs, particularly the agency cost arising from the divergence of interest between management and shareholders. In the case of SOEs, the state is the large shareholder. In the early stage of economic reform in China there was plenty of room for firm managers to

[29] Joseph D. Piotroski and Tianyu Zhang, "Politicians and the IPO Decision: The Impact of Impending Political Promotions on IPO Activity in China" (2014) 111(1) *Journal of Financial Economics* 111–136.

[30] Ibid.

[31] Mingyi Hung, T. J. Wong and Tianyu Zhang, "Political Considerations in the Decision of Chinese SOEs to List in Hong Kong" (2012) 53 *Journal of Accounting and Economics* 435–449.

[32] Ibid., p. 448.

[33] Zhonggong Zhongyang Guowuyuan Guanyu Shenhua Guoyouqiye Gaige de Zhidao Yijian (中共中央、国务院关于深化国有企业改革的指导意见) [Guiding Opinions of the CPC Central Committee and the State Council on Deepening the Reform of State-Owned Enterprises] (issued by the State Council on August 24, 2015).

misappropriate corporate assets. The agency problem was acute, as there were no effective mechanisms in place to deal with the opportunism of the managers.[34] Government officials, as the representatives of the state shareholders, were not able and willing to monitor a company's operation. The challenge here is how to incentivize the corporate management to work diligently for the best benefits of the company.

Cross-listing then presents a good mechanism to address the above issue. It bonds Chinese companies to the more stringent and more effective regime of corporate governance and market regulation in the overseas listing place. On the one hand, it puts more checks and balances on the managers and helps align the interests of the managers with those of the shareholders. On the other hand, the SOEs have to treat regulation more seriously in the overseas listing place than they do in the domestic market. In practice, the Chinese regulators may not be able to regulate SOEs in the same way as other companies simply because the SOEs are politically powerful and privileged. By contrast, overseas-listed SOEs cannot enjoy the same favorable treatment in the face of foreign regulators; however, due to various reasons such as political considerations, only a small number of SOEs sought to be listed overseas, particularly in the US markets. In recent years, the number of overseas-listed SOEs has been decreasing, and as of the start of 2024, all Chinese SOEs had been delisted from US exchanges.[35]

3.3.3 Other Methodological Issues

There can be other methodological issues that account for the lack of strong empirical evidence on the legal bonding effect in the case of overseas-listed Chinese companies. For instance, given the complexity of isolating the stock price effect of various other factors, the empirical studies available thus far should probably be viewed as preliminary for a full understanding of the phenomenon of Chinese companies' overseas listing. The same issue is faced by researchers looking at cross-listing in other markets, that is, how to properly attribute empirical findings on the stock price effects to the legal bonding theory and not the other plausible explanations that may give rise to similar predictions.

[34] Karen Lin, Bo Li and Yan Guo, "State-Owned Enterprises in China: A Review of 40 Years of Research and Practice" (2020) 13(1) *China Journal of Accounting Researching* 31–55.

[35] The US–China Economic and Security Review Commission, "Chinese Companies Listed on Major US Stock Exchanges," 2024, www.uscc.gov/sites/default/files/2024-01/Chinese__Companies_Listed_on_US_Stock_Exchanges_01_2024.pdf.

There is an additional layer of difficulty in isolating the price effect of legal bonding upon Chinese companies. Except for a number of special routes, such as the Qualified Foreign Institutional Investors (QFIIs), Stock Connect Programs between Shanghai/Shenzhen stock exchanges with Hong Kong Stock Exchange, the Chinese securities market is largely closed to foreign investors, in contrast with other origin countries often studied in cross-listing research, such as Mexico. The Chinese market is, therefore, structurally fragmented to begin with. With such effects in place, perhaps methodologies that indirectly look into changes in corporate activities could reveal better insights into legal bonding from a different angle. Possible observable corporate behavior includes changes in CSR performance,[36] the number of connected transactions,[37] or the number of independent directors on the board.

3.4 Political-Economy Factors Affecting the Legal Bonding Effect

The bonding effect may also be affected by various political-economy factors, that is, relevant stakeholders involved in the overseas listing of Chinese companies may behave in an institutional environment that is not envisaged by the legal bonding hypothesis. On the one hand, the host jurisdictions of overseas-listed Chinese companies may be tempted or pressured to take a relaxed approach to regulating them in order to attract and retain listings of Chinese companies in the face of increasingly fierce competition for listing businesses in international capital markets. On the other hand, overseas listings of Chinese companies may be motivated by other considerations, thus reducing the bonding effect.

3.4.1 Host Jurisdictions Seeking to Attract Chinese Companies

The attitude of the regulators of the listing place toward foreign issuers is important for the legal bonding mechanism to function, and it may be

[36] Haina Shi, Xin Zhang and Jing Zhou, "Cross-listing and CSR Performance: Evidence from AH Shares" (2018) 12 *Frontiers of Business Research in China* 11.

[37] Fang Ji (计方) and Xing Liu (刘星), "Jiaocha Shangshi, Bangding Jiashuo yu Da Gudong Liyi Qinzhan——Jiyu Guanlian Jiaoyi Shijiao de Shizheng Yanjiu" (交叉上市、绑定假说与大股东利益侵占——基于关联交易视角的实证研究) [Cross-listing, Bonding Hypothesis and Interest-Expropriation of Large Shareholders Based on the Perspective of Related Party Transactions] (2011) 33(04) *Dangdai Jingji Kexue (当代经济科学) [Modern Economic Science]* 105–114.

determined by the goal of host jurisdictions seeking to attract and retain the listings of Chinese companies. Indeed, there has been regulatory competition in international capital markets, and various interest groups may interact to shape the institutional environment in which overseas-listed Chinese companies are regulated.[38]

Regulators are often mindful of the competitiveness of the securities markets that they regulate, and thus, the regulators of the host jurisdiction may choose to take a more relaxed attitude toward foreign issuers. For example, the inclination of regulators toward favoring competition for listing can be seen from the regime for foreign private issuers (FPIs) in the US, under which foreign private issuers are subject to a lower level of regulation than that for domestic issuers in relation to various requirements such as disclosure requirements, reporting frequency and board committee composition requirements. The insistence on strict audit oversight by the PCAOB is another good example. The PCAOB has, until recently, allowed China-based auditors to register and operate despite not being able to monitor their work. In the first place, it was the US government and regulators that had given the green light for many years, allowing Chinese companies to list in the US without audit checking. As a result, the US securities markets could attract a large number of high-quality Chinese companies, particularly in the high-tech sector.

Likewise, in the face of increasing competition for listing businesses, stock exchanges have strong incentives to make listing criteria more flexible to accommodate foreign issuers instead of bonding them to more stringent standards. This arguably occurred in 2018 when the Hong Kong Stock Exchange revised its listing rules to introduce the "weighted voting right" regime, which is widely preferred by the founders of private high-tech companies to retain corporate control after listing.[39]

As for the issuers, as much as they may want to get the benefit of legal bonding in terms of higher valuation, there is also a tendency for them to try to evade rigorous regulation. This is true, at least for their managers, who would be more closely regulated in a developed jurisdiction. Here

[38] Fredrick Tung, "From Monopolists to Markets?: A Political Economy of Issuer Choice in International Securities Regulation" (2002) *Wisconsin Law Review* 1363; Erica Fung, "Regulatory Competition in International Capital Markets: Evidence from China in 2004–2005" (2006) 3 *NYU Journal of Law & Business* 244.

[39] Robin Hui Huang, Wei Zhang and Kelvin Siu Cheung Lee, "The (Re)introduction of Dual-Class Share Structures in Hong Kong: A Historical and Comparative Analysis" (2020) 20(1) *Journal of Corporate Law Studies* 121.

again, the agency problem is the crux of the issue. Compared with the task of corporate restructuring according to the regulatory requirements of the listing place, it can be more difficult to get the Chinese managers to adapt to them. For instance, Chinese managers may not readily agree with the emphasis on disclosure duty as advised by their overseas professional advisers.[40] Given the mindset of corporate management to avoid regulatory burdens whenever possible, it is quite plausible that they would take advantage of various problems associated with cross-border regulatory cooperation, such as jurisdictional ambiguities, regulatory conflicts and judgment recognition obstacles. This, in turn, has weakened the legal bonding effects of cross-listing.

3.4.2 *Other Motivations for Chinese Companies Seeking Overseas Listings*

There are other motivations for Chinese companies to get listed overseas, thus reducing the bonding effect. To begin with, many cases of overseas listing may be explained based on market segmentation or the liquidity theory.[41] The Chinese capital market has long been somehow isolated from the international market. For instance, foreigners are restricted from investing in the Chinese markets, and there are also restrictions on cross-border capital flow and currency conversion. Gaining access to the pool of international investors and liquidity has been an important factor that many Chinese companies consider in pursuing overseas listing, particularly in the early period when the Chinese market was less open to the outside world. Companies listed in overseas markets can enjoy the liquidity advantage when conducting cross-border corporate activities, such as merger and acquisition (M&A) transactions. Even today, the market segmentation theory remains a useful explanation for the overseas listing of many Chinese companies, as China continues to impose capital control on cross-border investments and its currency, namely Renminbi, is not yet freely convertible. Overseas listings can

40 Geoffrey Sant, Charles M. Yablon, Stephen A. Radin, Kayvan Sadeghi, Christopher Seeger and Richard H. Silberberg, "Symposium: Chinese Companies and U.S. Class Actions: Securities Litigation and Product Liability" (2014) 23 *Cardozo Journal of International and Comparative Law* 738.

41 Stephen R. Foerster and G. Andrew Karolyi, "The Effects of Market Segmentation and Investor Recognition on Asset Prices: Evidence from Foreign Stocks Listing in the United States" (1999) 54(3) *Journal of Finance* 981–1013.

allow Chinese companies and their Chinese founders to raise funds and have liquidity in international financial markets.

Moreover, the limited capacity of the Chinese capital markets may be another reason for Chinese companies to seek overseas listing.[42] Until recently, China has only had two national stock exchanges and can accommodate a limited number of companies to get listed every year. Worse still, SOEs generally enjoy a favorable treatment in getting listing opportunities. As such, the less privileged companies, such as private companies and smaller companies, may have to seek listing overseas.

The type of industry a firm belongs to also has a bearing on its listing decision. For many Chinese internet companies, overseas markets, especially the US, may be preferred due to the more friendly environment for high-tech businesses, such as the listing criteria and the valuation model. More mature listing destinations usually require more and better information disclosure, which can help reduce the monitoring cost of investors, thereby improving a firm's valuation.[43] When a company gains better visibility in the market, more investors may add its stock to their portfolio.[44] Compared to its home market, the overseas-listed company can have the benefit of a higher level of analyst coverage in the international market.

Further, if a company is listed in a well-respected overseas market, it may send out a stronger signal about its investment worthiness than would be the case if it were domestically listed. This is the central thesis of the "reputational bonding" theory under which cross-listed firms may benefit from enhanced reputation even if the more robust law of the listing place is not effectively enforced in practice.[45] This reputational bonding theory shares a common feature with the legal bonding theory, that is, a company can hope to improve its corporate governance and share price by getting listed in a more developed overseas market and thus bonding with it legally and/or reputationally. Hence, they can be referred to collectively as "the bonding theory."

[42] For a more detailed discussion of the inadequacies in the Chinese IPO regime, see Robin Hui Huang, *Securities and Capital Markets Law in China* (Oxford University Press, 2014), pp. 53–56.

[43] Steven Huddart, John S. Hughes and Markus Brunnermeier (1999), "Disclosure Requirements and Stock Exchange Listing Choice in an International Context" (1999) 26 *Journal of Accounting and Economics* 237–269.

[44] Stephen R. Foerster and G. Andrew Karolyi, "The Effects of Market Segmentation and Investor Recognition on Asset Prices: Evidence from Foreign Stocks Listing in the United States" (1999) 54(3) *Journal of Finance* 981–1013.

[45] *See* note 16.

The bonding theory may be simplistic because it overlooks the internal decision-making mechanism of the company and considers the bonding effects of overseas listing to be linear. The ultimate decision-makers within the company are the controlling shareholders and the bonding effects of overseas listing on them can be more complex than the bonding theory suggests. The controlling shareholders may benefit from a higher share price of the company in proportion to their shareholding, while at the same time, may suffer from a more stringent regulation regime in the sense of reduced ability to extract private benefits of control. The decision-making process of the controlling shareholders will be determined by the aggregate of the cash flow gains and the private benefits of control. This theory has become known as the "private benefit of control" hypothesis.[46] As it builds on the bonding theory and examines the impact of bonding effects in a more nuanced way, it can be seen as the more sophisticated version of the bonding theory.[47]

Empirical studies have confirmed the validity of the "private benefit of control" hypothesis by looking at non-US companies that cross-list in the US.[48] As controlling shareholders may benefit privately from their controlling power, they may choose not to get the company to list overseas if the bonding effect of cross-listing may result in a decrease in their private benefits. However, if the increase in the value of the company after listing brings sufficient benefits to the controlling shareholder to compensate for the decrease in private benefits, the controlling shareholder may decide to have the company listed overseas. For instance, when the controlling shareholding is significantly concentrated, the gain that the controlling shareholder may obtain from the increase in cash flow after listing may outweigh the "loss" in private benefits.[49]

[46] Craig Doidge, G. Andrew Karolyi, Karl V. Lins, Darius P. Miller and Rene M. Stulz, "Private Benefits of Control, Ownership, and the Cross-listing Decision" (2009) 64(1) *Journal of Finance* 425–466.

[47] Indeed, in the earlier stage of development of the "private benefits of control" hypothesis, it was intended to generate evidence to support the bonding hypothesis. See Craig Doidge, "U.S. Cross-listings and the Private Benefits of Control: Evidence from Dual Class Firms." (2004) 72(3) *Journal of Financial Economics* 519–553.

[48] *See* note 46.

[49] Feng Li (李凤) and Yan Dong (董艳), "Da Gudong Siyou Shouyi Dui Haiwai Shangshi Juece de Yingxiang" (大股东私有收益对海外上市决策的影响——基于内地赴港上市企业的实证研究) [Private Benefits of Control and the Foreign-listing Decision: Based on the Data of Domestic Company Listed in Hong Kong] (2016) 16(1) *Jingjixue Jikan (经济学季刊) [China Economic Quarterly]* 415–440.

Given that Chinese companies usually have a high level of ownership concentration with a controlling shareholder, this "private benefits of control" hypothesis is particularly relevant to the overseas listing of Chinese companies. Indeed, this hypothesis has been supported by an earlier study examining Chinese companies cross-listed in Hong Kong from 2004 to 2011.[50] Simply put, there exists a "U-shaped" pattern regarding the impact of shareholding structure on the company's listing decision. When the level of shareholding concentration is not sufficiently high, the controlling shareholder may be reluctant to give up control and to cross-list, but the decision may turn around when the shareholding concentration level is high, so much so that the controlling shareholder can gain more from the value increase of the company than its loss in control-based private benefits.

In addition, the motivations for some Chinese companies to get listed overseas can go against the bonding theory. For instance, under the "avoiding hypothesis,"[51] rather than looking for better corporate governance rules in the listing destination, the cross-listed companies may be more interested in evading their home country's regulatory oversight. This hypothesis may be particularly relevant to the case of Chinese companies, to the extent that some industries, such as internet businesses and education services, are subject to stricter regulation in China and may not be listed domestically. Other factors, such as geographical proximity, may play an important role in the decision-making process of Chinese companies as to where to get listed. The choice of listing place is related to the company's business operation strategy.[52]

Finally, international politics could exert a profound influence on the decision to list overseas. In recent years, against the broad backdrop of growing tension between the US and China, the US has tightened oversight on Chinese companies in relation to audit work papers.[53] In the shadow of delisting risks, many US-listed Chinese companies adopted the so-called homecoming plan – going back to China and/or Hong Kong for listing. This homecoming phenomenon has been labelled "reverse cross-listing of Chinese companies" and has occurred before in

50 Ibid.

51 Amir N. Licht, "Cross-listing and Corporate Governance: Bonding or Avoiding?" (2003) 4(1) *Chicago Journal of International Law* 141.

52 Sergei Sarkissian and Michael J. Schill, "The Overseas Listing Decision: New Evidence of Proximity Preference" (2004) 17(3) *Review of Financial Studies* 769–809.

53 Robin Hui Huang, "The US–China Audit Oversight Dispute: Causes, Solutions, and Implications for Hong Kong" (2021) 54(1) *The International Lawyer* 151.

the 2000s when regulatory compliance costs increased significantly for US-listed Chinese companies as a result of the enactment of the Sarbanes–Oxley Act.[54] However, this recent wave of reverse cross-listing of Chinese companies is different both in terms of the scale of reverse cross-listing and the nature of the reason behind it.

In practice, the overseas listing of Chinese companies is usually motivated by a combination of the reasons discussed earlier. The presence and entanglement of the various reasons make it harder to accurately measure the effect of legal bonding in empirical analysis. Nevertheless, the existence of the other reasons does not necessarily preclude the legal bonding theory, and they should not be viewed as mutually exclusive in explaining the overseas listing of Chinese companies. Together, they paint a well-rounded picture of the overseas listing of Chinese companies, and the effect of each of them would vary across periods, depending on the circumstances of individual companies, such as their ownership structure, the industry they belong to or their initial corporate governance level.

3.5 Regulatory Issues Affecting the Legal Bonding Effect

Regulatory issues may seriously hinder the functioning of the legal bonding mechanism in several ways. First, there are significant uncertainties in the substantive rules of the Chinese regulatory framework for overseas listing of Chinese companies. This makes it more difficult for the market to assess and price the regulatory gap between Chinese law and those in overseas listing destinations. Second, there are many challenges in cross-border misconduct monitoring and detection. Needless to say, if market misconduct cannot be effectively monitored and detected, there will be no law enforcement, and the law will remain on paper only. Finally, even if misconduct is detected, there are still various obstacles to the enforcement of laws on overseas-listed Chinese companies. This creates significant difficulties in holding misbehaving overseas-listed companies accountable to the same level as domestic companies.

Overall, regulatory issues are key to the proper functioning of the legal bonding mechanism and, thus, will be the focus of this research project.

54 Nicholas Calcina Howson and Vikramaditya S. Khanna, "Reverse Cross-listings: The Coming Race to List in Emerging Markets and an Enhanced Understanding of Classical Bonding" (2014) 47(3) *Cornell International Law Journal* 607–629.

3.5.1 *Uncertainties and Complexities of China's Regulatory Regime*

China's regulatory regime for overseas listing has been evolving over the past three decades.[55] On February 17, 2023, the CSRC issued the Interim Measures for the Administration of Overseas Securities Offering and Listing by Domestic Enterprises (2023 Measures on Overseas Listing), representing an overhaul of China's regulatory regime for overseas listings of Chinese companies.[56] A very important new requirement imposed by this rule is the introduction of a recordation regime for all overseas listing of Chinese companies, covering both direct and indirect overseas listings.[57] Under this new requirement, a domestic enterprise conducting overseas offering and listing should undergo the recordation formalities with the CSRC, submit the recordation report, legal opinions and other relevant materials, and truthfully, accurately and completely explain the information on shareholders.[58]

This recordation regime has important implications for an overseas listing of Chinese companies. Among them, the issue arises as to whether it confirms the legal status of the Variable Interest Entities (VIE) structure commonly used in indirect overseas listing activities, that is, whether the VIE structure will gain legality if it goes through the recordation process. As will be discussed in Chapter 6, I argue that the legality of the VIE structure is more likely to be confirmed with the recordation regime, but there is still lingering uncertainty.[59]

There are other sources of uncertainty in the Chinese regulatory regime for overseas listings of Chinese companies. For instance, as overseas listings will lead to foreign investment in Chinese companies, some of which may operate in sensitive industries, national security review of foreign investment is an integral part of the discussion on overseas listings of Chinese companies. Over the years, China has gradually established a comprehensive legal framework for national security review of foreign investment. Recent efforts were made to refine the public enforcement

55 For more details on the history of China's regulatory regime for overseas listings of Chinese companies, see Chapter 3.

56 Jingnei Qiye Jingwai Faxing Zhengquan He Shangshi Guanli Shixing Banfa (境内企业境外发行证券和上市管理试行办法) [Interim Measures for the Administration of Overseas Securities Offering and Listing by Domestic Enterprises] (issued by the CSRC on February 17, 2023, effective from March 31, 2023).

57 Ibid., art. 2.

58 Ibid., art. 13.

59 For a more detailed discussion of the VIE issue, see Chapter 6.

mechanism of the review in tandem with a new "pre-establishment national treatment plus negative list" system under the 2020 Foreign Investment Law. There are many factors affecting China's national security review regime for foreign investment, including the ongoing (and escalating) US–China competition (or conflict) at the international level and the evolution of state or party capitalism at the domestic level.[60]

National security is a broad term that includes many different types of security. In recent years, data security has become an increasingly important issue and has significantly impacted the overseas listing of Chinese companies.[61] This has been well demonstrated in the case of DiDi and the relevant requirement of data security clearance in the recently issued 2023 Measures on Overseas Listing.

Moreover, with the increasing internationalization of its securities market, China has recently introduced Article 2(4) of the 2019 Securities Law in order to deal with the important issue of extraterritorial jurisdiction over cross-border securities transactions.[62] While it represents an important development, the provision is couched in very broad terms, bringing uncertainties and difficulties to its application in practice.

Under the legal bonding theory, overseas-listed companies bond themselves to the more robust regulation of the listing place, thereby enhancing their corporate governance and business performance. This means that the more the regulation of the home jurisdiction lags behind that of the host jurisdiction, the stronger the bonding effect would be. However, if it is difficult to assess the gap between the regulation at home and overseas due to the uncertainties of the regulation on one side, the legal bonding effect cannot be effectively reflected in the stock price of overseas-listed companies. Further, it may also be a source of sampling bias for empirical research as overseas-listed Chinese companies have to go through a screening mechanism explicitly or implicitly imposed by the Chinese authorities.

3.5.2 *Hurdles in Cross-border Misconduct Monitoring and Detection*

More robust regulation in overseas jurisdictions would only be meaningful if they were rigorously enforced. In practice, there exist multiple

[60] For more details, see Chapter 5.
[61] For more details, see Chapter 3.
[62] For more details, see Chapter 4.

hurdles in the process of monitoring and detecting misconduct of overseas-listed Chinese companies. Indeed, although the Chinese capital markets law has significantly improved in terms of institution-building and law development, a noticeable gap still exists between it and its counterparts in the US and Hong Kong. It is thus important to examine the extent to which the legal bonding effect may be undercut by enforcement issues arising from the cross-border nature of overseas listings.

To enforce the law against misconduct of Chinese companies monitoring and detecting the misconduct is required, a process which is often plagued by the lack of transparency in the business operation and financial position of Chinese companies. Foreign regulators have until recently been denied access to the audit work paper concerning Chinese companies.[63] In the US, the audit oversight regime of the PCAOB relies on monitoring the audit firms that provide services to listed companies. Foreign audit firms that provide service to foreign companies listed in the US also need to be registered with the PCAOB and fall into the scope of regular onsite assessment. However, China-based audit firms had long refused to submit their work to the PCAOB for review, arguing that the information may constitute state secrets and could not be sent overseas without the approval of Chinese authorities.[64] Following some major auditing scandals of Chinese companies listed in the US that caused huge losses to investors in recent years, the US began to take a tougher stance by passing the "Holding Foreign Companies Accountable Act" (HFCAA) in 2020, under which Chinese companies may be forcibly delisted if the PCAOB is not able to inspect their relevant audit work papers. Under the specter of the HFCAA, the PCAOB and China's regulators reached an agreement to give the PCAOB complete access to the audit materials of US-listed Chinese companies in August 2022, and shortly thereafter, the PCAOB carried out its inspection of relevant audit materials for the first time under the agreement.

Similarly, as a popular destination for Chinese companies to list overseas, Hong Kong has long faced the same audit oversight problem as seen in the US, with some cases having been brought by the SFC against noncomplying auditors.[65] Since 2019, the Hong Kong regulator and Chinese authorities have reached an agreement that allows Chinese

[63] Robin Hui Huang, "The US–China Audit Oversight Dispute: Causes, Solutions, and Implications for Hong Kong" (2021) 54(1) *The International Lawyer* 151.

[64] Ibid.

[65] *SFC v. E & Y* (a firm) [2013] HKCFI 402; [2013] 6 HKC 156; HCMP 1818/2012.

companies' audit papers to be examined by the Hong Kong audit watchdog, namely the Financial Reporting Council (FRC). The first access to audit papers of Chinese companies was received near the end of 2020.[66] Then, FRC completed an investigation in the following June in relation to an auditing firm's failure to identify material misstatements in earnings figures presented by a China-based company. This is the first such investigation enabled by assistance from the Ministry of Finance under the Memorandum of Understanding.[67] The exchanged audit working document has enabled the FRC to pinpoint a failure in obtaining audit evidence on the part of the auditor, in which the auditors had not applied competent standards in drawing their overall conclusion.

Another important aspect of monitoring involves the surveillance of market misconduct, such as insider dealing.[68] To combat insider dealing, jurisdictions have generally established market surveillance mechanisms to detect abnormal transactions. However, surveillance can become more complicated in the cross-listing context, where companies have their primary business location outside of their listing jurisdictions. On top of that, further difficulties arise as China-based companies often cross-list in multiple locations – Shanghai/Shenzhen, Hong Kong and/or New York. Price-sensitive information may be formed in one jurisdiction, while insider trade may covertly take place in another. Then, besides the conventional company shares, an insider may opt for trading in a multitude of derivative asset classes which are offered in overseas markets for the China-based listed companies. These all create new challenges for effective market surveillance and hamper the efficacy of the regulation of overseas-listed Chinese companies.

3.5.3 *Difficulties of Securities Law Enforcement*

Enforcement strategies of securities law have traditionally been divided into two broad categories, namely, public enforcement and private enforcement. In general, public enforcement is initiated by a state official such as a regulator or a prosecutor, while private enforcement is by a

[66] Enoch Yiu, "'Statesecrets' no more: Hong Kong Regulator Gains Access to HKEX-listed Chinese Firms' Audit Papers in Breakthrough," *South China Morning Post*, December 10, 2020, www.scmp.com/business/banking-finance/article/3113210/state-secrets-no-more-hong-kong-regulator-gains-access.

[67] Financial Reporting Counsel, "Press Release," July 2, 2021, www.afrc.org.hk/media/nnanyteu/frc_completes_investigation_02072021_eng.pdf.

[68] For more details, see Chapter 8.

private party in the form of civil actions for compensation or rescission. Sections 3.5.3.1 and 3.5.3.2 will discuss the difficulties associated with these two types of enforcement in turn.

3.5.3.1 Public Enforcement

Where a contravention is detected by the SFC in Hong Kong, it can either bring the company and/or the directors to the Market Misconduct Tribunal (MMT) or the High Court for enforcement action. The actual number of public enforcement cases is meaningful both in terms of gauging the intensity of action taken by the regulator as well as in signaling deterrence to the issuers. A low figure of actual cases may not give a pronounced deterrent effect, which is perhaps the case in Hong Kong with regard to China-based issuers.

This research conducts a survey of all enforcement actions taken by the SFC from 2005 to mid-2021[69] against companies with a majority of operations in China, whether registered in Mainland, Hong Kong or overseas. As Table 3.1 shows, there were thirty instances of such enforcement actions, including enforcement actions against the company, its director or company chairman, as well as three instances where sanctions were imposed on sponsoring investment banks for IPO applications of Chinese companies.[70] Over half of these enforcement actions were undertaken during the period of 2017 to 2021, hence, over the extended period since the first Hong Kong-listed Chinese companies, there had been no enforcement actions. The target companies are also predominantly smaller private companies. In only one instance was an H-share company taken to court, where seven managers of the dual-listed Shandong Molong Petroleum Machinery were disqualified.[71] In another instance, the state-owned CITIC Group was taken to the MMT.[72]

[69] In earlier years, the power to bring a complaint against the issuer to the MMT rested with the Financial Secretary of Hong Kong Special Administrative Region (HKSAR), so the survey also includes cases brought by the Financial Secretary. For a discussion of the history of the MMT, see Robin Hui Huang, "Xianggang Zhengquan Shichang Shidang Xingwei Shencaichu Zhidu Jiqi Qishi" (香港证券市场失当行为审裁处制度及其启示) [The Institution of the Market Misconduct Tribunal in Hong Kong and Its Implications for Mainland China] (2018) 1 *Touzizhe (投资者) [Investors]* 184–202.

[70] Announcements on enforcement actions by SFC are available at apps.sfc.hk/edistributionWeb/gateway/TC/news-and-announcements/news/enforcement-news/. Multiple directors may be prosecuted in each instance.

[71] *HCMP 1094/2019*, proceedings under section 214 of the Securities and Futures Ordinance.

[72] Eventually, the prosecution failed, and the directors were acquitted by the MMT.

Table 3.1 *SFC enforcement actions against China-based companies in Hong Kong*

	Enforcement action counts	Red-chips / H-shares	P-chips
2021 (-Jun)	4	1	3
2020	4	0	4
2019	4	0	4
2018	5	0	5*
2017	4	0	4*
2016	1	0	1
2015	1	0	1
2014	4	1	3*
2013	0	0	0
2012	0	0	0
2011	1	0	1
2010	0	0	0
2009	2	0	2
2008	1	0	1
2007	1	0	1
2006	0	0	0
2005	0	0	0
	32	2	30

Source: SFC Enforcement news, Market Misconduct Tribunal.
Note: *Including enforcement action concerning negligent/fraudulent application in unapproved IPO.

Overall, the number of actions is not significant, and the effect of deterrence could not be said to be strong, especially in the long period between 1993 and 2014. Some institutional factors may help explain the low number of enforcement actions.

First, there are many difficulties in cross-border regulatory cooperation. In the case of cross-listed firms, the senior management, major assets and core business activity are typically outside of the listing jurisdiction. This is especially true for the small financial city of Hong Kong. With respect to China-based companies, sanctions of corporate misconduct often require evidence from the Mainland. Although regulatory cooperation has been gradually enhanced between Hong Kong and the Mainland, it progresses at a rate far slower than the growth of cross-listing. This is due to many important issues, which can be broadly divided into two categories: substantive rules on the definitions of market

Table 3.2 *SEC enforcement actions against Chinese issuers in the US*

	Case count
2021	0
2020	1
2019	0
2018	0
2017	0
2016	0
2015	2
2014	3
2013	7
2012	3
2011	0
2010	0
	16

Source: US Securities and Exchange Commission, Litigation Releases Archive.

misconduct and penalties for such misconduct; and enforcement mechanisms in relation to information exchange, regulatory architecture and extradition arrangement.[73]

Likewise, as shown in Table 3.2, looking at the enforcement activity of the SEC in the US, the case count against China-based companies is also small. As an illustration, in the year 2020 there were 302 instances where the SEC brought a complaint to federal courts, and only one of them concerned a Chinese issuer, that is, Luckin Coffee.[74] Apart from this case and the wave of cases between 2012 and 2015 (following an explosion of Chinese companies' backdoor listing), there had been little enforcement against Chinese issuers in most of the survey period.

Second, there is no extradition arrangement available between Hong Kong and Mainland China, as well as between the US and China.[75] This is problematic, especially for more serious cases of fraud and misconduct which warrant criminal sanctions. Without an extradition arrangement,

[73] For more details, see Chapter 8.

[74] *SEC v. Luckin Coffee, Inc.*, Civil Action no. 1:20-cv-10631.

[75] Jesse Fried and Ehud Kamar, "China and the Rise of Law-Proof Insiders" (2022) 48 *Journal of Corporation Law*, 227.

it would be difficult to proceed with the prosecution of a particular case. This would not have been the case for enforcement actions between European countries or between the US and Canada.

Lastly, it is sometimes difficult to negotiate and make a decision regarding which jurisdiction should act in tackling the misconduct of cross-listed issuers. Many types of corporate misconduct, such as fraudulent financial reporting, insider dealing and market manipulation, can fall into the jurisdiction of multiple regulators. Often, there can be no straightforward answer, and this may give rise to uncertainty in the scope of jurisdiction and the enforcement process.

3.5.3.2 Private Enforcement

In some jurisdictions, such as the US, private enforcement in the form of securities class action takes a role comparable to, or even greater than, public enforcement. For Hong Kong, a major obstacle to private enforcement concerns the cost. To begin with, the legal cost in Hong Kong is among the highest in the world. Adding on to the matter, there is no class action regime in Hong Kong. In the US, small investors can join in a class action litigation against listed companies and do not need to pay legal fees thanks to the contingency fee arrangement. In Hong Kong, however, this would be impossible due to the lack of class action regime. There is also no contingency fee arrangement whereby the lawyer can agree not to charge if the result of the case turns out to be unfavorable. As such, it would be practically impossible for small investors to bring lawsuits on their own.

Even if a claim is successful, there could be another obstacle, namely China's recognition and enforcement of foreign securities judgment.[76] In practice, most overseas-listed Chinese companies have most of their assets in China, making it necessary to go through Chinese courts to enforce the judgment delivered by the court of the listing place. However, there are many difficulties in this area, which undermine the efficacy of the regulation of cross-listed Chinese companies.[77]

On the other hand, it remains feasible for a company to use its resources to sue its director for their misfeasance against the company. A case in point is the case of China Shanshui, where a company sued its

[76] For a more detailed discussion of this issue, see Chapter 9.

[77] Jesse Fried and Ehud Kamar, "China and the Rise of Law-Proof Insiders" (2022) 48 *Journal of Corporation Law*, 226.

present and previous directors.[78] A related suit was also brought by the minority shareholders of the company through the statutory derivative action regime under the Hong Kong company law.[79] The statutory derivative action allows a member of the company, with the leave of the court, to bring proceedings on behalf of the company in respect of misconduct committed against the company.[80] However, this type of proceeding has not been frequently observed in the Hong Kong courts against China-based companies, resulting in a level of private enforcement lower than it should be. Ultimately, this weakens the checks and balances on issuers.

For private enforcement in the US, despite the availability of class action litigation, US investors have faced the same obstacle (even to a larger extent) in terms of judgment recognition and enforcement against China-based companies.[81] While there is a rising trend of litigation against Chinese companies, the judgment enforcement issue has made litigation less meaningful. Lower chances of enforcing securities judgments also lower the settlement values of securities cases.

3.6 Conclusion

Chinese companies listing overseas have recently attracted considerable attention in the realm of international financial markets. They represent one of the largest groups of companies that have sought listing in foreign markets, both in terms of the number of companies and the amount of market capitalization. The rationale behind this phenomenon warrants serious examination. There are some theories, particularly the legal bonding theory, that have been developed to explain company listing across borders in general, but it is unclear whether they fit well with the China case.

On the face of it, it seems that the legal bonding theory should be able to provide a good explanation for overseas listing of Chinese companies, as there is a significant disparity of capital market regulation between their home jurisdiction, namely China, and overseas host jurisdictions, particularly the US and Hong Kong. As a result of overseas listing, Chinese companies can be bonded to the more robust regulation of the

[78] *HCA 548/2019*, and a series of related lawsuits.
[79] *Yu Yuchuan & Ors v. China Shanshui Investment Company Limited* (HCMP) 360/2015.
[80] Companies Ordinance (Cap 622), sections 722, 732.
[81] For a more detailed discussion of this issue, see Chapter 9.

listing places. Under the bonding theory, these companies should consequently have better corporate governance and more confidence from investors, thereby producing a higher stock price with a bonding premium. Yet a review of relevant empirical studies shows that there are only ambiguous or, at best, weak effects of legal bonding.

It is thus interesting to investigate why the legal bonding effect is not as strong as expected. There are three factors that can be identified to help explain the empirical anomaly.

First, some technical or methodological issues may contribute to the lower-than-expected bonding effect in the case of overseas-listed Chinese companies. For instance, the empirical analysis of the legal bonding effects for Chinese companies may be affected by the selection of the research period. The bonding effects tend to be much larger in the early years of the opening up of the Chinese capital market, such as in the 1990s. During this period, China just leapt into the international financial markets from a planned economy, and the legal bonding effect could be most significant. However, data availability tends to be a more severe issue for this period, and thus, most empirical studies select a later study period, such as after the new millennium or even after the 2008 global financial crisis. Moreover, Chinese state-owned enterprises may present a special situation which may distort legal bonding effects. The listing of an SOE could be initiated not for economic reasons but rather out of political considerations or sometimes personal decisions of government officials.

Second, the bonding effect may also be affected by various political-economic factors. On the one hand, the host jurisdictions of overseas-listed Chinese companies may be tempted or pressured to take a relaxed approach to regulating them in order to attract and retain listings of Chinese companies in the face of increasingly fierce competition for listing businesses in international capital markets. On the other hand, overseas listings of Chinese companies may be motivated by other considerations, thus reducing the bonding effect. For instance, overseas listings of Chinese companies may be motivated by such factors as gaining access to the international market, overcoming the difficulty of getting listed in the Chinese domestic markets, obtaining reputational bonding effects, seeking private benefits of control from overseas listing and responding to geopolitical issues.

Third and most importantly, regulatory issues may seriously hinder the functioning of the legal bonding mechanism in several ways. To begin with, there are significant uncertainties in the substantive rules of the

Chinese regulatory framework for overseas listing of Chinese companies. This makes it more difficult for the market to assess and price the regulatory gap between Chinese law and those in overseas listing destinations. It may also be a source of sampling bias for empirical research as overseas-listed Chinese companies have to go through a screening mechanism explicitly or implicitly imposed by the Chinese authorities. Further, there are many challenges in cross-border misconduct monitoring and detection. Plainly, if market misconduct cannot be effectively monitored and detected, there will be no law enforcement, and the law will remain on paper only. Last but not least, even if misconduct is detected, there are still various obstacles to the enforcement of laws on overseas-listed Chinese companies, including both public and private enforcement modes of law. This creates significant difficulties in holding misbehaving overseas-listed companies accountable to the same level as domestic companies.

Overall, regulatory issues are key to the proper functioning of the legal bonding mechanism and, thus, will be the focus of this research project. This chapter lays a solid foundation and a roadmap for the following chapters, which will discuss the relevant regulatory issues in more detail and make suggestions for improvement.

4

Extraterritorial Jurisdiction of China's New Securities Law

4.1 Introduction

With increasing economic globalization and technological advancement, cross-border securities transactions have seen an upward trend. Issues of conflicts of jurisdiction (and in some circumstances, also the attendant issue of conflicts of law) have been raised due to the cross-border nature of such securities transactions. For instance, one company may offer securities and have them listed in a foreign securities market; further, the securities of a domestically listed company can be traded among foreign investors. In such circumstances, disputes may arise as to whether the securities law of the home jurisdiction or that of the foreign jurisdiction should govern the transaction, including the various forms of related misconduct, particularly misstatements, insider trading and market manipulation.

The issue of jurisdiction for cross-border securities transactions is of great significance not only for a country's sovereignty but also for the interests of participating companies and investors. Hence, there is a great need to examine the issue of extraterritorial jurisdiction, which generally means that under legally given circumstances, domestic courts can have jurisdiction upon overseas matters and apply their own domestic laws to regulate them, albeit in a different jurisdiction altogether.[1]

Over the past four decades, the Chinese economy has seen impressive growth and now ranks as the world's second largest. A growing number of Chinese companies have sought listings overseas, and simultaneously, more channels have become available for Chinese investors to access foreign securities markets.[2] China has also been considering the

[1] For a more detailed discussion of the concept and typology of jurisdiction, see Section 4.2.1.

[2] For official data on the upward trend of cross-border securities transactions, see Section 4.2.3.

possibility of accepting the listing of foreign companies on the Chinese markets. These market developments present legal issues of extraterritorial jurisdiction which, if not properly addressed, would hinder the further opening-up and internationalization of the Chinese securities market. Hence, in the recent overhaul of its securities law passed in December 2019 which has been in effect from March 2020 (PRC Securities Law),[3] China explicitly introduces a new provision on extraterritorial jurisdiction. However, due to the lack of detail, it is unclear how the extraterritorial jurisdiction of the Chinese securities law may be triggered and applied.

This chapter aims to critically examine the extraterritorial jurisdiction of Chinese securities law, and based on such examination, set out suggestions for improvement. Owing to the advanced development and global influence of its securities markets, the United States (US) is a pioneer in the theory and practice of extraterritorial jurisdiction, and therefore this chapter will draw upon the US experience in this regard. Section 4.2 briefly introduces basic concepts about jurisdiction and provides background. Section 4.3 discusses the problems of China's legal system and securities law, with a focus on the Luckin Coffee scandal as a case study. Section 4.4 discusses the history, development and present situations of extraterritorial jurisdiction of US securities law. Section 4.5 provides a comparison between the two countries and policy recommendations for China. A conclusion is drawn in Section 4.6.

4.2 Background: Concepts and Developments

4.2.1 The Concept and Typology of Jurisdiction

Under public international law, the term "jurisdiction" is closely related to the notion of sovereignty.[4] Sovereignty means that each country has exclusive powers and rights to govern all matters within its borders.[5] In other words, "jurisdiction" indicates the power of a country to regulate nationals and properties by adopting domestic laws within its territory.

[3] Zhonghua Renmin Gongheguo Zhengquanfa (中华人民共和国证券法) [Securities Law of the PRC] (promulgated by the National People's Congress on December 29, 1998, effective on July 1, 1999) (last amended on December 28, 2019, effective from March 1, 2020).

[4] Cedric Ryngaert, *Jurisdiction in International Law* (Oxford University Press, 2015), p. 5.

[5] Hannah L. Buxbaum, "Transnational Regulatory Litigation" (2006) 46 *Virginia Journal of International Law* 251, 268.

This concept also refers to the territorial principle, which is the most fundamental principle within the scope of jurisdiction.[6]

At the doctrinal level, however, the concept of "jurisdiction" has long been subject to debate because of its inaccuracy. It is necessary to first discuss the typology of jurisdiction, as different types of jurisdiction have varying legal meanings and functions. Under the traditional international law theory, there are three types of jurisdiction: legislative jurisdiction (prescriptive jurisdiction), judicial jurisdiction (adjudication jurisdiction) and executive jurisdiction (enforcement jurisdiction).[7] Legislative jurisdiction means that a country's legislative body has authority to enact and apply laws; judicial jurisdiction relates to the power of the courts to accept and hear cases; executive jurisdiction refers to a country's ability to exercise authority of administration in accordance with its laws. In general, a country can have legislative jurisdiction over extraterritorial matters without contravening international law (e.g., treaty law and customary law),[8] while judicial and executive jurisdictions are strictly limited within its territory.[9] Thus, a country can stipulate that a specific law or rule is applicable to overseas matters under certain conditions. The inconsistency between domestic law and international law does not necessarily violate international law,[10] and it may constitute a violation only in special circumstances. By contrast, if the judicial and executive jurisdiction are directly enforced by countries beyond territorial boundaries, it would generally contravene the territorial principle and encroach the sovereignty of other nations. In practice, there are controversies on the scope and application of these two types of jurisdiction. The term "jurisdiction" in this chapter is used to cover all three types and it will be specified which type is referred to in the relevant discussion.

In addition, there are several important principles governing the issue of jurisdiction in international law: the territorial principle, personality principle, protective principle and universality principle.[11] To start with, the territorial principle means that a country has the right to administer

[6] Cedric Ryngaert, *Jurisdiction in International Law* (Oxford University Press, 2015), p. 49.

[7] Robert Jennings and Arthur Watts (eds.), *Oppenheim's International Law* (Longman, 2008).

[8] *The case of S.S. Lotus (Fr. v. Turk.)*, 1927 P.C.I.J. (ser. A) No. 10 (Sept. 7), at 18–19.

[9] Ibid.

[10] Ian Brownlie, *Principles of Public International Law* (Oxford University Press, 2008).

[11] Cedric Ryngaert, *Jurisdiction in International Law* (Oxford University Press, 2015), p. 101.

all affairs within its territory. Second, the personality principle can be further divided into the active and passive personality principle. The active one implies that a country has the power to govern its own nationals, regardless of whether the nationals act domestically or abroad.[12] By contrast, the passive one indicates that a country has jurisdiction on overseas conduct that prejudices its nationals' interests.[13] In other words, the active personality principle focuses on the nationality of perpetrators while the passive personality principle is concerned with the nationality of victims. Third, the protective principle means that a country possesses rights to exercise jurisdiction over any behavior that poses threat to its security or interests, even though those actions are conducted abroad.[14] Finally, under the universality principle, every country has jurisdiction on internationally recognized criminal behavior such as war crimes, genocide and torture.[15] These principles are very important to ascertaining the nature and extent of extraterritorial jurisdiction in the specific context of securities law, which will be discussed in the section below.

4.2.2 *Extraterritorial Jurisdiction of Securities Law*

In general, extraterritorial jurisdiction refers to a situation where a country extends its legal power or applies its laws to other countries under particular conditions. Traditionally, private international law decides on the issue of "extraterritoriality" by choosing one essential element and then examining the place where the essential element is found.[16] As an exception to the traditional territorial principle, extraterritorial jurisdiction is based on the personality, protective and universality principles. Extraterritorial jurisdiction was once expressly denied in international law. The court in *S.S. Lotus* held that a country could not exercise jurisdiction beyond its territory unless allowed by international custom or conventions.[17]

[12] Cedric Ryngaert, *Jurisdiction in International Law* (Oxford University Press, 2015), p. 104.

[13] Ibid., p. 110.

[14] Ibid., p. 114.

[15] Ibid., p. 121.

[16] Anthony J. Colangelo, "What Is Extraterritorial Jurisdiction?" (2014) 99 *Cornell Law Review* 1303; This principle is also reflected in *Morrison v. National Australia Bank Ltd* 130 S. Ct 2869 at 2884 (2010).

[17] *The case of S.S. Lotus (Fr. v. Turk.)*, 1927 P.C.I.J. (ser. A) No. 10 (Sept. 7), at 18–19.

Nowadays, due to the increasing interconnectedness of securities markets, the extraterritorial jurisdiction of securities law has come to be applied by a growing number of countries, particularly the US. Extraterritorial jurisdiction of securities law can be applied to a broad range of securities activities relating to cross-border listing and/or trading of securities. As noted above, the personality, protective and universality principles provide theoretical underpinnings for extraterritorial jurisdiction. For instance, extraterritorial jurisdiction of securities law can be triggered by the personality principle where the nationals of a state are the perpetrator or the victim of securities misconduct overseas; the protective principle may provide the basis for the exercise of extraterritorial jurisdiction in the name of protecting national interests from securities misconduct overseas; the universality principle may be used to justify exercising extraterritorial jurisdiction in serious criminal securities offenses such as insider trading. In practice, the issue of extraterritorial jurisdiction usually arises when there is a need to deal with cross-border securities misconduct such as misrepresentation, insider trading and market manipulation.

4.2.3 China's Need to Regulate Cross-border Securities Transactions

With the impressive development of China's securities market and the general economic growth, the issue of extraterritorial jurisdiction of securities law has become increasingly significant for China. Since the early 1990s, China has gradually established a vibrant domestic securities market, which is now ranked the world's second largest in terms of market capitalization.[18] Simultaneously, a large number of Chinese companies choose to get listed or dual-listed overseas for various reasons. For instance, many Chinese companies, particularly privately owned companies, cannot get listed domestically and therefore, must seek listings overseas. China has traditionally adopted a merits-review regulatory system for securities offerings, under which securities offerings must receive approval from the securities regulator, namely, the China

[18] China Securities Regulatory Commission, *2020 Annual Report of China Securities Regulatory Commission*, p. 22. China has a total of three national stock exchanges now: Shanghai Stock Exchange and Shenzhen Stock Exchange were established in the early 1990s while Beijing Stock Exchange was set up in September 2021.

Securities Regulatory Commission (CSRC).[19] In practice, the merits-review system favors state-owned enterprises (SOEs), and many non-SOEs have no choice but to turn to overseas markets for listings.

Hong Kong and the US are the two most popular destinations for overseas listings of Chinese companies. As of June 2019, Chinese companies represented almost 60 percent of the companies listed in Hong Kong, over 70 percent of the market capitalization and nearly 80 percent in terms of the volume of turnover.[20] For Chinese companies listed in the US markets, the majority (around 180 companies) are listed on Nasdaq, many of which are tech companies or smaller-sized companies. There are around eighty Chinese companies listed on the New York Stock Exchanfe (NYSE), which tend to be larger companies operating in more traditional industries.[21]

On the other hand, Chinese investors have more access to foreign securities markets both indirectly and directly. Due to China's policy of capital account control for foreign investment, Chinese investors cannot freely trade in securities listed in overseas markets. In order to broaden the investment choices for the Chinese public and to alleviate the problem of excess liquidity within China, the Chinese government announced on April 18, 2006 that Chinese investors can indirectly invest in overseas securities markets through the Qualified Domestic Institutional Investors (QDII).

In more recent years, China has tried to establish various mechanisms to allow Chinese investors to invest directly in overseas markets. In November 2014, the Shanghai–Hong Kong Stock Connect was set up to link the two stock exchanges in Shanghai and Hong Kong, so that investors from each side can have direct access to the other market; this was soon followed by a similar Shenzhen–Hong Kong Stock Connect in December 2016; and in June 2019, the Shanghai–London Stock Connect established links between the Shanghai Stock Exchange and the London Stock Exchange. These programs open the door for the two-way traffic of cross-border securities trading, in the sense that Chinese investors can trade in securities listed overseas while foreign investors can trade in those listed in China.

[19] Robin Hui Huang, *Securities and Capital Markets Law in China* (Oxford University Press, 2014), ch. 3.

[20] Robin Hui Huang, "The US–China Audit Oversight Dispute: Causes, Solutions, and Implications for Hong Kong" (2021) 54(1) *The International Lawyer* 151.

[21] Ibid.

While the above development has greatly facilitated the cross-border trading of securities and has improved the internationalization of the Chinese securities market, it has also brought about a new challenge of regulating cross-border securities misconduct. In fact, the issue relates not only to the companies which are based in China and listed overseas but may also cover purely foreign companies in which Chinese nationals have invested. To be sure, the securities regulatory regimes in the listing/trading places, such as the US and Hong Kong, can be generally expected to provide adequate protection to Chinese investors dealing with securities there. However, there may be instances where the Chinese investors may prefer to bring litigation under the Chinese securities law in a Chinese court. For instance, China has established a regime for aggrieved investors to pursue compensation claims arising from securities misstatement, which is dubbed Chinese-style class action with the advantages of a light evidentiary burden and a high recovery rate.[22] By contrast, Hong Kong has no class action regime but rather relies on public enforcement of securies law to protect investors.[23] While the US has a robust regime for securities class action, Chinese investors may, in some cases, want to litigate in China due to factors such as litigation costs, prospects of success, recovery rates and the issue of cross-border judgment enforcement.

Moreover, with the increasing internationalization of Chinese markets there is a growing risk that the order of the Chinese domestic securities markets may be disrupted by activities conducted overseas. Apart from the typical cross-border securities misconduct such as insider trading and market manipulation, a recent example is the unauthorized provision of overseas trading services to Chinese domestic investors. It was reported that some overseas securities firms provided online services for Chinese investors to trade securities in overseas markets such as the US and Hong Kong, without holding a license from the Chinese regulators.[24]

22 Robin Hui Huang, "Class Action in China: Opportunities and Challenges" in Brian Fitzpatrick and Randall Thomas (eds.), *Cambridge International Handbook of Class Actions* (Cambridge University Press, 2021), pp. 350–365; Robin Hui Huang, "Private Enforcement of Securities Law in China: A Ten-Year Retrospective and Empirical Assessment" (2013) 61(4) *American Journal of Comparative Law* 757.

23 Donald, David C. and Paul W. H. Cheuk, "Hong Kong's Public Enforcement Model of Investor Protection" (2017) 4 *Asian Journal of Law & Society* 349.

24 Wang Yuanyuan (王媛媛), "Futu、Laohu Gengda de Jinrong Anquan Wenti Hai Zai Houmian" (富途、老虎更大的金融安全问题还在后面 它们连合法经营资质都没有) [Futu and Tiger Securities Have Bigger Problems of Financial Security Including the Lack of Business Qualifications], *21st Century Business Herald*, October 16, 2021, finance.eastmoney.com/a/202110162142602074.html.

In addition, these so-called internet cross-border securities firms were also criticized for transferring the personal information of Chinese investors outside China in violation of the personal information protection law.[25] Due to various reasons such as resources constraints and lack of regulatory priority or political will, the regulators in overseas markets may not take action in a timely and adequate manner, and thus it would be necessary for the Chinese regulators to exercise extraterritorial jurisdiction over those issues.

In sum, owing to the growing number of cross-border securities transactions that may impact on Chinese investors, Chinese companies and the Chinese domestic securities markets, there is a pressing need for China to deal with the issue of extraterritorial jurisdiction of securities law.

4.3 The Chinese Law: Progress and Problems

4.3.1 Historical Development

Over the years, in recognition of the need to regulate cross-border securities transactions, China made a series of legislative efforts. The current legal regime is comprised of several laws and regulations as follows.

As early as in 1994, the State Council issued the *Special Provisions of the State Council Concerning the Floatation and Listing Abroad of Stocks by Limited Stock Companies*, stipulating that the laws of the PRC can apply to disputes involving Chinese companies listed in foreign securities markets.[26] However, this regulation is couched in very general terms without setting out clear and workable details.

In 2010, the *Law of the People's Republic of China on Choice of Law for Foreign-Related Civil Relationships*[27] was enacted to clarify the application of laws concerning foreign-related civil relations, including securities transactions. Under Article 39 of this law, the laws at the locality of the

[25] Ibid.

[26] Guowuyuan Guanyu Gufen Youxian Gongsi Jingwai Muji Gufen ji Shangshi de Tebie Guiding (国务院关于股份有限公司境外募集股份及上市的特别规定) [Special Provisions of the State Council Concerning the Floatation and Listing Abroad of Stocks by Limited Stock Companies] (issued by State Council on August 4, 1994, effective on August 4, 1994), art. 29.

[27] Zhonghua Renmin Gongheguo Shewai Minshi Guanxi Falv Shiyongfa (中华人民共和国涉外民事关系法律适用法) [Law of the People's Republic of China on Choice of Law for Foreign-Related Civil Relationships] (issued by Standing Committee of the National People's Congress on October 28, 2010, effective on April 1, 2011).

realization of the rights of securities or other laws which have the closest relation with the securities shall apply to such securities.[28] As the provision relates to the application of law, it falls within the category of legislative jurisdiction. However, it does not provide guidance on how to determine important issues such as "the locality of the realization of the rights" and "the closest relation."

The key legislation in this area is the *Civil Procedure Law of the People's Republic of China*,[29] which lays down a set of provisions about judicial jurisdiction over cases involving contractual disputes, shareholders and company disputes, tort disputes and other property disputes respectively.[30] Further, the Supreme People's Court (SPC) issued the *Judicial Interpretation on the Application of the Civil Procedure Law of the People's Republic of China*[31] to provide more guidance on the various types of foreign-related civil cases which are subject to the jurisdiction of Chinese laws. However, there is no provision specifically addressing judicial jurisdiction of securities disputes.

As a primary law to regulate the national securities markets, the Securities Law of the PRC was first enacted in 1998 and did not include any explicit provision on extraterritorial jurisdiction until the recent reform, which was passed on December 28, 2019 and took effect from March 1, 2020.[32] Article 2(4) is a newly added provision specifically addressing extraterritorial jurisdiction, stating that:

[28] Zhonghua Renmin Gongheguo Shewai Minshi Guanxi Falv Shiyongfa (中华人民共和国涉外民事关系法律适用法) [Law of the People's Republic of China on Choice of Law for Foreign-Related Civil Relationships] (issued by Standing Committee of the National People's Congress on October 28, 2010, effective on April 1, 2011), art. 39

[29] Zhonghua Renmin Gongheguo Minshi Susongfa (中华人民共和国民事诉讼法) [The Civil Procedure Law of the People's Republic of China] (issued by the National People's Congress on April 9, 1991, revised in 2007, 2012, 2017 and 2021).

[30] Zhonghua Renmin Gongheguo Minshi Susongfa (中华人民共和国民事诉讼法) [The Civil Procedure Law of the People's Republic of China] (issued by the National People's Congress on April 9, 1991, revised in 2007, 2012, 2017 and 2021), arts. 24, 27, 29, 35, 266.

[31] Zuigao Renmin Fayuan Guanyu Shiyong <Zhonghua Renmin Gongheguo Minshi Susongfa> de Jieshi (最高人民法院关于适用《中华人民共和国民事诉讼法》的解释) [Interpretation of the Supreme People's Court on the Application of the Civil Procedure Law of the People's Republic of China] (issued by Supreme People's Court on January 30, 2015, effective on February 4, 2015, revised in 2020 and 2022). It should be noted that under the Chinese legislative system, the judicial interpretation carries the force of law and can be cited as legal basis for adjudicating cases.

[32] Zhonghua Renmin Gongheguo Zhengquanfa (中华人民共和国证券法) [Securities Law of the PRC] (promulgated by the National People's Congress on December 29, 1998, effective on July 1, 1999) (last amended on December 28, 2019, effective from March 1, 2020).

> Where the offering and trading of securities outside the People's Republic of China disrupt the order of the domestic market of the People's Republic of China and infringe upon the lawful rights and interests of domestic investors, the violator shall be punished in accordance with the relevant provisions of this Law and shall be subject to legal liability.

In sum, the extraterritorial jurisdiction of the securities law in China has a relatively short history and there is only one specific provision on the issue, namely, Article 2(4) of the 2019 Securities Law. To be certain, Article 2(4) marks a critical watershed in the history of extraterritoriality of Chinese securities law, but it suffers from a number of problems which will be discussed in the next section.

4.3.2 Article 2(4) of PRC Securities Law and Its Problems

As discussed above, under the 2019 reform of the Chinese securities law, Article 2(4) explicitly provides for extraterritorial jurisdiction for the very first time. Specifically, it is made clear that the law may apply to relevant securities activities even if they occur outside China. Extraterritorial jurisdiction covers both the offering and trading of securities outside China. Further, extraterritorial jurisdiction may arise when the relevant securities activities disrupt the order of the Chinese securities markets and infringe upon the lawful interests of the Chinese investors.

No doubt, Article 2(4) is an important development in the area of extraterritorial jurisdiction, representing one of the most significant changes brought about by the 2019 reform of the Chinese securities law. It provides an important legal tool for China to protect Chinese investors and its securities markets from misconduct committed in relation to cross-border securities listings and transactions. However, the legal regime is not without problems. Indeed, there are several problems that may affect the application of Article 2(4).

To start with, there is a theoretical issue about the nature of extraterritorial jurisdiction under Article 2(4). Indeed, a literal reading of Article 2(4) does not clearly indicate which type of jurisdiction it refers to. Some commentators are of the view that Article 2(4) is regarding legislative jurisdiction and thus expands the application of the PRC Securities Law beyond China's borders.[33] Others believe that Article 2(4) is about

[33] Liu Xinyu (刘歆宇), "Ruixing Caiwu Zaojiaan Wuda Falv Jiaodian: Zuiduo Faduoshao, Shifou Shiyong Changbiguanxia" (瑞幸财务造假案五大法律焦点：最多罚多少，是否适用长臂管辖) [The Five Major Legal Focuses of Ruixing's Financial Fraud Case: What

judicial and executive jurisdiction so that Chinese courts and the CSRC can have jurisdiction on securities activities outside China.[34]

Second, Article 2(4) is worded in broad terms with some vagueness of expression, which may lead to uncertainties in relation to its application. For instance, what would constitute the disruption of the order of the Chinese markets? How do we determine the nature and extent of infringements on the interests of Chinese investors? In fact, while the English translation of Article 2(4) provided by a widely used Chinese law database, namely, PKULAW, has an "and" between the "market disruption" prong and the "investor infringement" prong,[35] there is no such conjunction in the original Chinese text. In other words, Article 2(4) is actually silent on the relationship of the two prongs. As a result, it is not fully clear whether the two prongs need to both be satisfied or whether only satisfying one prong would suffice to sustain extraterritorial jurisdiction.

Finally, there is a lack of clarity as to how Article 2(4) interacts with other relevant laws and rules. Under Article 2(4), the essential test of extraterritorial jurisdiction is the effect of the relevant securities transactions on the Chinese market and investors. As noted in the preceding paragraph, it is not fully clear how the effect test is structured on paper, let alone how it will be applied in practice. Large discretion is left to courts and relevant authorities, thereby causing legal uncertainty and conflicts of jurisdictions. Further, as discussed earlier, some relevant laws and regulations in China refer to other elements of extraterritorial jurisdiction such as conduct.[36]

Hence, there is a great need to conduct a holistic and contextualized examination of the Chinese regime for extraterritorial jurisdiction over foreign-related securities cases.

the Maximum Penalty is and Whether Long-Arm Jurisdiction Applies], *Pengpai Xinwen (澎湃新闻) [The Paper]*, April 3, 2020, www.thepaper.cn/newsDetail_forward_6824214.

34 Chen Yixin (陈一新) and Tangxin (汤欣), "Woguo Zhengquanfa Yuwaiguaxia Tiaokuan De Shiyong – Yi Ruixing Zaojia Shijian Wei Zhongxin" (我国证券法域外管辖条款的适用——以瑞幸造假事件为中心) [The Application of the Extraterritorial Jurisdiction of Chinese Securities Law – Focus on Luckin Coffee Fraud] (2020) *Gongsi Falv Pinglun (公司法律评论) [Company Law Review]*.

35 Zhonghua Renmin Gongheguo Zhengquanfa (中华人民共和国证券法) [Securities Law of the PRC] (promulgated by the National People's Congress on December 29, 1998, effective on July 1, 1999) (last amended on December 28, 2019, March 1, 2020), art. 2(4).

36 *See* Section 4.3.1.

4.3.3 *A Case Study:* Luckin Coffee

The recent high-profile case of *Luckin Coffee* has generated a heated debate on when and how Article 2(4) should be applied in practice. Luckin Coffee is a China-based company which was listed on the US market in 2019. On April 2, 2020, this company revealed that its revenue was inflated by around RMB 2.2 billion (US$310 million) from the second quarter to the fourth quarter of 2019.[37] As a result, the market value of Luckin Coffee plummetted with a spillover effect that damaged the general reputation of Chinese companies listed overseas. The CSRC communicated with the SEC about the case of *Luckin Coffee* and conducted an investigation into it.[38] As Luckin Coffee was listed on the US securities markets, this investigation was technically the first time the CSRC had exercised extraterritorial executive jurisidiction under Article 2(4).[39] Some Chinese investors reportedly attempted to bring a civil suit to recover their investment losses before the Intermediate People's Court of Xiamen City (where Luckin Coffee's operational headquarters are located); however, the court only requested these investors to supplement evidence but did not indicate whether it would accept this case.[40] As the case arises from securities misstatements of an overseas-listed company, the key issues are whether Chinese courts have extraterritorial jurisdiction over this case under the 2019 Securities Law, and if so, how should they exercise their jurisdiction in this case?

[37] Liu Yujing and Louise Moon, "Luckin Coffee's Founder Says Sorry as Nasdaq Prepares to Kick Out His Stock for Fraud, in the First Expulsion of a Chinese Company," *South China Morning Post*, May 19, 2020, www.scmp.com/business/companies/article/3085132/nasdaq-readies-delist-luckin-coffee-chinas-answer-starbucks.

[38] Brenda Goh and Zhang Yan, "China says to penalise Luckin Coffee for accounting fraud," *Reuters*, July 31, 2020, www.reuters.com/article/us-luckin-coffee-investigation-idUSKCN24W1XF.

[39] Sun Tingyang (孙庭阳), "Zhongguo Zhengjianhui Changbiguaxia Shouxiu, Hecha Ruixingkafei" (中国证监会"长臂管辖"首秀，核查瑞幸咖啡) [The "Long Arm Jurisdiction" Debut of CSRC, Inspecting Luckin Coffee] *Jinjing Wang (经济网) [Ceweekly]*, April 27, 2020, www.ceweekly.cn/2020/0427/295412.shtml.

[40] ZhouYing (周莹) "Ruixingkafei Susong Jinzhan Zhuizong: Jingnei Susong Rengzai Zhunbei Lian Cailiao Jieduan, Jingwai Jiti Susong Yiyou Touzizhe Shenqing Shouxiyuangao" (瑞幸咖啡诉讼进展追踪：境内诉讼仍在准备立案材料阶段 境外集体诉讼已有投资者申请首席原告) [The Litigation Progress of Luckin Coffee: Domestic Litigation is Still in the Stage of Filing Materials while Investors in Overseas Class-Action Lawsuits Have Applied for Chief Accuser] *21Shiji Jingji Baodao (21世纪经济报道) [21st Century Business Herald]*, June 29, 2020, m.21jingji.com/article/20200629/herald/f25b0b8c29b8bd075333c7d8ca5ec418.html.

Before discussing PRC courts' jurisdiction, it is worth noting the nonretroactivity principle of the law, whereby a law can only apply to matters occurring after its promulgation. Because the PRC Securities Law came into effect on March 1, 2020, while the Luckin Coffee scandal happened on January 31, 2020, some scholars believe that Article 2(4) cannot be applicable to this case.[41] However, in China, substantive law follows the doctrine of observing old laws, while procedural law follows the doctrine of observing new laws.[42] In other words, if Article 2(4) is considered as a substantive rule, then the nonretroactivity principle should apply to prevent its application to the case of *Luckin Coffee*. On the other hand, if Article 2(4) is treated as a procedural rule, it can be applied retrospectively to the case of *Luckin Coffee*. Assuming that Article 2(4) has retrospective effect, the issue boils down to whether the requirements of Article 2(4) are satisfied so as to give the Chinese courts extraterritorial jurisdiction over the case. As discussed earlier, however, the wording of Article 2(4) is very general, and Article 2(4) falls short of providing clear guidance.

In sum, the case of *Luckin Coffee* demonstrates the importance of the extraterritorial jurisdiction of Chinese securities law as a practical issue. There is a pressing need to solve the various problems with the relevant Chinese law as discussed earlier. Thus, the following sections will examine the experiences of overseas jurisdictions, notably the US, with a view of finding appropriate ways to improve the Chinese legal regime.

4.4 The US Experiences: Law and Practice

4.4.1 Overview

4.4.1.1 The Presumption against Extraterritoriality and Its Exception

To understand the extraterritorial jurisdiction of the US securities law, it is necessary to first look at the presumption against extraterritoriality.

[41] Deng Jianping (邓建平) and Mou Wenhui (牟纹慧), "Ruixing shijian yu xin zhengquanfa de yuwai guanxiaquan (瑞幸事件与新《证券法》的域外管辖权) [The Luckin Case and the Extraterritorial Jurisdiction of the New Securities Law]" (2020) Caikuai yuekan (财会月刊) [Finance and Accounting Monthly] 135, 138.

[42] Zhu Ting (朱婷), "Ruixin Zaojia Shijian: Xin Zhengquanfa 'Changbiguanxia' de Shijinshi" (瑞幸造假事件：新《证券法》"长臂管辖"的试金石) [The Luckin Coffee Fraud Incident: The Touchstone of "Long-Arm Jurisdiction" in the New Securities Law], *Sohu*, April 28, 2020, www.sohu.com/a/391748169_120032.

This presumption means that domestic laws or regulations cannot be applied to overseas activities unless there are clear provisions allowing so.

The history of this presumption can be traced back to *United States v. Palmer.*[43] The most famous case explaining this presumption is *American Banana Co v. United Fruit Co.*[44] In this case, the Supreme Court refused to exercise its jurisdiction – despite the fact that both the plaintiff and the defendant were American companies, on the grounds that the alleged misconduct occurred outside the US.[45] Thus, the key point of this case is that the operation and effect of domestic laws should be confined within US territory.[46] In 1949, a clear statement of this presumption was given in *Foley Bros., Inc. v. Filardo*,[47] where the court stated "legislation of Congress, unless a contrary intent appears, is meant to apply only within the territorial jurisdiction of the United States."[48]

There are two important points to note about the presumption against extraterritoriality. First, a legal presumption can be either an irrebuttable presumption or a rebuttable presumption. In the above quote from *Foley Bros., Inc. v. Filardo*, the phrase "unless a contrary intent" indicates an exception to the presumption, leaving an opportunity to exercise extraterritorial jurisdiction. Consequently, the presumption against extraterritoriality is a rebuttable presumption. Second, the presumption against extraterritoriality in substance is concerned about legislative jurisdiction. Again, based on the quote from *Foley Bros*, this presumption deals with the issue of whether US laws can apply to behaviors outside the territorial jurisdiction of the US. This refers to the concept of legislative jurisdiction.

4.4.1.2 Legislative Framework

The US has built up a comprehensive legal regime for its securities markets, with the Securities Act of 1933 ("Securities Act")[49] and the Securities Exchange Act of 1934 ("Exchange Act")[50] being at its core.

43 *United States v. Palmer*, 16 U.S. 610 at 611 (1818).
44 *American Banana Co. v. United Fruit Co.*, 213 U.S. 347 (1909).
45 Ibid., at 355.
46 Ibid., at 357.
47 *Foley Bros., Inc. v. Filardo*, 336 U.S. 281 (1949).
48 Ibid., at 285.
49 Full text available at www.govinfo.gov/content/pkg/COMPS-1884/pdf/COMPS-1884.pdf.
50 Full text available at www.govinfo.gov/content/pkg/COMPS-1885/pdf/COMPS-1885.pdf.

The Securities Act mainly regulates securities offerings, stipulating that the interstate commerce includes cross-border securities commerce or communication means among the US and any foreign country.[51] Under s.4A(c), an issuer using instruments of interstate commerce shall also be liable for material misstatements and omissions.[52] Further, s.17(a) is concerned with fraudulent or misleading conduct in offering securities with the use of interstate commerce.[53] Moreover, s.5 provides that as long as an issuer applies means or instruments in interstate commerce when offering one security, no matter in domestic or overseas markets, they must follow the registration requirements under the Securities Act.[54] The above sections are related to the extraterritoriality of the Securities Act.

The Exchange Act focuses on securities transactions and also applies to interstate commerce, which is defined in a similar way as the Securities Act.[55] Under the broad provision of s.10(b), any person shall be liable for making manipulative devices, provided that he uses instruments in interstate commerce.[56] Further, s.30(a) states that brokers or dealers will be liable if they affect American securities transacted in foreign countries and violate SEC's regulations through interstate commerce,[57] while s.30 (b) indicates that only if the extraterritorial securities business contravenes SEC's rules for preventing traders from evading Exchange Act, can the Act be applied to monitor those businesses.[58]

In addition, s.929P(b)(1) of the Dodd–Frank Wall Street Reform and Consumer Protection Act[59] ("Dodd–Frank Act") added a new section of extraterritorial jurisdiction of anti-fraud provisions to s.22 of the Securities Act. The provision states that US courts have jurisdiction over overseas transactions if the conduct in the US are crucial steps to the violation or such conduct will foreseeably affect the US.[60] Meanwhile, s.929P(b)(2) added a similar section about extraterritorial jurisdiction on anti-fraud rules to s.27 of the Exchange Act.

51 Securities Act (n 29), s. 2(a)(7).
52 Ibid., s. 4A(c)
53 Ibid., s. 17(a)
54 Ibid., s. 5.
55 Exchange Act, s. 3(a)(17).
56 Exchange Act, s. 10(b).
57 Ibid., s. 30.
58 Ibid., s. 30(b).
59 Full text available at www.congress.gov/111/plaws/publ203/PLAW-111publ203.pdf.
60 Ibid., s. 929P(b)(1).

Finally, the SEC Rule 10b-5,[61] issued under s10 of the Exchange Act, has long been a well-known catch-all anti-fraud provision in the US securities regulation. Another relevant provision is Regulation S under s.5 of the Securities Act.[62]

4.4.2 *Before the* Morrison *Case of 2010*

Prior to the case of *Morrison* in 2010, the jurisprudence of extraterritorial jurisdiction of the US securities law was predominantly developed by the Second Circuit Court of Appeals (the 2nd Cir).[63] At the relevant time, there were many securities actions brought under s.10(b) of the Exchange Act and Rule 10b-5, which could broadly be divided into two categories, namely, the so-called Foreign-Squared and Foreign-Cubed cases. Foreign-Squared cases involve transactions where US investors buy securities of foreign companies on foreign securities exchanges,[64] while Foreign-Cubed cases arise from transactions where foreign investors purchase foreign securities on foreign securities exchanges.[65] The US courts used to exercise their jurisdiction of securities law in these cases by applying three tests, namely, the Effect Test, the Conduct Test and the Effect-Conduct test. However, in practice, the US courts tend to combine legislative jurisdiction with judicial jurisdiction. When such tests were satisfied, the US courts usually held that they had judicial jurisdiction, and then simply applied the US securities law.

4.4.2.1 Effect Test

The Effect Test was first established in *Schoenbaum v. Firstbrook*.[66] The plaintiff was an American investor, while one of the defendants was a

[61] Code of Federal Regulations, Title 17, s. 240 10b-5, text available at www.ecfr.gov/cgi-bin/text-idx?SID=133fd1aae548e8fcd69f3a1fafc67362&mc=true&node=se17.4.240_110b_65&rgn=div8.

[62] Sara Hanks, *Regulation S: The Safe Harbor for Offshore Securities Transactions* (Bureau of National Affairs, 2006).

[63] Roberta S. Karmel, "The Second Circuit's Role in Expanding the SEC's Jurisdiction Abroad" (1991) 65 *St. John's Law Review* 743.

[64] Jennifer Mitchell Coupland, "A Bright Idea: A Bright-Line Test for Extraterritoriality in F-Cubed Securities Fraud Private Causes of Action" (2012) 32 *Northwestern Journal of International Law & Business* 541.

[65] Kelley Morris White, "Is Extraterritorial Jurisdiction Still Alive: Determining the Scope of U.S. Extraterritorial Jurisdiction in Securities Cases in the Aftermath of *Morrison v. National Australia Bank*" (2012) 37 *North Carolina Journal of International Law and Commercial Regulation* 1187, 1199.

[66] *Schoenbaum v. Firstbrook*, 405 F.2d 200 (2d Cir. 1968).

Canadian petroleum firm whose shares were registered in the US but all of its business activities were operated within Canada. The petroleum firm did not disclose the discovery of a large oil field until one year later. During this period, the petroleum firm allowed two other defendants to buy its shares at the then prevailing market price, and all such selling and buying activities occurred in Canada. The plaintiff suspected that the defendants did not fully disclose information and thus brought an action in the US. The 2nd Cir held that although the unlawful acts occurred in Canada, the related securities were registered in the US, and thus those acts could have impacts on the American securities markets and investors.[67] In sum, if an act has a detrimental effect[68] or a sufficiently serious effect,[69] then the presumption against extraterritoriality is rebutted and the US courts can exercise extraterritorial jurisdiction by applying its securities law.[70]

Nevertheless, the Effect Test is not without criticism.[71] First, the standard of having "effects or detrimental effects" is too vague and may lead to uncertainties in practice. Different courts may have different views over "effect" for the same unlawful conduct.[72] Further, under international law, it is inappropriate to exercise jurisdiction primarily based on an effect, especially when this effect is only a result instead of a component of a crime.[73] Some scholars consider that the *Schoenbaum* case adopted the Effect Test because the securities concerned were offered in the US and the transactions had impacts in the US securities market.[74] Thus, when the relevant securities are not registered in the US, but the transactions merely have effects on the US securities markets, would the Effect Test still be applicable?

67 *Schoenbaum v. Firstbrook* 405 F.2d 200 at 206–208 (2d Cir. 1968); see also James D. Cox, Robert W. Hillman and Donald C. Langevoort, *Securities Regulations: Case and Materials* (Wolters Kluwer Law & Business, 2019).

68 *Strassheim v. Daily*, 221 U.S. 280, 285, 31 S.Ct. 558, 560, 55 L.Ed. 735 (1911).

69 *Schoenbaum v. Firstbrook* 405 F.2d 200 at 209 (2d Cir. 1968).

70 *Schoenbaum v. Firstbrook* 405 F.2d 200 (2d Cir. 1968).

71 Raphael G. Toman, "The Extraterritorial Reach of the U.S. Securities Laws and Non-conventional Securities: Recent Developments after *Morrison* and Dodd-Frank" (2018) 14 *New York University Journal of Law & Business* 657.

72 Hannah L. Buxbaum, "Multinational Class Actions under Federal Securities Law: Managing Jurisdictional Conflict" (2007) 46 *Columbia Journal of Transnational Law* 14, 42–43.

73 Robert Jennings and Arthur Watts (eds.), *Oppenheim's International Law* (Longman, 2008), pp. 335–336.

74 Mark Roppel, "Extraterritorial Application of Securities Laws between the United States and Canada" (1988) 24 *Gonzaga Law Review* 391, 414.

In recognition of the above issues, the 2nd Cir refined the Effect Test in *Bersch v Drexel Firestone.*[75] In this case, the 2nd Cir clarified that there are several requirements of the Effect Test: first, the "effects" should be substantial effects instead of general effects;[76] second, the "effects" must be on individuals who have interests in the related securities, instead of on the general economy and investors as a whole.[77] This case refines the standard of the Effect Test to a more reasonable and operative standard. Also, the 7th Cir held that the "effects" must be substantial and foreseeable in *Kauthar SDN BHD v. Sternberg*[78] and *Tamari v. Bache & Co. S.A.L.*[79]

4.4.2.2 Conduct Test

While the Effect Test emphasizes the effects of cross-border securities transactions, the Conduct Test focuses on the conduct of the transactions. The Conduct Test was formulated in *Leasco Data Processing Equipment Corp. v. Maxwell,*[80] where an American plaintiff brought proceedings against a British defendant because the latter made many false statements which induced the former to buy its shares. The transaction was completed on the London Stock Exchange (LSE). The court declared its jurisdiction on the basis of two conditions: first, the conduct occurred within the US;[81] second, the conduct was substantial and not merely preparatory, constituting an important link of the casual chain in the impugned transaction.[82]

However, even though the Conduct Test has been followed in many later cases, different courts have applied it in different ways. On the one hand, the 2nd Cir and the US Court of Appeals for the District of Columbia Circuit[83] strictly followed the conditions set up in *Leasco.* On the other hand, the Third Circuit, Eighth Circuit and Ninth Circuit Court of Appeals, in *SEC v. Kasser,*[84] *Continental Grain (Australia) Pty.*

[75] *Bersch v. Drexel Firestone*, 519 F.2d 974 (2d Cir. 1975).
[76] Ibid., at 992.
[77] Ibid.
[78] *Kauthar SDN BHD v. Sternberg*, 149 F.3d 659 at 665 (7th Cir. 1998).
[79] *Tamari v. Bache Co.* (Lebanon) S.A.L., 730 F.2d 1103 at 1108 (7th Cir. 1984).
[80] *Leasco Data Processing Equipment Corp. v. Maxwell*, 468 F.2d 1326 (1970).
[81] Ibid., at 1333.
[82] Ibid., at 1338.
[83] *Zoelsch v. Arthur Anderson & Co.*, 824 F.2d 27, 31 (D.C. Cir.1987).
[84] *SEC v. Kasser*, 548 F.2d 109, 114 (3rd Cir. 1977).

Ltd v. Pacific Oilseeds Inc.[85] and *Grunenthal GmbH v. Hotz*[86] respectively, applied a "lenient" Conduct Test where the US securities law has extraterritorial jurisdiction as long as the defendant's conduct both relates to the fraudulent activity and negatively affects US securities markets.

4.4.2.3 Effect-Conduct Test

Some US courts have chosen to combine the aforementioned two tests when deciding on the issue of extraterritorial jurisdiction. For instance, *Itoba Ltd. v. Lep Group PLC*[87] developed the Effect-Conduct Test. The plaintiff was a British company and its parent company offered and listed shares on the NYSE, while the defendant was a British company dual-listed on the LSE and NASDAQ. Based on the documents provided by the defendant to the SEC, the plaintiff bought shares of the defendant company listed on the LSE. However, after the transaction, the share price of the defendant company dropped sharply due to alleged misstatements in the SEC-registered documents, and as a result, the plaintiff brought an action in the US.

The district court rejected this action at first instance because the transaction was conducted outside the US and it did not significantly affect the US securities markets. The 2nd Cir overruled the district court's decision, indicating that a combination of the Effect Test and the Conduct Test may be applied to justify the exercise of jurisdiction.[88] In this case, the plaintiff relied on documents provided in the US securities markets to buy shares in the defendant company, causing direct losses to the plaintiff and indirectly to the shareholders of the plaintiff's parent company which was listed on the NYSE.[89] Thus, the Effect-Conduct Test was satisfied to afford the US court jurisdiction in this case.

4.4.3 *Transactional Test (*Morrison *Case)*

Morrison v. National Australia Bank Ltd.[90] is a turning point in the development of extraterritorial jurisdiction of the US securities law.

[85] *Continental Grain (Australia) Pty. Ltd. v. Pacific Oilseeds Inc.*, 592 F.2d 409 (8th Cir. 1979).
[86] *Grunenthal GmbH v. Hotz*, 712 F.2d 421, 425 (9th Cir. 1983).
[87] *Itoba Ltd. v. Lep Group PLC*, 54 F.3d 118 (2nd Cir. 1995).
[88] Ibid., at 124.
[89] Ibid., at 123.
[90] *Morrison v. National Australia Bank Ltd.*, 130 S. Ct 2869 (2010).

In this case, Australian investor plaintiffs brought action in the US court against the National Australia Bank, an Australian company listed in the Australian Securities Exchange, because the latter announced a significant write-down in assets due to an alleged fraud committed by its M&A target in the US. The US Supreme Court finally ruled that there lacked a cause of action and s.10(b) of the Exchange Act did not allow for extraterritorial jurisdiction in this case.

The Supreme Court distinguished between the extraterritorial judicial jurisdiction and the extraterritorial legislative jurisdiction.[91] Before the *Morrison* case, the 2nd Cir confused judicial jurisdiction with legislative jurisdiction when dealing with the issue of extraterritorial jurisdiction. However, *Morrison* expressly distinguished between these two types of "jurisdiction," thus separating the following two questions: whether the US courts have the power to hear an extraterritorial securities case, and whether the case can be heard under the substantive rules of the US securities law.

The Supreme Court created a new Transactional Test, under which if key transactional activities (including offering, selling and purchasing) are carried out within a country's territory, the whole transaction would be regarded as occurring in that country, and thus its securities law can apply.[92] In other words, when transactional activities occur in foreign markets, the US courts would not apply relevant rules to adjudicate the case, even though certain unlawful conduct is carried out in the US and has effects on the US market. Under the Transactional Test, Foreign-Cubed claims can no longer be brought in the US courts on the basis of the Exchange Act.[93]

4.4.4 *Dodd–Frank Act*

After *Morrison*, the US Congress passed the Dodd–Frank Act, which clarifies the Effect Test and the Conduct Test, and authorizes their application to actions brought by the US government or the SEC.[94] The means that the extraterritorial effect of the US securities law may

[91] Ibid., at 2877.

[92] Ibid., at 2874.

[93] Genevieve Beyea, "*Morrison v. National Australia Bank* and the Future of Extraterritorial Application of the US Securities Law" (2011) 72 *Ohio State Law Journal* 537, 539–574.

[94] Dodd–Frank Act, s.929P(b).

vary depending on whether the foreign-related case is brought by a private party or the US government.

In cases where the claimants are private bodies, the courts typically follow the *Morrison* decision to apply the Tranactional Test. One noteworthy case is *In re Vivendi Universal, S.A. Securities Litigation.*[95] Vivendi was a company listed in the Paris Bourse. Shareholders of Vivendi from the US, the UK and France brought a class action against Vivendi before a US district court, claiming that Vivendi made misleading statements about its financial health and caused them to suffer losses. In this case, a jury decided that Vivendi violated s10(b) of the Exchange Act. However, after the *Morrison* decision was made by the Supreme Court, the district court dismissed the plaintiffs' s10(b) claims on the grounds that the case fell outside the reach of s10(b) according to the *Morrison* decision.[96] It is also important to note that the 2nd Cir has changed its previous approach and has followed *Morrison* to distinguish between judicial jurisdiction and legislative jurisdiction.[97]

As for cases that are brought by the US government or the SEC, the Effect or Conduct Test has generally been applied according to s929P(b) of the Dodd–Frank Act.[98] One interesting example is *SEC v. Tiger Asia Management, LLC, et al.*[99] The defendant Tiger Asia was a US hedge fund based in New York and had securities trading activities in Hong Kong. The SEC brought proceedings against Tiger Asia on the basis of s.17(a) of the Securities Act and s.10(b) of the Exchange Act, because the defendant allegedly received insider information and carried out securities transactions in New Jersey. As noted above, the Dodd–Frank Act grants judicial jurisdiction over cases brought by the US government. Thus, the US District Court for the District of New Jersey accepted this

[95] *In re Vivendi Universal, S.A. Securities Litigation*, No. 02 Civ. 5571 (RJH) (S.D.N.Y. Feb. 23, 2011) 765 F. Supp. 2d 512 (S.D.N.Y. 2011).

[96] Ibid., at 526–527, 533–534.

[97] *See*, for example, *Absolute Activist Value Master Fund Ltd. v. Ficeto*, 677 F.3d 60 at 66–67 (2d Cir. 2012) (stating that if a US court has judicial jurisdiction on the relevant securities case according to s.27 of the Exchange Act, then the court could decide whether s.10(b) of the Exchange Act is applicable); *Parkcentral Global Hub Limited v. Porsche Automobile Holdings SE*, 763 F.3d 198 at 216–218 (2nd Cir. 2014) (refusing to apply s.10(b) and Rule 10b-5 extraterritorially, because "the relevant actions in this case are so predominantly German").

[98] *See*, for example, *SEC v. Scoville*, 913 F.3d 1204 (10th Cir. 2019); *SEC v. Traffic Monsoon, LLC*, 245 F.Supp.3d 1275 (D. Utah 2017); *SEC v. Chicago Convention Center, LLC*, 961 F.Supp.2d 905 (N.D. Ill. 2013).

[99] Civil Action No. 12-cv-7601 (The US District Court for the District of New Jersey, 2012).

case, and the key issue was whether US securities law can be applied. The court relied on the Dodd–Frank Act to apply the Conduct Test to allow extraterritotial application of US securities law.[100]

4.5 Comparative Analysis and Policy Suggestions

4.5.1 General Observations

Broadly speaking, the US regime for extraterritorial jurisdiction of securities law is probably the most developed in the world, having established various tests and corresponding supervision mechanisms. By contrast, the Chinese regime is still in its early stages of development. There is a great need for further guidance on the exercise of extraterritorial jurisdiction and for a more effective institutional framework to facilitate its development in China.

As for the issue regarding the typology of jurisdiction, there are important differences between the US and China. In the US, before *Morrison*, the courts always blended the concepts of legislative jurisdiction and judicial jurisdiction. As discussed earlier, when the 2nd Cir dealt with cross-border cases, it used the Effect Test and Conduct Test to decide the application of the US securities law. If those tests were satisfied, the US courts had the power to hear extraterritorial cases and simultaneously apply the US securities law. However, the US Supreme Court in *Morrison* changed this situation, drawing a clear distinction between legislative and judicial jurisdiction. After this case, the US courts have tended to discuss judicial jurisdiction, namely, whether they have authority to adjudicate a case, and legislative jurisdiction, namely, whether the US securities law can be applied, separately.[101]

[100] Civil Action No. 12-cv-7601 (The US District Court for the District of New Jersey, 2012), p. 3.

[101] After the case of *Morrison*, scholars also started to treat the two types of jurisdiction separately, examining the possibility of relying on US courts to apply foreign securities law to foreign transanctions. *See*, for example, Hannah L. Buxbaum, "Remedies for Foreign Investors under U.S. Federal Securities Law" (2012) 75 *Law & Contemporary Problems* 161, 183. ("[T]he prospects for asserting claims arising out of foreign transactions on the basis of foreign governing law seem slim."); Wolf-Georg Ringe and Alexander Hellgardt, "The International Dimension of Issuer Liability and Choice of Law from a Transatlantic Perspective" (2011) 31 *Oxford Journal of Legal Studies* 23, 50–51 (proposing that investors of cross-listed companies can choose securities liability rules). In fact, long before *Morrison*, Professor Roberta Romanno made the "issuer choice" proposal under which issuers and investors choose the relevant securities law to govern their transactions in the international capital markets. See Roberta Romano,

In contrast, China has treated judicial jurisdiction and legislative jurisdiction distinctively from the very beginning in its development of the regime of extraterritorial jurisdiction. The judicial jurisdiction of Chinese courts over cross-border securities litigation is governed by the civil procedure law, while the application of Chinese securities law in those cases refer to corresponding substantive law. Specifically, on the one hand, the issue of whether Chinese courts have power to hear cross-border securities cases is addressed in ss 24, 27, 29, 35 and 266 of the Civil Procedure Law of the PRC; on the other hand, Article 2(4) of the PRC Securities Law is essentially about legislative jurisdiction, setting out the criteria for applying substantive provisions of securities law in the context of extraterritorial cases.

On March 16, 2021, the SPC issued a rule on the scope of judicial jurisdiction for the newly established Beijing Financial Court.[102] Under this rule, the Beijing Financial Court, established on March 18, 2021, has jurisdiction over cases brought by Chinese domestic investors who are aggrieved by securities activities conducted overseas.[103] Clearly, this rule is concerned about the aspect of judicial jurisdiction in relation to cross-border securities cases under China's new securities law.

Further, on April 22, 2021, the SPC issued the revised rule on the scope of judicial jurisdiction for the Shanghai Financial Court,[104] which was established on August 20, 2018, as the first specialist court for finance-related cases in China. The revised rule expands the judicial jurisdiction of the Shanghai Financial Court to cover cases that are brought by Chinese domestic investors in relation to securities activities conducted overseas.[105] Hence, both the Shanghai Financial Court and the Beijing

"The Need for Competition in International Securities Regulation" (2001) 2 *Theoretical Inquiries in Law* 1, 6–7. While this idea of choice of law is hard to implement in practice, it is conceptually appealing and shows the importance of separating jurisdictional and legislative jurisdiction.

102 Zuigao Renmin Fayuan Guanyu Beijing Jinrong Fayuan Anjian Guanxia de Guiding《最高人民法院关于北京金融法院案件管辖的规定》[The Rule of the Supreme People's Court on the Scope of Jurisdiction of Beijing Financial Court] (issued by the Supreme People's Court on March 16, 2021). The Beijing Financial Court is the second specialist court to hear financial cases, with the first one being the Shanghai Financial Court which was established in August 2018.

103 Ibid., art. 2.

104 Zuigao Renmin Fayuan Guanyu Beijing Jinrong Fayuan Anjian Guanxia de Guiding《最高人民法院关于上海金融法院案件管辖的规定》[The Rule of the Supreme People's Court on the Scope of Jurisdiction of Shanghai Financial Court] (issued by the Supreme People's Court on August 7, 2018, revised on April 22, 2021).

105 Ibid., art. 2.

Financial Court have judicial jurisdiction over cases brought under Article 2(4) of the 2019 Securities Law.

In relation to the criteria for extraterritorial jurisdiction, the US has formulated a series of tests, including the Effect Test, Conduct Test, Effect-Conduct Test and Transactional Test. By contrast, the Chinese securities law in this area is at its infancy stage. At present, there is only one explicit provision about extraterritorial jurisdiction in Chinese securities law, which was introduced in 2019 and vaguely refers to only one standard similar to the US "Effect Test." To date, no relevant cases have been heard.

Finally, the US and China each have a principal securities regulator which has the power to regulate securities transactions domestically and extraterritorially. In the US, the SEC has been very active in exercising extraterritorial jurisdiction and thus has contributed to the rich body of case law in the area. By contrast, the Chinese securities market watchdog, namely, the CSRC, does not have significant experience in exercising extraterritorial jurisdiction. As China continues to open up its securities market with increasing cross-border transactions, there is a great need for China to provide more guidance on the issue of extraterritorial jurisdiction of its securities law.

4.5.2 Improving the Tests for Extraterritorial Jurisdiction

As discussed earlier, Article 2(4) is the only provision in the PRC Securities Law specifically addressing extraterritorial jurisdiction. As important as it may be, it has several problems, including its vague language and insufficient guidance. Since the US has developed a rich body of experiences of statutory rules and court cases on extraterritorial jurisdiction of securities law, China can critically learn from them and carefully make adaptations to suit its local conditions.

To start with, it should be made clear that extraterritorial jurisdiction may arise if any of the two prongs under Article 2(4) is satisfied, namely, the "market disruption" prong and the "investor infringement" prong. As discussed earlier,[106] due to the ambiguous wording of Article 2(4), the relationship of the two prongs is not fully clear. This would allow China to better protect its domestic securities market and investors, which is consistent with the overarching goal of the Chinese securities law and the

[106] *See* Section 4.3.2.

US experiences.[107] Moreover, in June 2021, China promulgated the Data Security Law, which also provides for extraterritorial jurisdiction when the relevant data processing activities outside China "harm the national security, public interest, *or* lawful rights and interests of citizens and organizations of China."[108] There is clearly a conjunction of "or" between the triggering events of extraterritorial jurisdiction in the original Chinese text. Hence, it is consistent to clarify that extraterritorial jurisdiction can be triggered by any of the two prongs under Article 2(4) of the Chinese securities law.

Thus, in principle, we suggest a phased reform agenda to improve the tests for extraterritorial jurisdiction under the Chinese securities law. In the short run, since the two prongs under Article 2(4) are very similar to the Effect Test in the US, efforts should be made to refine them in light of the Effect Test of the US securities law; in the long run, there is a need to go beyond the Effect Test to consider other relevant tests. These two phases of improvement will be discussed in more detail as follows.

In the short run, drawing on the rich body of US case law on the Effect Test, China can provide more guidance on what constitutes the standard of disrupting the market order or infringing individuals' interests. For example, Article 2(4) can be revised to be read as "only when the effect or result of cross-border fraudulent conduct on Chinese securities markets is substantial, direct and foreseeable, can this law be applied to these frauds." In addition, more guidance should be provided on the elements of "substantial," "direct" and "foreseeable."

Specifically, it can be made clear that the term "substantial" requires two conditions: first, the interests of investors in China should have been harmed; second, illegal securities activities should have been mainly aimed at domestic investors in Mainland China. In other words, domestic investors whose interests are infringed account for a relatively large percentage of all victims. Moreover, the causation theory of tort law can be used to define the meaning of "direct" since securities fraud is

[107] 2019 Securities Law, art. 1 (stating that this law is enacted for the purposes of "protecting the lawful rights and interests of investors, maintaining the social and economic order and safeguarding public interest").

[108] Zhonghua Renmin Gongheguo Shuju Anquan Fa (中华人民共和国数据安全法) (Data Security Law of the People's Republic of China) (adopted at the 29th session of the Standing Committee of the Thirteenth National People's Congress of the People's Republic of China on June 10, 2021, effective September 1, 2021), art. 2 (emphasis added).

generally regarded as a form of tort.[109] Thus, the requirement of "direct" can be specified in the following ways: first, unlawful acts are factual causes of domestic investors' damage, which shows these acts are indispensable conditions for the infringed interests; second, the damage caused must be a reasonably foreseeable result of the unlawful acts, not being too remote. As for the term "foreseeable," it should be clarified that it focuses more on the perpetrators' perspective. The harm caused by the illegal behavior to investors must have been foreseen by the perpetrators. If the harm is merely incidental or coincidental, or otherwise exceeds the reasonable expectation of the perpetrators, they should not be liable for the relevant losses.

In the longer run, on the basis of US experiences, China may introduce more tests, such as the Conduct Test and the Transactional Test, in order to provide for a more flexible extraterritorial jurisdiction regime to meet the needs of the market. As discussed earlier, the Effect Test has shortcomings, and thus the US has devised other tests.[110] In the US, the different tests can be used in a flexible way, depending on who initiates the action. As discussed before, the Dodd–Frank Act altered the outcome of *Morrison* to confer a right of action for the SEC or government actions, but not private actions. China is advised to make clear that there should be a different approach under Article2(4) depending on who the plaintiff is: if foreign-related cases are raised by the CSRC and satisfy the broader tests such as the Effect or Conduct Test, then Chinese courts can exercise jurisdiction; conversely, if those cases are raised by private investors, then Chinese courts should apply the stricter Transactional Test, focusing on where the trading behavior occurred. The CSRC is the Chinese equivalent of the SEC in the US and should be given the same privilege as that of the SEC under the Dodd–Frank Act. Indeed, as a national securities market regulator in China, the CSRC generally aims to protect public interests and more importantly, represents the sovereignty of financial regulation. Hence, compared to private investors, the CSRC should have greater room to bring extraterritorial cases. These varied tests can bring more flexibility for China to consider different factors in achieving its legislative goals.

It should be noted that China needs to adopt a critical approach when borrowing US experiences to improve its regime for extraterritorial

[109] Donald H. J. Hermann, "Extraterritorial Criminal Jurisdiction in Securities Laws Regulation" (1986) 16 *Cumberland Law Review*, 207, 228.

[110] *See* Section 4.4.

jurisdiction of securities law. As discussed earlier, the US law in this area is still evolving, despite already having built up a relatively comprehensive framework comprised of statutory provisions and cases.

There remains uncertainty and confusion over the meaning and application of the various tests for extraterritorial jurisdiction under the US law. The scope and effects of the various tests, particularly the Transactional Test under the *Morrison* decision, have long been the subject of intense debate in the US.

To start with, as noted before, the Transactional Test excludes Foreign-Cubed claims, in which foreign plaintiffs sue foreign issuers for losses on transactions on foreign exchanges.[111] Under the prevailing view of the Transactional Test, the US securities law will not apply to Foreign-Cubed transactions even if they involve the underlying securities of a sponsored American Depositary Receipt (ADR) listed on a US domestic exchange.[112] This would negatively affect the bonding premium for some cross-listed firms, to the extent that the more rigorous US law regime will only benefit the ADR traders in the US, but not the investors trading shares of the same company listed in the home market.

Second, the Transactional Test may also affect Foreign-Squared claims brought by domestic plaintiffs against foreign issuers for losses on transactions on foreign exchanges. The US District Court for the Southern District of New York has adopted this position, stating that the *Morrison* decision is applicable to Foreign-Squared cases as well.[113] This has attracted much criticism, as the US securities law may not afford protection to US investors who suffer from losses from purchasing the securities of foreign issuers in foreign stock markets.[114] As discussed earlier, many Chinese investors currently trade securities in overseas markets such as the US and Hong Kong, and one of the objectives of extraterritoriality application of the Chinese securities law is to protect them.

[111] *See* Section 4.4.3.

[112] Richard Painter, Douglas Dunham and Ellen Quackenbos, "When Courts and Congress Don't Say What They Mean: Initial Reactions to *Morrison v. National Australia Bank* and to the Extraterritorial Jurisdiction Provisions of the Dodd–FrankAct" (2011) 20 *Minnesota Journal of International Law* 1, 11.

[113] *See*, for example, *Cornwell v. Credit Suisse Group*, 729 F. Supp. 2d 620 (S.D.N.Y. 2010); *In re Royal Bank of Scotland Grp. PLC Sec. Litig.*, 765 F. Supp. 2d 327, 336 (S.D.N.Y 2011).

[114] Nidhi M. Geevarghese, "A Shocking Loss of Investor Protection: The Implications of *Morrison v. National Australia Bank*" (2011) 6 *Brooklyn Journal of Corporate, Financial & Commercial Law* 235.

Hence, as noted earlier, this chapter makes the proposal that China adopts and improves the Effect Test in the short term.

Third, some commentators have pointed out that the US securities markets may risk becoming a "safe harbor" for cross-border securities fraud as long as offering and purchasing activities are not within the US.[115] In fact, this concern was already voiced in the *Morrison* case. For instance, Justice Stevens concurred in the final judgment but disagreed with the Court's reasoning, stating that:

> Imagine ... an American investor who buys shares in a company listed only on an overseas exchange. That company has a major American subsidiary with executives based in New York City; and it was in New York City that the executives masterminded and implemented a massive deception which artificially inflated the stock price – and which will, upon its disclosure, cause the price to plummet ... [The] investors would, under the Court's new test, be barred from seeking relief under § 10(b).[116]

Moreover, the relationship between the *Morrison* decision and the Dodd–Frank Act needs further clarification. It has been argued that s.929P(b) of the Dodd–Frank Act intends to overturn *Morrison* because it gives legal effect to extraterritorial jurisdiction, which is an exception to the presumption against extraterritoriality.[117] However, there is a counterargument that s.929P(b) does not completely negate *Morrison*. As discussed before, the judicial jurisdiction is distinct from legislative jurisdiction. The "jurisdiction" in s.929P(b) refers to judicial jurisdiction, which gives the US courts the power to hear cases. It is opined that the *Morrison* case does not cast doubt on the courts' judicial jurisdiction, but instead deals with the issue of the extraterritorial application of s.10(b) of the Exchange Act, which is essentially an issue of legislative jurisdiction.[118] Hence, *Morrison* should still apply in securities cases where a proceeding is initiated by a private person.

[115] *See*, for example, Kelley Morris White, "Is Extraterritorial Jurisdiction Still Alive: Determining the Scope of U.S. Extraterritorial Jurisdiction in Securities Cases in the Aftermath of *Morrison v. National Australia Bank*" (2012) 37 *North Carolina Journal of International Law and Commercial Regulation* 1187, 1217.

[116] *Morrison v. National Australia Bank Ltd.*, 130 S. Ct. 2869, 2888 (2010) (Stevens, J., concurring).

[117] Kelley Morris White, "Is Extraterritorial Jurisdiction Still Alive: Determining the Scope of U.S. Extraterritorial Jurisdiction in Securities Cases in the Aftermath of *Morrison v. National Australia Bank*" (2012) 37 *North Carolina Journal of International Law and Commercial Regulation* 1187, 1229.

[118] J. William Hicks, *International Dimensions of U.S. Securities Law* (Thomson West, 2020) part V, ch. 11, IV§ 11:50.

It should be noted, however, that perhaps due to the issue of ambiguity, the US courts seem to have more flexibility now in determining the issue of extraterritorial jurisdiction. As the relationship between the *Morrison* decision and the Dodd–Frank Act is not fully clear, the US courts have been divided over the extraterritorial effect of the securities law. In practice, despite the seemingly restrictive ruling of *Morrison*, the US securities law has continued to be frequently used extraterritorially. One recent empirical study examined 388 cross-border securities cases after *Morrison*, finding that it does not have a material impact on the situation of extraterritorial jurisdiction of the US securities law, and the possibility of cross-border securities cases being governed by the US securities law does not decrease significantly.[119]

Hence, as discussed earlier, China is advised to take a staged approach to adopting the various tests in applying extraterritorial jurisdiction of securities law to advance both national and international interests. China needs to issue implementation rules to provide more guidance on the circumstances where extraterritorial jurisdiction of securities law may be triggered and exercised. In doing so, China should clearly distinguish between legislative jurisdiction and judicial jurisdiction. This can help avoid the issue of legal uncertainty that has long existed under the US law.

Last but not least, the legal transplantation process needs to take into account China's local conditions, such as the need for exercising extraterritorial jurisdiction to protect Chinese investors, and the constraints of juridical resources in China. The next section will use the case of *Luckin Coffee* to provide a detailed analysis of the factors that China may consider in putting extraterritorial jurisdiction into practice.

4.5.3 *Adopting Multilateralism and Pragmaticism: The Case of* Luckin Coffee

Reverting back to the case of *Luckin Coffee*, this chapter argues that the extraterritorial jurisdiction of Chinese securities law should not be exercised in this case. We will use this case study to illustrate the Chinese approach toward the extraterritorial application of securities law and to identify relevant factors which may affect the development of the Chinese

[119] Robert Bartlett, Matthew D. Cain, Jill E. Fisch and Stephen Davidoff Solomon, "The Myth of Morrison: Securities Fraud Litigation against Foreign Issuers" (2019) 74 *Business Lawyer* 967.

approach. Further, we will make suggestions as to how China should exercise extraterritorial jurisdiction of securities law to achieve the purposes for which the laws were introduced.

On April 30, 2021, it was reported that some Luckin Coffee investors had filed a civil case for compensation before the Shanghai Financial Court.[120] However, according to our interview with a high-level judge of the Shanghai Financial Court, the case was received but not yet accepted, as the court is very cautious about the exercise of extraterritorial jurisdiction, especially considering that this would be the very first case of its kind if it were to be accepted.[121] Irrespective of the final fate of this case, it has already demonstrated the cautious attitude of Chinese courts toward extraterritorial jurisdiction. We argue that the Shanghai Financial Court's caution toward the case of *Luckin Coffee* is well justified due to the high level of political sensitivity and technical complexity involved. Below is a more detailed discussion on the specific reasons for our argument that the case of *Luckin Coffee* does not present a strong case for the exercise of extraterritorial jurisdiction of Chinese securities law.

4.5.3.1 Nonretroactive Application of Law

As discussed above, the PRC Securities Law came into effect on March 1, 2020, but Luckin Coffee allegedly committed misstatements before that. An issue thus arises as to whether the case of *Luckin Coffee* can be retroactively covered by the PRC Securities Law, particularly Article 2(4) which explicitly sets out extraterritorial jurisdiction.

Generally, nonretroactivity is a fundamental legal principle, which means a law cannot apply to cases that occurred before its promulgation. In China, there is also a principle that the "substantive law" follows the "old law" while the "procedural law" complies with the "new law."[122] As noted earlier, China differentiates legislative jurisdiction and judicial jurisdiction, which corresponds to the substantive law and procedure law respectively. Article 2(4) of the PRC Securities Law is about legislative

[120] "Ruixing Kafei Yu Jingnei Bei Qisu Huo Wei Zhonggaigu Shouli" (瑞幸咖啡于境内被起诉 或为中概股首例) [Luckin Coffee was Sued in China to Probably Become the First Such Case Involving China-Concept Stocks], available at www.163.com/dy/article/G8RMKP6605199LJK.html.

[121] WeChat interview, April 30, 2021.

[122] Yu Xi (余希), "Minshi Susongfa Sujili Wenti Tantao" (民事诉讼法溯及力问题探讨) [Discussion on the Retroactivity of Civil Procedure Law] (2020) 3 *Shoudu Shifan Daxue Xuebao (Shehui Kexueban) (首都师范大学学报 (社会科学版)) [Journal of Capital Normal University (Social Science Edition)]* 151.

jurisdiction, which relates to a substantive rule. As a result, the principle that the "substantive law" follows the "old law" should apply. Therefore, the PRC Securities Law has no extraterritorial effect on the *Luckin Coffee* case.

4.5.3.2 Not Meeting the Effect Test

Even if Article 2(4) could operate retroactively, it would not apply to the *Luckin Coffee* case as the two criteria under Article 2(4) are not satisfied.

As for the first criterion of disrupting the order of the Chinese securities market, there is some difference of opinion over whether it is satisfied. On one view, although the main operations of Luckin Coffee were within China, the offering and trading of its shares occurred mostly in the US securities markets. It thus seems to follow that the case of *Luckin Coffee* does not meet the requirement of disturbing the market order.[123] However, a counterargument is that Luckin Coffee's operation and development were dependent on domestic consumers and markets, therefore, its financial misstatements would have adversely affected the market order in China.[124] We argue that the *Luckin Coffee* case has a negative effect on the reputation of overseas-listed Chinese companies, but it does not seem to directly affect the order of the Chinese securities markets.

As for the second criterion of infringing upon the lawful rights and interests of domestic investors in China, Luckin Coffee's misrepresentation does not seem to meet this test either. First, under the shareholding structure of Luckin Coffee, the top five shareholders including executives and institutions hold around 61 percent of shares,[125] which

[123] Li Youxing (李有星) and Pan Zheng (潘政), "Ruixing Kafei Xujia Chenshu An Falv Shiyong Tantao – Yi Zhongmei Zhengquanfa Bijiao Wei Shijiao" (瑞幸咖啡虚假陈述案法律适用探讨—以中美证券法比较为视角) [Discussion on the Application of Law on Luckin Coffee False Statement Case: From the Perspective of the Comparison of the US and Chinese Securities Laws] (2020) 9 *Falv Shiyong (法律适用) [Journal of Law Application]* 118, 128.

[124] Jiang Zheng (蒋政) and Wei Jie (魏婕), "Ruixing Shijian Fajiao Zhongmei Kuajing Zhengquan Jianguan Fengbao Kaiqi" (瑞幸事件发酵 中美跨境证券监管风暴开启) [The Fermentation of Luckin Coffee Case, Cross-border Securities Regulatory Storm Begins], *China Business Journal*, May 2, 2020, www.cb.com.cn/index/show/jr/cv/cv12518527247.

[125] Han Hongling (韩洪灵), Chen Shuaidi (陈帅弟), Lu Xumi (陆旭米) and Chen Hanwen (陈汉文), "Ruixing Shijian yu Zhongmei Kuajing Zhengquan Jianguan Hezuo: Huigu yu Zhanwang (瑞幸事件与中美跨境证券监管合作：回顾与展望) [The Luckin Coffee Case and Cross-border Securities Regulatory Cooperation between China and the US: Review and Outlook]" (2020) 9 *Kuaiji Zhiyou (会计之友) [Friends of Accounting]* 6.

means Luckin Coffee's executives and some institutions account for a high proportion. In addition, as mentioned earlier, domestic investors in China cannot freely buy securities listed on overseas markets. Instead, they can only invest in overseas securities markets through QDII. Furthermore, Luckin Coffee's prospectus indicates that it is listed in the US and its target investors are not Chinese investors.[126] Although there is no accurate data available on the proportion of Chinese public shareholders in Luckin Coffee, it may be safe to estimate that this proportion is very small, and thus the criterion of infringing the interests of Chinese investors may not be satisfied.

4.5.3.3 Adherence to the Principle of International Comity

In considering whether to exercise extraterritorial jurisdiction of its securities law, China should pay attention to the principle of international comity, which is a fundamental principle of private international law aimed at reducing conflicts of jurisdiction. Cross-border securities transactions may be subject to the jurisdiction of multiple countries, and thus, jurisdictional conflicts will inevitably arise. If the extraterritorial jurisdiction of the Chinese securities law were to be expanded excessively, it would lead to conflicts with other countries' jurisdiction.

With more than thirty years of rapid development, the Chinese securities market has become increasingly connected with the rest of the world, and as such, it is important for China to establish good relationships with other markets to improve the efficacy of regulatory cooperation. Moreover, the US courts clearly have jurisdiction over the *Luckin Coffee* case and have already handled relevant cases against *Luckin Coffee* under the US securities law.[127] If China were to exercise jurisdiction over the *Luckin Coffee* case, it may cause jurisdictional conflicts. Thus, we argue that China should adhere to the principle of international comity and refrain from exercising extraterritorial jurisdiction over the *Luckin Coffee* case.

Of course, if required, China should endeavor to provide relevant judicial assistance, such as evidence gathering, the service of judicial

[126] Luckin Coffee Inc., "Luckin Coffee's Form of Prospectus," May 16, 2019, investor.luckincoffee.com/static-files/62ae7fff-d256–461e-9012-a47bfdc3a686.

[127] On October 26, 2021, Luckin Coffee reached a settlement of the class action brought in the US. Jonathan Stempel, "Luckin Coffee in $175 mln class action settlement over accounting fraud" www.reuters.com/business/retail-consumer/luckin-coffee-reaches-175-million-class-action-settlement-over-accounting-fraud-2021-10-26/.

documents as well as recognition and enforcement of judgments.[128] Indeed, it seems sensible to allow the US courts to deal with the *Luckin Coffee* case, for three main reasons. First, the US courts are generally much more experienced to handle cases of extraterritorial jurisdiction. Second, as Luckin Coffee was listed in the US, it is more convenient for the US courts to collect relevant evidence. Third, it is fair to say that the US courts can adequately protect the Chinese investors who were harmed by the misstatements of Luckin Coffee.

4.5.3.4 The Constraints of Judicial Resources

Exercising extraterritorial jurisdiction requires the consumption of judicial resources, which is a very practical factor to consider in formulating the policy of extraterritorial jurisdiction.[129] As cross-border securities disputes are usually more complicated due to the involvement of multiple jurisdictions, they may take up a significant amount of judicial resources. This can be a particularly acute problem for China where judicial resources are generally limited. Indeed, Chinese courts, especially basic-level courts, have long been under-resourced in terms of staff and funding,[130] due to various reasons such as the reform of the case-filing system, the significant increase in the number of cases adjudicated in recent years and the slow increase in the number of judges. For instance, during the five-year period of 2015 to 2020, the number of concluded cases rocketed by about 40 percent from approximately 8,851 million to 12,397 million, while the number of judges increased from 189,000 to 197,000, representing only a small increase of 4.23 percent.[131]

128 2019 Securities Law, art. 177 (providing for cross-border regulatory cooperation).

129 Daniel S. Kahn, "The Collapsing Jurisdictional Boundaries of the Antifraud Provisions of the U.S. Securities Laws: The Supreme Court and Congress Ready to Redress Forty Years of Ambiguity" (2010) 6 *New York University Journal of Law & Business* 365, 409–410.

130 Yang Lixin (杨立新), "Jiceng Sifa Ziyuan Buzu de Kunjing ji Wanshanlujing" (基层司法资源不足的困境及完善路径) [The Predicament of Insufficient Judicial Resources at the Basic Level and Its Improvement] (2020) 5 *Renmin Luntan (人民论坛) [People"s Tribune]* 112.

131 Zuigao Renmin Fayuan Gongzuo Baogao (最高人民法院工作报告) [Work Report of the Supreme People's Court] (May 25, 2020), www.court.gov.cn/zixun-xiangqing-231301.html; Zhongguo Fayuan Wang (中国法院网), "Renzui Renfa Congkuan Zhidu Tuijin Anjian Fanjianfenliu" (认罪认罚从宽制度推进案件繁简分流) [The System of Lenient Punishment for the Admission of Guilt and Acceptance of Punishment Promotes the Diversion of Complicated Cases]" (July 20, 2020), www.chinacourt.org/article/detail/2020/07/id/5360734.shtml.

Moreover, compared with other types of civil cases, securities civil cases are more complicated and thus, require a more demanding skillset of experience from judges. In 2001, the Chinese courts simply refused to accept securities civil cases on the grounds that those cases were too difficult for them to adjudicate; one year later, the SPC acceded to public pressure to accept such cases, and decided that the first trial of securities civil cases should be conducted by intermediate courts, rather than primary courts, as the former were more experienced and better-resourced to meet the challenge.[132] If securities civil cases in a purely domestic context pose significant difficulty for Chinese courts, the situation will only be worse when it comes to cross-border securities civil cases where there will be additional novel issues of extraterritorial jurisdiction and conflicts of law.

4.5.3.5 Future Implications

As discussed in Sections 4.5.3.1–4.5.3.4, there are four main factors which may play against the Shanghai Financial Court exercising extraterritorial jurisdiction of securities law in the case of *Luckin Coffee*. This may provide a beacon of light for other courts to identify whether similar cases will be covered by Article 2(4) of the 2019 Securities Law. To be sure, some of the factors are more specific to the case of *Luckin Coffee* while others may have wider implications. For instance, the nonretroactive application of law may be less likely to impact on other cases, given that the new securities law has been in effect since March 2020. Moreover, the constraints of juridical resources may become less important a factor to consider as China has continued to reform the judicial system and inject more resources into it.[133]

In July 2021, the General Office of the Chinese Communist Party Central Committee and the General Office of the State Council

[132] For a detailed discussion of the development of securities private litigation in China, *see* Robin Hui Huang, "Private Enforcement of Securities Law in China: A Ten-Year Retrospective and Empirical Assessment" (2013) 61(4) *American Journal of Comparative Law* 757–798.

[133] On Feburary 27, 2022, the Supreme People's Court formally submitted a plan to the National People's Congress that the third specialist financial court be established in the twin cities of Chengdu and Chongqing to hear financial cases in China's western region. Yue Hongbin (岳弘彬) and Niu Yong (牛镛), "Woguo Ni Sheli Chengyu Jinrong Fayuan" (我国拟设立成渝金融法院) [China Plans to Establish Chengdu & Chongqing Financial Court], Feburary 27, 2022, politics.people.com.cn/BIG5/n1/2022/0227/c1001-32360674.html.

specifically pointed out the need to improve the system for extraterritorial application of securities law in a policy document issued in July 2021, stating that the development of judicial interpretations and supporting rules on extraterritorial application of securities law should be accelerated, and the specific circumstances for extraterritorial jurisdiction of securities law should be refined.[134] This chapter represents an attempt to make contributions in this regard by discussing extraterritorial jurisdiction of securities law in the *sui generis* context of China. In short, the nebulous expression of Article2(4) causes uncertainties over the nature, scope and test of extraterritoriality jurisdiction of China's new securities law. China is advised to critically learn from the extensive experiences of the US law to clarify and enrich Article2(4) in consideration of its local conditions.

4.6 Conclusion

In the recent overhaul of its securities law, China has explicitly introduced a provision on extraterritorial jurisdiction, namely Article 2(4) of the 2019 Securities Law. While this provision represents an important development, it is not without problems. Due to the simplistic expressions and broad terms used in the provision, there are worrying uncertainties over the nature, scope and test of extraterritorial jurisdiction of securities law in China. These problems, if left unaddressed, may adversely affect the capacity of the Chinese securities law to handle cross-border securities transactions and ultimately hamper the inter nationalization process of the Chinese securities market.

In a search for solutions to the aforementioned problems, this chapter compares the Chinese law with that of the US, a leading jurisdiction in the area of extraterritorial jurisdiction of securities law. The US has extensive experience relating to extraterritorial jurisdiction of securities law, with a series of court-created tests in place such as the Effect Test, the Conduct Test, the Effect-Conduct Test and the Transnational Test. In principle, Article 2(4) of the 2019 Securities Law is broadly similar to the Effect Test in the US, but it is not entirely clear how the test can be

134 Guangyu Yifa Congyan Daji Zhengquan Weifa Huodong de Yijian (关于依法从严打击证券违法活动的意见) [Opinions on Strictly Cracking Down on Illegal Securities Activities in Accordance with the Law] (issued by the General Office of the Chinese Communist Party Central Committee and the General Office of the State Council on July 6, 2021), art. 21.

applied in practice. Using the recent *Luckin Coffee* scandal as a case study, this chapter highlights the factors China may consider in applying Article 2(4), including the tests of national interests, the principle of international comity and the issue of judicial recourse constraints. This chapter argues that China should draw upon US experiences to clarify and enrich the test for exercising extraterritorial jurisdiction under Article 2(4). In doing so, China must adopt a critical approach, as the US law has its own problems and there is a great need to properly consider China's local conditions. While the *Luckin Coffee* case may not present a good occasion for applying Article 2(4), it will only be a matter of time before China exercises extraterritorial jurisdiction of its securities law for the purposes of regulating cross-border securities transactions and protecting investors.

5

China's National Security Review of Foreign Investment

5.1 Introduction

Drawing upon the experiences of other jurisdictions, particularly the United States, China has gradually established its national security review (NSR) regime for foreign investment.[1] The basic national-level laws enacted by the National People's Congress include the 2015 National Security Law[2] and the 2020 Foreign Investment Law.[3] To implement the laws, the Ministry of Commerce (MOFCOM) and the National Development and Reform Commission (NDRC) under the State Council have issued relevant rules to provide guidance on the NSR of foreign investment in China. On the other hand, a growing number of Chinese enterprises have gone overseas under the "going global" policy of the Chinese government.[4] In this process, these outbound Chinese enterprises have increasingly encountered the issue of national security review for their investment and business in host countries overseas. For example, in 2005, China National Offshore Oil Corporation launched a bid for Unocal, the then ninth-largest oil company in the United States, but the deal was vehemently opposed by some members of the US Congress owing to national security concerns, which forced China

[1] For the definition of foreign investment and the notion of NSR under the Chinese law, see Section 5.3.1.1.

[2] *See* Zhonghua Renmin Gongheguo Guojia Anquan Fa (中华人民共和国国家安全法) [National Security Law of the People's Republic of China] (promulgated by the National People's Congress, July 1, 2015, effective July 1, 2015) [hereinafter National Security Law].

[3] *See* Zhonghua Renmin Gongheguo Waishang Touzi Fa (中华人民共和国外商投资法) [Foreign Investment Law of the People's Republic of China] (promulgated by the National People's Congress, March 15, 2019, effective January 1, 2020) [hereinafter Foreign Investment Law].

[4] *See* Council on Foreign Relations, "China's Approach to Global Governance," www.cfr.org/china-global-governance/.

National Offshore Oil Corporation to withdraw the offer in the end.[5] In July 2013, another Chinese company experienced similar difficulties in the case of Ralls, in which the Committee on Foreign Investment in the United States (CFIUS) decision to block foreign investment was challenged for the first time in history.[6]

In the United States, CFIUS, a multiagency government body chaired by the Secretary of the Treasury, is responsible for reviewing foreign investments for national security considerations.[7] The CFIUS can take measures relevant to its mandate, such as limiting a foreign investor's access to a US company's R&D information, and in extreme cases, the CFIUS can advise the parties to abandon a deal.[8] If a formal ban or divestment order is needed, the CFIUS can submit the matter to the president.[9] The CFIUS's jurisdiction has remained unchanged in the past thirty-five years since the US Congress first passed the 1988 Exon–Florio Amendment, which added Section 721 to the Defense Production Act of 1950.[10] In 2018, the United States passed the Foreign Investment Risk Review Modernization Act (FIRRMA) to modernize and reshape its national security review system.[11] This new statute aims to strengthen the US government's ability to protect national security while preserving its open investment policy.[12] FIRRMA has significantly expanded the

[5] *See*, for example, Matt Pottinger, Russell Gold, Michael M. Phillips and Kate Linebaugh, "Cnooc Drops Offer for Unocal, Exposing US–Chinese Tensions," *Wall Street Journal*, August 3. 2005, www.wsj.com/articles/SB112295744495102393.

[6] *Ralls Corp. v. Committee on Foreign Investment in the United States*, 758 F.3d 296, 296 (D.C. Cir. 2014).

[7] The Committee on Foreign Investment in the United States (CFIUS), U.S. Department of the Treasury, home.treasury.gov/policy-issues/international/the-committee-on-foreign-investment-in-the-united-states-cfius.

[8] CFIUS Monitoring and Enforcement, U.S. Department of the Treasury, home.treasury.gov/policy-issues/international/the-committee-on-foreign-investment-in-the-united-states-cfius/cfius-monitoring-and-enforcement.

[9] Jeanne Whalen, "TikTok Was Just the Beginning: Trump Administration Is Stepping Up Scrutiny of Past Chinese Tech Investments," *The Washington Post*, September 29, 2020, www.washingtonpost.com/technology/2020/09/29/cfius-review-past-chinese-investment/.

[10] CFIUS Laws and Guidance, U.S. Department of the Treasury, home.treasury.gov/policy-issues/international/the-committee-on-foreign-investment-in-the-united-states-cfius/cfius-laws-and-guidance.

[11] Foreign Investment Risk Review Modernization Act of 2018, H.R. 5841, 115th Cong. (2d Sess. 2018).

[12] Ibid.

scope of transactions reviewable by the CFIUS so that current concerns can be addressed more effectively.[13]

With the escalation of China–US trade frictions, the US government has made more frequent use of national security review to restrict Chinese enterprises from carrying out business activities in the United States. Since the passing of FIRRMA, there has been a growing number of national security review cases against Chinese "national strategic buyers"[14] investing in the US market. For example, Huawei Technologies Co., Ltd. (Huawei) is listed as a national security threat and thus forbidden to conduct certain business activities in the United States.[15] Another example is TikTok, a social media company from China, which was temporarily removed from app stores on the ground of endangering national security in the United States.[16]

This chapter aims to critically examine China's national security review regime of foreign investment and compare it with that of the United States. Section 5.2 discusses the four stages of the evolutional trajectory of national security review in China and summarizes their unique characteristics. Section 5.3 analyses the key elements of the current regime for national security review in China, including review procedures, legal effects and enforcement mechanisms. This is followed by Section 5.4 which looks at the national security review regime in the United States. Section 5.5 compares the law and practice of national security review in China and the United States, revealing the jurisdictional differences and similarities. Section 5.6 tries to identify the factors contributing to the convergences and divergences between China and the United States and discusses the implications for the future development of national security review.

5.2 The Evolution of China's NSR

The Foreign Investment Law, enacted in 2020, marks the accomplishment of China's long-planned comprehensive NSR regime.[17] The

[13] *See FIRRMA FAQs,* U.S. Department of the Treasury, home.treasury.gov/system/files/206/FIRRMA-FAQs.pdf.

[14] *See* Jeffrey N. Gordon and Curtis J. Milhaupt, "China as a National Strategic Buyer: Toward a Multilateral Regime for Cross-Border M&A" (2019) *Columbia Business Law Review* 192–193.

[15] *See,* for example, Christopher Balding and Donald C. Clarke, "Who Owns Huawei?" (2019) (unpublished paper) (available through SSRN), 11, papers.ssrn.com/sol3/papers.cfm?abstract_id=3372669.

[16] *See* Whalen, above note 9.

[17] *See* Foreign Investment Law (promulgated by the National People's Congress, March 15, 2019, effective January 1, 2020).

formation of the Chinese national security review system is a response to the rapid increase in foreign direct investment (FDI) and Mergers & Acquisitions (M&A) in China.[18] China's system tries to maintain a balance between ensuring national security and embracing foreign investment.[19] While China's NSR regime seems to be immediately triggered by several failed acquisitions made by Chinese companies in the United States,[20] it is also a long-term strategy for China to cope with the challenges brought by the general economic globalization and the specific China–US tension. The development of China's NSR regime can be broadly divided into four stages.

5.2.1 *Stage 1 (1979–2003): Market Entry Restrictions*

At the first stage, China's national security review system was based on the examination and approval of enterprise establishment and industry access for greenfield investment.[21] Upon opening up to the world, China reviewed foreign investment and domestic investment in similar ways. The concept of national security first appeared in the 1995 Interim Provisions on Guiding the Orientation of Foreign Investment.[22] Under this scheme, foreign-invested projects were categorized as projects that were either encouraged, permitted, restricted or prohibited.[23]

The legal regime did not provide detailed guidance on what factors the government would consider when reviewing foreign investment in China. The underdevelopment of China's national security review during this period can be explained by economic reasons. Cross-border M&As in the 1990s accounted for only a very small portion of the total

[18] *See* Qingxiu Bu, "China's National Security Review: A Tit-for-Tat Response" (2012) 6 *Law and Financial Markets Review* 343, 345. (describing the respective increases and associated national security concerns).

[19] Ibid., at 343.

[20] Souvik Saha, "CFIUS Now Made in China: Dueling National Security Review Frameworks as a Countermeasure to Economic Espionage in the Age of Globalization" (2012) 33 *Northwestern Journal of International Law and Business* 199, 215.

[21] For more discussions on greenfield investment in China, see Robin Hui Huang, "The Regulation of Foreign Investment in Post-WTO China: A Political Economy Analysis" (2009) 23 *Columbia Journal of Asian Law* 185, 187–188.

[22] Zhidao Waishang Touzi Fangxiang Zanxing Guiding (指导外商投资方向暂行规定) [Provisional Regulations on Direction Guide to Foreign Investment] (promulgated by the State Development Planning Commission, the State Economic & Trade Commission and the Ministry of Civil Affairs, June 20, 1995, effective June 20, 1995).

[23] Ibid., art. 4.

FDI in China.[24] It was not until China promised to embrace more foreign investment as part of its World Trade Organization (WTO) accession commitments in 2001 that foreign investment started flocking into China.

5.2.2 *Stage 2 (2003–2015): NSR for Foreign M&A*

During the second stage, China's national security review became an increasingly important tool to regulate foreign M&As. The Interim Provisions on Mergers and Acquisitions of Domestic Enterprises by Foreign Investors (the Foreign M&A Provisions) were issued in 2003.[25] These provisions aimed to deal with rapidly growing foreign M&As of domestic companies after China's WTO accession.[26] Article 19 required foreign investors to submit a report of national security if the government had deemed it necessary.[27] The 2008 Anti-Monopoly Law was enacted to combat monopolistic business activities in China.[28] It introduced a specific provision, Article 31, to deal with national security issues in relation to M&As.[29] Under this provision, NSR is conducted where a foreign investor merged with or acquired a domestic enterprise and where national security issues were involved.[30] Further, in 2006 and 2009, the MOFCOM issued and revised the Provisions on

[24] Huan Zou and Paul Simpson, "Cross-border Mergers and Acquisitions in China: An Industry Panel Study, 1991–2005" (2008) 14 *Asia Pacific Business Review* 491, 492–493.

[25] Waiguo Touzizhe Binggou Jingnei Qiye Zanxing Guiding (外国投资者并购境内企业暂行规定) [Interim Provisions on Mergers and Acquisitions of Domestic Enterprises by Foreign Investors] (promulgated by the Ministry of Foreign Trade and Economic Cooperation, the State Taxation Administration, the State Administration for Industry and Commerce, and the State Administration of Foreign Exchange, March 7, 2003, effective April 12, 2003) [hereinafter 2003 Foreign M&A Provisions].

[26] China's Foreign Direct Investment Hits US$ 53 bln in 2003, January 14, 2004, Consulate-General of the People's Republic of China in Chicago, www.chinaconsulatechicago.org/eng/zt/aboutchina/t58507.html; Eric Jensen, "Balancing Security and Growth: Defining National Security Review of Foreign Investment in China" (2010) 19 *Pacific Rim Law & Policy Journal* 161, 165–166.

[27] 2003 Foreign M&A Provisions, art. 19.

[28] Zhonghua Renmin Gongheguo Fanlongduan Fa (中华人民共和国反垄断法) [Anti-Monopoly Law of the People's Republic of China] (promulgated by the National People"s Congress, August 30, 2007, effective August 1, 2008) [hereinafter Anti-Monopoly Law].

[29] Ibid., art. 31.

[30] Ibid.

M&A of a Domestic Enterprise by Foreign Investors.[31] However, all the rules noted above just mentioned the importance of NSR, without providing detailed guidance on its application.

In 2011, the State Council issued the Notice of the General Office on the Establishment of the Security Review System for Mergers and Acquisitions of Domestic Enterprises by Foreign Investors (2011 M&A NSR Notice).[32] This regulation provides some detailed guidance on the application of NSR in relation to foreign M&A transactions targeting domestic enterprises. It makes clear that the NSR mainly applies to foreign M&As in several key industries such as national defense and important infrastructural facilities.[33] Subsequently, in the same year, the MOFCOM issued the Provisions on the Implementation of the Security Review System for Mergers and Acquisitions of Domestic Enterprises by Foreign Investors (2011 M&A NSR Provisions).[34] This regulation provides the legal basis for establishing a mechanism of interdepartmental Joint Meetings under the State Council to handle NSR issues,[35] and sets out the procedure for conducting a national security review.[36]

5.2.3 *Stage 3 (2015–2020): NSR in General*

In 2015, China enacted the National Security Law (2015 NSL), elevating national security to the status of national-level strategy for the first time.

[31] Guanyu Waiguo Touzizhe Binggou Jingnei Qiye de Guiding (关于外国投资者并购境内企业的规定) [Provisions on M&A of a Domestic Enterprise by Foreign Investors] (promulgated by the MOFCOM, August 6, 2006, revised June 22, 2009). For more details, see Robin Hui Huang, "China's New Regulation on Foreign M&A: Green Light or Red Flag?" (2007) 30 *University of New South Wales Law Journal* 802–803.

[32] Guowuyuan Bangongting Guanyu Jianli Waiguo Touzizhe Binggou Jingnei Qiye Anquan Shencha Zhidu De Tongzhi (国务院办公厅关于建立外国投资者并购境内企业安全审查制度的通知) [Notice of the General Office of the State Council on the Establishment of the Security Review System for Mergers and Acquisitions of Domestic Enterprises by Foreign Investors] (promulgated by the State Council, February 3, 2011, effective March 3, 2011) [hereinafter 2011 M&A NSR Notice].

[33] Ibid., art. 1.

[34] Shangwubu Shishi Waiguo Touzizhe Binggou Jingnei Qiye Anquan Shencha Zhidu De Guiding (商务部实施外国投资者并购境内企业安全审查制度的规定) [Provisions of the MOFCOM on the Implementation of the Security Review System for Mergers and Acquisitions of Domestic Enterprises by Foreign Investors] (promulgated by the MOFCOM, August 25, 2011, effective September 1, 2011) [hereinafter 2011 M&A NSR Provisions].

[35] Ibid., art. 3.

[36] Ibid., art. 4.

The law authorizes the government to formulate guidelines for achieving specific national security objectives, strategies and policies in key fields.[37] When ensuring national security, the government is required to consider economic and social development.[38] The state's basic economic system and the socialist market economy order must be protected from economic security risks, especially among important industries and crucial economic fields.[39] Apart from listing a number of key aspects of state security, the law also contains a provision to give the government broad discretionary power.[40]

Under the 2015 NSL, the government is authorized to establish mechanisms for conducting NSR in various areas, such as foreign investment transactions, specified materials, key technologies, internet information technology products and services and construction projects involving national security issues.[41] Relevant departments of the central government are empowered to make and implement national security review decisions.[42] Local governments are responsible for national security review within their respective administrative regions.[43] Overall, the 2015 NSL, as a formal law at the national level, confirms the importance of NSR in the specific area of foreign investment, but does not add much substance to the then-existing regime for conducting NSR for foreign investment.

5.2.4 *Stage 4 (from 2020): NSR for Foreign Investment*

The fourth stage is characterized by the formation of a comprehensive NSR framework for all foreign investments. The 2020 Foreign Investment Law clarifies the scope of China's NSR regime, setting up a "pre-establishment national treatment plus negative list" system.[44] Foreign investors may not invest in a field on the "negative list for access

[37] National Security Law (promulgated by the National People's Congress, July 1, 2015, effective July 1, 2015), art. 6.
[38] Ibid., art. 8.
[39] Ibid., art. 19.
[40] Ibid., art. 34.
[41] Ibid., art. 59.
[42] Ibid., art. 60.
[43] Ibid., art. 61.
[44] Foreign Investment Law (promulgated by the National People's Congress, March 15, 2019, effective January 1, 2020), art. 4.

of foreign investment,"[45] while national treatment will be accorded to foreign investment outside of the negative list.[46] If a foreign investment project is not on the negative list, it will be deemed not to be a threat to China's national security.[47]

To further facilitate the application of NSR, the NDRC issued the Measures for the Security Review of Foreign Investment (the 2020 NSR Measures) on November 27, 2020, which entered into force on January 18, 2021.[48] This rule extends the NSR regime from foreign M&A transactions to cover greenfield foreign investment. Further, it introduces two types of review processes, namely, general review and special review.[49] Under the leadership of the NDRC and the MOFCOM, the Office of the Working Mechanism was established to take responsibility for the routine NSR work, replacing the former "Joint Meeting" mechanism.[50] Interestingly, the new office is located in the NDRC, which means that the NDRC replaces the MOFCOM as the leading NSR regulator.[51] In summary, the 2020 NSR Measures have made significant improvements on China's NSR regime in terms of its scope of application and procedures.

Finally, China has continuously improved the "negative list" system as a key component of the NSR regime. In 2015, the State Council issued the Opinions of the State Council on Implementing the Market Access Negative List Regime, providing guidance for the establishment of a negative list system for domestic and foreign investments, respectively, for the first time.[52] Since 2018, the NDRC and the MOFCOM have jointly issued the Special Administrative Measures for Foreign

45 Ibid., art. 28.

46 Ibid., art. 4.

47 Ibid., art. 6.

48 Waishang Touzi Anquan Shencha Banfa (外商投资安全审查办法) [Measures for the Security Review of Foreign Investments] (promulgated by the NDRC, November 27, 2020, effective January 18, 2021) [hereinafter 2020 NSR Measures].

49 Ibid., art. 8.

50 Ibid., art. 3.

51 Ibid. This provision puts the NDRC in front of the MOFCOM, which means the NDRC outranks the MOFCOM in dealing with NSR issues.

52 Guowuyuan Guanyu Shixing Shichang Zhunru Fumian Qingdan Zhidu De Yijian (国务院关于实行市场准入负面清单制度的意见) [Opinions of the State Council on Implementing the Market Access Negative List Regime] (promulgated by the State Council, October 2, 2015, effective December 1, 2015), www.chinadaily.com.cn/business/2015-11/13/content_22446386.htm.

Investment Access Negative List (Negative List Measures).[53] The 2020 Export Control Law[54] and the 2020 Provisions on the Unreliable Entity List (the Unreliable Entity List Provision)[55] were promulgated to supplement the negative list system.

5.3 China's Current NSR Regime

The 2020 Foreign Investment Law and the 2020 NSR Measures are the main components of China's current NSR regime. Further, the two regulations issued in 2011 to deal with M&A transactions are still in effect, namely, the 2011 M&A NSR Notice and the 2011 M&A NSR Provisions. When it comes to reviewing foreign M&A transactions, the specific rules in the two M&A regulations issued in 2011 will apply where the 2020 Foreign Investment Law and the 2020 NSR Measures are silent or unclear on relevant matters.

5.3.1 Overview

5.3.1.1 Key Concepts

Under the 2011 M&A NSR Notice, the scope of NSR includes foreign M&A of domestic enterprises in key areas such as military industries, major and sensitive military facilities and other entities relating to national defense security.[56] NSR can be triggered if a foreign investor becomes the controlling shareholder or actual controller of a domestic enterprise through M&A.[57] If the foreign investor's share of a domestic enterprise exceeds 50 percent, or has enough voting power to exert a

53 The most updated version was issued in 2021. See Waishang Touzi Zhunru Tebie Guanli Cuoshi Fumian Qingdan Erling Eryi Nian Ban (外商投资准入特别管理措施（负面清单）（2021年版）) [Special Administrative Measures for Foreign Investment Access Negative List] (promulgated by the NDRC and the MOFCOM, December 27, 2021, effective January 1, 2022) [hereinafter 2021 Negative List Measures].

54 Zhonghua Renmin Gongheguo Chukou Guanzhi Fa (中华人民共和国出口管制法) [The Export Control Law of the People's Republic of China] (promulgated by the National People's Congress, October 17, 2020, effective December 1, 2020) [hereinafter the 2020 Export Control Law].

55 Bukekao Shiti Qingdan (不可靠实体清单规定) [The Provisions on the Unreliable Entity List] (promulgated by the State Council, September 19, 2020, effective September 19, 2020).

56 2011 M&A NSR Notice, arts. 1.1–1.2.

57 Ibid., arts. 1.1, 1.3.

material impact on corporate resolutions, the investor will be regarded as having actual control of the domestic enterprise.[58]

Under the 2020 Foreign Investment Law, foreign investors and foreign-funded enterprises conducting investment activities within China are prohibited from compromising China's national security.[59] A "foreign investment" means investment activities within mainland China directly or indirectly conducted by foreign natural persons, enterprises and other organizations.[60] A "foreign-funded enterprise" means an enterprise formed and registered within mainland China under Chinese laws in which all or part of the investment is made by a foreign investor.[61] The 2015 NSL defines "national security" as a status in which major state interests are not threatened internally or externally.[62]

The 2020 NSR Measures provide further guidance on the relevant terms. For instance, "foreign investment" means the investing activities conducted by a foreign investor directly or indirectly in China, including investing in a new project or by the formation of an enterprise, investing via M&A or investing by any other means.[63]

The NSR regime covers the following industries: (1) foreign investment in the arms industry. This includes an ancillary to the arms industry, or any other field related to national defense security.[64] The law also mentions foreign investments in sensitive areas surrounding a military installation or an arms industry facility;[65] (2) foreign investment in several key manufacturing and other industries where the foreign investor has actual control. The law enumerates extensively the industries, such as critical equipment manufacturing, important agricultural products and key technology, followed by a catch-all provision (any other important fields related to national security);[66] (3) where a foreign investor's purchase of stock in a Chinese listed company affects national security, the specific national security review rules shall be formulated by the CSRC in conjunction with the Office of the Working Mechanism.[67]

58 Ibid., art. 1.3.

59 Ibid., art. 6.

60 Ibid., art. 2.

61 Ibid.

62 National Security Law of the People's Republic of China 2015 (2015 NSL) (中华人民共和国国家安全法), art. 2.

63 2020 NSR Measures, art. 2.

64 Ibid., art. 4.

65 Ibid.

66 Ibid.

67 Ibid., art. 22.

5.3.1.2 Office of the Working Mechanism Decision-Making Factors

The 2020 NSR Measures do not clarify what factors the Office of the Working Mechanism may consider when making decisions. Thus, the 2011 M&A NSR Notice continues to be relevant in shedding light on the factors that the Office of the Working Mechanism may consider in the NSR exercise:

> (1) The influence of M&A transactions on the national defense security must be reviewed, including the ability for producing domestic products and providing domestic services required for national defense and the relevant equipment and facilities.
> (2) The influence of M&A transactions on the stable operation of the national economy.
> (3) The influence of M&A transactions on the order of basic social life.
> (4) The influence of M&A transactions on the capacity of research and development of key technologies involving national security.[68]

Article 7 of the 2020 Unreliable Entity List Provisions enumerates the relevant factors which may lead to a foreign entity being considered unreliable, including: (1) the degree of danger to national sovereignty, security or development interests of China; (2) the degree of damage to the legitimate rights and interests of enterprises, other organizations or individuals of China; (3) whether there is compliance with internationally accepted economic and trade rules; and (4) other factors that shall be considered.[69]

5.3.2 Review Agencies

5.3.2.1 The Agency That Accepts Applications

Under the 2011 M&A NSR Notice, the MOFCOM is the agency authorized to accept NSR applications for foreign M&A deals.[70] The NSR application is usually made by foreign investors. The foreign investor needs to file an application with the MOFCOM, which will then request that members of the Joint Meeting review the transaction within five working days.[71] If the applicant fails to apply, the local department of

[68] 2011 M&A NSR Notice, art. 2.

[69] The Provisions on the Unreliable Entity List (promulgated by the State Council, September 19, 2020, effective September 19, 2020), art. 7.

[70] 2011 M&A NSR Provisions, art. 1.

[71] Ibid., art. 3.

commerce shall require the applicant to file an application within five working days and report the relevant situations to the MOFCOM.[72] There are other ways to initiate the NSR process. For instance, the relevant department of the State Council,[73] a national industrial association, an enterprise of the same profession or an upstream/downstream enterprise may propose a security review to the MOFCOM. Further, the members of the Joint Meeting may decide to conduct a security review if they deem it necessary.[74]

The 2020 NSR Measures refine the review procedures, stipulating three ways to initiate the NSR process: (1) a foreign investor is obligated to proactively report the foreign investment within certain sensitive areas to the Office of the Working Mechanism; (2) the Office of the Working Mechanism has the power to require the foreign investor to report the investment within these areas;[75] (3) a relevant agency, enterprise, social group or member of the general public among others may propose a security review to the Office of the Working Mechanism if it deems that necessary.[76]

5.3.2.2 The Agency That Makes Decisions

Although the MOFCOM is responsible for accepting NSR applications from foreign investors, it does not make the final decision on the application. The 2011 M&A NSR Notice established a system of Joint Meeting for making review decisions.[77] Members of the Joint Meeting were from the State Council, the NDRC, the MOFCOM and other relevant departments.[78] However, the 2011 M&A NSR Notice did not clearly delineate the division of power between the NDRC and the MOFCOM.

The 2020 Foreign Investment Law extends the NSR regime from foreign M&A transactions to all foreign investments, stating that the NSR regime is administered by the commerce department and the investment department.[79] Later, the 2020 NSR Measures were issued to

[72] Ibid., art. 2

[73] The State Council (国务院) is the Chinese central government.

[74] 2011 M&A NSR Notice, art. 4.

[75] 2020 NSR Measures, art. 4.

[76] Ibid., art. 15.

[77] 2011 M&A NSR Notice (promulgated by the State Council, February 3, 2011, effective March 3, 2011), art. 3.

[78] Ibid., art. 3.

[79] Foreign Investment Law, art. 7.

establish a Working Mechanism for carrying out the NSR of foreign investment.[80] Under the joint leadership of the NDRC and the MOFCOM, the Office of the Working Mechanism is responsible for the routine work of NSR.[81] Importantly, the Office of the Working Mechanism is located within the NDRC,[82] which is empowered to formulate and implement strategies of national economic and social development and to coordinate economic and social development. As such, the NDRC seems to take on a more important role in the NSR process than the MOFCOM under the 2020 NSR Measures.

5.3.3 *Review Procedures*

5.3.3.1 Filing Procedures and Documents

The 2011 M&A NSR Provisions set out procedural rules for the NSR process. If the NSR application documents submitted are complete, the MOFCOM will notify the applicant in writing of receipt of the application. If the transaction falls within the scope of M&A security review, the MOFCOM shall notify the applicant in writing within fifteen working days and, within five working days thereafter, submit it to the Joint Meeting for review.

The 2020 NSR Measures refine the filing procedures. Under Article 4 of this instrument, if foreign investors want to make investments in China in relevant areas of national security concerns, they have an affirmative duty to report the investment to the Office of the Working Mechanism prior to actually making the investment. Article 6 requires the submission of relevant documents and information for the reporting purposes.[83]

Within fifteen working days of receiving the relevant materials, the Office of the Working Mechanism will decide whether a security review is required.[84] The foreign investor will be notified in writing to continue the investment if the Office of the Working Mechanism finds that the investment does not require national security review.[85] If a national security review is required, then the Office of the Working Mechanism

80 2020 NSR Measures, art. 3.
81 Ibid.
82 Ibid.
83 Ibid., art. 6.
84 Ibid., art. 7.
85 Ibid.

will take the case further to the review stage, which will be discussed in more detail in the following sections.

5.3.3.2 Formal Review and Informal Consultation

The 2011 M&A NSR Notice provides for two kinds of review processes: general review and special review. For a transaction that may give rise to national security concerns, a general review will first be conducted and, if the transaction fails to pass the general review, a special review will follow.[86] Under the 2020 NSR Measures, the general review shall be completed by the Office of the Working Mechanism within thirty working days.[87] After the general review, the Office of the Working Mechanism decides whether to initiate a special review.[88]

There may be a voluntary informal consultation process between the foreign investor and the MOFCOM. The foreign investor may submit a consultation application to the MOFCOM to discuss its case before filing a formal application. The consultation is not a procedure that the foreign investor must go through before filing a formal application, and the result of the consultation will not have any binding legal effect.[89] This informal consultation mechanism offers a useful channel for foreign investors to communicate with the regulators before embarking on the burdensome NSR process.

5.3.4 Review Decisions

Under the 2020 NSR Measures, the Office of the Working Mechanism can make three types of decisions. First, if the foreign investment does not affect national security, it will pass the security review. Second, if the reported foreign investment affects national security, it will prohibit the investment. The foreign investor should stop the investment or dispose of its equities or assets and take necessary measures to eliminate the harmful effect on national security.[90] Third, if the imposition of conditions accepted by the foreign investor in writing is sufficient to eliminate the effect on national security, the security review can be passed

[86] 2011 M&A NSR Notice, art. 4.
[87] 2020 NSR Measures, art. 8.
[88] Ibid., art. 8.
[89] 2011 M&A NSR Provisions, art. 4; 2020 NSR Measures, art. 5.
[90] 2020 NSR Measures, art. 12.

conditionally. The party shall make the investment subject to the imposed conditions.[91]

There are certain legal consequences for foreign investors who violate the NSR regime. For instance, where a foreign investor within the reporting scope fails to report, the Office of the Working Mechanism shall order the foreign investor to report or dispose of its resultant equities or assets within a specified period and take necessary measures to eliminate the effect on national security.[92] Further, where a foreign investor provides any false material or conceals any relevant information, the Office of the Working Mechanism shall order it to take corrective action or revoke the relevant decision, or order the party to dispose of its resultant equities or assets within a specified period and take necessary measures to eliminate the effect on national security.[93] Moreover, where any foreign investor fails to make the investment in compliance with the imposed conditions, the Office of the Working Mechanism shall order it to take corrective action or order it to dispose of its resultant equities or assets within a specified period and take necessary measures to eliminate the effect on national security.[94] Finally, if the foreign investor does not comply with the law, it will receive negative credit, which shall be included in the relevant credit information system of the state.[95]

5.4 The NSR Regime in the United States

5.4.1 Overview

Compared to China, the United States has a much longer history of national security review.[96] The Defense Production Act of 1950 is the major legal instrument for NSR in the United States, and it has been supplemented by other laws such as the Foreign Investment and National Security Act of 2007.[97] During the 1980s, several high-profile foreign takeovers of American enterprises led to the enactment of the 1988

91 Ibid.
92 2020 NSR Measures, art. 16.
93 Ibid., art. 17.
94 Ibid., art. 18.
95 Ibid., art. 19.
96 *See* Sam Karson, "Caught between Superpowers: Alaska's Economic Relationship with China Amidst the New Cold War" (2019) 36 *Alaska Law Review* 47.
97 Foreign Investment and National Security Act of 2007 (FINSA), Pub. L. No. 110–149, 121 Stat. 246.

Exon–Florio Amendment.[98] Section 721 of the Defense Production Act of 1950 was introduced as the legal basis for the establishment of the CFIUS, which is authorized to conduct the NSR review of relevant M&A transactions.[99]

5.4.2 The 1950 Defense Production Act

5.4.2.1 Substantive Rules

Section 721 of the Defense Production Act covers any merger, acquisition or takeover that is proposed or pending by or with any foreign person, and that could result in foreign control of any person engaged in interstate commerce in the United States.[100] However, the law does not provide a clear definition of national security; instead, it enumerates several factors for the government to take into account.[101] In general, there must be a possibility that a foreign company may obtain sensitive technology or may dominate an industry deemed critical for national defense.[102] The NSR regime applies to the so-called foreign government-controlled transaction, namely, transactions that could result in the control of any person engaged in interstate commerce in the United States by a foreign government or an entity controlled by a foreign government.[103] "National security" refers to issues relating to "homeland security," including critical infrastructure.[104]

The eleven consideration factors are specified in Section 721(f), covering major aspects of the capacity of domestic industries to meet national defense requirements.[105] For instance, the CFIUS will consider the potential effects of the proposed transaction on sales of military goods, equipment or technology to any country that supports terrorism, and on the United States' international technological leadership, critical

[98] CFIUS Laws and Guidance, U.S. Department of the Treasury, home.treasury.gov/policy-issues/international/the-committee-on-foreign-investment-in-the-united-states-cfius/cfius-laws-and-guidance.

[99] Christina E. Holzer, "Committee on Foreign Investment in the United States and Judicial Review" (2014) 13 *Journal of International Business and Law* 169, 170–172.

[100] Defense Production Act of 1950 § 721(a)(3), 50 U.S.C. § 4501 (2023).

[101] Yang Wang, "Incorporating the Third Branch of Government into US National Security Review of Foreign Investment" (2016) 38 *Houston Journal of International Law* 323, 325.

[102] Defense Production Act of 1950 § 721(a)(4), 50 U.S.C. § 4501 (2023).

[103] Ibid., §§ 721(a)(4).

[104] Ibid., §§ 721(a)(5)–(6).

[105] Ibid., at § 721(f).

infrastructure and critical technologies.[106] Foreign government-controlled transactions will be reviewed with more care.[107] There is a catch-all provision, which allows the president and the CFIUS to consider "other factors" as appropriate during the NSR process.[108]

5.4.2.2 Procedural Rules

As a multiagency committee, the CFIUS is mandated to perform the function of conducting NSR for relevant foreign investments in the United States.[109] When the CFIUS was established in 1975, it was perceived as a paper tiger due to its lack of enforcement power.[110] In response to growing concerns about foreign takeovers, the US Congress passed the Omnibus Trade and Competitiveness Act of 1988.[111] It included the Exon–Florio Amendment, endowing the CFIUS with greater authority.[112] Any party or parties to any covered transaction is able to initiate a review of the transaction by submitting a written notice to the chairperson of the CFIUS. Upon receiving written notification of any covered transaction, the president can review the transaction through the CFIUS to determine its effects on national security.[113] The review should be completed within thirty days.[114] Besides the foreign investor, the president or the CFIUS may initiate a review if the foreign investor submits false or misleading material information, omitted material information or intentionally and materially breaches a mitigation agreement.[115]

The review may be accompanied by an investigation process under certain conditions. The CFIUS will immediately conduct a national security investigation and take any necessary actions if a review of a

[106] Ibid., at § 721(f).
[107] Ibid., at § 721(f)(8).
[108] Ibid., at § 721(b)(1)(A).
[109] Ibid., at § 721(k).
[110] Souvik Saha, "CFIUS Now Made in China: Dueling National Security Review Frameworks as a Countermeasure to Economic Espionage in the Age of Globalization" (2012) 33 *Northwestern Journal of International Law and Business* 199, 215.
[111] Omnibus Trade and Competitiveness Act of 1988, Pub. L. No. 100-418, § 5021, 102 Stat. 1107, 1425–1426 (codified at 50 USC app. § 2170 (2012)).
[112] Souvik Saha, "CFIUS Now Made in China: Dueling National Security Review Frameworks as a Countermeasure to Economic Espionage in the Age of Globalization" (2012) 33 *Northwestern Journal of International Law and Business* 199, 215.
[113] Ibid., § 721(b)(1)(A).
[114] Ibid., § 721(b)(1)(E).
[115] Ibid., § 721(b)(1)(D).

covered transaction produces relevant findings, including but not limited to: first, the transaction threatens to impair national security, which has not been mitigated during or prior to the review; second, the transaction is a foreign government-controlled transaction; third, the transaction would result in control of any critical infrastructure of or within the United States by or on behalf of any foreign person.[116] The CFIUS must determine that the transaction could impair national security, which has not been mitigated by assurances provided or renewed with the approval of the CFIUS.[117] When the lead agency recommends and the CFIUS concurs, the CFIUS will conduct an investigation.[118] An investigation should be completed within forty-five days.[119] There are exceptions to the investigation when the Secretary of the Treasury and the head of the lead agency jointly determine that the transaction will not impair the national security.[120]

Certain actions and findings of the president under Section 721(d) are nonreviewable.[121] Under Section 721(d)(1), the president may take action to suspend or prohibit any covered transaction that threatens to impair national security and direct the attorney general to seek appropriate relief in the district courts to enforce the action.[122] Furthermore, the findings of the president under Section 721(d)(4) shall not be subject to judicial review.[123] This has been criticized as a violation of the due process rights of investors and an abuse of power by the executive branch.[124] Further, it has been argued that the CFIUS may pose a threat to economic productivity in an arbitrary and capricious manner.[125]

Although the presidential findings and actions are exempted from judicial review under Section 721, the CFIUS decision may arguably be subject to judicial review.[126] The case of Ralls is the first judicial review case that challenged the CFIUS's decision to block a foreign

[116] Ibid., § 721(b)(2)(A)(B).
[117] Ibid., § 721(b)(2)(B).
[118] Ibid., § 721(b)(2)(ii).
[119] Ibid., § 721(b)(2)(C).
[120] Ibid., § 721(b)(2)(D)(i).
[121] Ibid., § 721(e).
[122] Ibid., § 721(d)(1).
[123] Ibid., § 721(e).
[124] Wang, above note 101, at 327.
[125] Saha, above note 20, at 200.
[126] 50 U.S.C. § 2170(c) (2011). When CFIUS gives foreign entities a negative review, none of them have ever sought judicial review before the case of *Ralls*. See Holzer, above note 99, at 181.

investment.[127] In 2012, Ralls Corporation, a Chinese-owned Delaware company, planned to develop windfarms near the military zone of the US Navy.[128] The CFIUS blocked the transaction based on national security grounds, backed by President Obama's Presidential Order.[129] Ralls filed a lawsuit for declaratory and injunctive relief against the CFIUS, claiming the violation of its due process rights.[130] Ralls asserted that the CFIUS acted arbitrarily and capriciously beyond the scope of its empowerment,[131] and the District Court had jurisdiction over the claim. The complaint was dismissed by the district court,[132] but on appeal, the D.C. Circuit held that a constitutional claim challenging the process preceding the presidential action is reviewable despite the fact that final actions of the president are nonreviewable.[133] Ralls may set a dangerous precedent for judicial interference in national security and diplomacy.[134] However, the president's power to block transactions based on CFIUS recommendations remains unchanged.

5.4.3 The 2018 FIRRMA

The United States has failed to adequately screen foreign investment that has been pouring in from China and other countries in recent years, particularly low-profile venture-capital investments.[135] In response, the United States passed FIRRMA on August 13, 2018, to boost the CFIUS's funding and powers.[136] FIRRMA formed one part of a comprehensive defense bill for Fiscal Year 2019, signed by President Trump, and was largely a response to the Trump Administration's concerns over Chinese

[127] "Ralls and US Government Settle Only CFIUS Suit in History," *Steptoe*, October 14, 2015, www.steptoeinternationalcomplianceblog.com/2015/10/ralls-and-u-s-government-settle-only-cfius-suit-in-history/.

[128] *See Ralls Corp. v. Comm. on Foreign Inv. in U.S.*, 926 F. Supp. 2d 71 at 75–76 (D.D.C. 2013).

[129] Ibid., at 76.

[130] Ibid.

[131] Ibid., at 81.

[132] *Ralls Corp. v. Comm. on Foreign Inv. in the U.S.*, 926 F. Supp. 2d 71, 71 (D.D.C. 2013).

[133] *See* generally *Ralls Corp. v. Comm. on Foreign Inv. in the U.S.*, 758 F.3d 296 (D.C. Cir. 2014).

[134] Christopher M. Fitzpatrick, "Where Ralls Went Wrong: CFIUS, the Courts, and the Balance of Liberty and Security" (2016) 101 *Cornell Law Review* 1087, 1096.

[135] Whalen, above note 9.

[136] FIRRMA, § 1702(b)(5); Sam Karson, "Caught between Superpowers: Alaska's Economic Relationship with China Amidst the New Cold War" (2019) 36 *Alaska Law Review* 47.

investment in the United States. Specifically, it mainly seeks to prevent the transfer of US technology by Chinese investors.[137]

FIRRMA has systematically amended the current national security review regime in the United States. Although the law was not applied exclusively to Chinese investments, it primarily targets China.[138] It expands the scope of covered transactions and broadens the purview of the CFIUS.[139] The Department of the Treasury regards this law to be revolutionary for the landscape of foreign investment and the NSR regime in the United States.[140] However, these changes may also increase the possibility of politicizing NSR and compressing review relief channels.

5.4.3.1 Substantive Rules

Generally, FIRRMA covers any merger, acquisition or takeover that is proposed or pending after August 23, 1988, by or with any foreign person.[141] These transactions could result in foreign control of any US business, including those carried out through a joint venture.[142] The law can trace back to foreign deals struck as early as August 23, 1988[143] and, thus, all the investments in the recent era of globalization since the 1990s will be examined and reviewed. Section 1702(c) of FIRRMA lists factors to be considered.[144] For instance, the CFIUS must consider whether a covered transaction involves a "country of special concern" that has shown a strategic goal of acquiring a type of critical technology or critical infrastructure that would affect US leadership in areas related to national security.[145]

Specifically, there are four new types of covered transactions: (1) a purchase, lease or concession by or to a foreign person of real estate

[137] Paul B. Edelberg, "Can Chinese Companies Still Invest in the United States: The Impact of FIRRMA" (2019) 16 *US–China Law Review* 12, 13.

[138] Ibid.

[139] U.S. Department of the Treasury, "FIRRMA FAQs," at 1, home.treasury.gov/system/files/206/FIRRMA-FAQs.pdf.

[140] Ibid.

[141] *See* Foreign Investment Risk Review Modernization Act of 2018 (FIRRMA), H.R. 5515, § 1703(4)(B) (2018).

[142] Ibid., § 1703(4)(B) (2018).

[143] This provision can be used to target offshore joint ventures which have been formed in the past years. To avoid CFIUS, US companies used to transfer their assets to offshore joint ventures (including Chinese joint ventures). See Edelberg, above note 137.

[144] Ibid., § 1702(c).

[145] Ibid.

located in proximity to sensitive government facilities, which may function as part of an air or maritime port or provide the foreign person with the ability to collect intelligence; (2) any other investments by a foreign person in any critical technologies, critical infrastructure and sensitive personal data of American citizens, which are collectively referred to as the "TID" business; (3) any change in a foreign investor's rights resulting in foreign control of a US business or an "other investment" in the third category above; (4) any other transaction, transfer, agreement or arrangement designed to circumvent CFIUS jurisdiction.[146]

There are two highlights in FIRRMA reform, namely, certain sensitive real estate investments and the TID investments.[147] On one hand, for the foreign acquisition of real estate, the law focuses on the proximity of the real estate to certain specified military and other government installations.[148] On the other hand, the CFIUS's jurisdiction is expanded to cover small, noncontrolling investments in the TID business.[149] FIRRMA covers these two types of investments, even if the foreign party does not gain control over the business.[150]

The CFIUS is particularly focused on foreign companies that collect sensitive personal information. It will pay special attention to foreign investment in critical technologies such as chip and battery technology and biotechnology.[151] In practice, the federal government has been sending national security officials to tech leaders to caution them about accepting Chinese investments.[152]

5.4.3.2 Procedural Rules

In order to make the NSR more efficient, FIRRMA makes several important changes to the filing process. The new "declarations" procedure grants the CFIUS wide discretionary power to require parties to file

146 Ibid., § 1703(a)(4); see U.S. Department of the Treasury, "Summary of the Foreign Investment Risk Review Modernization Act of 2018," home.treasury.gov/system/files/206/Summary-of-FIRRMA.pdf.

147 *See* Timothy J. Keeler, Duane W. Layton and Mickey Leibner, "US Treasury Finalizes Regulations to Expand CFIUS Reviews of Foreign Investment in the US," *Mayer Brown*, January 15, 2020, www.mayerbrown.com/en/perspectives-events/publications/2020/01/us-treasury-finalizes-regulations-to-expand-cfius-reviews-of-foreign-investment-in-the-us.

148 Ibid.

149 Ibid.

150 Ibid.

151 Ibid., § 1703(6).

152 Whalen, above note 9.

before closing a transaction.[153] To allow the CFIUS to better carry out its work, the review timelines are expanded: The CFIUS's review period is increased from thirty days to forty-five days, and the period of an investigation is extended for an additional fifteen-day period under extraordinary circumstances.[154] In addition to the timelines, the law strengthens the requirements on the use of mitigation agreements, including compliance plans.[155] It gives special hiring authority to the CFIUS and establishes a fund for collection of new CFIUS filing fees.[156]

FIRRMA also provides for exceptions to the filing requirement.[157] These exemptions generally apply to investors from "excepted foreign states" (the UK, Canada and Australia) and investment funds managed exclusively and ultimately controlled by US nationals.[158]

It is important to note that Section 1719(b) mandates periodic reports on Chinese investments in the United States.[159] Every two years after the enactment of FIRRMA through 2026, the Secretary of Commerce must submit to the US Congress and the CFIUS a report on foreign direct investment transactions made by Chinese entities in the United States.[160] This requirement seems to be a response to China's initiative of "Made in China 2025," under which the Chinese government aims to raise the domestic content of core components and materials to 70 percent by 2025.[161] The US government reached a consensus that the "Made in China 2025" initiative poses a special national security threat to the US economy and technological advantages. Indeed, one of the explicit objectives of FIRRMA is to prevent the transfer of technology to Chinese companies.[162]

153 FIRRMA, § 1706.

154 Ibid., § 1709.

155 Ibid., § 1718.

156 Ibid., § 1723(3).

157 For instance, Section 1706 (v)(IV)(bb)(CC) of the 2018 FIRRMA provides exceptions for a foreign investor to submit a declaration.

158 *See* Christine Daya, "New Regulations Reinforce CFIUS's Expanded Role with Respect to Foreign Investments in the United States," *DLA Piper*, January 16, 2020, www.dlapiper.com/en/us/insights/publications/2020/01/new-regulations-reinforce-cfius-expanded-role/.

159 Foreign Investment Risk Review Modernization Act of 2018, H.R. 5515, § 1719(b) (2018).

160 *See* FIRRMA, § 1719(b)(1), 50 U.S.C. § 4565.

161 *See* Melissa Cyrill, "What Is Made in China 2025 and Why Has It Made the World So Nervous?" *China Briefing*, December 28, 2018, www.china-briefing.com/news/made-in-china-2025-explained/.

162 *See* Edelberg, above note 137, at 14.

5.4.4 *The 2022 Executive Order*

To cope with evolving national security risks, President Biden signed an executive order on September 15, 2022.[163] It is the first executive order to provide formal presidential direction on national security review.[164] The 2022 Executive Order explicitly ties the CFIUS' role with the US government's overall national security priorities. It was mainly targeted at risks from a "country of special concern,"[165] which has been emphasized by Section 1702(c) of FIRRMA. The executive order is a result of heightened geopolitical competition between the US and China.[166]

In conjunction with the old factors,[167] the 2022 Executive Order added several new national security factors.[168] After the reforms, the CFIUS received greater powers and responsibilities. On October 20, 2022, the CFIUS released its first-ever enforcement and penalty guidelines, which came just a few weeks after President Biden issued an executive order.[169] The 2018 FIRRMA lists the following consideration factors: (1) a "country of special concern"; (2) control of critical infrastructure, energy asset, critical material or critical technology; (3) foreign person's US law compliance history; (4) control of US industries and commercial activity, including the availability of human resources, products, technology, materials and other supplies and services; (5) sensitive data; (6) cybersecurity risks. In contrast, the consideration factors set out in the 2022 Executive Order include: (1) resilience of critical US supply chains,

163 *See* Exec. Order No. 14,083, 87 Fed. Reg. 57,369 (September 15, 2022) (The White House Executive Order on Ensuring Robust Consideration of Evolving National Security Risks by the Committee on Foreign Investment in the United States); The White House, "Fact Sheet: President Biden Signs Executive Order to Ensure Robust Reviews of Evolving National Security Risks by the Committee on Foreign Investment in the United States" (2022), www.whitehouse.gov/briefing-room/statements-releases/2022/09/15/fact-sheet-president-biden-signs-executive-order-to-ensure-robust-reviews-of-evolving-national-security-risks-by-the-committee-on-foreign-investment-in-the-united-states/.

164 Ibid.

165 *See* The White House, above note 163.

166 *See* K. Atwood, "President Biden Issues Executive Order on Ensuring Robust Consideration of Evolving National Security Risks by the Committee on Foreign Investment in the United States" (2023) 117 *American Journal of International Law* 340, 341.

167 *See* Defense Production Act § 721(f), 50 U.S.C. § 4565; Foreign Investment Risk Review Modernization Act of 2018 § 1702(c), 50 U.S.C. § 4565.

168 *See* Exec. Order No. 14,083, 87 Fed. Reg. 57,369, § 2.

169 *See* U.S. Department of the Treasury, "CFIUS Enforcement and Penalty Guidelines" (2022), home.treasury.gov/policy-issues/international/the-committee-on-foreign-investment-in-the-united-states-cfius/cfius-enforcement-and-penalty-guidelines.

including those outside of the defense industrial base; (2) US technological leadership in key areas (microelectronics, AI, biotechnology and biomanufacturing, quantum computing, advanced clean energy and climate adaptation technologies); (3) industry investment trends; (4) cybersecurity risks; (5) sensitive data.

The reforms reflect the evolutionary nature of US national security review laws and policies.[170] The 2018 FIRRMA and the 2022 Executive Order have some common grounds. First, both address geopolitical risks from China, which is arguably the United States' top rival in the world. Second, both emphasize personal data protection and cybersecurity, stressing critical technologies and infrastructure. However, their focuses are different. While the 2018 FIRRMA focuses on the more traditional spheres of national security, the 2022 Executive Order aims at filling loopholes in NSR practices. The CFIUS began to bring new factors into consideration, such as the resilience of critical US supply chains and US technological leadership in AI and other key areas.

There are several possible explanations for the evolution of the US NSR regime. First, the 2018 FIRRMA was enacted in an era when the Sino-US trade war was just beginning. Among others, the Trump administration's main goal was to ensure the United States' economic interests and network security and to prevent intellectual property theft, brain drain and job losses. The cases of Huawei and TikTok were rare examples that cannot indicate a full-scale Sino-US tech war.[171] When Biden took office, the tech war was fully underway, as the 2022 CHIPS and Science Act illustrate. The Science Act requires that funded recipients do not build certain facilities in China.[172] The Biden administration needed to further impose a technological blockade on China to ensure its leading position in key areas such as artificial intelligence technology.[173] Second, the COVID-19 pandemic has exerted great impacts on the Sino-US relationship. As the world's factory, China implemented a stringent

170 *See* The White House, above note 163.

171 *See* Grant Schneider, "President Trump Unveils America's First Cybersecurity Strategy in 15 Years," National Security & Defense, September 20, 2018, trumpwhitehouse.archives.gov/articles/president-trump-unveils-americas-first-cybersecurity-strategy-15-years/.

172 *See* Chips and Science Act of 2022, Pub. L. No. 117–167, 136 Stat. 1366.

173 *See* Ellen Nakashima and David J. Lynch, "Biden Order Proposes New Restrictions on China Tech Investment," *Washington Post*, August 9, 2023, www.washingtonpost.com/national-security/2023/08/09/china-ban-technology-biden-military/.

Zero-COVID policy that led to serious supply chain crises in the US.[174] Therefore, the 2022 Executive Order attaches great importance to the United States' supply chain security and economic independence from China.

5.5 A China–US Comparison of NSR: Law and Practice

The preceding sections have discussed the NSR regime in China and the United States separately. This section will look at them together from a comparative perspective. The examination will include both the law on the books and the law in practice. This comparative study is important not only because China and the United States are two important jurisdictions but also because they actually interact to influence the way the NSR regime evolves in each of them.

5.5.1 Comparing the Law on the Books

In China, the enactment of the 2020 Foreign Investment Law laid the legal basis for establishing a comprehensive NSR framework for all foreign investments, including foreign M&A transactions and greenfield investment.[175] The 2021 NSR Measures added more details to the implementation of the review decision-making and enforcement process. The 2011 M&A NSR Notice and the 2011 M&A NSR Provisions continue to apply as specific rules for foreign M&A transactions. The MOFCOM serves as the agency that accepts NSR applications, while the Office of the Working Mechanism located within the NDRC is tasked with making decisions. The foreign investor as well as other organizations can initiate the NSR. There is an informal consultation process between the foreign investor and the Chinese regulators.

In the United States, the 2018 FIRRMA and the 2022 Executive Order expanded the NSR regime from covering only foreign takeovers to cover foreign acquisition of real estate and the TID business.[176] To make the review mechanism more efficient, the review process was streamlined and the CFIUS was granted more discretionary powers. As the United

[174] *See* Martin Farrer, "Zero-Covid Policy Is Costing China Its Role as the World's Workshop," *Guardian*, December 3, 2022, www.theguardian.com/world/2022/dec/03/zero-covid-policy-is-costing-china-its-role-as-the-worlds-workshop.

[175] *See* above Section 5.2.

[176] *See* above Section 5.4.

States' biggest rival, China seems to be the major target of the NSR reforms in the US. For instance, the real estate investments and the TID investments are highlighted in the backdrop of the China–US trade and tech wars. The periodic reporting regime on Chinese investments in the United States is also closely related to China's "Made in China 2025" initiative.

Table 5.1 summarizes some important aspects of the NSR regime in China and the United States.

5.5.1.1 The Convergence

As Table 5.1 shows, there are some convergences in terms of the law on the books between China and the United States. First, the common feature of the review agency is the interdepartmental attribute of both the Office of the Working Mechanism and the CFIUS. The review periods in both countries are at least thirty days. These arrangements ensure the efficient and smooth operation of the national security review among the governmental departments.

Second, the NSR scopes of the two countries are quite broad, since they cover all kinds of sensitive foreign investments that may impact national security. China forbids foreign investors from substantially evading the review in any form.[177] Both jurisdictions have significantly broadened the applicable scope of their NSR regimes from traditionally sensitive industries to nonsensitive industries. For example, the 2018 FIRRMA and the 2022 Executive Order expanded the security review to real estate and other traditionally nonsensitive areas. The term "national security" in both countries is not limited to specific areas of domestic industries, leaving the government with flexible discretionary powers.[178]

Lastly, both countries have excluded the courts from the national security review process. They have explicitly shut down the judicial remedy channel for foreign investors to challenge review decisions. As mentioned earlier, FIRRMA also explicitly excludes any judicial review of the president's and the CFIUS's decisions on foreign investment. After the 2022 Executive Order was issued, the CFIUS received

[177] *See* 2011 M&A NSR Provisions, art. 9 (including forms such as holding shares on behalf of others, trust, multilevel reinvestment, leasing, loans, agreement-based control and overseas transactions).

[178] *See* H. L. Fu and Richard Cullen, "National Security Law in China" (1996) 34 *Columbia Journal of Transnational Law* 449, 451–452.

Table 5.1 *Key elements of the NSR regime in China and the United States*

	China	The United States
Legal sources	2020 Foreign Investment Law 2020 NSR Measures; 2011 M&A NSR Notice; 2011 M&A NSR Provisions	1950 Defense Production Act 2018 FIRRMA 2022 Executive Order
Reviewer	Office of the Working Mechanism in the NDRC	CFIUS
Review scope	(1) Greenfield investment, (2) M&A of domestic enterprises, and (3) other investment by foreign investors	Any merger, acquisition or takeover by or with any foreign person that could result in foreign control of any US business
Review period	30 days for general review; 60 days for special review (may be extended under exceptional circumstances)	30 days review period; 45 days investigation period
Consideration factors	4 factors	Over 10 factors
Judicial review	No	No

greater powers and responsibilities. In China, the 2020 Foreign Investment Law explicitly stipulates that a decision legally made upon a security review shall be final in terms of legal effect.[179] This arrangement can be viewed as a response to the reforms in the United States.

5.5.1.2 The Divergence

Although their national security regimes are similar in some respects, there are significantly more differences or divergences between China and the United States.

First, China's NSR framework is far from complete and clear, leaving the government with tremendous discretionary powers. The 2020 NSR Measures contain very few provisions on how the system works in detail. Compared with the United States, there is much less legislative and judicial monitoring of the governmental decisions in China.

[179] *See* Foreign Investment Law of 2020 (promulgated by the 13th National People's Congress, March 15, 2019, effective January 1, 2020), art. 35.

In comparison, the US government has been constrained by the detailed provisions of statutes. Due to the evolving nature of the national security review regime, the United States has enumerated many more factors to be considered by the CFIUS.[180]

Second, unlike the US practice, China's NSR incorporates a negative list regime. The 2021 Negative List Measures provide an updated negative list that regulates the market access of foreign investments in China. The number of forbidden or restricted foreign investment items on the negative list has been continuously reduced to speed up the process of opening up key areas of service industry in China. Traditional restrictions on the ratio of foreign shareholdings in securities companies, securities investment fund management companies, futures companies and life insurance companies have been abolished.[181] However, bans on foreign investment in certain internet service industries are still maintained for cybersecurity concerns.[182] Foreign investments on the negative list are not granted licensing, enterprise registration or other related matters.[183]

Third, China has lower transparency in terms of NSR decision-making processes. There may be wider room for informal consultation and shadow screening in China. Most review outcomes are not disclosed on the government's official website. The media only covers the most famous and controversial cases. Through the informal consultation process, the Chinese government may notify foreign investors in private that their investments will not pass the national security review. As a result, they will probably relinquish their plan to apply for a formal review.[184] The NSR regime of China may thus sometimes function in a

[180] *See* The White House, above note 163.

[181] *See* Tuijin Gengao Shuiping Duiwai Kaifang Yi Kaifang Cu Gaige Cu Fazhan Guojia Fazhan Gaige Wei Youguan Fuzeren Jiu Erling Erling Nianban Waishang Touzi Zhunru Fumian Qingdan Da Jizhe Wen (推进更高水平对外开放，以开放促改革促发展——国家发展改革委有关负责人就2020年版外商投资准入负面清单答记者问) [Promoting A Higher Level of Opening Up and Promoting Reform and Development through Opening Up], National Development and Reform Commission, June 24, 2020, www.gov.cn/zhengce/2020-06/24/content_5521526.html.

[182] *See* 2021 Negative List Measures (promulgated by the NDRC and the MOFCOM, December 27, 2021, effective January 1, 2022) Category VII; *see generally* Robin Hui Huang, Charles Chao Wang and Olivia Xin Zhang, "The Development and Regulation of Robo-Advisors in Hong Kong: Empirical and Comparative Perspectives" (2022) 22 *Journal of Corporate Law Studies* 229 (providing more discussion on China's national interests in cybersecurity).

[183] *See* 2021 Negative List Measures, art. 2. (China).

[184] Ibid., at arts. 4, 5 (providing informal consultation rules).

disguised manner. For example, the foreign investments in China may be blocked by the Chinese government for anti-monopoly reasons. The case of Coca-Cola's attempted acquisition of Huiyuan Juice is a good example.[185] In the United States, the CFIUS's review decisions are usually disclosed to the public, although its review standards may be politicized.

Fourth, China's NSR legislative history has been accompanied by legal transplantation efforts.[186] The path dependence of selectively borrowing overseas rules explains why China's NSR regime has been based on flexible departmental statutes instead of national-level laws. The American NSR regime has a long history in congressional legislation, while the Chinese national security review regime has less experience. The four stages of Chinese national security review development show that China established its NSR framework for M&A and foreign investment in a short amount of time and have based it on western experiences. That said, it only borrows from elements of the US experience selectively.

Last, but not least, China did not clearly state whether the law has a retrospective effect on foreign investments, while FIRRMA has a retrospective effect of thirty years. This may be explained by the relatively short history of China's accession into the WTO.[187] The United States has a much longer history of attracting foreign investments.[188] China has transplanted the NSR regime from foreign countries since the 1990s. However, it was not until China's accession into the WTO that foreign investments started pouring into China. The Chinese NSR regime was

[185] Although the MOFCOM's decision to block the transaction was stated to be based purely on anti-monopoly concerns, there has been widespread speculation of national economic security disquiet about the potential loss of famous Chinese brands to foreigner investors. See Yuwen Li and Cheng Bian, "A New Dimension of Foreign Investment Law in China: Evolution and Impacts of the National Security Review System" (2016) 24 *Asia Pacific Law Review* 149, 154.

[186] *See generally* Robin Hui Huang and Charles Chao Wang, "The Mandatory Bid Rule Under China's Takeover Law: A Comparative and Empirical Perspective" (2020) 53 *The International Lawyer* 195 (discussing history and features of China's legal transplantation); Robin Hui Huang and Charles Chao Wang, "The Law and Practice of Substantial Shareholding Disclosure in China: Comparative Perspectives and Recent Developments" (2020) 48 *Securities Regulation Law Journal* 216.

[187] *See* Bob Davis, "When the World Opened the Gates of China," *Wall Street Journal* (July 27, 2018), www.wsj.com/articles/when-the-world-opened-the-gates-of-china-1532701482.

[188] *See* Section 5.4.

built in a piecemeal, ad hoc way, which is consistent with the trial-and-error nature of China's economic reforms over the past several decades.[189]

5.5.2 *Comparing the Law in Practice*

5.5.2.1 The United States

In practice, the CFIUS has reviewed only a small fraction of foreign investment in the United States.[190] Nevertheless, Chinese investment in the United States has been a major target for the NSR mechanism. There are several possible causes for this phenomenon. First, the trade relationship between both countries has created dramatically lopsided trade deficits. Second, China's massive investment in US debt provides political leverage in the United States. Third, China's current FDI policy in the United States poses a more direct threat.[191] From 1990 to 2016, the CFIUS blocked several takeover attempts of US enterprises by Chinese companies based on national security, as seen in Table 5.2.[192] The first security review case that successfully withstood judicial review in the United States was the case of *Ralls v. Corp. v. Comm. on Foreign Inv. in the U.S.*[193] Huawei has been the main target of the US government in the last decade. Huawei claims itself to be privately owned by the trade union

189 *See generally* Robin Hui Huang, "The Regulation of Foreign Investment in Post-WTO China: A Political Economy Analysis" (2009) 23 *Columbia Journal of Asian Law* 185 (providing additional discussions on greenfield investment in China).

190 In 2010, the FDI entering the US totaled $194 billion. See Christina E. Holzer, "Committee on Foreign Investment in the United States and Judicial Review" (2014) 13 *Journal of International Business & Law* 169, 174. However, the number of notices reviewed were ninety-three with thirty-five investigations and no presidential action.

191 *See* Souvik Saha, "CFIUS Now Made in China: Dueling National Security Review Frameworks as a Countermeasure to Economic Espionage in the Age of Globalization" (2012) 33 *Northwestern Journal of International Law and Business* 199–205.

192 *See* Tu Xinquan (屠新泉) & Zhou Jinkai (周金凯), "Meiguo Guojia Anquan Shencha Zhidu Dui Zhongguo Guoyou Qiye Zaimei Touzi De Yingxiang Ji Duice Fenxi" (美国国家安全审查制度对中国国有企业在美投资的影响及对策分析) [The Influence of the USA National Security Review of Foreign Merger and Acquisition Towards State-Owned Enterprises of China and the Related Suggestions] (2016) 031(005) *Qing Hua Daxue Xuebao (清华大学学报) [Journal of Tsinghua University]* 74–83.

193 *See Ralls Corp. v. Comm. on Foreign Inv. in the U.S.*, 926 F. Supp. 71, 80 (D.D.C. 2013), *rev'd and remanded*, *Ralls Corp. v. Comm. on Foreign Inv. in the U.S.*, 758 F.3d 296, 326 (D.C. Cir. 2014).

Table 5.2 *Chinese companies blocked by the CFIUS from 1990 to 2016*

Year	Acquirer v. target	Industry	The reasons for rejection by the CFIUS
1990	*China National Aero-Technology Import & Export Corporation v. Mamco*	Aviation Technology	The deal involves US export controls on China
2005	*China National Offshore Oil Corporation v. Unocal Corporation*	Energy	China National Offshore Oil Corporation is under the control of Chinese government
2007	*Huawei and Bain Capital v. 3Com*	High-tech telecommunication network	Huawei has a military background
2009	*Northwest Nonferrous International Investment Co v. First Gold*	Mining	The project is too close to the naval training base and may be controlled by Chinese government
2010	*Huawei v. 2Wire*	High-tech telecommunication network	Huawei has a military background
2010	*Huawei v. Motorola mobile network infrastructure*	High-tech telecommunication network	Huawei has a military background
2010	*Tangshan Caofeidian Investment Group v. Emcore*	Energy smelting	Concerns about the leakage of core technology

Table 5.2 (*cont.*)

Year	Acquirer v. target	Industry	The reasons for rejection by the CFIUS
2010	*Anshan Iron and Steel Group Co., Ltd v. US Steel Development Co.*	Smelting	As a state-owned enterprise, the acquirer may obtain the new steel production technology and in US defense infrastructure
2010	*Huawei、ZTE v. Sprint*	High-tech telecommunication network	The acquirers have close relationships with the Chinese government
2011	*Huawei v. 3Leaf*	High-tech telecommunication network	Huawei has a military background and is subsidized by the government
2012	*Ralls v. Terna (Butter Creek)*	Energy	The project is too close to the naval training base and may be controlled by the Chinese government for obtaining military information
2015	*Tsinghua Unigroup v. MicronTechnology*	Semiconductor technology	The deal may lead to leakage of core technology
2016	*Tsinghua Unigroup v. Western Digital Corp*	Storage technology	The deal involves core high technology

committee, but it is viewed by many people as a de facto state-owned enterprise (SOE).[194]

In recent years, the US NSR regime has restricted Chinese investment tremendously, especially in US technology companies. These investment restrictions will apply to any trade deal between the United States and China, causing Chinese investments in US businesses to fall by 95 percent as compared to 2016.[195] In 2020, the US government decided to ban the use of WeChat in the United States on the basis of national security concerns. In response to President Trump's Executive Orders, the Department of Commerce announced prohibitions on transactions relating to WeChat and TikTok on September 18, 2020, because these apps threatened the US national security.[196] Subsequently, US Magistrate Judge Laurel Beeler issued a preliminary injunction to block the US Commerce Department order. After that, the US Justice Department asked Judge Beeler to put on hold her preliminary injunction, concluding that WeChat constituted a threat to the national security and foreign policy of the United States. The Justice Department argued that WeChat acts as a tool for the Chinese government to control information dissemination and influence US WeChat users.[197] According to the court, the US Department of justice did not provide substantial evidence to support that "such a broad swipe at WeChat was necessary to address a national security threat."[198] Judge Beeler admitted the significance of the government's overarching national security concerns. However, she doubted the sufficiency of the evidence: "While the government has established that China's activities raise significant national security concerns – it has put

[194] Taking into consideration the functions of trade unions in China, some scholars argue that Huawei may be deemed effectively state-owned. *See*, for example, Balding and Clarke, above note 15, at 11.

[195] *See* Steve Dickinson, "CFIUS Shuts Down Chinese Investment in U.S. Technology," *China Law Blog*, 16 January 2019, www.chinalawblog.com/2019/01/cfius-shuts-down-chinese-investment-in-u-s-technology.html.

[196] *See* "US Justice Department Asks Judge to Allow WeChat ban: Apple and Google Stores Face Potential Bans on Allowing Downloads of Tencent App," *Nikkei Asia*, September 25, 2020, asia.nikkei.com/Politics/International-relations/US-China-tensions/US-Justice-Department-asks-judge-to-allow-WeChat-ban.

[197] *See* Katy Stech Ferek, "Justice Department Appeals Injunction against WeChat," *Wall Street Journal*, October 2, 2020, www.wsj.com/articles/justice-department-appeals-injunction-against-wechat-11601663698.

[198] Steven Overly, "Judge Hits Pause on Trump Administration's WeChat Ban," *Politico*, September 20, 2020, www.politico.com/news/2020/09/20/judge-wechat-ban-418764.

in scant little evidence that its effective ban of WeChat for all US users addresses those concerns."[199]

The ban of WeChat shows that the US government attaches great importance to the review of the country of origin of a foreign investment, namely, which country the investor comes from. Whether the country is an ally or competitor is an important basis for judging whether a foreign investment may pose a threat to US national security. Concerning WeChat, the Department of Justice believes that WeChat has the ability to collect information abroad, and its servers can be accessed freely by the Chinese government. There is a perceived risk that China may easily infringe the personal privacy of WeChat users, thereby damaging the network information security of the United States.[200]

Another representative case is the US block of ByteDance's acquisition deal. In 2020, the CFIUS conducted an exhaustive review of Chinese company ByteDance's acquisition of Musical.ly (now known as TikTok). It then recommended the TikTok ban to the president to protect US users' personal data. On August 14, 2020, President Trump issued an order prohibiting ByteDance's acquisition of TikTok. ByteDance was required to divest all interests and rights in any assets or property used to support the operation of TikTok, and any data obtained from TikTok users.[201]

The TikTok case indicates that the US federal government has stepped up its efforts to scrutinize past Chinese investments, even for older deals executed years ago. Since the ban of TikTok, the CFIUS has contacted dozens of US companies to screen shareholders for national-security risks. There seems to be no clear time limit on such foreign investments. The US federal government can ban a foreign investor from transactions which have taken place long before it initiates the NSR or investigation procedures. After the CFIUS gathers details from the foreign companies, it can decide whether to probe the matter further and can even force the foreign investor to divest its interests or rights in relation to the impugned investment.[202]

199 Ibid.

200 Stech Ferek, above note 197.

201 *See* U.S. Department of the Treasury, "Statement by Secretary Steven T. Mnuchin on the President's Decision Regarding the Acquisition by ByteDance Ltd. of the US Business of musical.ly," August 14, 2020, home.treasury.gov/news/press-releases/sm1094.

202 *See* Whalen, above note 9.

There were two new trends under the Biden administration. First, the CFIUS became increasingly focused on Chinese investment cases in American high-tech and data security industries.[203] According to the CFIUS annual report, there was a total of forty-four official declarations from Chinese investors in 2021.[204] China overtook Japan in accounting for the highest proportion among all countries.[205] Most of the industries involved finance, information and services. Second, the NSR functioned together with export control measures. On October 7, 2022, the Biden administration announced restrictions on exports to China of advanced integrated circuits and related technology.[206] The export control measures were responsive to the United States' current strategic goals set in the Executive Order, the CHIPS and Science Act, and the Biden administration's National Security Strategy.[207]

5.5.2.2 China

The author of this book searched the database of Chinese courts and the official websites of the NDRC and the MOFCOM but did not find any judicial or regulatory decision regarding the NSR of foreign investment in China.[208] The low transparency in the review process shows how sensitive the foreign investment issue is to the Chinese government. However, some of the most influential and representative cases of review can still be found in the media.

China's Xugong Group Construction Machinery Co.'s decision not to proceed with plans to sell a stake to US private equity group Carlyle was a clear example of the underdevelopment of China's national security review regime at that time.[209] In October 2005, Carlyle signed an

[203] *See* U.S. Department of the Treasury, "Treasury Releases CFIUS Annual Report for 2021," August 2, 2022, home.treasury.gov/news/press-releases/jy0904.

[204] Ibid.

[205] Ibid.

[206] "Biden Administration Restricts U.S. Exports of Advanced Computing and Semiconductor Manufacturing Equipment, Software, and Technology to China," *Dorsey & Whitney, LLP*, November 28, 2022, www.dorsey.com/newsresources/publications/client-alerts/2022/11/us-adds-strict-limits-on-technology-exports.

[207] *See* The White House, "National Security Strategy," October 2022, www.whitehouse.gov/wp-content/uploads/2022/10/Biden-Harris-Administrations-National-Security-Strategy-10.2022.pdf.

[208] *See* discussion in Sections 5.3 and 5.4.

[209] Tom Miller, "Carlyle, Xugong Ditch Contentious Stake Deal," *South China Morning Post*, July 24, 2008, www.scmp.com/article/646361/carlyle-xugong-ditch-contentious-stake-deal.

investment agreement with Xugong, agreeing to acquire 85 percent of Xugong shares for $375 million.[210] However, after having waited for three years for the approval of the Chinese government, Carlyle had to abandon its bid because the investment agreement expired.[211] The deal would have been the biggest foreign acquisition of a leading State-owned company in China.[212] To relieve the concerns of the Chinese government, Carlyle made several concessions, for example, by cutting its acquisition to 45 percent.[213] However, there were still serious concerns that China could lose its critical technologies to foreign competitors.[214] On the other hand, the foreign investment was sensitive partly because Xugong was controlled by the local government of Xuzhou.[215] China is a socialist country, and the state-controlled enterprises constitute the cornerstones of the domestic economy. One of the central government's responsibilities has been to prevent losses of state assets.[216]

Coca-Cola's attempted acquisition of Huiyuan Juice is an example of China's foreign merger control regime under the 2008 Anti-Monopoly Law.[217] In 2009, the Chinese government rejected Coca-Cola's planned $2.4 billion acquisition of China's top juice-maker Huiyuan Juice for anti-monopoly reasons.[218] The acquisition deal would have been the largest buyout ever of a Chinese company by a foreign rival, and thus the rejection has been seen as a sign of protectionism.[219] This indicates that MOFCOM does not welcome foreign acquisitions of Chinese companies with prominent brands.[220] Although the MOFCOM's

[210] Wan Zhihong, "Carlyle Abandons Xugong Dream," *China Daily*, July 24, 2008, www.chinadaily.com.cn/bizchina/2008-07/24/content_6873004.htm.

[211] Ibid.

[212] Ibid.

[213] Ibid.

[214] Ibid.

[215] Ibid.

[216] Xinhua News Agency, "China to Curb SOEs Assets Losses," *China Daily*, December 1, 2004, www.china.org.cn/english/government/113697.htm.

[217] Michael Wei and Tony Munroe, "China rejects $2.4 billion coke bid for Huiyuan juice," *Reuters*, March 18, 2009, www.reuters.com/article/us-huiyuan-cocacola-idUSTRE52H0QH20090318.

[218] *See* Hannah C. L. Ha, "Coca-Cola/Huiyuan Deal Vetoed under China's Anti-Monopoly Law," *Mayer Brown*, March 19, 2009, www.mayerbrown.com/en/perspectives-events/publications/2009/03/cocacola–huiyuan-deal-vetoed-under-chinas-antimon.

[219] Ibid.

[220] *See* Michael Wei and Tony Munroe, "China rejects $2.4 billion coke bid for Huiyuan juice," *Reuters* (March 18, 2009), www.reuters.com/article/us-huiyuan-cocacola-idUSTRE52H0QH20090318.

decision was stated to be based purely on anti-monopoly concerns, there has been widespread speculation of nationalistic concerns about the potential loss of Chinese brands to foreigners.[221] Chinese authorities may broadly interpret preexisting regulations to review deals that may raise national security issues.[222] Coca-Cola's attempted acquisition of Huiyuan is essentially a case of NSR disguised as an anti-monopoly review.[223]

5.6 Explanations and Implications

5.6.1 *General Observations*

China and the United States have reformed their foreign investment NSR regimes. These reforms are aimed at strengthening the regimes in the face of globalized economic risks and challenges. There are certain common features between China and the United States from the perspectives of law and history. For example, both countries have established and empowered interdepartmental review agencies under the central or federal government. Both NSR regimes have also stipulated similar review periods, broadened the review scopes of domestic industries, and explicitly attempted to exclude the possibility of foreign investors seeking judicial remedies for adverse national security review decisions.

However, there have been even greater divergences between the two regimes. First, China's NSR framework is neither detailed nor complete, leaving the central government with tremendous discretionary powers. Second, the NSR regime has been cooperating with the negative list regime in China. Third, China has lower transparency of national security review decision-making processes. Fourth, China's legislative history of national security review has been accompanied by legal transplantation efforts of selectively borrowing foreign rules, which in turn explains the flexible departmental statutes of China's regime. Last, but not least, China did not clearly state whether the law has a retrospective effect on foreign investments.

221 *See* Li and Bian, above note 185, at 160.
222 *See* Ha, above note 218.
223 Yuwen Li and Cheng Bian, "A New Dimension of Foreign Investment Law in China: Evolution and Impacts of the National Security Review System" (2016) 24 *Asia Pacific Law Review* 149, 154.

5.6.2 *Explaining Jurisdictional Similarities and Differences*

5.6.2.1 Similarities

The similarities between the recent reforms of the Chinese and the United States' regimes are rooted in the increasingly complex global political economy after decades of globalization. Specifically, the reconfiguration of the global value chain and global supply chain has been pushing lawmakers toward a more conservative stance. There are several explanations for this observation.

For starters, major advanced economies worldwide have been more or less influenced by the ideology of economic nationalism in a new era of globalization. Since the 1980s, there has been an unprecedented wave of global industrial consolidation in the value chain. Specifically, the global big business revolution allows core firms in advanced economies to extensively sell off low-end manufacturing businesses to upgrade their core technologies, while developing economies also achieved their economic and technological upgrading opportunities.[224] Nevertheless, this has also led to growing unemployment in these advanced economies, while the developing countries are rapidly catching up.

Indeed, advanced economies have grown cognizant to the risks brought about by globalization. For instance, in 2016, blue-collar voters in key industrial swing states voted for Donald Trump in the US presidential election. In the eyes of some people, the phenomenal win for President Trump was brought about by the oft-forgotten population whose interests have been neglected by profit-driven globalists and multinational enterprises. As a double-edged sword, economic globalization brings about unemployment and national security concerns, albeit economic prosperity as well.

On the other hand, the developing countries are facing increasing pressure from the requirements of globalization as they climb toward the apex of the global value chain. They are latecomers in the game and want to catch up with, or even surpass, the advanced economies. To prevent this, the advanced economies have adopted protectionism, by kicking away the ladder after they have climbed up the value chain

[224] *See* Peter Nolan, Jin Zhang and Chunhang Liu, "The Global Business Revolution, the Cascade Effect, and the Challenge for Firms from Developing Countries" (2008) 32 *Cambridge Journal of Economics* 29; Daniele Archibugi and Carlo Pietrobelli, "The Globalisation of Technology and Its Implications for Developing Countries: Windows of Opportunity or Further Burden?" (2003) 70(9) *Technological Forecasting and Social Change* 861.

and then requiring latecomers to obey free trade rules in the global competition.[225] Therefore, it could be harder for developing countries to obtain advanced technology at the apex due to the limitations of their comparative advantages.

In the specific case of China, although the country has already grown into the world's second largest economy, it is still lagging behind in terms of leading technology. Therefore, in order to climb up in the global value chain, Chinese policymakers are motivated to adopt a protectionist mindset, including encouraging scientists and researchers to import leading technologies and building up a self-controlled high-tech supply chain. The rapid growth and ascension of China have threatened the leading position of advanced economies, especially the United States, and has resulted in the China–US relationship becoming an economic competition or even confrontation. This has been well illustrated in the escalating trade war and technology export restrictions.

Therefore, the trade war, as well as the competition of technology between China and the United States, has exerted great impacts on both countries. The reform of the Chinese NSR regime was partly inspired by the enactment of FIRRMA by the Trump administration. FIRRMA overhauled the American national security review regime to improve the protection of national interests against foreign investment risks in a globalized world, especially from China. The Trump administration's "America First" policy contributed to the strengthening of US national interests, which was echoed by the US Congress in its response to the "Made in China 2025" initiative. The "Made in China 2025" initiative explicitly states that China's technology market shall be controlled by Chinese companies,[226] which is a Chinese version of the "America First" policy.

5.6.2.2 Differences

The differences between China and the United States are caused by a diverse range of factors, which not only show the path-dependent features of their national security review regimes, but also reflect their divergent needs and national interests in the present era. Apart from the legal and institutional discrepancy between the two countries, there are also important differences in their stages of development. Specifically,

[225] *See* Ha-Joon Chang, "Kicking Away the Ladder: Infant Industry Promotion in Historical Perspective" (2003) 31 *Oxford Development Studies* 21, 29.

[226] *See* Cyrill, above note 161.

China is currently in a phase where it needs to maintain its attractiveness to global investors while protecting its national security. In contrast, the United States relies less heavily on external investments and enjoys a stable leadership in the global financial system. These factors are analyzed in more detail as follows.

First, their legal systems are different. The Chinese government has unfettered discretionary powers in the NSR decision-making process; the legislature and courts do not have the authority to review specific decisions made by the government over the NSR issue.[227] In comparison, the US government decisions are often challenged by the US Congress and courts. Thus, FIRRMA has to be very specific about the powers and obligations of the CFIUS.

Second, their political regimes are different. NSR is a highly political issue, especially for a socialist country such as China. The United States has long been a capitalist country that emphasizes political and economic freedom. Acknowledging its lack of sufficient political trust and recognition in the capitalist world,[228] the Chinese government should avoid frequently using the NSR in the economic field. It is advisable for China to deal with the issue through less controversial and less political ways, such as anti-monopoly reasons.

Third, China and the United States have sharply different domestic economic structures. The Chinese economy has maintained a socialist system where state-controlled enterprises are the cornerstones.[229] The Chinese central government aims to prevent loss of state assets and develop big SOE groups to compete in the global market.[230] The failure of the Xugong takeover by an American company was partly due to Xugong's SOE identity. In comparison, the United States is a capitalist country that prioritizes the prosperity of private firms. Foreign private firms investing in the United States would face fewer regulatory hurdles.

[227] China's judiciary is subject to many internal and external controls from different levels of government. *See* Congressional-Executive Commission on China, "Judicial Independence in the PRC," www.cecc.gov/judicial-independence-in-the-prc.

[228] *See* Chris Patten, "No Country in the World Should Ever Trust China's Communist Leaders Again," *MarketWatch*, September 29, 2020, www.marketwatch.com/story/no-country-in-the-world-should-ever-trust-chinas-communist-leaders-again-2020-09-29?mod=search_headline.

[229] David C. Donald, "Conceiving Corporate Governance for an Asian Environment" (2016) 12 *University of Pennsylvania Asian Law Review* 88, 99.

[230] Li-Wen Lin and Curtis J. Milhaupt, "We Are the (National) Champions: Understanding the Mechanisms of State Capitalism in China" (2013) 65 *Stanford Law Review* 697, 743.

Fourth, Chinese and American economies have different degrees of reliance on foreign investments. China has been relying on investment from the United States in recent years.[231] In 2019, Chinese companies invested $38.79 billion into US firms,[232] while the US investments in China were valued at $105.61 billion.[233] If China deals with the national security issue through anti-monopoly channels instead, the US government may be less likely to cut back on investments in China.

Fifth, China's selective borrowing of foreign national security review rules can be explained by the different social needs in historical development. Before joining the WTO, China did not need a comprehensive national security review framework due to the scarcity of foreign investment. After China's accession to the WTO, massive foreign acquisitions of famous domestic enterprises followed, making it imperative for the government to expedite the issuance of statutes tailored to the NSR of M&As.[234] When the 2015 National Security Law was enacted, it became necessary to integrate existing national security review rules and build a comprehensive regime for all investment.

Lastly, the United States generally has a greater advantage over China in terms of its economy and the presence of advanced technology. That is probably why the United States emphasizes the protection of sensitive technologies and TID businesses from China. The United States even mandates periodic reports on Chinese investments.[235] That is also the main reason why FIRRMA has a retrospective effect reaching back to 1988: to target China offshore joint ventures.[236] Because the negative list compiled by Chinese government is subject to changes year by year, this signifies to foreign investors that China may continue to open up to the global economy as its own economy and technical advantages grow.

[231] The Chinese government invested much of its foreign exchange reserves in US Treasury securities, being the world's largest holder of foreign exchange reserves in 2020. *See* Congressional Research Service, "US–China Investment Ties: Overview," January 15, 2021, sgp.fas.org/crs/row/IF11283.pdf.

[232] "Foreign direct investment from China into the United States from 2000 to 2021," *Statista*, July 31, 2023, www.statista.com/statistics/188935/foreign-direct-investment-from-china-in-the-united-states/.

[233] "Direct investment position of the United States in China from 2000 to 2021," *Statista*, July 31, 2023, www.statista.com/statistics/188629/united-states-direct-investments-in-china-since-2000/.

[234] *See* Huang, above note 31, at 810–811.

[235] Foreign Investment Risk Review Modernization Act of 2018, H.R. 5515, § 1719 (b) (2018).

[236] Edelberg, above note 137.

5.6.2.3 Functional Convergence

In comparative law, one should take both the formal and functional approaches in considering convergence and divergence.[237] This section adopts this research method to compare the NSR regimes between China and the United States. The legislature of the recipient country, though transplanted from other jurisdictions, may be adapted to follow local regulatory imperatives.[238] The development of Chinese NSR regime has been path-dependent on China's earlier legislative model, which was segregated and incremental.[239] There are several functional convergences between China and the United States.

China's use of anti-monopoly excuses to conduct NSRs illustrates the formal divergence and functional convergence between the national security review regimes of China and the US. Although the MOFCOM stated its decision to block Coca-Cola's acquisition of Huiyuan as one based purely on anti-monopoly concerns, there were hidden nationalistic concerns about the potential loss of Chinese brands to foreigners. The MOFCOM deliberately evaded the application of the national security review to avoid public skepticism, and the decision based on anti-monopoly reasons in fact undertook similar functions of the NSR.[240]

The NSR regime is facilitated by the negative list regime in China, making up for the government's discretionary use of powers and low transparency. The State Council can lift the bans in relevant fields for specific foreign investments.[241] The list has been maintained by MOFCOM,[242] which will decide whether to make an announcement to investigate a relevant foreign entity.[243] It shall make decisions including restricting or prohibiting the foreign entity in the list from investing in

[237] *See* Ronald J. Gilson, "Globalizing Corporate Governance: Convergence of Form or Function" (2001) 49 *American Journal of Comparative Law* 329, 337–339 (describing the different approaches).

[238] China has always been selectively adopting and adapting foreign rules to further the state's interests. Ibid., at 356–357.

[239] For more discussions on the path dependence theory, see Lucian Arye Bebchuk and Mark J. Roe, "A Theory of Path Dependence in Corporate Ownership and Governance" (1999) 52 *Stanford Law Review* 127.

[240] *See* Li and Bian, above note 185, at 167.

[241] *See* 2021 Negative List Measures (promulgated by the NDRC and the MOFCOM, December 27, 2021, effective January 1, 2022), art. 5.

[242] *See* The Provisions on the Unreliable Entity List (promulgated by the State Council, September 19, 2020, effective September 19, 2020), art. 4 (authorizing "relevant central departments" to organize and implement the regulatory system).

[243] Ibid., art. 5.

China.[244] The list is updated every year and disclosed on the government official website.

5.6.3 *Implications for the International Relationship*

Over the years, China has gradually established and strengthened its NSR system for foreign investment. In the post-financial crisis period of globalization, the legal foundations of the Chinese national security review system consisted of two legal instruments issued in 2011; after nearly a decade of legal experimentation in the foreign M&A business, the Chinese NSR system was comprehensively overhauled by the 2020 Foreign Investment Law and the 2020 NSR Measures.[245] As discussed earlier, this reform was partly inspired by the enactment of FIRRMA by the Trump administration, which overhauled the American NSR regime by prioritizing national interests over globalization efforts.[246]

First, the FIRRMA reform will cause more chilling effects on US–China political and economic relations in the short term. On January 13, 2020, the Treasury Department issued landmark regulations that dramatically expanded the scope of the CFIUS.[247] It requires a mandatory filing for the acquisition of a "substantial interest" in an American TID business by a foreign person in which a foreign government had a "substantial interest."[248] These regulations aim to scrutinize foreign investments that are made in critical technology firms, especially those controlled by the Chinese government. Silicon Valley companies have become more cautious about accepting foreign investments.[249] China-backed venture-capital funds have to curb their activities in the American high-tech industries and other sensitive areas.[250]

244 Ibid., art. 10.

245 *See* above Section 5.2.

246 *See* above Section 5.6.2.1

247 Mira R. Ricardel, "These New Rules Might End Tech's Reliance on Chinese Investors," *Fortune*, January 20, 2020, fortune.com/2020/01/20/cfius-rules-regulations-china-investment/.

248 Keeler, Layton and Leibner, above note 147.

249 Theodore Schleifer, "Silicon Valley Is Awash in Chinese and Saudi Cash: And No One Is Paying Attention (except Donald Trump)," *Vox*, May 1, 2019, www.vox.com/recode/2019/5/1/18511540/silicon-valley-foreign-money-china-saudi-arabia-cfius-firrma-geopolitics-venture-capital.

250 *See* Whalen, above note 9.

Second, the competition between China and the United States over the global economy order will dominate the NSR in the long run. China may address trade frictions with developed economies by commercial and legal means,[251] but the conflicts between the United States and China are structural and systematic. FIRRMA has been the US governmental effort to prevent Chinese private and government-controlled entities from acquiring American technologies. At the end of the day, it is also meant to prevent more competitive disadvantages for the US economy in the global competition. The US government has expressed its concerns over the potential adverse impacts of "Made in China 2025."[252] As mentioned, the Biden administration shifted the focus to new national security issues arising in the escalated China–US tech war and COVID pandemic.[253] The conflicts between China and developed economies in the making of trade rules are, by nature, a competition over the dominance of the global economic order.

Third, the state capitalism approach of SOEs and government-controlled private companies in China will face more challenges. It is not difficult to detect the relationship between FIRRMA's new reporting regime on Chinese investments and the "Made in China 2025" initiative. The US executive and legislative branches reached a consensus that the "Made in China 2025" initiative poses a special national security threat to the United States.[254] FIRRMA gives the US government more power to curtail the transfer of technology to foreign companies.[255] It even mandates periodic reports on Chinese investments in the United States.[256] Government-controlled enterprises will face more reviews and garner less trust in the world, as seen by the recent series of investment screening reforms in major economies. Privately owned enterprises are expected to be approved by the CFIUS as long as they do not impact the US national security.[257] However, China's private enterprises may also be

[251] *See* Pan Xiaoming, "A New Competitive Situation in the Digital Economy and China's Actions" (2020) 82 *China International Studies* 123, 139.

[252] *See* Edelberg, above note 137, at 13.

[253] *See* above Section 5.4.

[254] *See* Melissa Cyrill, "What Is Made in China 2025 and Why Has It Made the World So Nervous?" *China Briefing*, December 28, 2018, www.china-briefing.com/news/made-in-china-2025-explained/.

[255] FIRRMA, § 1702(b)(5); Sam Karson, "Caught between Superpowers: Alaska's Economic Relationship with China Amidst the New Cold War" (2019) 36 *Alaska Law Review* 47.

[256] Foreign Investment Risk Review Modernization Act of 2018, H.R. 5515, § 1719(b) (2018).

[257] Edelberg, above note 137, at 20.

reviewed if the US government deems it necessary to protect national security, as can be seen in the case of Huawei. Although Huawei claims to be a private company, the US government believes that the Chinese government can exert control over its businesses in many unofficial ways.[258] The Chinese national strategic buyers will have to prove their commercial and financial motives behind the cross-border investments.[259]

Finally, there would be far-reaching implications for the development of the global supply chain. On the one hand, the current wave of globalization that began in the 1980s might be seriously interrupted. As both the United States and China have taken measures to protect their core interests in technology development, the national security review systems adopted by the two countries could eventually result in the emergence of two parallel industrial supply chains in the world. One may even argue that the world is at risk of a new Cold War, particularly in the economic arena. Nevertheless, the increasing complexity of US–China mutual economic reliance could force both countries to conduct NSRs in a more elastic manner. For instance, the United States cannot get rid of the cheap and quality products manufactured by Chinese companies, and China still needs key components with advanced technology from US suppliers. Therefore, it may eventually lead to a new structure of the global economic system where there is fierce competition at the apex of the value chain while maintaining parallel "safe" supply chains. This means that foreign investments could continue to flow, at least in the industries with fewer concerns of national security, due to the complex China–US economic coupling and mutual reliance.

5.7 Conclusion

This chapter analyzed the NSR regimes of China and the United States from a comparative perspective after China established a comprehensive NSR legal framework in 2021. FIRRMA has made extensive reforms on the American national security review regime and has exerted great

[258] *See* Raymond Zhong, "Who Owns Huawei? The Company Tried to Explain. It Got Complicated," *New York Times*, April 25, 2019, www.nytimes.com/2019/04/25/technology/who-owns-huawei.html.

[259] *See* Jeffrey N. Gordon and Curtis J. Milhaupt, "China as a National Strategic Buyer: Toward a Multilateral Regime for Cross-border M&A" (2019) *Columbia Business Law Review* 192, 202.

influences over its Chinese counterpart. Both China and the United States have empowered interdepartmental review agencies under the central or federal government. By analyzing Chinese and US law and practice, this chapter shows many formal divergences between the two jurisdictions caused by their diverse legal and political systems. For example, China's NSR framework is not a detailed and complete one, leaving the central government with tremendous discretionary powers and thereby lowering transparency. The NSR regime has been cooperating with the negative list regime in China. China's NSR legislative history has been accompanied by legal transplantation efforts of selective borrowing foreign rules.

Based on these observations, this chapter explains why the Chinese and American NSR regimes have converged functionally. It indicates the importance of a functional comparison between the two national security review regimes of different jurisdictions. From a future prospect perspective, the reforms of the national security review regimes in China and the United States will have profound influences on each other and the world. In the short run, the legal development in both countries will cause tremendous chilling effects on US–China political and economic relations. In the long run, the competition between China and the United States over the global economic order will dominate and reshape both national security review regimes. The state capitalism approach of SOEs and government-controlled private companies in China will face greater challenges and hostility. Nevertheless, due to the complex coupling and mutual reliance of the China–US economy, foreign investments could continue to flow, at least in the industries less concerned with national security.

PART II

Specific Regulatory and Practical Issues

6

The Legality of the VIE Structure

A Theory of Strategic Ambiguity

6.1 Introduction

Since the "reform and opening-up" policy in the late 1970s, China has attracted an influx of foreign capital to fuel its rapidly growing economy.[1] To protect national security, China has imposed restrictions or prohibitions on foreign investment in certain industries, such as the internet services industry.[2] At the same time, many companies in these sensitive industries, particularly private-owned enterprises (POEs), need to raise funds for their business in the capital markets. However, for various reasons, compared to state-owned enterprises (SOEs), it has traditionally been much more difficult for the POEs to conduct securities offering and listing domestically. Hence, those companies may choose to get listed overseas, but this means that they will be open to foreign investors, thereby contravening relevant foreign investment restrictions. In the face of such a dilemma, many Chinese companies have used the so-called Variable Interest Entities (VIE) structure to list overseas: It is based on contractual arrangements rather than ownership links and thus may technically get around the foreign investment restrictions.

There has been a longstanding debate on whether it is legal to use the VIE structure for overseas listing because it arguably represents a way of law circumvention.[3] Indeed, many commentators have repeatedly suggested that the legality of VIEs be clarified,[4] but the Chinese authorities

[1] In this chapter, the term "China" refers to Mainland China unless otherwise indicated.

[2] Robin Hui Huang, "China's National Security Review of Foreign Investment: A Comparison with the United States" (2023) 57 *Vanderbilt Journal of Transnational Law* 1263.

[3] Shitong Qiao, "Finance against Law: The Case of China" (2023) 64(2) *Harvard International Law Review* 431.

[4] *See*, for example, Guo Li, "Chinese Style VIEs: Continuing to Sneak under Smog?" (2014) 47(3) *Cornell International Law Journal* 569 (suggesting that China end "the murky

have consistently refused to do so. Indeed, in March 2023 China introduced a recordation regime for an overseas listing of Chinese companies, but it remains unclear that the VIE structure will gain legality if it goes through the recordation process.[5]

Hence, while there has been a large body of literature on the legality of VIEs, significant research gaps exist. First, the Chinese authorities have continuously issued relevant laws and regulations in this area, including the aforementioned 2023 recordation regime for overseas listing, as well as some recent court cases.[6] These new developments call for more updated research to evaluate the trend of the attitudes of the Chinese authorities toward VIEs. Second, most existing literature has been focused on discussing the investment risks caused by the uncertain legality of VIEs and then urging China to clarify it. However, commendable as it may be, this line of research has proven less useful than expected, as it is based on some questionable understandings of the nature of the issue. Is it really because the Chinese authorities do not know that the undetermined status of VIEs poses significant investment risks to POEs and foreign investors? Is it just technical difficulty that prevents the Chinese authority from taking those suggestions to clarify the legality of VIEs? Do the Chinese authorities simply shirk their responsibilities in dealing with the issue? Are they totally unaware of the teaching of the "law and finance" school that investor protection problems stemming from the uncertain legality of VIEs would adversely affect the development of the market?

This chapter endeavors to develop a new theory for understanding the VIE issue, arguing that the uncertain legality of VIEs is an intended product of the "strategic ambiguity" policy of the Chinese authorities, as it allows them to decide the legality of VIEs in appropriate cases depending on the right balance that they want to strike between national security, on the one hand, and the need to facilitate overseas listing of Chinese companies, on the other hand. The phrase "strategic ambiguity" was first coined to describe the Chinese government's position on VIEs

situation surrounding the VIE" and set up a "less restrictive, more transparent, better defined, and more user friendly" regulatory framework for VIEs); Ma Mengwei, "The Perils and Prospects of China's Variable Interest Entities: Unraveling the Murky Rules and the Institutional Challenges Posed" (2013) 43(3) *Hong Kong Law Journal* 1061 (suggesting that China improve its rule-of-law system and build a level playing field for foreign investors).

[5] For more details, *see* Section 6.4.2.

[6] *See* Section 6.3.2.

in Hui Huang's (2014) book,[7] and was later used by more commentators to discuss the legal risks of VIEs to foreign investors.[8] However, there is still a great need to further develop the theory of strategic ambiguity to more fully answer the questions posed earlier, by investigating the extent to which legal ambiguity exists on paper and in practice, how it has evolved over time, what factors have contributed to the institutional environment in which the policy of strategic ambiguity operates and how to come to terms with it.

The new theory will have important theoretical and practical implications. It shows that it can be futile to continue to urge the Chinese authorities to clarify the legality of VIEs without first addressing the factors that cause them to adopt the strategic ambiguity policy. Indeed, the repeated suggestions for clarifying the legal status of the VIE structure have continued to fall on the deaf ears of the Chinese authorities for many years. After all, you can't wake a person who is pretending to be asleep. Hence, research should be more focused on understanding the underlying policy of strategic ambiguity, rather than simply urging the Chinese authorities to do the right thing. Further, the market operators and participants need to accept the harsh reality that the issue will not go away unless and until the underlying policy of strategic ambiguity is changed.

It is important to note that by developing the theory of strategic ambiguity, this chapter does not attempt to justify the Chinese government policy on VIEs but rather aims to provide a deeper understanding of what the Chinese authorities have done in the past and will do in the future. Indeed, the uncertainty over the legality of VIEs has brought significant risks to foreign investors.[9] However, it would be naïve to simply suggest the Chinese authorities have solved the issue, without properly examining the considerations they may have from their perspective.

This chapter proceeds as follows. Section 6.2 provides a background discussion of the concept and use of the VIE structure. Section 6.3 reviews the legal regime for the VIE structure, including the law on paper

[7] Robin Hui Huang, *Securities and Capital Markets Law in China* (Oxford University Press, 2014), 335–336.

[8] Fa Chen, "Variable Interest Entity Structures in China: Are Legal Uncertainties and Risks to Foreign Investors Part of China's Regulatory Policy?" (2021) 29(1) *Asia Pacific Law Review* 1.

[9] *See* Section 6.5.2.

and the law in practice. The law can be broadly divided into two categories, namely, the legality-related category and the regulation-focused category. The law in practice is to be examined through an empirical study of all relevant cases over the years. The discussion illustrates the nature and extent of the legality issue of VIEs. Section 6.4 develops a theory to argue that China adopts a policy of strategic ambiguity regarding the legality of the VIE structure, so as to juggle the need to regulate foreign investment to protect national security and the need to facilitate overseas listing of Chinese companies to promote economic development. Based on the above analysis, Section 6.5 discusses the future of the VIE structure, its practical implications for foreign investors and theoretical implications for the law and finance scholarship. Section 6.6 concludes.

6.2 Background Discussion

6.2.1 Concept Evolution and Operational Structure

The VIE structure originates from the accounting rules in the US, under which a company must include the financial information of another entity in its consolidated financial statement if it has "controlling financial interest" over the latter, and if it must bear the majority of the entity's losses.[10] The rule was introduced after the Enron incident, which aims at preventing companies from hiding their assets and losses. Innovative lawyers later utilized this rule to incorporate the financial information of a Chinese business into an offshore listing vehicle by way of intragroup contracting. Under the VIE structure, foreign investors of the overseas-listed Chinese company can obtain economic benefits from the onshore business in China through contractual arrangements rather than shareholding relationships, thus bypassing China's foreign investment restrictions on foreign ownership in certain industries.

In a typical VIE structure used for overseas listings of Chinese companies, there are mainly three layers of companies. The top layer is offshore companies, which serve as listing vehicles overseas, and foreign

[10] US Financial Accounting Standards Board, "Consolidation of Variable Interest Entities – An Interpretation of ARB No. 51" (FIN 46) (2003), www.fasb.org/page/PageContent?pageId=/reference-library/superseded-standards/summary-of-interpretation-no-46-revised-december-2003.html&bcpath=tff. It should be noted that FIN 46 was revised by FIN 46(R) on December 24, 2003 which was then replaced by Statement of Financial Accounting Standards No. 167 in June 2009.

investors are free to invest in them. The second layer of companies are onshore companies, which serve as holding vehicles within China and are usually 100 percent owned by the top-layer offshore companies, thus known as wholly foreign-owned enterprises (WFOEs).[11] The third layer comprises VIEs, which are Chinese companies that carry on actual business and generate profits. VIEs and WFOEs are connected through contractual mechanisms, as opposed to shareholding relationships, which allows VIEs to fall outside the foreign investment restrictions in special industries such as technology, media and telecom (TMT).

To illustrate how the VIE structure works, it is useful to examine the case of Sina, which first used the VIE structure to get listed in the US in 2000.[12] As this method of overseas listing was first used in the case of Sina, it has been commonly dubbed the "Sina Model."

As shown in Figure 6.1, STC, as a WFOE owned by foreign investors and registered as a foreign investment company in China, cannot directly engage in restricted or prohibited investments[13] such as the telecommunication services market. There are several VIE entities, such as the ICP company, and they are owned by senior management officers and others, all of whom are Chinese citizens or domestic companies. These VIE companies are not owned by foreigners and thus can hold the necessary licenses to operate internet services in China. The VIE contracts signed between STC and the ICP company will be discussed as an example to show how the VIE structure can help STC to obtain from the ICP company such benefits as economic interests, management power and control.

1. Exclusive Technical Services Agreement: STC provides technical services for its online advertising, value-added telecommunication and other respective related businesses to the ICP company for a service fee.
2. Exclusive Sales Agency Agreement: The ICP company grants STC the exclusive right to distribute, sell and provide agency services for all the products and services provided by the ICP company.

[11] By December 31, 2024 all foreign-invested enterprises (FIEs), including WFOEs, would need to make necessary amendments to their constitutional documents in compliance with the Company Law of the PRC. This means that FIEs are regulated in the same way as other companies in China and no longer exist as a special type of business organization.

[12] Annual Report of Sina, p. 76, www.sec.gov/ix?doc=/Archives/edgar/data/1094005/000110465920052758/sina-20191231x20f.htm.

[13] *See* Section 6.3.1.

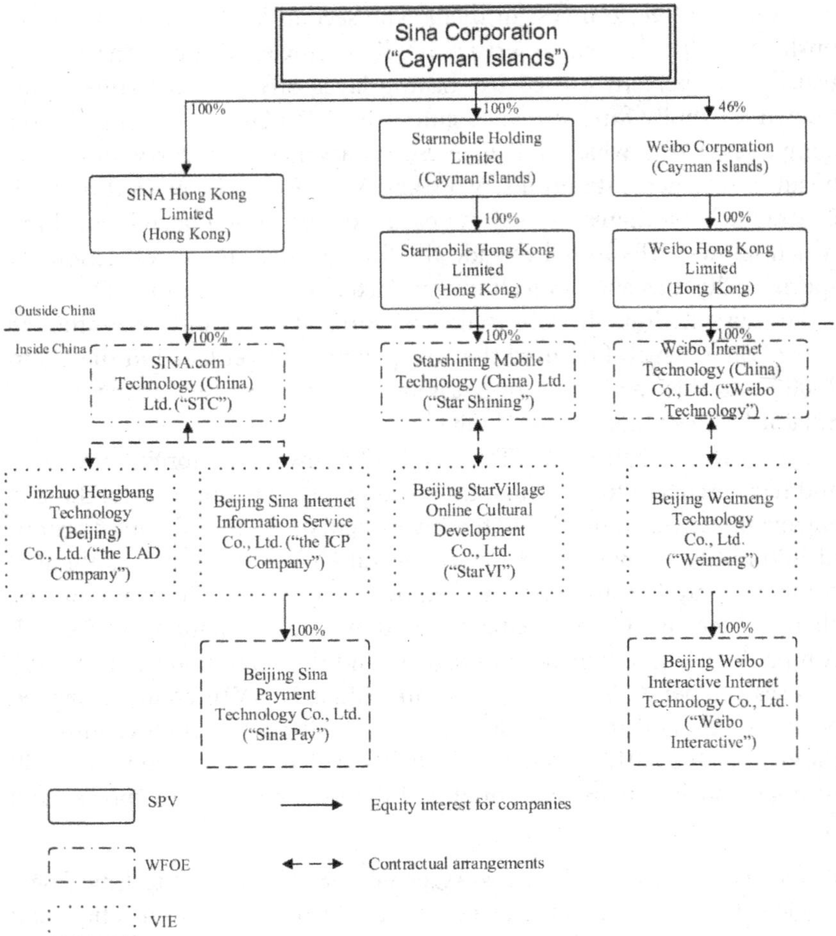

Figure 6.1 The VIE structure of Sina.

3. Trademark License Agreement: STC grants the ICP company annual trademark licenses to use the trademarks held by STC in specific areas, and the ICP company is obliged to pay license fees to STC.
4. Loan Agreements: STC grants interest-free loans to the shareholders of the ICP company for daily operations. Interest-free loans will only be repaid through share transfer.
5. Agreements on Authorization to Exercise Shareholder's Voting Power: Each shareholder of the ICP company irrevocably authorizes STC to exercise all of their voting power.

6. Share Transfer Agreements: Each shareholder of the ICP company grants STC an option to purchase shares in the ICP company at a purchase price equal to the amount of loans.
7. Share Pledge Agreements: Each shareholder of the ICP company has pledged all their shares in the ICP company to STC as collateral security for their obligations to pay off all debts to STC under the loan agreement and for the payment obligations of the ICP company under the trademark license agreement and the technical services agreement.

As a result, STC assumes a form of control akin to ownership and obtains the profits of the ICP company (domestic VIEs). The financial statements are thus consolidated from the bottom layer all the way to the top layer, enabling foreign investors to have de facto investment in the business as well as the top-layer overseas-listed company.

6.2.2 *Actual Use and Legality Debate*

Since Sina Corporation's successful foreign listing with a VIE structure in 2000, other Chinese companies have followed suit, notably in the US and Hong Kong. As of January 8, 2024 there were at least 265 Chinese companies listed on the major stock exchanges in the US, and about 166 of them, or 63 percent of all US-listed Chinese companies, adopted the VIE structure.[14]

In Hong Kong, there are two main ways that Chinese companies can get listed: an "H-share" structure or a "Red-chip" structure. H-share companies are enterprises incorporated in China and listed directly on the Hong Kong Exchanges and Clearing Limited (HKEX); Red-chip companies are enterprises incorporated outside of China (normally in Hong Kong or the Cayman Islands), which are controlled by China entities or individuals, and conduct most of their business within China.

As of June 2024, there were 343 H-share companies and 1,117 Red-chip companies listed on the Main Board of the HKEX.[15] There is no

[14] The US–China Economic and Security Review Commission, "Chinese Companies Listed on Major US Stock Exchanges" (2024), www.uscc.gov/research/chinese-companies-listed-major-us-stock-exchanges.

[15] HKEX, "HKEX Monthly Market Highlights" (2024), www.hkex.com.hk/Market-Data/Statistics/Consolidated-Reports/HKEX-Monthly-Market-Highlights?sc_lang=en.

accurate data on the percentage of Hong Kong-listed Chinese companies that adopt the VIE structure, but it is estimated to be similar to that figure in the US among Red-chip companies.

Interestingly, although the VIE structure has been widely used by numerous Chinese companies for many years, its legal status has never been entirely clear. Indeed, there is considerable ambiguity over the legality of VIEs under the current Chinese law and practice. The next section will thus conduct a comprehensive examination of the Chinese legal regime relating to VIEs, examining both the black-letter laws and relevant cases. This will help illustrate the extent of ambiguity over the legal status of VIEs and the level of difficulty in clarifying it.

6.3 Legal Regime

The VIE structure is not governed by a specific law in China, but rather a complex web of relevant provisions that are scattered throughout national laws and administrative regulations. Most existing studies tend to discuss them together, which usually makes it harder to focus on more relevant laws and see the extent of legal ambiguity and even conflict among them.

Hence, unlike existing studies, we try to provide a more logical discussion by grouping the generally scattered web of relevant laws and regulations into two categories: one category is directly related to the legality of the VIE structure, and the other category is essentially focused on the regulation of VIEs with an implicit assumption of its legality. The legality-related law category can be further divided into three sub-categories, including contract law, foreign investment law and industry-specific regulation. The regulation-focused law category is even more diverse, covering such issues as foreign exchange administration, foreign merger and acquisition approval, national security review, overseas listing recordation and the homecoming listing of Chinese companies. As the legality of VIEs is the main issue here, this part will focus on the legality-related law categories and relevant cases in practice. The regulation-focused law category will be discussed later to show that although some important regulations have recently been promulgated in this area, they do not substantially change the debate on the legality of VIEs.[16]

[16] *See* Section 6.4.2.

6.3.1 *Law on Paper*

6.3.1.1 Contract Validity

First and foremost, the validity of the VIE contract is the key legal issue and thus the legal analysis must start from contract law. Before China's first-ever Civil Code took effect in 2021,[17] the issue of contract validity was mainly governed by Article 52 of the Contract Law.[18] Of particular relevance to the VIE structure are the three grounds for contract invalidation under Articles 52(3), (4) and (5), under which a contract shall be void if it is found to "conceal an illegitimate purpose through a legal form," or "damage public interests" or "violate compulsory provisions of laws and administrative regulation." However, it was unclear what constitutes "an illegitimate purpose," "public interest" and "compulsory provisions."

After 2021, the Civil Code superseded the Contract Law, devoting a whole section with several provisions on contract invalidation.[19] As a key provision there, Article 153 of the Civil Code sets out two situations in which a contract is void:[20] (1) there is a violation of compulsory provisions of law or administrative regulation, which is similar to Article 52(5) of the Contract Law; and (2) there is an infringement of the so-called "public order and good customs" (Gongxu Liangsu公序良俗). According to the Supreme People's Court (SPC), the term "Gongxu Liangsu" is flexible enough to cover "public interest" which was previously stipulated under Articles 52(4) of the Contract Law.[21] Further, although the "illegitimate purpose" ground under Article 52(3) of the Contract Law is not explicitly reproduced in the Civil Code, it is not simply removed but actually absorbed into the ground of "violating compulsory provisions of law or administrative regulation," because the

[17] Zhonghua Renmin Gongheguo Minfadian (中华人民共和国民法典) [Civil Code of the People's Republic of China] (issued by the National People's Congress on May 28, 2020 effective on January 1, 2021) (hereinafter Civil Code).

[18] Zhonghua Renmin Gongheguo Hetong Fa (中华人民共和国合同法) [The Contract Law of the People's Republic of China] by the National People's Congress on March 15, 1999 effective on October 1, 1999 (hereinafter Contract Law).

[19] Civil Code, Book 1, Chapter 6, Section 3.

[20] Civil Code, art. 153.

[21] Zuigao Renmin Fayuan Minfadian Guanche Shishi Gongzuo Lingdao Xiaozhu (最高人民法院民法典贯彻实施工作领导小组) [Leadership Panel of the SPC on the Implementation of the Civil Code], *Understanding and Application of the Part of General Principles of the Civil Code of the PRC (中华人民共和国民法典总则编理解与适用)*, p. 754.

finding of "illegitimate purpose" usually coincides with "a violation of compulsory provisions of law or administrative regulation" in judicial practice.[22] Hence, Article 153 of the Civil Code broadly corresponds to Articles 52(3), (4) and (5) of the Contract Law.

Further, Article 153 of the Civil Code makes the issue of contract validity even more flexible (or uncertain) by adding an exception clause that violating some compulsory provisions may not lead to contract invalidity.[23] To be sure, this clause is not really new, but a codification of past judicial practice. In 2009, in response to the situation that the ground of violating compulsory provisions was excessively used to invalidate contracts, the SPC issued several judicial interpretations to urge courts to exercise caution, clarifying that compulsory provisions can be divided into two categories, namely, "validity-related compulsory provisions" and "administration-related compulsory provisions," and violating the latter should not lead to contract invalidity.[24]

In December 2023, the SPC issued a judicial interpretation on the contract part of the Civil Code, providing more details on when a contract should be declared void (hereinafter "Judicial Interpretation on Contract Part of Civil Code").[25] Article 16 stipulates that if a contract violates compulsory provisions of laws and administrative regulations but the legislative purpose of the compulsory provisions can be achieved by imposing criminal or administrative liability on the violator in certain

22 Ibid., p. 731.

23 Civil Code, art. 153(1).

24 Guanyu Shiyong <Zhonghua Renmin Gongheguo Hetong Fa> Ruogan Wenti de Jieshi (Er) (关于适用《中华人民共和国合同法》若干问题的解释(二)) [Interpretation II of Several Issues concerning the Application of the Contract Law of the People's Republic of China] by the Supreme People's Court on April 24, 2009 effective on May 13, 2009 art. 14; Guanyu Dangqian Xingshi xia Shenli Min Shang Shi Hetong Jiufen Anjian Ruogan Wenti de Zhidao Yijian (关于当前形势下审理民商事合同纠纷案件若干问题的指导意见) [Guiding Opinions on Several Issues Concerning the Trial of Cases of Disputes over Civil and Commercial Contracts under the Current Situation] by the Supreme People's Court on July 7, 2009 art. 15; Quanguo Fayuan Min Shang Shi Shenpan Gongzuo Huiyi Jiyao (全国法院民商事审判工作会议纪要) [Minutes of the National Courts' Civil and Commercial Trial Work Conference] by the Supreme People's Court on August 11, 2019, Section 30.

25 Zuigao Renmin Fayuan guanyu Shiyong <Zhonghua Renmin Gongheguo Minfa Dian> Hetongbian Tongze Ruogan Wenti de Jieshi (最高人民法院关于适用〈中华人民共和国民法典〉合同编通则若干问题的解释) (Interpretation by the Supreme People's Court of Several Issues Concerning the Application of Title One General Provisions of Book Three Contracts of the Civil Code of the People's Republic of China), issued by the SPC on December 4, 2024 effective from December 5, 2024.

circumstances, the court may not declare the contract to be void.[26] Conversely, Article 17 provides that even if a contract does not violate compulsory provisions of laws and administrative regulations, the court may still hold it to be void as long as it falls under any of the following circumstances: (1) it affects political, economic, military or other aspects of national security; (2) it affects social stability or fair competition, harms the public interest or otherwise disrupts the public order; (3) it deviates from social morality or family ethics, destroys personal dignity or otherwise violates good customs.[27]

Given that the VIE structure is used to circumvent restrictions on foreign investment, it is then important to examine whether those restrictions constitute "compulsory provisions of law or administrative regulation" under Article 153(1), and if so, whether they are "validity-related compulsory provisions" or "administration-related compulsory provisions." It should be noted that for Article 153(1) to apply, the relevant compulsory provisions violated must be contained in national laws passed by the National People's Congress or regulations issued by the State Council.[28] This does not mean, however, that the issue of contract validity cannot be affected by a violation of administrative rules issued by the departments under the State Council such as the Ministry of Commerce (MOFCOM) and the Ministry of Industry and Information Technology (MIIT). Rather, a violation of administrative rules may trigger the ground of infringing "public order and good customs" (Gongxu Liangsu公序良俗)under Article153(2).[29] Further, as noted above, the Judicial Interpretation on Contract Part of Civil Code has added more factors to consider in determining the validity of VIE contracts, such as the legislative purpose of the compulsory provisions, national security, public interest, public order and good customs. Plainly, they are of direct relevance to the issue of VIE contract validity. Relevant administrative rules regarding the VIE structure will thus be examined as well in the following sections.

[26] Judicial Interpretation on Contract Part of Civil Code, art. 16.

[27] Judicial Interpretation on Contract Part of Civil Code, art. 17.

[28] Civil Code, art. 153(1).

[29] Zuigao Renmin Fayuan Minfadian Guanche Shishi Gongzuo Lingdao Xiaozhu (最高人民法院民法典贯彻实施工作领导小组) [Leadership Panel of the SPC on the Implementation of the Civil Code], *Zhonghua Renming Gongheguo Minfadian Zongzebian Lijie yu Shiyong (中华人民共和国民法典总则编理解与适用) [Understanding and Application of the Part of General Principles of the Civil Code of the PRC]* (People's Court Press, 2020), pp. 764–765.

6.3.1.2 Foreign Investment

Before the enactment of the 2019 Foreign Investment Law,[30] there was no national law specifically for foreign investment and many basic concepts were left undefined. For instance, it was never clear whether "foreign investment" may refer only to foreigners' equity interest in Chinese companies or extend to cover other interests through contractual control. This provided a source of flexibility as well as uncertainty over the legality of the contractual arrangements under the VIE structure.

In 2015, the MOFCOM submitted a draft version of the Foreign Investment Law, making clear that the control of a domestic company or the holding interest of a domestic company via contract or trust shall be treated as "foreign investment,"[31] and that the imposition of decisive influence on a domestic company's operation, finance, personnel management or technology through contract or trust shall be treated as "control."[32] Had the above draft provisions been passed into law, it would have been clear that the VIE structure would be illegal unless it is affirmatively endorsed by relevant Chinese authorities. However, due to the lack of consensus on the above draft provisions during the consultation process, they were not adopted in the end.

As a result, the 2019 Foreign Investment Law contains no specific provisions concerning foreign control of domestic equity through contractual arrangements, but rather uses a broad delegation phrase, namely, "other ways of investments as stipulated by law, regulation and the State Council."[33] Under Article 4 of the Foreign Investment Law, China applies the administrative system of preestablishment national treatment plus a negative list to foreign investment, and the negative list shall be issued by or with the approval of the State Council.[34] In practice, the negative list is jointly issued and updated by the National Development

[30] Zhonghua Renmin Gongheguo Waishang Touzi Fa (中华人民共和国外商投资法) [Foreign Investment Law of the People's Republic of China] by the National People's Congress on March 15, 2019 effective on January 1, 2020.

[31] Zhonghua Renmin Gongheguo Waiguo Touzi Fa (Cao'an Zhengqiu Yijiangao) (中华人民共和国外国投资法(草案征求意见稿)) [Foreign Investment Law of the People's Republic of China (consultation draft)] by the Ministry of Commerce on January 19, 2015, art. 15.

[32] Ibid., art. 18.

[33] Foreign Investment Law, art. 2.

[34] Ibid., art. 4.

and Reform Commission (NDRC) and MOFCOM.[35] The negative list sets out two categories of business for foreign investment: (1) prohibited business, namely, business which is simply prohibited for foreigners; and (2) restricted business, namely, business which foreigners must get approval to conduct.[36] If foreign investment violates the provisions of the negative list, it shall assume relevant legal liability.[37]

To facilitate the implementation of the Foreign Investment Law, the SPC issued a judicial interpretation to provide that the court shall support applications for invalidating investment contracts that involve foreign investment on the negative list.[38] Again, the SPC just mentions some examples of "investment contracts," leaving open the issue of whether the VIE contract may fall within the ambit of the term.[39]

6.3.1.3 Industry-Specific Regulations

In addition, there are industry-specific regulations governing foreign investment. For instance, since 1993, the authority responsible for regulating telecommunication services ruled that no foreign investors shall be permitted to enter the telecommunication services industry or participate in its business operations.[40] Telecommunication services were listed in

[35] Guojia Fazhan Gaigewei Shangwubu Guanyu Yinfa <Shichang Zhunru Fumian Qingdan (2022 nian ban)> de Tongzhi (国家发展改革委 商务部关于印发《市场准入负面清单(2022年版)》的通知) [Notice of on the Issuance of the 2022 version of Market Access Negative List] (issued by the National Development and Reform Commission and the Ministry of Commerce on March 12, 2022).

[36] Before the promulgation of the Foreign Investment Law, foreign investment projects were generally classified into four categories, namely "encouraged," "permitted," "restricted" and "prohibited." Zhidao Waishang Touzi Fangxiang Guiding (指导外商投资方向规定) [Regulations on Direction Guide to Foreign Investment] issued by the State Council in February 2002, effective on April 1, 2002.

[37] Foreign Investment Law, art. 36.

[38] Article 3 and 4, Zuigao Renmin Fayuan Guanyu Shiyong <Zhonghua Renmin Gongheguo Waishang Touzi Fa> Ruogan Wenti de Jieshi (最高人民法院关于适用《中华人民共和国外商投资法》若干问题的解释) [The interpretation by the Supreme People's Court on several issues about the application of the Foreign Investment Law of the People's Republic of China] by the Supreme People's Court on December 16, 2019, effective on January 1, 2020.

[39] Ibid., art. 1.

[40] Guanyu Jinyibu Jiaqiang Dianxin Yewu Shichang Guanli Yijian de Tongzhi (关于进一步加强电信业务市场管理意见的通知) [Notice on Further Strengthening the Administration of Telecommunication Services Market] by the Ministry of Post and Telecommunications on August 3, 1993.

the prohibited category in the first version of the Catalogue for the Guidance of Foreign Investment Industries.[41]

On July 13, 2006 the Ministry of Information Industry (MII) (now known as the MIIT) issued the Circular on Intensifying the Administration of Foreign Investment in Value-added Telecommunications Services,[42] which imposes stringent requirements on foreign investment in the industry: (1) telecommunication enterprises in China shall not lease, transfer or sell any license for telecommunication business in any form, or provide resources, places and facilities or any other conditions for any foreign investor to engage in any illegal telecommunication operations by any means in China; (2) key assets (such as domain names of the internet and registered trademarks) of the business must be directly held by the VIEs and the People's Republic of China (PRC) individuals, telecommunication enterprises must have the necessary places and facilities to operate the business and have in place its own security system; and (3) examination and approval of the administrative department for the information industry of the State Council are required for PRC domestic telecommunication enterprises which wish to go for offshore listing.

On September 28, 2009 the General Administration of Press and Publication (GAPP) issued a circular which expressly prohibits foreign investment from indirectly controlling or participating in the online game business of Chinese companies through contractual arrangements. This is the first time that Chinese regulators have explicitly prohibited the use of contractual agreements in certain industries. That said, it is peculiar that no enforcement action has been taken against any online game companies using the VIE structure to get listed overseas. Take Taomee Holdings Limited (Taomee) as an example; Taomee is a company specializing in online games, which is the regulatory scope of the GAPP circular. Instead of making any approval or clarification, Taomee still underwent an IPO on the New York

[41] Waishang Touzi Chanye Zhidao Mulu (外商投资产业指导目录) [Catalogue for The Guidance of Foreign Investment Industries] by the State Development and Reform Commission and Others on June 20, 1995.

[42] Xinxi Chanyebu Guanyu Jiaqiang Waishang Touzi Jingying Zengzhi Dianxin Yewu Guanli de Tongzhi (信息产业部关于加强外商投资经营增值电信业务管理的通知) [Circular on Intensifying the Administration of Foreign Investment in Value-Added Telecommunications Services] (issued by the Ministry of Information Industry on July 13, 2006).

Exchange after consultation with its lawyers. Taomee identified the risk of violating GAPP regulations in its prospectus, but immediately assured investors that, without the participation of the regulator directly responsible (in this case, the Ministry of Culture), it was unlikely that the GAPP alone would take any enforcement action.[43] The subsequent successful IPO seems to reflect the accuracy of Taomee's understanding to a certain degree. As far as the GAPP regulations are concerned, there are very few available cases suggesting that any company had ever been subject to the penalty.

Restrictions on telecommunications and value-added telecommunications services have eased as more internet companies listed in Hong Kong and the US. In the Shanghai Free Trade Zone (Shanghai FTZ), the MIIT and the Shanghai government took the innovative step to further liberalize restrictions on value-added telecommunication services. Not only can the foreign investment proportion exceed 50 percent, but several prohibited areas now also welcome the participation of foreign investors.[44] The MIIT closely administered the reform process in the Shanghai FTZ so that the experience might be extended to other FTZs and local areas. Apparently, the implementation of the pilot program has received positive feedback. The online data processing business was introduced to the whole country, and the MIIT further permitted the shareholding proportion of foreign investment to reach 100 percent.[45]

In the education industry, foreigners are prohibited from participating in all stages of education – from pre-primary to high school and higher education. Only qualified foreign investors can participate in the form of

[43] Taomee Holdings Limited, Form 424 (B)(4) (2011), pp. 23–24, www.sec.gov/Archives/edgar/data/0001507051/000119312511162606/d424b4.htm#rom118192_2.

[44] Guanyu Zhongguo (Shanghai) Ziyou Maoyi Shiyanqu Jinyibu Duiwai Kaifang Zengzhi Dianxin Yewu de Yijian (关于中国（上海）自由贸易试验区进一步对外开放增值电信业务的意见) [Opinions on Further Opening Up the Value-Added Telecommunication Services in China (Shanghai) Pilot Free Trade Zone] by the Ministry of Industry and Information Technology and the Shanghai Municipal People's Government on January 6, 2014.

[45] Guanyu Fangkai Zaixian Shuju Chuli yu Jiaoyi Chuli Yewu (Jing Ying lei Dianzi Shangwu) Waizi Gubi Xianzhi de Tonggao (关于放开在线数据处理与交易处理业务（经营类电子商务）外资股比限制的通告) [Notice on Removing the Restrictions on Foreign Equity Ratios in Online Data Processing and Transaction Processing (Operating E-commerce) Business] by the Ministry of Industry and Information Technology on June 19, 2015.

"foreign educational institutions,"[46] and such cooperation must be dominated by their Chinese counterparts.[47]

6.3.2 *Law in Practice*

As discussed in Section 6.3.1, the Chinese law does not provide clear rules on the legality of VIEs. In order to see how the issue is dealt with in practice, it is useful to look at relevant cases.

6.3.2.1 Earlier Cases

The first important case appeared in 2012 when the SPC delivered a final judgment in the Chinachem Financial Services (Chinachem) case.[48] There, Chinachem entered into a shareholding entrustment agreement with China SME Investment Development (SME), under which SME agrees to hold the shares of China Minsheng Bank on behalf of Chinachem. Later, the value of the entrusted shares increased significantly, and SME claimed to be the legal owner of those shares, on the grounds that the shareholding entrustment agreement should be invalid because its main purpose was to circumvent restrictions on foreign investment in Chinese financial institutions. The SPC supported the allegation made by SME, stating that the agreement should be void *ab initio*. However, based on the principle of fairness, the SPC ordered SME to pay Chinachem an amount of compensation.[49]

It should be noted that this case did not actually involve the use of VIE structures, but it is highly relevant to the issue of VIE contract validity. The shareholding entrustment agreement disputed in this case was very

[46] Zhonghua Renmin Gongheguo Zhongwai Hezuo Banxue Tiaoli (中华人民共和国中外合作办学条例) [Regulations of the People's Republic of China on Chinese–Foreign Cooperative Education] by the State Council on March 1, 2003, effective on September 1, 2003 and amended on March 2, 2019.

[47] Waishang Touzi Zhunru Tebie Guanli Cuoshi (Fumian Qingdan) (2020 nian ban) (外商投资准入特别管理措施（负面清单）（2020年版）) [Special Administrative Measures on Foreign Investment (Negative List) (2020 Version)] by the National Development and Reform Commission and the Ministry of Commerce on June 23, 2020 effective on July 23, 2020.

[48] Huamao Jinrong Fuwu Youxian Gongsi yu Zhongguo Zhongxiao Qiye Touzi Youxian Gongsi Guquan Jiufen Shangsuan (华懋金融服务有限公司与中国中小企业投资有限公司股权纠纷上诉案) [The Appeal Case of Shareholding Dispute between Huamao Financial Services Limited and China SME Investment Limited] (2012) Min Si Zhong Zi Di 30 Hao ((2012)民四终字第30号) [(2012) Min Si Zhong Zi No. 30] By the Supreme People's Court on October 29, 2012.

[49] Ibid.

similar to the VIE contract in that they shared a common purpose to circumvent China's foreign investment regulation. As discussed before, the circumvention of compulsory provisions in laws and administrative rules may render the relevant contract void under China's Civil Code.[50] The judicial attitude toward the legality of the shareholding entrustment agreement in this case can thus shed important light on that of the VIE structure. Indeed, the Chinachem case has been widely seen a relevant case in the discussion of the validity of VIE contracts, with many commentators arguing by analogy that it shows judicial disapproval of the VIE structure.[51]

It was also reported that Shanghai Branch of the China International Economic and Trade Arbitration Commission (CIETAC) declared the VIE structure invalid in a 2011 case.[52] In this case, the VIE entity was a Chinese company which conducted business in the internet game industry and held relevant licenses. Foreign investors exerted control over the VIE entity through a set of VIE contracts. The relationship between the Chinese founders and foreign investors became sour, and thus the Chinese founders wanted to take back control of the VIE entity by seeking to invalidate the VIE structure. Shanghai CIETAC opined that the VIE structure enabled foreign investors to de facto participate in and control the management of the internet game business, thereby contravening the relevant foreign investment restrictions. Hence, Shanghai CIETAC held that the VIE structure should be void, because it was used to "conceal an illegitimate purpose through a legal form," or "violate compulsory provisions of laws and administrative regulation" under the Chinese contract law.

6.3.2.2 Recent Cases

Since 2016, there has been a significant change in the judicial attitude toward the legality of the VIE structure. In the 2016 case of Anbo Education, the SPC upheld the validity of a VIE structure used in the education industry.[53] In this case, a VIE structure was implemented to

[50] *See* Section 6.3.1.1.

[51] Charles Comey, Paul McKenzie, et al., "China VIEs: Recent Developments and Observations" (2013), www.lexology.com/library/detail.aspx?g=90f823b1-02cb-4b6a-aabb-de857e45c246.

[52] Kong Huanzhi (孔焕志) and Sui Xueqin (隋雪芹), "贸仲上海第一起VIE仲裁案 Shanghai CIETAC's Fingding on VIE Case Raises Plenty of Questions" (2012) 1 商法 *China Business Law Journal* 90.

[53] Changsha Yaxing Zhiye Fazhan Youxian Gongsi yu Beijing Shida Anbo Jiaoyu Keji Youxian Zeren Gongsi Hezuo Hetong Jiufen Shangsuan (长沙亚兴置业发展有限公司

allow foreign investors to contractually control a VIE entity which conducted education business in China. The SPC stressed the fact that the VIE entity was actually managed by Chinese citizens and foreign investors did not participate in the management, and thus held that foreign investment restrictions should not apply to make the VIE contract invalid. According to this case, the key issue is whether foreign investors are directly involved in the operation and management of VIE entities.

One year later, in the 2017 case of *Zhao Yuping v. Han Gengcheng et al.*, the Court of Haidian District of Beijing City went further to hold that the VIE structure is valid as there are neither mandatory rules to prohibit it under the Chinese law nor any infringement of the so-called "public order and good customs."[54] The court also referred to the Anbo Education case to state that "the VIE structure reflects the true expression of the minds of relevant contractual parties, and invalidating it would harm the safety of commercial transactions and the legitimate interests of the honest, law-abiding parities."[55]

In 2019, there were two important cases which clearly supported the legality of the VIE structure. In the case of *Tang Qiushi v. Yang Huiqin*,[56] a court in the Sichuan Province simply held that the VIE contract should be valid because it reflected the true intentions of relevant contracting parties, and it did not violate Article 52 of the Contract Law.

In the other case of *Wang Feng v. Fujian Wangge Ltd.*,[57] the plaintiff invested in the VIE entity, and the investment contract stipulated that the

与北京师大安博教育科技有限责任公司合作合同纠纷上诉案) [The Appeal Case of Cooperation Contract Dispute between Changsha Yaxing Real Estate Development Co., Ltd. and Beijing Shida Ambo Education Technology Co., Ltd.] (2015) Min Er Zhong Zi Di 117 Hao ((2015)民二终字第117号) [(2015) Min Er Zhong Zi No. 117] By the Supreme People's Court on July 2, 2016.

[54] Zhao Yuping yu Han Gengchen deng Sunhai Gongsi Liyi Zeren Jiufen Yishen Minshi Panjueshu (赵宇平与韩庚辰等损害公司利益责任纠纷一审民事判决书) [First-Instance Civil Judgment on Dispute over Liability for Damaging Company Interests between Zhao Yuping and Han Gengchen et al.] (2017) Jing 0108 Min Chu 31402 Hao ((2017)京0108民初31402号) [(2017) Jing 0108 Min Chu No. 31402] By the Beijing City Haidian District Court on December 29, 2017, p. 12.

[55] Ibid., p. 14.

[56] Tang Qiushi yu Yang Huiqin Hetong Jiufen Yishen Minshi Panjueshu (唐秋实与杨辉琴合同纠纷一审民事判决书) [First-Instance Civil Judgment on Contract Dispute between Tang Qiushi and Yang Huiqin] (2019) Chuan 0191 Min Chu 4663 Hao ((2019)川0191民初4663号) [(2019) Chuan 0191 Min Chu No. 4663] By the Chengdu New Technology Development Zone People's Court on December 19, 2019.

[57] Wang Fen, Wangge (Fujian) Zhineng Keji Youxian Gongsi Hetong Jiufen Ershen Minshi Panjueshu (王芬、网格（福建）智能科技有限公司合同纠纷二审民事判决

shares in the VIE entity would transform into shares in the overseas listing entity at the same value once the company was successfully listed overseas. The plaintiff sought a refund of investment while keeping the shares in the overseas listing entity, on the grounds that the investment made through the VIE structure was invalid. The Intermediate Court of Fuzhou City held that there is no shareholding or investment relationship between the VIE entity and the overseas listed company under the VIE structure, and that the Chinese law did not expressly prohibit the VIE structure. The court even stated that relevant state authorities actually acquiesce in the use of the VIE structure.[58] Importantly, in this case, the Information Bureau of Fujian Province presented a document to the court that the overseas listing of the defendant company through the VIE structure was consistent with the national policy and did not constitute evasion of any law and regulations.[59]

6.4 A Theory of Strategic Ambiguity

6.4.1 *The Meaning of Strategic Ambiguity*

As shown in Section 6.3, the Chinese law, both on paper and in practice, is still not fully clear about the legal status of the VIE structure, but there seems to be a trend toward judicial recognition of its legality. The VIE structure seems to be legal by default unless there are special circumstances.

However, several caveats need to be made about the above observation. First, despite the trend toward recognizing the legality of VIEs, Chinese courts are not monolithic. There are heterogenic approaches to the values underlying VIE regulation. Second, cases do not have legal effects in China and are not binding on later cases. It remains to be seen whether other courts will follow them. Third, the VIE structure can be used in many different contexts and its legality may need to be judged on the individual circumstances of each case. For instance, the VIE structure can be used not only for overseas listing, but also mergers and acquisitions in a purely domestic context. Even within the category of overseas listing, the legality of VIEs may be affected by various factors, such as the

书) [Second-Instance Civil Judgment on Contract Dispute between Wang Fen and Wange (Fujian) Intelligent Technology Co., Ltd.] (2019) Min 01 Min Zhong 950 Hao ((2019)闽01民终950号) [(2019) Min 01 Min Zhong No. 950] By the Fuzhou Intermediate People's Court on March 18, 2019.

58 Ibid., p. 7.

59 Ibid., p. 7.

industry in which the VIEs operates, the importance of the VIEs and the level of support given by the local government.

Despite these technical difficulties, there have been significant technical reasoning efforts made by Chinese judges. On the surface, the case law analysis centers on private disputes between shareholders, to which the state is not a party. However, the issue of state interest or national security is implied in those cases when the judges decide on whether the VIE structure should be seen as a way to circumvent China's foreign investment restrictions. As national security is a broad and sensitive issue, Chinese authorities will usually refer to a more specific basis for their decisions such as anti-monopoly law and foreign investment law.[60] Hence, the protection of state interests is always a key issue in the cases, whether or not it is explicitly mentioned in the judgments.

Hence, while there is some technical difficulty in clarifying the legality of VIEs, the key issue remains how to balance protecting state interest or national security on the one hand and facilitating economic development and overseas listings of Chinese companies on the other hand. Striking a proper balance here is no easy task, as the two goals may conflict directly as a matter of law. Indeed, the Chinese authorities are caught between a rock and a hard place: they cannot expressly legitimize the VIE structure as there is a need to use foreign investment restrictions to protect state interests; neither can they simply declare the VIE structure invalid as many Chinese companies would be denied access to foreign investment and international capital markets through overseas listings.

In the face of the above dilemma, it seems natural for Chinese authorities to take a strategy that makes the legal status of VIEs ambiguous. This policy of strategic ambiguity offers flexibility for the Chinese government in striking a balance between facilitating overseas listing of Chinese companies and controlling the risks of foreign investment.[61] The ambiguous status of the VIE structure allows China to receive the inflow of foreign investment even in restricted or prohibited industries, while preserving the power to block it if and when there are serious national security risks caused. It is thus not surprising that the Chinese authorities

[60] Robin Hui Huang, "China's National Security Review of Foreign Investment: A Comparison with the United States" (2023) 57 *Vanderbilt Journal of Transnational Law* 1263, 1293 (discussing a national security case disguised as an anti-monopoly issue).

[61] Robin Hui Huang, *Securities and Capital Markets Law in China* (Oxford University Press, 2014), pp. 335–336; Michael J. Enrigh, "China's Inward Investment: Approach and Impact" in Julien Chaisse (ed.), *China's International Investment Strategy: Bilateral, Regional, and Global Law and Policy* (Oxford University Press, 2019), p. 28.

have simply ignored repeated suggestions to clarify the legality of VIEs, because the policy of strategic ambiguity requires them to refrain from providing a direct, clear-cut answer to that issue.

Finally, there are two important points to be made about the thesis of strategic ambiguity.[62] First, among various vitiating factors, illegality is the most difficult one in terms of its level of certainty and predictability in virtually all legal systems, including developed jurisdictions. For instance, the development of the doctrine of illegality, especially in the common law world, has become a mess over the last two centuries. One should not expect that a crystal-clear solution can be given by any jurisdiction, and China is not an exception in this sense. However, while it may not be uncommon to see ambiguity over contractual validity in other areas of law and even in developed legal systems, the VIE case in China is still peculiar because the ambiguity is a product of strategic policy. Second, the key players relating to the issue of strategic ambiguity include not only the courts as law enforcers, but also law makers including legislators and relevant regulators. As a private law issue, the validity of VIE contracts is to be determined by the Chinese courts. However, in adjudicating such disputes, the court will need to decide on whether the VIE structure has violated or circumvented relevant laws or administrative rules. This means that the Chinese legislators and regulators can have important impact on the decision-making process of the courts. Indeed, they are reluctant to articulate rules with a high level of controversy in a clear-cut way, and in actual VIE cases, if one litigation party could get relevant regulators to issue an opinion on the interpretation of the relevant rule and thus the legality of VIE contracts, they would usually win the case.[63] Hence, although no Chinese regulator on its own has the power to decide which particular contract is void due to illegality, it still plays an important role in relation to the issue. It is thus necessary to examine the factors affecting the behaviors of relevant regulators at both institutional and individual levels.

6.4.2 *Application of the Policy of Strategic Ambiguity*

6.4.2.1 The 2023 Recordation Regime

On February 17, 2023 the CSRC issued the Interim Measures for the Administration of Overseas Securities Offering and Listing by Domestic

[62] Thanks to the anonymous reviewer for raising these points.
[63] *See* Section 6.3.2.

Enterprises (2023 Measures on Overseas Listing), introducing a recordation regime for overseas listing of Chinese companies.[64] A domestic enterprise conducting overseas offering and listing should undergo the recordation formalities with the CSRC, submit the recordation report, legal opinions and other relevant materials, and truthfully, accurately and completely explain the information on shareholders.[65] This recordation requirement applies to both direct and indirect overseas listing.[66] Under the direct overseas listing mode, China-registered companies directly issue their shares such as H-shares and get listed on an overseas market; under the indirect overseas listing mode, Chinese companies operating business in China get listed indirectly through an overseas-registered listing vehicle, and the latter has either equity or contractual control over the former.

This recordation regime has important implications for overseas listing of Chinese companies. Among them, the issue arises as to whether it solves the legality issue of the VIE structure used in indirect overseas listing activities, that is, whether the VIE structure will gain legality if it goes through the recordation process. We argue that the legality of the VIE structure is more likely to be confirmed with the recordation regime, but there is still lingering uncertainty.

First, there is simply no reference to the legality of the VIE structure in the 2023 Measures on Overseas Listing, so there is no legal basis to assume that the legality issue of the VIE structure is solved by the recordation regime. Second, the recordation regime, as the name suggests, is to require companies to file their overseas listing activities with the CSRC, rather than give regulatory approval to them, including the use of the VIE structure. In fact, even if the recordation regime could be seen as a de facto approval system, it does not necessarily mean that the CSRC gives its endorsement to the legality of the VIE structure. For instance, under the previous merit-review regime for securities offerings, the CSRC had been empowered to approve IPO applications in China, but it was expressly stipulated that the approval does not constitute endorsement of the investment-worthiness of relevant securities.[67]

64 Jingnei Qiye Jingwai Faxing Zhengquan he Shangshi Guanli Shixing Banfa (境内企业境外发行证券和上市管理试行办法) [Interim Measures for the Administration of Overseas Securities Offering and Listing by Domestic Enterprises] (issued by the CSRC on February 17, 2023, effective from March 31, 2023).

65 Ibid., art. 13.

66 Ibid., art. 2.

67 Huang, above note 7, pp. 54–56.

Third, the recordation regime is designed to "create a more transparent and predictable institutional environment and support enterprises in using overseas capital markets to develop business in a standardized manner." This is a response to the recent problems that overseas-listed Chinese companies have caused: according to the CSRC:

> in recent years, with the deepening of the opening up of the capital market, some new conditions and new problems appear in the overseas offering and listing by domestic enterprises, for example, some enterprises conducting overseas offering and listing caused bad impact by committing financial frauds, and some domestic enterprises deliberately circumvented the regulation to conduct overseas offering and listing, which violated national industrial policies and even endangered national security.[68]

The CSRC referred to "the new problems" that have occurred "in recent years," such as financial frauds (the *Luckin Coffee* case in 2020) and national security violations (the *Didi* case in 2022). By contrast, the legality of the VIE structure has been an issue for many years, and there is little surprise that it was not listed as an example.

In fact, the 2023 recordation regime is the final crystallization of two consultation papers that the State Council and the CSRC issued on December 24, 2021, namely, the State Council's Regulations on the Administration of Domestic Enterprises' Overseas Issuance and Listing of Securities (Consultation Paper)[69] and the Measures on the Filing Administration of Domestic Enterprises' Overseas Issuance and Listing of Securities (Consultation Paper).[70] At the press conference on these consultation papers, the CSRC spokesperson simply stated that

[68] Guanyu <Jingnei Qiye Jingwai Faxing Zhengquan he Shangshi Guanli Shixing Banfa (关于《境内企业境外发行证券和上市管理试行办法》的说明) [Explanations on <Interim Measures for the Administration of Overseas Securities Offering and Listing by Domestic Enterprises>] (issued by the CSRC on February 17, 2023).

[69] Guowuyuan Guanyu Jingnei Qiye Jingwai Faxing Zhengquan he Shangshi de Guanli Guiding (Cao'an Zhengqiu Yijian Gao) (国务院关于境内企业境外发行证券和上市的管理规定（草案征求意见稿））[State Council's Regulations on the Administration of Domestic Enterprises' Overseas Issuance and Listing of Securities (Consultation Paper)] (promulgated by the CSRC on December 24, 2021) (hereinafter Regulation on Overseas Listing).

[70] Jingnei Qiye Jingwai Faxing Zhengquan he Shangshi Bei'an Guanli Banfa (Zhengqiu Yijian Gao) (境内企业境外发行证券和上市备案管理办法（征求意见稿））[Measures on the Filing Administration of Domestic Enterprises' Overseas Issuance and Listing of Securities (Consultation Paper)] (promulgated by the CSRC on December 24, 2021) (hereinafter Filing Measures for Overseas Listing).

companies with a VIE structure can seek overseas listing after going through the recordation process, provided that they satisfy the relevant requirements of domestic laws and regulations.[71] However, the recordation effect is conditional upon compliance with other relevant laws and regulations, including those regarding foreign investment. As such, it is still unclear whether the recordation process is meant to confirm the legality of the VIE structure. In short, the filing process seems to represent only the regulator's record of the company's overseas listing, rather than the regulator's endorsement of the VIE structure used in the listing.

6.4.2.2 Other Examples

As discussed earlier, VIE-related laws can be broadly divided into two categories, namely, the legality-related law category and the regulation-focused law category. The 2023 Measures on Overseas Listing clearly falls into the second category, as it is focused on the regulation of overseas listing of Chinese companies and is not directly related to the legality of the VIE structure. There are many other examples of this category.

One such example is the Provisions of the MOFCOM on the Implementation of the Security Review System for Mergers and Acquisitions of Domestic Enterprises by Foreign Investors (2011 M&A Review Provisions).[72] Although the VIE structure is based on contractual arrangements rather than ownership ties, it gives rise to the power of control, which is known as "contractual control." This has important implications for calculating market dominance and conducting national security reviews in the context of foreign mergers and acquisitions (M&A).[73] Under Article 9 of the 2011 M&A Review Provisions, one should look at the substance and impact of foreign M&A deals in determining whether they fall into the scope of M&A security review, and foreign investors should not substantially

[71] CSRC, "Zhengjianhui Youguan Fuzeren Da Jizhe Wen" (证监会有关负责人答记者问) [Officials from the CSRC Answered Reporter Questions], December 24, 2021, www.csrc.gov.cn/csrc/c100028/c1662240/content.shtml.

[72] Shangwubu Shishi Waiguo Touzizhe Binggou Jingnei Qiye Anquan Shencha Zhidu de Guiding (商务部实施外国投资者并购境内企业安全审查制度的规定) [Provisions of the MOFCOM on the Implementation of the Security Review System for Mergers and Acquisitions of Domestic Enterprises by Foreign Investors] (promulgated by the MOFCOM, August 25, 2011 effective September 1, 2011).

[73] Robin Hui Huang, "China's National Security Review of Foreign Investment: A Comparison with the United States" (2023) 57 *Vanderbilt Journal of Transnational Law* 1263–1303.

circumvent M&A security review in any way, such as contractual control through the use of the VIE structure.

The second example is the famous Document 37 issued by the State Administration of Foreign Exchange (SAFE) on July 4, 2014.[74] Under the SAFE Document 37, before contributing capital to a special-purpose company with its legal assets or interests within or outside China, a domestic resident should apply to the SAFE for undergoing the foreign exchange registration procedure for overseas investment.[75] Document 37 provides the channel through which Chinese domestic individual investors can legally hold shares in overseas-listed companies and get the investment return back to China. Hence, if the founders of Chinese companies want to establish a special-purpose company as the listing vehicle overseas, they need to comply with Document 37. This mechanism is usually used to facilitate the Red-chip structure for the overseas listing of Chinese companies. The Red-chip structure may also have an element of the VIE structure for companies which operate in an industry restricted for foreign investment. In other words, the SAFE allows Chinese companies with the VIE structure to do the foreign exchange registration.

Another example is the recent regime to allow Red-chip companies to get listed back in China without having to dismantle their VIE structures. On March 30, 2018 the CSRC issued the Opinions Released on Launching Pilot Program of Issuance of Stocks or Depositary Receipts within China by Innovative Enterprises (2018 Pilot Program Opinions), in order to attract Red-chip companies (which are established by Chinese people in foreign jurisdictions) to return to China for listing.[76] Under the 2018 Pilot Program Opinions, Red-chip companies in high-tech

[74] Guojia Waihui Guanliju Guanyu Jingnei Jumin Tongguo Teshu Mudi Gongsi Jingwai Tourongzi ji Fancheng Touzi Waihui Guanli Youguan Wenti de Tongzhi (国家外汇管理局关于境内居民通过特殊目的公司境外投融资及返程投资外汇管理有关问题的通知) [Notice of the State Administration of Foreign Exchange on Issues Concerning Foreign Exchange Administration of the Overseas Investment and Financing and the Round-Tripping Investment Made by Domestic Residents through Special-Purpose Companies] (issued by the SAFE on July 4, 2014) (hereinafter Document No. 37).

[75] Ibid., art. 3.

[76] Guanyu Kaizhan Chuangxin Qiye Jingnei Faxing Gupiao Huo Cuntuo Pingzheng Shidian de Ruogan Yijian (关于开展创新企业境内发行股票或存托凭证试点的若干意见) [Opinions Released on Launching Pilot Program of Issuance of Stocks or Depositary Receipts within China by Innovative Enterprises] (promulgated by the CSRC, April 12, 2018 effective April 12, 2018) [hereinafter the 2018 Pilot Program Opinions].

industries, including those with VIE structures, can apply to get listed in China.

Moreover, on December 28, 2021 the NDRC and MOFCOM jointly issued the 2021 version of the Negative List for Foreign Investment Access (hereinafter "2021 Negative List").[77] According to the 2021 Negative List, two new requirements have been added for Chinese companies to list overseas. First, for domestic companies engaged in businesses in areas where foreign investment is prohibited, their overseas listing plans must be reviewed and approved by relevant national industry authorities. Second, foreign investors are not allowed to participate in business operations and management.[78] Further, the shareholding level by foreign investors in overseas-listed Chinese companies should be subjected to the same regulatory requirements as the investment of foreign investors in domestically listed Chinese companies.[79] For instance, in such companies, the total shares held by foreign investors should not exceed 30 percent.[80] Again, this requirement applies to both direct and indirect listings, including those listings effected through the VIE structure. It is worth noting that the above new requirements will only be applicable to new listings.[81]

Hence, the 2023 recordation regime is not the first regulation that recognizes the existence of the VIE structure and tries to regulate its use in the context of overseas listing. As shown in Section 6.3.1, other regulations in the regulation-focused law category are intended to cover the use of the VIE structure in other contexts, such as foreign M&A national security review, foreign exchange administration, foreign investment and the homecoming listing of Red-chip companies. A common feature of these regulations is that they do not constitute an official endorsement of the legality of the VIE structure but rather recognize

[77] Waishang Touzi Zhunru Tebie Guanli Cuoshi (Fumian Qingdan) (2021 nian ban) (外商投资准入特别管理措施（负面清单）（2021年版）) [Special Administrative Measures for Foreign Investment Access (Negative List) (2021 Edition)] (jointly promulgated by the NDRC and MOFCOM on December 28, 2021 effective January 1, 2022) (hereinafter 2021 Negative List).

[78] 2021 Negative List, art. 6.

[79] Ibid.

[80] Shangwubu Xinwen Bangongshi (商务部新闻办公室) [The Press Office of the Ministry of Commerce], "Shangwubu Youguan Fuzeren Jiu 2021 Nian Ban Waizi Zhunru Fumian Qingdan Da Jizhe Wen" (商务部有关负责人就2021年版外资准入负面清单答记者问) [Officials from the MOFCOM Answered Reporter Questions], December 27, 2021, www.mofcom.gov.cn/article/zcjd/jdtzhz/202112/20211203232235.shtml.

[81] Ibid.

the status quo of the use of the VIE structure. Hence, the regulation-focused law category aims to regulate other matters on the assumption of the legality of the VIE structure and cannot be referred to as conclusive evidence to support the legality of the VIE structure.

Indeed, although the CSRC has issued various rules to regulate the use of the VIE structure in many different contexts, its position on the legality of the VIE structure has never been clear. In 2011, an internal CSRC report was reported to take a tough stance on the VIE structure amid growing security threats in the internet industry.[82] The internal report even suggested prohibiting the use of the VIE structure in several phases. To prevent any sudden disruption to the existing market, existing VIE companies will enjoy certain grandfathered terms, and new VIE companies awaiting listing approval shall be banned. However, in another informal report published on the CSRC's website, the CSRC's attitude was rather cautious, suggesting that arbitrary denial of the VIE structure might impact the long-term creativity of Chinese enterprises, and the positive effect and economic advantages generated by the VIE structure should be recognized.[83]

In sum, although the CSRC, NDRC and MOFCOM have tightened their regulation over overseas listing of Chinese companies, neither of them has expressed a clear position on the legality of the VIE structure. Despite the recent wave of new regulations governing the overseas listings of Chinese companies, the policy of strategic ambiguity seems to remain unchanged for the legal status of the VIE structure.

6.4.3 *Factors Contributing to the Policy of Strategic Ambiguity*

As discussed earlier, the Chinese authorities have never clarified the legality of VIEs, not because of technical difficulty in doing so, but rather due to the policy of strategic ambiguity. In fact, as will be discussed below, the Chinese authorities are acutely aware that the limbo status of VIEs has caused significant investment risks to foreign investors and impeded overseas listing of Chinese companies. Nevertheless, despite

82 Liu Yan (刘燕), "Zai 'Moren Hefa' Zhong Baofa de Falv Fengxian—Xieyi Kongzhi-VIE Moshi Xia Fengxian Shijian ji Anli Shuping" (在"默认合法"中爆发的法律风险——协议控制VIE模式下风险事件及案例述评) [Legal Risks in "Implicit Legality" – A Review of Risk Events and Cases under the Agreement Control or VIE Model] (2013) 9 *Zhengquan Fayuan (证券法苑) [Securities Law Review]* 1,10.

83 Ibid., 11.

repeated suggestions and calls for dealing with the issue, Chinese regulatory authorities have remained silent in line with the policy of strategic ambiguity.

Hence, it is important to investigate why the Chinese authorities have adopted and implemented this policy. This section will thus identify and examine various factors that have contributed to the constitution of the institutional environment in which the policy of strategic ambiguity operates.

6.4.3.1 The Need for Balancing Economic Development and National Security

The policy of strategic ambiguity over the legality of VIEs can be mainly attributed to the pragmatic mentality of the Chinese authorities, as it enables them to decide the issue in individual cases depending on the right balance that needs to be struck between facilitating economic development and protecting national security.

On the one hand, the VIE structure plays an important role in the overseas listing of Chinese companies, which enables Chinese companies to acquire the foreign capital and technology necessary to catch up with or even surpass their global competitors. As foreign investment is important to China's economic growth, particularly in the technology industries, it would be impractical and harmful if the VIE structure were to be declared illegal, which would deprive Chinese companies of access to foreign investment. Apart from capital supply, overseas listing may also help Chinese companies to improve their management skills and corporate governance.

In practice, many influential Chinese companies have been listed in overseas markets, notably the US and Hong Kong. Many of them have adopted the VIE structure, and some – including Alibaba, Baidu and Tencent – are among the most influential enterprises in China. Any major change of policy regarding the VIE structure would not only have a significant impact on them but would also cause huge volatility in the relevant markets. This would ultimately undermine the confidence of international investors in the investment value of all Chinese companies.

On the other hand, national security concerns have prevented Chinese regulators from confirming the legality of the VIE structure. Indeed, if the VIE structure were to be made unequivocally legal, it would make a mockery of China's foreign investment regime, as the VIE structure could easily be used as a backdoor for foreign investors to break into certain industries that would otherwise be restricted or even prohibited from foreign investment. Not only would this amount to a slap in the face to Chinese regulators, it could also lead to real national security risks. Take the internet services industry as an example: With the rapid development of information technology, data has become a strategic resource which can affect innovative processes and production activities. Countries have already begun to struggle for the control of data to obtain a strategic advantage in global competition for the next generation of innovation. Internet services companies control a massive amount of customer data, and if the industry were to open up widely to foreign investment through the VIE structure, serious concerns would emerge over data security and sovereignty.

In sum, the policy of strategic ambiguity offers a convenient tool for the Chinese authorities to juggle competing demands. Indeed, there is a great need for China to ensure Chinese ownership and control in certain industries which are considered strategically important to national security. It should be noted that the Chinese ownership does not have to be state ownership. In practice, the Chinese authorities have various informal means of controlling China-based firms, regardless of whether they are SOEs or POEs.[84]

However, the policy of strategic ambiguity brings significant investment risks to foreign investors and impedes overseas listings of Chinese companies. One may thus ask whether there are potential alternative policies that would balance better between national security and economic growth. In particular, would it be better to have an arrangement that requires *ex ante* state approval for holding a significant stake or control block in companies that are important for national security?

The *ex ante* state approval would be certainly better for foreign investors because it can remove the uncertainty over the legality of VIEs and the resultant investment risks. However, it may not be a better arrangement for the Chinese authorities, as it takes away their discretionary power and brings potential liability to them. Apart from the goal of facilitating foreign investment, the Chinese authorities need to protect state interests and national security. Arguably, the latter is more important and harder for them to handle. In general, the effect of economic development contributed by foreign investment is hard to measure in individual cases they approve, but the issue of national security can occur

[84] Tamar Groswald Ozery, "The Politicization of Corporate Governance: A Viable Alternative?" (2022) 70 *American Journal of Comparative Law* 43, 63 (discussing various informal means that the Chinese government uses to control private-sector firms).

directly in those cases. Simply put, government officials may be held liable if the cases approved by them turn out to be a problem of national security. This risk can be exacerbated by the fact that the concept of national security is very broad and highly sensitive.[85] Naturally, government officials will have every incentive to avoid giving *ex ante* approval or "safe harbours." Indeed, *ex ante* approval would effectively transform investment risks on the part of foreign investors into political risks on the part of Chinese authorities. At a fundamental level, the Chinese government will not put economic considerations before national security and thus will prefer *ex post* determination as a safety net.[86]

Again, it is worth noting that the above analysis does not attempt to justify the policy of strategic ambiguity, nor posit that *ex post* determination is better than *ex ante* approval. Rather, it tries to reveal the inconvenient truth that it seems just wishful thinking to expect the Chinese authorities to take the suggestion to clarify the legality of VIEs either through statutory provisions or *ex ante* approvals. Indeed, from the perspective of the Chinese authorities, the policy of strategic ambiguity can better meet their need to strike a balance between promoting economic development and protecting national security.

6.4.3.2 Interest Group Politics of Regulatory Agencies

The second reason for the policy of strategic ambiguity is related to interest group politics among different regulators. Since the interests of industry regulators vary widely, regulators may not agree on how to deal with the issue of the legality of the VIE structure. In the traditional East Asian developmental state model, economic development policies are usually issued continuously by a superagency.[87] However, it has been pointed out that there is bureaucratic competition among Chinese ministries in formulating policies to serve their departmental interests.[88] The

[85] Robin Hui Huang, "China's National Security Review of Foreign Investment: A Comparison with the United States" (2023) 57 *Vanderbilt Journal of Transnational Law* 1263.

[86] Cf. Wei Shen, "Will the Door Open Wider in the Aftermath of Alibaba?: Placing (or Misplacing) Foreign Investment in a Chinese Public Law Frame" (2012) 42(2) *Hong Kong Law Journal*, 275, 306 (suggesting that China "think business" first and "improve the situation by laying out general standards and principles of behavior").

[87] Stephan Haggard, *Developmental States* (Elements in the Politics of Development) (Cambridge University Press, 2018).

[88] Yingyao Wang, "Policy Articulation and Paradigm Transformation: The Bureaucratic Origin of China's Industrial Policy" (2021) 28(1) *Review of International Political Economy* 204–231.

various regulatory agencies may want to expand their respective powers, leading to a turf war between them.

The CSRC, as China's securities market watchdog, has long required Chinese companies to obtain its approval for overseas direct listings.[89] However, the use of the VIE structure has led many companies to circumvent CSRC's supervision of their overseas listings. Therefore, the CSRC's efforts to strengthen the supervision of the VIE structure serve to discharge its responsibility and enhance its position as a securities regulator. At the same time, the CSRC has an interest in internationalizing the Chinese capital markets and facilitating the overseas listing of Chinese companies by way of the VIE structure. A report published by the CSRC warns that arbitrary invalidation of the VIE structure will affect the long-term growth of Chinese enterprises.[90]

Similarly, industry authorities, such as the MIIT, generally adopt a quite pragmatic attitude toward companies in their respective industries that use the VIE structure to get listed overseas. As mentioned in Section 3.2, although they make rules to restrict foreign investment in their industries, industry regulators have not vigorously enforced them to prevent companies from getting listed abroad through the VIE structure. In the information technology industry, for instance, restrictions on foreign investment apply to all companies, including those which do not endanger national security and could greatly contribute to economic growth and technological innovation. At the same time, the MIIT has incentives to use foreign capital to promote the development of the internet industry in China. Hence, in the eyes of the MIIT, the CSRC's review requirement for overseas listings may run counter to its objective of promoting the development of the internet industry.

By contrast, MOFCOM may be in a more complicated position because it has direct responsibility for balancing economic development and national security. On one hand, as the regulator of foreign investment, it must deal with national security risks brought by companies that bypass regulations to gain access to foreign capital. On the other hand, it is tasked with making good use of foreign capital to promote national

89 Guanyu Gufen Youxian Gongsi Jingwai Faxing Gupiao he Shangshi Shenbao Wenjian ji Shenhe Chengxu de Jianguan Zhiyin (关于股份有限公司境外发行股票和上市申报文件及审核程序的监管指引) [Guidelines for Supervising the Application Documents and Examination Procedures for the Overseas Stock Issuance and Listing of Limited Companies] (promulgated by the CSRC on December 20, 2012 effect on January 1, 2013).

90 Liu, above note 82, pp. 1, 11.

economic development and technological innovation. Therefore, due to its mixed departmental interests, MOFCOM has been ambivalent about the legality of the VIE structure.

Interest group politics also manifests itself in the way that the various regulators interact with each other in their self-interests. According to media reports, the CSRC submitted a report to the State Council as early as 2011, recommending that the VIE structure be declared illegal.[91] Although the CSRC's claim is based on the protection of national security, this is still widely seen as an attempt to restore powers that the VIE structure has bypassed.[92] However, the proposal was not finally accepted by the State Council because other regulators such as MOFCOM and MIIT did not agree to it. Under the CSRC's 2023 Measures on Overseas Listing as discussed in Section 6.4.2.1, the tenet was to adopt a unified filing process for overseas listings, whether direct or indirect, including listings via the VIE structure.[93] This would extend the CSRC's supervisory power to all companies that use the VIE structure to go public overseas.

The inter-agency conflict has been further exacerbated by the fact that regulators usually care only about their own regulatory responsibilities, without paying adequate attention to issues that do not fall squarely within their regulatory spheres but may have an impact on other regulators. For instance, MOFCOM only provides a negative list of industries that are forbidden or restricted from foreign investments, and it is up to the CSRC and relevant industry authorities to handle the difficult issue of whether companies in these industries could go public overseas or not.[94]

6.4.3.3 Rent-Seeking Activities of Regulatory Officials

At the individual level, a reason behind the policy of strategic ambiguity may be that it provides rent-seeking opportunities for regulatory officials. This in turn creates an incentive for regulators to continue to embrace strategic ambiguity. There are four types of rent-seeking activities,

[91] Hu Zhongbin (胡中彬), "VIE Jianguan Dingdiao Xinlao Huaduan Guowuyuan Fazhiban Yi Jieru" (VIE监管定调新老划断 国务院法制办已介入) [The Supervision of VIE Will be Based on the Principle of "Old People Old Rule, New People New Rule" The Legislative Affairs Office of the State Council has intervened in], September 23, 2022, finance.sina.com.cn/chuangye/ipo/20110923/225010532638.shtml.

[92] Ibid.

[93] "Filing Measures for Overseas Listing," art. 2; "Regulation on Overseas Listing," art. 28.

[94] 2021 Negative List, art. 6.

namely, petty theft, grand theft, speed money and access money.[95] Among them, speed money and access money are more likely to be involved in financial regulation. Speed money means that in developing countries such as China, businesses or citizens pay petty bribes to bureaucracies to get around hurdles or speed things up.[96] Under this circumstance, if the regulations are ambiguous, there will be more room for self-interpretation in law enforcement, which may allow regulators to obtain more rent-seeking benefits. For example, the ambiguity surrounding the legality of the VIE structure could, in theory, allow regulatory officials to assert that the companies adopting such a structure have de facto bypassed foreign investment restrictions and therefore demand bribes. It can also be manifested in the form of selective enforcement as the regulator can have the final say in cases of ambiguity.

Even worse is access money, which by definition refers to high-stake payments given to prominent officials by commercial actors, not merely for speed, but also access to exclusive and valued privileges.[97] Under such a model, these commercial actors could even bribe to lobby for favorable regulatory policies.[98] For instance, Guo Jingyi, the former deputy director of the Department of Treaty and Law of MOFCOM, was internally investigated by the Communist Party of China (CPC) in 2008 and sentenced in 2010 for accepting bribes in the formulation of laws and regulations related to foreign mergers and acquisitions.[99] Specifically, under the rules restricting foreign investment, there was room for foreign investors to enter restricted industries through contractual arrangements, including the VIE structure. Foreign investors could easily bypass these regulations as they only restrict foreign direct investment.[100] Since the MOFCOM regulations on foreign investment were mainly formulated during Guo's tenure, the ambiguity of these regulations regarding the

95 Yuen Yuen Ang, *China's Gilded Age: The Paradox of Economic Boom and Vast Corruption* (Cambridge University Press, 2020), p. 10.

96 Ibid.

97 Ibid.

98 Ibid., p. 28.

99 "Guo Jingyi An Qianshe Li Jiacheng Qingnian Jishu Guanliao Jiti Qingfu" (郭京毅案牵涉李嘉诚青年技术官僚集体倾覆) [The Guo Jingyi Case Involves Li Ka-shing and the Collective Overthrow of Young Technocrats], *TechWeb*, June 10, 2010, m.techweb.com.cn/article/2010-06-10/620036.shtml.

100 "The Inspector of the Ministry of Commerce is under investigation: Suspected of taking bribes in the process of making laws," *ChinaNews*, September 4, 2008, www.chinanews.com.cn/cj/gncj/news/2008/09-04/1370918.shtml.

legality of the VIE structure has been seen as evidence of rent-seeking activities of corrupt regulators in the law-making process.[101]

6.5 Prospects and Implications

6.5.1 The Future of the VIE Structure

In the foreseeable future, the VIE's ambiguous legality stance is likely to continue, as there is little sign that Chinese authorities will drastically change the policy of strategic ambiguity. Indeed, the various factors contributing to the adoption of the policy will likely persist in the years to come.

Specifically, Chinese authorities may continue to pursue the policy of strategic ambiguity to provide useful leeway over the legality of VIEs. A blanket ban on the VIE structure would thwart the effort to attract foreign investment. As such, it is unlikely that the VIE structure will be prohibited by the Chinese authorities under the current national policy of foreign investment. Meanwhile, with the increasing uncertainty of the political and economic environment in recent years, both at the national and international levels, China has become more concerned about national security risks, particularly those emanating from foreign investment.[102] Under the policy of strategic ambiguity, Chinese authorities will have more wiggle room to maneuver in balancing economic benefits with national security concerns.

Again, it should be noted that this is just our honest assessment of the future development, and not an attempt to justify or advocate for the continuation of the policy of strategic ambiguity. Indeed, the limbo status of VIEs brings significant investment risks to foreign investors and hampers overseas listings of Chinese companies. However, as discussed earlier, it is unlikely that the Chinese authorities will adopt an *ex ante* approval system for VIEs to remove those risks.[103] At the same time, the VIE structure will continue to provide an important method to facilitate indirect overseas listing, which is crucial for Chinese companies, particularly private-owned high-tech companies, to gain access to international capital markets. Hence, although the Chinese authorities will not change

[101] Ibid.

[102] Robin Hui Huang, "China's National Security Review of Foreign Investment: A Comparison with the United States" (2023) 57 *Vanderbilt Journal of Transnational Law* 1263.

[103] *See* Section 6.4.3.

from *ex post* determination to *ex ante* approval, they may take measures to alleviate the issue of VIEs' uncertain legality.

For instance, under the 2023 Measures on Overseas Listing, the CSRC adopted a recordation system for overseas listings of Chinese companies.[104] As discussed in Section 6.4.2, this regime is just for recordation purposes and does not have the legal effect of approval. In other words, when a company with the VIE structure successfully goes through the recordation process, it does not necessarily mean that the CSRC confirms the legality of the VIE. However, the recordation process could significantly increase the chance that the recorded VIEs would be declared valid should a dispute arise. Of course, this will depend on how the recordation regime works in practice, a question that is still too early to tell at present.

Another point to note is that while the VIE structure may continue to be used in the overseas listings of Chinese companies, its utility may gradually decrease due to the continuing relaxation of foreign investment control and overseas listing regulation in the future.

In general, the VIE structure is used to circumvent two restrictions: one is the restriction on foreign investment access, and the other is the review of overseas direct listings. Over the years, China's negative list for foreign investment has continued to shrink. For instance, compared with the first version of the negative list issued in 2016, the 2021 Negative List reduces the number of restricted industries to only thirty-one, representing a significant cut from the ninety-three industries on the 2016 Negative List.[105] Therefore, there will be less need for Chinese companies to use the VIE structure to obtain foreign investment.

Further, the recordation regime introduced by the CSRC in 2023 applies to both direct and indirect overseas listings. This differs from the previous rule under which the CSRC's approval was required only for direct overseas listings, a burdensome requirement that companies may wish to bypass through indirect listing. Hence, for Chinese companies that conduct indirect overseas listings, it would be less meaningful to use the VIE structure to circumvent the CSRC's approval requirement.

[104] *See* Section 6.4.2.

[105] "The 2021 version of the negative list for foreign investment access is released, and the terms are reduced for the fifth consecutive year," *Xinhua Agency*, December 28, 2021, www.xinhuanet.com/money/20211228/84286d4413b847279fc8a1b8cf05bcf8/c.html.

6.5.2 *Practical Implications for Foreign Investors and Regulators*

Overseas-listed companies are exposed to the risk of losing control over their VIEs because the former possess mere contractual rights rather than a shareholding relationship with the latter. In this situation, there is a real chance that the controlling shareholder of the VIE may not obey the instructions of the listed company and may even take away the control of the VIE without the consent of the listed company.

As the overseas-listed companies do not have equity interest over their VIEs but a series of contractual arrangements, such a degree of control is less effective than direct ownership. Consequently, the founder, senior management or shareholder of VIEs plays a central role in VIE structures. Here, potential risks will arise if there is any change of positions involving their interests. In particular, if PRC individuals or VIEs fail to comply with the contractual arrangements, there could be immense difficulties for foreign investors to assert their rights. This risk to foreign investors has been well illustrated in many cases, such as the *GigaMedia* case in 2010[106] and the *Alibaba* case in 2011.[107]

Hence, overseas securities regulators have been deeply concerned about Chinese companies that are listed in their markets through the VIE structure. The US Securities and Exchange Commission (SEC) has used two main regulatory tools for the VIE structure. The first one is to warn investors of potential legal risks associated with the VIE structure used by Chinese companies through the SEC website and other channels.[108] The other one is to require Chinese companies to disclose relevant information about VIE risks in SEC filings. On December 20, 2021 the Division of Corporation Finance of the SEC posted the "Sample Letter to China-Based Companies" on the Division's homepage.[109] According to this letter, China-based companies need to disclose

[106] In this case, GigaMedia tried to remove the founder of the VIEs, but the founder refused to step down. For more details, see Guo Li, "Chinese Style VIEs: Continuing to Sneak under Smog?" (2014) 47(3) *Cornell International Law Journal* 569, 585.

[107] In this case, Jack Ma, the controller of the VIE (Zhejiang Alibaba) transferred its payment business (Alipay) out of the Alibaba Group without obtaining approval from other shareholders. For more details, see Wei Shen, "Will the Door Open Wider in the Aftermath of Alibaba?: Placing (or Misplacing) Foreign Investment in a Chinese Public Law Frame" (2012) 42(2) *Hong Kong Law Journal* 275, 276–279.

[108] US SEC, "Disclosure Considerations for China-Based Issuers" (2020), www.sec.gov/corpfin/disclosure-considerations-china-based-issuers.

[109] US SEC, "Sample Letter to China-Based Companies" (2021), www.sec.gov/corpfin/sample-letter-china-based-companies.

specifically whether they use a VIE structure, whether they use a Cayman company as the main body of listing and the legal risks they face under Chinese law.[110]

In Hong Kong, the HKEX has formulated Listing Decision No. HKEX-LD43–3 ("Listing Decision") to supervise Chinese companies that use the VIE structure to list on the HKEX.[111] In addition to the requirement for disclosure of relevant information similar to that in the US, the HKEX also requires relevant companies to provide a legal opinion letter from Chinese lawyers, which should confirm that the adoption of the VIE structure by the company complies with Chinese laws and regulations.[112] In addition, the HKEX strictly limits the use of the VIE structure to cases where it is needed due to foreign investment restrictions.[113] Apart from the circumvention of foreign investment restrictions, the VIE structure can bring other advantages, such as flexibility. Therefore, in practice, some companies may wish to use the VIE structure even if they are not subject to foreign investment restrictions. The HKEX has tried to prevent the overuse of the VIE structure – that is, the use of VIE structure is not permitted where the company belongs to an industry without foreign investment restrictions.

While the overseas regulators' concerns regarding the VIE structure of Chinese companies are reasonable, there is no need for excessive anxiety. As argued earlier, although the Chinese government has yet to clarify the legality of VIEs, uncertainties surrounding the VIE structure have been gradually decreasing. Although the Chinese authorities have continued to avoid providing a clear confirmation on the issue, recent developments such as the 2023 Measures on Overseas Listing may have made the issue less worrisome than before. Further, if foreign investors are not directly involved in the business operation and management of the VIE entities, the VIE structure will be more likely to be considered legal.

In any case, as discussed before, Chinese regulators will likely continue to pursue a policy of strategic ambiguity regarding the VIE structure, and thus overseas regulators will have to learn how to live with this ambiguity. Specifically, overseas regulators would benefit from a proper understanding of China's policy of strategic ambiguity on the VIE legality issue

110 Ibid.

111 HKEX Listing Decision HKEX-LD43–3 (issued in 2005, last updated in January 2022), en-rules.hkex.com.hk/sites/default/files/net_file_store/LD43-3.pdf.

112 HKEX, "HKEX Listing Decision," arts. 18, 18A, 18B.

113 HKEX, "HKEX Listing Decision," art. 17.

as discussed earlier, in the sense that it could help them better assess the level of risks posed by the limbo status of VIEs in a given case and as a general matter. Indeed, from a political-economy perspective, the VIE legality issue is much more nuanced than suggested by a traditional doctrinal analysis. For instance, the issue may vary depending on some relevant factors such as the industry the VIE entity belongs to and the level of involvement foreign investors have in the management of the VIE entity. Hence, it may not be wise to simplistically take a black-or-white approach to the issue and adopt overly stringent regulatory measures. Indeed, over-regulation is a real problem to be avoided here, as it would increase the cost of overseas listings for Chinese companies and decrease the number of high-quality China-based listed companies for overseas exchanges.

6.5.3 *Theoretical Implications for the "Law and Finance" Debate*

The thesis of strategic ambiguity put forward in this chapter has important theoretical implications, particularly for the "law and finance" debate. As will be discussed below, it has been argued that China's VIE issue presents examples of "finance without law" or "finance against law," thereby negating the "law and finance" teaching that legal protection is important to the market development. However, under our theory of strategic ambiguity, there are many laws and regulations in this area, and the VIE structure does not run against the law. We argue that China's VIE case, viewed from our theory of strategic ambiguity, does not really challenge the "law and finance" theory, but rather enriches the substance of the latter in the sense that legal protection can be implicit or ambiguous.

6.5.3.1 Is There Really "Finance without Law" in the Case of VIE?

It has been argued that China's VIE structure presents an example of "finance without law" and extralegal mechanisms such as politics and reputation "work in the absence of law."[114] However, as discussed earlier, there is actually a large web of laws and regulations that China has

[114] Shitong Qiao, "Finance without Law: The Case of China," *The CLS Blue Sky Blog* (Columbia Law School's Blog on Corporations and The Capital Markets), September 20, 2022, clsbluesky.law.columbia.edu/2022/09/20/finance-without-law-the-case-of-china/.

gradually established for the VIE structure over the years, including the category of legality-related laws (such as contract law, foreign investment law and industry-specific rules)[115] and the category of regulation-focused laws (such as 2023 Measures on Overseas Listing, 2021 Negative List, 2018 Pilot Program Opinions, 2014 SAFE Document 37 and 2011 M&A Review Provisions).[116]

To be sure, the category of legality-related VIE laws has some inner tensions and resultant uncertainties, but this does not mean that there is no law. In fact, in many other areas of law, there is often a certain level of uncertainty due to conflicting rules (which is not uncommon in Chinese law) or differing interpretations of the same rule (which is quite common even in the US), such as the meaning of abuse under the corporate veil-piercing regime,[117] the application of directors' fiduciary duties, the definition of securities, the scope of insider trading,[118] the standard of due diligence defence under the securities misstatement liability regime,[119] the characterization of Fintech[120] and so on.

At a more fundamental level, the uncertainty of the VIE regime in China stems from the policy of strategic ambiguity. Indeed, it would be more appropriate to see the uncertainty of the VIE structure as an intended product of conscious regulatory action than a disastrous outcome of irresponsible regulatory inaction. As discussed earlier, the regulators have issued an array of regulation-focused VIE laws about such issues as foreign exchange administration, foreign merger and acquisition approval, national security review, overseas-listing recordation and the homecoming listing of Chinese companies. This category of regulation-focused VIE laws serves to regulate the use of the VIE structure while purposely leaving the legality of VIEs to be governed by the other category of legality-related VIE laws. This way, the Chinese authorities can allow the VIE structure to be used for overseas listing of Chinese

115 *See* Section 6.3.1.

116 *See* Section 6.4.2.

117 *See*, for example, Robin Hui Huang, "Piercing the Corporate Veil in China: Where Is It Now and Where Is It Heading?" (2012) 60(3) *American Journal of Comparative Law* 743.

118 *See*, for example, Robin Hui Huang, *International Securities Markets: Insider Trading Law in China* (Kluwer Law International, 2006).

119 *See*, for example, Robin Hui Huang, "Private Enforcement of Securities Law in China: A Ten-Year Retrospective and Empirical Assessment" (2013) 61(4) *American Journal of Comparative Law* 757.

120 *See*, for example, Robin Hui Huang, *Fintech Regulation in China: Principles, Policies and Practices* (Cambridge University Press, 2021).

companies in a well-regulated way while retaining the flexibility to disallow it to protect national security in certain circumstances.

Finally, extralegal mechanisms such as politics and reputation may play an important role in VIEs, but they work in the shadow of and not in the absence of law. There is a legal regime for the VIE structure in China and extralegal mechanisms only work to supplement rather than substitute the law. Due to the uncertainty of the VIE law, there does exist some room for the functioning of politics and reputation in the area. They may influence the way that the law is interpreted and enforced but still need to act within the framework of the law.

6.5.3.2 Is There Really "Finance against Law" in the Case of VIE?

Perhaps in recognition of the obvious problems as noted above, the "finance without law" argument later changed its name to "finance against law" at the final stage of publication.[121] The "finance against law" argument has two key features: first, financial development violates legal prohibitions and restrictions; second, there are two risks, including the lack of judicial enforcement of contracts and the expropriation of investment by the state.[122] Again, questions arise as to whether the case of VIE is really an example of "finance against law."

According to the "finance against law" argument, the VIE structure violates foreign investment law in China, but it is debatable whether this is the case. Based on a doctrinal analysis, it could be argued that VIE-based contract control does not constitute "foreign investment" as defined under the foreign investment law. Specifically, as the VIE structure gives rise to contract control rather than a shareholding relationship, the VIE contracts may not be considered as foreign investment contracts, and therefore their legality should not be affected by foreign investment restrictions. This point was made by the court in the 2017 case of *Zhao Yuping v. Han Gengcheng et al.*[123]

The Chinese regulators were actively involved in the creation of the VIE structure as a practical way to juggle the need to restrict foreign investment to protect national security and the need to promote economic development through an overseas listing of Chinese companies. In the case of Sina, the VIE structure was actually proposed by the

[121] *See* Qiao, above note 3.
[122] Ibid., 438.
[123] *See* Section 6.3.2.3.

Chinese regulator and was later accepted by Sina to become widely known as the "Sina Model."[124] This development process of the VIE structure was also confirmed by a member of the legal team who worked for the overseas listing of Sina.[125] This shows that while there appears some tension within the VIE legal regime, the VIE structure is not generally a violation of legal prohibitions on foreign investment in the eyes of Chinese authorities.

Further, instead of arguing that there is no law for VIE in China, the "finance against law" argument claims that there is no "legal protection for investors," because the VIE contracts are "unlikely to be enforced in Chinese courts."[126] The "finance without law" argument made an even stronger claim that "contracts under the VIE structure are not enforceable."[127] From both theoretical and practical perspectives, these points about VIE contract enforceability are not strictly correct. On the one hand, the relevant contract law provisions in China are so flexible that the use of the VIE structure can be reasonably accommodated.[128] On the other hand, as shown earlier, there have been several cases where the Chinese courts upheld the validity of VIE contracts and enforced them.[129] Thus far, no court cases have been found where VIE contracts were clearly declared illegal and unenforceable. Although China does not have a formal case law precedent system, those cases show the judicial attitude toward the VIE structure and have important reference value for other courts.

In practice, the VIE structure has long been regarded as possessing "implicit legality" in China.[130] This means that the VIE structure will usually have legal recognition from Chinese courts and regulators save in very special circumstances. As discussed earlier, for instance, some authorities such as the MII and the GAPP have issued clear rules to prohibit the use of the VIE structure to facilitate the overseas listing of companies in their respective industries.[131] However, this is obviously different from state expropriation of investment. To date, there have been

[124] David Sheff, *China Dawn: The Story of a Technology and Business Revolution* (HarperCollins, 2002) 199–203.

[125] Interview, June 18, 2023, Hong Kong.

[126] Ibid., 431.

[127] *See* above note 114.

[128] *See* Section 6.3.1.

[129] *See* Section 6.3.2.

[130] Liu, above note 82, p. 1.

[131] *See* Section 6.3.1.

virtually no reported cases where the VIE structure is declared illegal and foreign investment is expropriated by the state.

Hence, viewed from the perspective of the VIE regime, there are several problems with the "finance against law" argument. On the one hand, it seems that the "finance against law" argument equates conflicts of law with violations of law. Despite some tension within the VIE regime, it would stretch a point to find legal violations. On the other hand, even in the case of "finance against law," it is simply not true that there is no legal protection for investors due to the lack of judicial enforcement of contracts and state expropriation of investment. Interestingly, the "finance against law" argument also sees the Islamic banking system as an example, because it circumvents the Sharia law.[132] But the question is: Are contracts simply not judicially enforceable under the Islamic banking system? Do investments in the Islamic banking system easily fall prey to state expropriation? As shown in the case of VIE, there is considerable legal protection for investors, judging from both the law on paper and the law in practice.

6.5.3.3 Does the Case of VIE Really Challenge the "Law and Finance" Theory?

As discussed in the preceding sections, the case of VIE does not really lend support to the "finance without law" and the "finance against law" arguments which seek to challenge the "law and finance" theory. Instead, the case of VIE fits in well with the "law and finance" theory under which financial development is positively correlated with legal protection for investors.[133]

To start with, if the legality of VIEs had become more certain, the VIE-facilitated overseas listing market could have been larger and more developed. As discussed earlier, due to the uncertainty over the limbo status of VIEs, there are significant risks for foreign investors.[134] Plainly, this will increase the transaction costs of using the VIE structure for overseas listings and even prevent it altogether.

[132] Qiao, above note 3, pp. 431, 439.

[133] *See*, for example, Rafael La Porta, Florencio Lopez-de-Silanes, Andrei Shleifer and Robert W. Vishny (LLSV), "Legal Determinants of External Finance" (1997) 52 *Journal of Finance* 1131; LLSV, "Law and Finance" (1998) 106 *Journal of Political Economy* 1113.

[134] *See* Section 6.5.2.

Hence, over the years, Chinese regulators have tried to make the legality of VIEs more certain. As discussed earlier, a recent and significant example is that the CSRC issued the 2023 recordation regime for overseas listing of Chinese companies, including those with the VIE structure.[135] Further, as discussed earlier, since 2016, there has been a clear judicial trend for recognizing the legality of VIEs.[136] Indeed, the uncertainty of the VIE's legal status is actually not as high as argued by the "finance against law" thesis. This may explain that despite the uncertainty surrounding the legality of the VIE structure, the market for VIE-facilitated overseas listing has seen significant growth since the Sina Model was invented in 2000.

Theoretically, as the law and finance theory teaches us, it would be ideal for the further development of the VIE market if the legality issue concerning VIEs could be completely eradicated to provide investors with a full panoply of protection. However, as discussed earlier, China will likely continue the policy of strategic ambiguity over the legality of VIEs.[137] Hence, it is unlikely that the legality issue will be completely eliminated in the foreseeable future.

Indeed, the complexity of the VIE regime in China is due to the fact that the development of the VIE market is not the only goal but rather needs to be balanced with the other goal of regulating foreign investment to protect national security. The policy of strategic ambiguity is adopted as a pragmatic tool to provide flexibility for the Chinese authorities to maintain the balance. In this sense, the VIE regime, as a whole, works as intended to balance the two goals noted above. The flexibility/uncertainty of the VIE regime is a purposeful and delicate top-level design of the Chinese authorities. Hence, the case of VIE does not really challenge the law and finance theory and the lingering uncertainty of its legality is essentially a result of practical considerations.

6.6 Conclusion

The legality of the VIE structure has long been a subject of debate since it was first used by Sina Corporation to effectuate its US listing in 2000. Under the VIE structure, foreign investors of overseas-listed Chinese companies can benefit from their onshore business in China through

[135] *See* Section 6.4.2.
[136] *See* Section 6.3.2.
[137] *See* Section 6.5.1.

contractual control rather than a shareholding relationship, thus bypassing relevant prohibitions or restrictions on foreign investment in China. However, it has never been fully clear about the legality of the VIE structure used for overseas listing of Chinese companies.

This chapter develops a theory of strategic ambiguity, arguing that China adopts a policy of strategic ambiguity about the legality of VIEs. This policy usefully gives China important leeway in regulating the use of the VIE structure so as to balance the need to regulate foreign investment to protect national security and the need to facilitate overseas listing to promote economic growth. There are also institutional reasons behind this policy, including interest group politics of regulatory agencies and the rent-seeking activities of regulatory officials.

China will likely continue to implement the policy of strategic ambiguity, and thus the uncertainty over the legality of VIEs will persist in the foreseeable future. In March 2023, the CSRC introduced a recordation regime for all overseas listings of Chinese companies, but it remains unclear whether the VIE structure will gain legality if it goes through the recordation process.

However, the level of uncertainty is not as high as perceived by some commentators arguing that the VIE market presents an example of "finance without law" or "finance against law." Contrary to the "finance without law" argument claiming that the VIE structure operates without law, there is actually a large web of relevant laws and regulations that China has gradually established for the VIE structure, including the category of legality-related laws and the category of regulation-focused laws. Further, an empirical study of all relevant cases shows that there has been a clear trend of judicial recognition of the VIE structure over the years. As such, contrary to the "finance against law" argument claiming that there is no legal protection for investors in the VIE market, the VIE regime, both on paper and in practice, provides reasonably good protection for investors and ensures that the VIE structure is used in a well-regulated manner. This has important practical implications for the overseas listing of Chinese companies and foreign investors therein, as well as theoretical implications for the international discourse on the relationship between law and finance.

7

Audit Oversight Issues Concerning Overseas-Listed Chinese Companies

7.1 Introduction

Audit oversight is a significant issue in the context of a company conducting listings across borders. In practice, the auditing of overseas-listed companies is usually undertaken by local accounting firms, raising the issue of whether the regulators of the host market can reach the local accounting firms and relevant documents in their possession, particularly audit working papers.

In general, the US and Hong Kong are the two most popular listing destinations for Chinese companies.[1] It is thus important to focus on these two jurisdictions when examining the issue of cross-border audit oversight from a Chinese perspective. In the US, the audit oversight regime demands inspection and investigative power on all audit firms that provide services to listed companies, including foreign audit firms. This requirement has been in place since the enactment of the Sarbanes–Oxley Act 2002, which created the Public Company Accounting Oversight Board regime (PCAOB) as a specialized audit oversight body in the US. The extraterritorial power is often in conflict with the laws and sovereignty of the home jurisdictions of the listed companies. Demanding foreign audit firms to turn over documentation produced during the auditing process puts them into the vortex of this conflict, as domestic law in foreign jurisdictions may forbid them to do so.

Until recently, this conflict of law has been one of the most serious disputes between the US and Chinese securities regulators due to the cross-border listing of many Chinese issuers (known as China Concept Stocks) on the US stock market.[2] Over the years, some of the Chinese

[1] *See* Chapter 2.

[2] Robin Hui Huang, "The US–China Audit Oversight Dispute: Causes, Solutions, and Implications for Hong Kong" (2021) 54(1) *The International Lawyer* 151.

Concept Stocks have been found to commit fraudulent accounting practices, resulting in severe losses for US investors. However, the PCAOB has long faced obstacles placed by China to its effort to get access to audit working papers of Chinese Concept Stocks, which is necessary for it to carry out audit oversight functions.

The US–China dispute over cross-border audit oversight issues was resolved through a regulatory cooperation agreement in late 2022, but it remains to be seen whether and how the agreement will be implemented effectively as expected. This agreement has been reached under the shadow of the Holding Foreign Companies Accountable Act (HFCAA) that the US passed in 2020, which contains a threat of delisting all Chinese Concept Stocks in certain circumstances.[3] The agreement seems to be an emergency measure on the part of China to avoid the potential consequence of the HFCAA. To properly understand the evolution of the China–US audit oversight dispute, this chapter will first trace the US's PCAOB from its creation, particularly in relation to its extraterritorial oversight power and international inspection practice. The audit oversight regime of China and its restriction on audit working papers from outside access will then be reviewed.

This chapter will also discuss the experience of Hong Kong in relation to the cross-border audit oversight issues concerning overseas-listed Chinese companies. Indeed, until recently, Hong Kong has had similar cross-border audit oversight issues to those experienced by the US. The issue is of practical significance as Hong Kong is expecting more initial public offerings (IPOs) of Chinese companies, including those that will be "homecoming" from US listing. Further, Hong Kong plays an important role in the 2022 agreement reached between the US and China, in the sense that audit working papers of US-listed Chinese companies will be sent to Hong Kong for US regulators to inspect.[4]

Overall, this chapter will examine the experiences of the US and Hong Kong in seeking access to audit working papers of Chinese companies listed in their markets, analyzing the various factors that have contributed to the constitution of the institutional environment shaping the past, present and future of the audit oversight issues concerning overseas-listed Chinese companies.

[3] For more details, *see* Section 7.6.

[4] For more details, *see* Section 7.6.

7.2 Audit Oversight Regime in the US

7.2.1 The Establishment of the PCAOB

As a general rule of securities regulation, listed companies are required to periodically report their financial statements so that investors can obtain material information about the companies to inform their investment decisions. Independent examination of financial records and financial statements by auditing firms is, therefore, an indispensable part of this process to ensure that such information is truthful, accurate and complete. To this end, the conduct of auditors themselves is held to their professional standards and relevant laws. The auditing standard in the US has a long history of development, which can be traced to the 1900s. In 1917, the American Institute of Certified Public Accountants (AICPA) first formed a special committee for establishing auditing standards, and in 1978, this became the Auditing Standards Board.[5] For a long time, the auditing profession was left to self-regulation conducted by their industry association.

The self-regulatory landscape for the auditing profession was drastically changed following the Enron scandal. In March 2002, Arthur Andersen, one of the then "big-five" accounting firms in the world, was criminally charged for its involvement in Enron's accounting fraud case as Enron's auditor.[6] In the same year, another Arthur Andersen client, WorldCom, collapsed in yet another accounting scandal, again sending shockwaves throughout the financial markets.[7] The involvement of Arthur Andersen in the accounting scandals of Enron and WorldCom demonstrated that auditors' self-regulation was ineffective. The US Congress investigated this issue, concluding that the system of oversight by the auditing profession itself was no longer sufficient, and substantial changes had to be made.[8]

Hence in June 2002, the US Congress passed the Sarbanes–Oxley Act, creating the PCAOB as an independent nonprofit body to oversee the auditing of public companies.[9] The Sarbanes–Oxley Act also introduced

[5] Georgetown Law, *Accounting Research Guide*, guides.ll.georgetown.edu/accounting/auditing-standards.

[6] *United States of America v. Arthur Andersen, LLP*, 374 F.3d 281 (5th Cir. 2004).

[7] George J. Benston, "The Quality of Corporate Financial Statements and Their Auditors before and after Enron," *Cato Institute Policy Analysis*, November 6, 2003, p. 12, www.cato.org/sites/cato.org/files/pubs/pdf/pa497.pdf.

[8] *See* Conference report filed in House (07/24/2002), H.R.3763.

[9] Public Law 107-204, 116 Stat. 745.

a wide range of measures in mandating higher corporate responsibility standards, enhancing financial disclosure requirements, increasing punishment toward white-collar crime and creating new corporate fraud crimes. The PCAOB is empowered to "protect the interest of investors and further the public interest in the preparation of informative, accurate, and independent audit reports."[10] For the first time in US history, the auditors of public companies were put under independent and external oversight.

The PCAOB consists of five board members appointed by the Securities and Exchange Commission (SEC) after consultation with the Fed and the Treasury.[11] The board members are drawn from leading accounting firm partners, legal scholars and lawyers with public administration experience, but importantly, only two members can be accountants at any given time.[12] The funding of the PCAOB comes from fees allocated to issuers, brokers and dealers, and registered accounting firms also pay an annual fee to cover the costs of reviewing audit reports.[13] The oversight responsibility over the PCAOB lies with the SEC, which would review and approve its rules, standards and annual budget.[14] The SEC can also review disciplinary actions taken by the PCAOB and may make modifications to them.[15] In sum, the PCAOB plays a vital role in overseeing auditing issues of US-listed companies, contributing to the regulation of the US capital markets.

7.2.2 The Extraterritorial Jurisdiction of the PCAOB

The first obligation for auditors of US-listed companies is to be registered with the PCAOB and come under its jurisdiction. It is unlawful for an unregistered accounting firm to prepare or issue audit reports for any US-listed companies. Hence, any audit firm, domestic or foreign, that wants to prepare an audit report for a US-listed company or plays a substantial role in the preparation must be registered with the PCAOB.[16]

10 Section 101(a) of the Sarbanes–Oxley Act.
11 Sections 101(e)(1) and 101(e)(4) of the Sarbanes–Oxley Act.
12 Section 101(e)(2) of the Sarbanes–Oxley Act.
13 Rule 7100, Rule 2202, PCAOB Bylaws and Rules.
14 Sections 101(h), 107 and 109(b) of the Sarbanes–Oxley Act.
15 Section 107(c) of the Sarbanes–Oxley Act.
16 Rule 2100, PCAOB Bylaws and Rules. For a full list of registered US and non-US audit firms, *see* pcaobus.org/oversight/registration/registered-firms.

Each registered audit firm must file an annual report with the PCAOB.[17] Registration is done electronically on a standard form, and in determining whether to accept the registration, the PCAOB considers if the registrant has violated any rules or regulations or if it fails to provide complete and accurate information.[18]

Registered accounting firms are required to be periodically inspected by the PCAOB to assess compliance with auditing standards.[19] Audit firms with more than 100 issuer clients need to be annually inspected, and firms that provide audit reports for fewer clients are inspected at least triennially.[20] The particular sets of audits to be reviewed in each firm are selected in a risk-based way, focusing on those that have heightened risks of financial misstatement. In general, the PCAOB inspects relevant documentation, interviews with personnel and reviews the firm's internal control policy.[21] The PCAOB may conduct a "surprise inspection" if necessary.[22] The outcomes of the inspections are publicly disclosed in an individual report for each firm, and in case of deficiencies, may lead to a reprimand or enforcement action against the firm.

These requirements apply equally to domestic and foreign accounting firms that are registered with the PCAOB. Under the Sarbanes–Oxley Act, any foreign accounting firm that prepares an audit report for a US-listed company will be subject to regulatory oversight and enforcement "in the same manner and to the same extent" as a domestic accounting firm.[23] In other words, the PCAOB has extraterritorial jurisdiction over foreign accounting firms. For instance, having found deficiencies in its practice, a Canada-based accounting firm that audited a US-listed Canadian mining company was fined, ordered to conduct training and

[17] Rule 2200, PCAOB Bylaws and Rules.

[18] PCAOB, "Frequently Asked Questions Regarding Registration with the Board," December 4, 2017, pcaobus.org/Registration/Information/Documents/Registration_FAQ.pdf.

[19] Section 104(a) of the Sarbanes–Oxley Act.

[20] Section 104(b)(1) of the Sarbanes–Oxley Act.

[21] PCAOB, "PCAOB Inspection Procedures: What Does the PCAOB Inspect and How Are Inspections Conducted?" pcaobus.org/Inspections/Pages/PCAOB-inspection-procedures-what-does-PCAOB-inspect-how-inspections-conducted.aspx.

[22] As noted by the comment from accounting firms during the PCAOB rulemaking. EY, "PCAOB Rulemaking Docket Matter No. 006, Proposed Rules on Inspections of Registered Public Accounting Firms," August 18, 2003, pcaobus.org/Rulemaking/Docket%20006/010_Ernst_and_Young_LLP.pdf.

[23] Section 106(a)(1) of the Sarbanes–Oxley Act.

to submit a written report to the PCAOB.[24] The same goes for a Brazilian branch of Deloitte, which was fined US$ 8 million by the PCAOB and ordered to retain a third-party independent monitor to review the firm's practice.[25]

Central to the audit working paper dispute is the power that the PCAOB holds to demand a registered accounting firm to produce audit working papers for inspection upon request.[26] Even if a foreign accounting firm does not issue audit reports, the PCAOB can determine that it nonetheless plays a substantial role in the preparation of the report and thus is subjected to the same registration and inspection requirement. Importantly, there are two deeming provisions in this regard. Under the first deeming provision, if a foreign accounting firm provides service for a registered accounting firm and issues an opinion or performs services which form part of any audit report, the foreign accounting firm will be deemed to have consented to produce its audit working papers for PCAOB's inspection, and subject to the jurisdiction of US courts for enforcement of any request for production of working papers.[27] Under the second deeming provision, if a US accounting firm engages the service of a foreign accounting firm in preparation of any audit report, it will be deemed as having consented to supply audit working papers produced in the work of that foreign firm and further deemed to have secured the agreement of the foreign firm to produce the document as a condition of relying on the work of that foreign firm.[28] The accounting firms are constantly reminded of these obligations, as they have to affirm their consent to comply with these rules in their annual filings to the PCAOB.[29]

In sum, an accounting firm that performs the auditing of US-listed overseas companies is required to produce relevant documents for PCAOB's inspection. Failing compliance with such requirements, the SEC may bring action to seek mandatory provision of relevant information.[30] This rule has equal application to domestic and foreign

[24] PCAOB Release No. 105-2018-020, dated October 16, 2018.

[25] PCAOB Release No. 105-2016-031, dated December 5, 2016.

[26] Section 106 of the Sarbanes–Oxley Act.

[27] Section 106(b)(1) of the Sarbanes–Oxley Act.

[28] Section 106(b)(2) of the Sarbanes–Oxley Act.

[29] Part IX of Form 2 Annual Report Form, affirming that the registered firm has "secured from each of its associated persons … consents to cooperate in and comply with any request for testimony or the production of documents made by the Board."

[30] Section 102(e) of the Sarbanes–Oxley Act.

accounting firms that are registered with the PCAOB and engage in the auditing business of US-listed companies.

7.2.3 *PCAOB's Practice of Overseeing Foreign Auditors*

Soon after its establishment, the PCAOB began the regular cycle of inspections of US accounting firms. In the first cycle, it conducted 982 such inspections and completed annual inspections on the largest US domestic firms.[31] In 2005, it initiated the inspection of foreign accounting firms, but it was not an easy task given the logistical and jurisdictional hurdles. As noted earlier, the PCAOB must inspect smaller registered accounting firms at least once within three years.[32] When the deadline for the first cycle of inspections came, the PCAOB had 129 foreign firms, or nearly half of the total, still pending inspection. Only Canada was immediately onboard and with the cooperation agreement signed. Among those that refused inspections were registered accounting firms from seventeen jurisdictions, including China, the UK, France, Germany, Luxembourg Korea and so on.[33] The PCAOB, therefore had to extend the time for inspection, with a timeline set to inspect all of these audit firms by the end of 2012.[34]

The delay in inspection was largely due to the noncooperation of foreign accounting firms and their regulators at home.[35] They refused to cooperate with PCAOB in relation to inspections due to restrictions under local laws or objections based on national sovereignty. The regulators of the various European jurisdictions are among the most vocal critics. The Federation of European Accountants commented that the PCAOB essentially forced non-US firms to choose between violating either the laws of their home country or the PCAOB rules and that such a dilemma calls into question the integrity of the PCAOB's policy.[36] The

[31] PCAOB Release No. 2009-003 (June 25, 2009).

[32] PCAOB Rule 4003.

[33] PCAOB, "Updated Information on PCAOB International Inspections," December 31, 2010, pcaobus.org/International/Inspections/Pages/122010_UpdatedInformation.aspx.

[34] PCAOB Release No. 2008-007 (December 4, 2008), p. 11.

[35] Ibid., p. 5.

[36] Fédération des Experts comptables Européens (Federation of European Accountants), "FEE Comments on PCAOB Release No. 2008-007, Rulemaking Docket Matter No. 027, Rule Amendments Concerning the Timing of Certain Inspections of Non-US Firms, and Other Issues Relating to Inspections of Non-US Firms," January 27, 2009, pcaobus.org/Rulemaking/Docket%20027/001_FEE.pdf.

industry association of French audit firms stated that they could not be considered responsible for any delay or hindrance to PCAOB's inspection, as it was due to legal conflicts with the French professional secrecy laws, and that the only practicable solution is mutual recognition and full reliance on foreign national oversight bodies.[37] Specifically, the French Penal Code prohibits the disclosure of secret information by persons entrusted with it because of their profession, such as being an auditor.[38] The exception to it is where it is required by law, but still, it refers to local law, not foreign.[39] Contravention of this French law on protecting professional privileges is punishable by imprisonment of up to one year. In short, the extraterritorial jurisdiction of the Sarbanes–Oxley Act was at odds with many foreign jurisdictions, leading to some discontent in the early years of PCAOB's foreign audit inspection.

As the US was the first country in the world to establish an independent audit oversight body with far-reaching powers and extraterritorial jurisdiction, objections from foreign jurisdictions were understandable. While the foreign regulators were standing by their own national laws and doubting the PCAOB's proclaimed extraterritorial jurisdiction, there was a great need to ensure the quality of information disclosure by strengthening oversight of auditors working for US-listed companies. The PCAOB commented that there were important differences between its inspection and that of other regulators and that few other countries spent as much on enforcement of financial reporting and auditing as the US did.[40] It was the PCAOB's mandate and longstanding initiative to promote cooperation between regulators, to the extent that it can place full reliance on the monitoring work of foreign regulators.[41] In a 2007 policy statement, the PCAOB set out the criteria for a foreign oversight entity to be considered qualified for its full reliance, including up to twenty-three detailed essential criteria listed under five principles.[42]

37 Campagnie Nationale des Commissaires aux Comptes (CNCC), letter dated February 2, 2009, assets.pcaobus.org/pcaob-dev/docs/default-source/rulemaking/docket_027/013_cncc.pdf?sfvrsn=601ca18d_0.

38 Article 226-13 of the French Penal Code.

39 Article 226-14 of the French Penal Code.

40 PCAOB, "Statement on Consideration of Proposing Release of Full Reliance Policy Statement," December 5, 2007, pcaobus.org/news-events/speeches/speech-detail/statement-on-consideration-of-proposing-release-of-full-reliance-policy-statement_91.

41 PCAOB Rule 4012.

42 PCAOB, "Guidance Regarding Implementation of PCAOB Rule 4012," pcaobus.org/Inspections/Documents/2007_12-05_release_2007-011.pdf.

Succinctly, the foreign oversight body must be transparent, independent and perform its work with adequacy and integrity. It should also be properly staffed, adequately funded, with the source of funding not subject to interference or undue influence by external parties and have a good record of historical performance in investigation and enforcement.

Over time, with the example of the PCAOB, and perhaps also due to its insistence to assert jurisdiction and common standards, almost all advanced or emerging market countries have now established independent audit oversight boards of their own. The International Forum of Independent Audit Regulators (IFIAR) has been formed to coordinate these independent audit oversight bodies, and the PCAOB has come into cooperative agreements with these national counterparts.[43] Canada was one of the earliest jurisdictions to establish such an independent oversight body, namely the Canadian Public Accountability Board, which was announced in July 2002, just one month after the passage of the Sarbanes–Oxley Act.[44] It was also the first jurisdiction to sign a cooperative agreement with the US in 2005. The next major jurisdictions to sign such agreements with the PCAOB were the UK, Switzerland and Japan in 2011, followed by France and other European countries from 2013 onward. Presently, a total of twenty-six non-US regulators have made cooperative arrangements with the PCAOB, including China, by way of a Statement of Protocol and/or Data Protection Agreement.[45] While the negotiation process between the regulators is not disclosed, it can be assumed that these cooperating jurisdictions have fulfilled the criteria listed by the PCAOB in the 2007 policy statement.

In general, there are three main modes for the PCAOB to conduct inspections of foreign audit firms. First, the PCAOB and local regulators may conduct joint inspections. Under this mode, the PCAOB would coordinate with the local regulator to form a joint team to conduct on-site inspection of foreign audit firms in satisfaction of the inspection requirements of both regulators. Canada is a good example of this mode. Second, the PCAOB can rely on the inspection work performed by the

[43] China's regulator is not a member of IFIAR. China does not have a separate body for audit oversight, as will be introduced in Section 7.3.

[44] Canadian Public Accountability Board, "Re: PCAOB Rulemaking Docket Matter No. 001," March 28, 2003, pcaobus.org/Rulemaking/Docket%20001/010_CPAB_Canada.pdf.

[45] PCAOB, "PCAOB Cooperative Arrangements with Non-U.S. Regulators," pcaobus.org/oversight/international/regulatorycooperation.

local regulator in the foreign jurisdiction on a sliding scale of reliance that takes into account the rigor and independence of the foreign regulator.[46] In the case of "full reliance" deemed appropriate, the PCAOB will not need to send their own team to the foreign jurisdiction.[47] Interestingly, the flow of reliance may also go in the opposite direction. For instance, the Financial Reporting Council of the UK stated that it "relies to a significant degree on the work of the [PCAOB]."[48] Third, the PCAOB conducts the inspection "on its own in coordination with the home country regulator."[49] Under this mode, an overseas inspection may be conducted by the PCAOB's team alone. However, the local regulator may observe the inspection,[50] with a good example of this mode being Brazil.[51]

7.3 China's Audit Oversight Regime

7.3.1 Accounting Profession and Oversight in China

The development and regulation of the audit profession in China has followed a very different path from that in the US. Compared with its counterpart in the US, China's audit profession has a much shorter history. The audit profession in the US has developed "from the bottom up" as a market institution, whereas the Chinese counterpart was created "from the top down"[52] with a political undertone.

For instance, in 2009, the Chinese government published a plan for the accounting industry to establish a tiered structure of "10-200-7000" firms according to their sizes,[53] stating that the government would provide

46 PCAOB Rule 4011.

47 PCAOB Rule 4012.

48 Financial Reporting Council (UK), "Professional Oversight Board Consultation Document: Monitoring the Work of the Third Country Auditors," March 2012, at para 2.12, www.frc.org.uk/consultations/consultation-document-monitoring-the-work-of-third-country-auditors/.

49 PCAOB, "Inspections of Non-U.S. Firms," pcaobus.org/oversight/inspections/non-us-firm-inspections.

50 PCAOB Release No. 2009-003 (June 25, 2009), p. 5.

51 Lewis H. Ferguson, speech at 6th Annual Conferência Brasileira de Contabilidade e Auditoria Independente, pcaobus.org/News/Speech/Pages/Ferguson-speech-Brazil-global-audit-oversight-06-13-2016.aspx.

52 Shuwen Deng and Richard H. Macve, "How China Has Built an Accounting and Auditing Profession with Potential Global Impact" (2018) *SSRN*, available at ssrn.com/abstract=3102253.

53 "10-200-7000" means that the Chinese State Council planned the industry to have 10 large accounting firm, 200 medium-sized firms, and 7,000 small firms.

"political protection," entry barrier and various government support to the largest firms.[54] In this policy statement, it was explicitly noted that companies listed in foreign markets, especially SOEs, should choose those accounting firms that are beneficial "to protecting the safety of national economic information."[55] Further, China has been aggressively pushing for the localization of accounting firms. In 2012, the Ministry of Finance issued a detailed scheme that targeted the Big Four accounting firms.[56] It stated that they had too large a proportion of foreign partners and needed to have more Chinese partners. Further, it requires that the managing partner be a Chinese national.[57]

In terms of the audit oversight regime, China has not set up a separate supervisory body specifically for the audits of listed companies. At present, the supervision work is jointly conducted by the CSRC and the Ministry of Finance. The two agencies are both under the direct leadership of the State Council. As the capital market watchdog, the CSRC is generally concerned with the financial reporting of listed companies. Specifically, the Accounting Department (Chief Accountant Office) within the CSRC performs the function of supervising audit firms that work for listed companies. In practice, it randomly inspects a percentage of those audit firms every year. The Ministry of Finance is responsible for administering all accounting firms in the country, whether they prepare audit reports for listed companies or not. Where a problem is detected with respect to an audit firm working for listed companies, the Ministry of Finance and the CSRC will work together to conduct investigations and take enforcement actions.

7.3.2 Regulations on Access to Audit Documents

With regard to access to audit documents, the Chinese regime is very complex and stringent, being composed of multiple pieces of legislation

54 Guanyu Jiakuai Fazhan Woguo Zhuce Kuaijishi Hangye de Ruogan Yijian (关于加快发展我国注册会计师行业的若干意见) [Opinion on Accelerating the Development of Our Country's CPA Industry] (issued on March 10, 2009 by the State Council of China).

55 Ibid., para. 4.2.

56 Zhongwa Hezuo Kuaijishi Shiwusuo Bentuhua Zhuanzhi Fangan (中外合作会计师事务所本土化转制方案) [Scheme for the Localization Restructuring of Chinese–Foreign Cooperative Accounting Firms] (jointly issued by Ministry of Finance, the State Administration for Industry and Commerce, the Ministry of Commerce, the State Administration of Foreign Exchange and the China Securities Regulatory Commission, on May 2, 2012).

57 Ibid., art. 11.

and administrative regulations.[58] The laws and regulations can be broadly divided into two categories: one is about general issues of data privacy and protection, and the other is about regulatory issues specific to audit documents.

It begins with the general provision for the confidentiality duty of accountants under the Certified Public Accountants (CPA) Law of the PRC.[59] Then, for the audits of listed companies, there are specific prohibitions on transferring documents outside of the PRC. For instance, the 2019 Securities Law of the PRC requires that a securities service institution (such as audit firms, law firms, etc.) shall properly store clients' documents, verification materials and working papers, and may not divulge such materials.[60] Furthermore, it is expressly stipulated that overseas securities regulators (such as the SEC) are prohibited from conducting any investigation, evidence collection or other activities within China.[61]

Central to the dispute to access audit documents is the law regarding state secrets. The State Secrets Law of 2010 prohibits transferring overseas any document or item containing state secrets.[62] Yet, there are a lot of ambiguities both in the scope of state secrets and the procedure of determining what constitutes state secrets.[63] The law covers a wide range

58 For a detailed discussion of the early history of the regulatory regime, see Robin Hui Huang, "'Yiguoliangzhi' Beijing Xia de Xianggang yu Neidi Zhengquan Jianguan Hezuo Tizhi: Lishi Yanbian yu Qianjing Zhanwang" ("一国两制"背景下的香港与内地证券监管合作体制：历史演变与前景展望) [The Prospect and Evolution of the Securities Regulatory Cooperative Regime between Hong Kong and Mainland China under the "One Country, Two Systems" Arrangement] (2017) 5 *Bijiaofa Yanjiu* 比较法研究 *[Journal of Comparative Law]* 12, 19–21.

59 Zhonghua Renmin Gongheguo Zhuce Kuaijishi Fa (中华人民共和国注册会计师法) [Certified Public Accountants Law of the People's Republic of China] (passed October 31, 1993 effective January 1, 1994, as amended August 31, 2014), art. 19.

60 Zhonghua Renmin Gongheguo Zhengquan Fa (中华人民共和国证券法) [Securities Law of the People's Republic of China] (passed December 29, 1998 as amended August 28, 2004, October 27, 2005, June 29, 2013, August 31, 2014 and December 28, 2019), art. 162.

61 Securities Law of the PRC, art. 177.

62 Zhonghua Renmin Gongheguo Baoshou Guojia Mimi Fa (中华人民共和国保守国家秘密法) [Law of the People's Republic of China on Guarding State Secrets] (passed September 5, 1988 as amended April 29, 2010) (State Secrets Law), art. 26.

63 Robin Hui Huang, "'Yiguoliangzhi' Beijing Xia de Xianggang yu Neidi Zhengquan Jianguan Hezuo Tizhi: Lishi Yanbian yu Qianjing Zhanwang" ("一国两制"背景下的香港与内地证券监管合作体制：历史演变与前景展望) [The Prospect and Evolution of the Securities Regulatory Cooperative Regime between Hong Kong and Mainland China under the "One Country, Two Systems" Arrangement] (2017) 5 *Bijiaofa Yanjiu* 比较法研究 *[Journal of Comparative Law]* 12.

of matters that may be classified as state secrets, with one of the categories termed "secret matters in national economic and social development."[64] The range of information put forward as state secrets by litigants in the Chinese court is wide, including information on payment of social security fees, financial information of a company that contracted with the military, transaction information of properties and lands relating to certain government agencies or any documents that were created as an extension of classified documents.[65] While not all cases were substantiated by the court, the range of information that may be suggested as state secrets signifies a considerable litigation risk faced by auditing firms if they were to hand over their audit information to an overseas party.

The State Secrets Law also contains a catchall provision, where even if a piece of information is not marked as classified, but one "should have known" that it concerned national security and national interest, one would still be prosecuted in the same manner.[66] Another extra complexity in the law is that during the court process, the information that constitutes a state secret, and of what secretive level, could be identified at that time by state secrets protection agencies of various levels.[67] This means that a piece of information can be retroactively recognized as a state secret after a matter goes to court. It may not be conclusively ascertained whether a particular document contains state secrets until consultation with relevant government agencies. If prosecuted, the punishment set down in the law is harsh. According to a judicial

[64] State Secrets Law, art. 9.

[65] Liumou Yu Nanjingshi Renliziyuan he Shehuibaozhangju Xingzhengfuyi Xingzheng Panjueshu (刘某与南京市人力资源和社会保障局行政复议行政判决书) (Railway Transport Court of Nanjing 2019) CLI.C.78071137 (Lawinfochina); Zhaomou、Wangmou yu Jiangsu Baoke Dianzi Youxiangongsi Mingshi Panjueshu (赵某、王某与江苏宝科电子有限公司民事判决书) (Court of Yangzhou Economic Zone 2018) CLI.C.94846250 (Lawinfochina); Huangmou deng yu Ziranziyuanbu deng Xingxigongkai Xingzheng Pangjushu (黄某等与自然资源部等信息公开行政判决书) (Court of Tongzhou District 2019) CLI.C.97328639 (Lawinfochina); Shanghai Jingxie Gongsi Su Jiandeshi Qita Xinxi Gongkaian (上海经协公司诉建德市政府其他信息公开案) (Higher People's Court of Zhejiang 2012) CLI.C.861533 (Lawinfochina).

[66] State Secrets Law, art. 5.

[67] Zuigao Renmin Fayuan Guanyu Shenli Wei Jingwai Qiequ, Citan, Shoumai, Feifa Tigong Guojia Mimi, Qingbao Anjian Juti Yingyong Falv Ruogan Wenti De Jieshi (最高人民法院关于审理为境外窃取、刺探、收买、非法提供国家秘密、情报案件具体应用法律若干问题的解释) [Supreme People's Court Interpretation of Certain Issues Regarding Application of State Secrets Law] (issued by the Supreme People's Court, effective on January 22, 2001), art. 7.

interpretation issued by the Supreme People's Court, any person who unlawfully supplies "three or more items" of state secrets is to be regarded as acting in an "especially serious circumstance" and shall be sentenced to imprisonment of a minimum of ten years.[68]

A relevant regulation that, for the first time, directly links the handling of audit documents to the State Secret Law is the so-called Circular 29 issued by the CSRC in 2009.[69] Circular 29 states that "any archives, including working papers, which are created in China . . . in the course of any overseas issuance and listing of the securities shall be stored in China . . ."[70] and that if the documents involve any state secrets, national security or other substantial interests of the state, then prior approval is required from competent authorities for them to be transferred out of the PRC. Circular 29 also requires that where overseas securities regulators conduct an inspection of companies listed overseas and may involve documents that contain state secrets, the listed company or the auditing firm should report to the competent authorities to obtain approval.[71]

In 2023, Circular 29 was superseded by the Provisions on Strengthening Confidentiality and Archives Administration of Overseas Securities Offering and Listing by Domestic Companies ("Circular 44").[72] The general principle of Circular 44 is that data collected and generated by securities companies and securities service providers, such as underwriters, accounting firms and law firms, in connection with an "overseas listing" should (1) be stored in the PRC; and (2) not be transferred outside of the PRC without prior approval. In the context of services provided by accounting firms in connection with "an overseas listing," it

68 Ibid,, art. 3.

69 Guanyu Jiaqiang Zaijingwai Faxing Zhengquan Yu Shangshi Xiangguan Baomi He Dangan Guanli Gongzuo (关于加强在境外发行证券与上市相关保密和档案管理工作) [The Regulation on Strengthening Confidentiality and Archives Administration Relating to Overseas Issuance and Listing of Securities] (issued by the CSRC on October 20, 2009).

70 Circular 29, art. 6.

71 Circular 29, art. 8.

72 Guangyu Jiaqiang Jingnei Qiye Jingwai Faxing Zhengquan he Shangshi Xiangguan Baomi he DangAn Guanli Gongzuo de Guiding (关于加强境内企业境外发行证券和上市相关保密和档案管理工作的规定) [The Provisions on Strengthening Confidentiality and Archives Administration of Overseas Securities Offering and Listing by Domestic Companies] (Announcement [2023] No. 44) (jointly issued by the CSRC, the Ministry of Finance, the National Administration of State Secrets Protection and the National Archives Administration of China on February 24, 2023 effective from March 31, 2023).

is important to highlight that this covers not just services in connection with an initial public offering itself but also audit services in connection with annual audits of those overseas listed entities. Under Circular 44, securities service providers (including audit firms) should keep safe the documents and materials obtained from domestic companies that may contain state secrets or leakage of which may be detrimental to national security or the public interest, in compliance with national regulations on confidentiality and archives administration; and any disclosure of these documents and materials to other relevant entities or individuals would need to comply with the relevant procedures stipulated by applicable national regulations protecting state secrets.[73] Further, it states, specifically in relation to audit working papers, that "working papers produced in the Chinese mainland by securities companies and securities service providers in the process of undertaking businesses related to overseas offering and listing by domestic companies shall be retained in the Chinese mainland. Where such documents need to be transferred or transmitted outside the Chinese mainland, relevant approval procedures stipulated by national regulations shall be followed."[74]

There are also other administrative rules on the specific issue of access to auditing documents, particularly for foreign entities. For instance, in 2015, the Ministry of Finance (MOF) issued an important rule to regulate the way that accounting firms provide auditing services for the overseas listing of Chinese enterprises ("Interim Provisions on Auditing Services").[75] This rule referred to Circular 29 to reiterate the prohibition on transferring audit documents overseas without prior approval.[76] As we will discuss later, the MOF issued the issue in quick response to a case where a Hong Kong court ordered an accounting firm to produce audit documents generated in its work for the overseas listing of a Chinese company.[77] In 2016, the MOF and the National Archives Administration of China (NAAC) issued another important rule to regulate the management of auditing archives of accounting

[73] Ibid., art. 6.

[74] Ibid., art. 9.

[75] Kuaijishi Shiwusuo Congshi Zhongguo Neidi Qiye Jingwai Shangshi Shenji Yewu Zanxing Guiding (会计师事务所从事中国内地企业境外上市审计业务暂行规定) [Interim Provisions on Accounting Firms' Provision of Auditing Services for the Overseas Listing of Enterprises in Chinese Mainland] (issued by the Ministry of Finance on May 26, 2015, effective from July 1, 2015).

[76] Ibid., art. 12.

[77] *See* Section 7.4.

firms ("Auditing Archives Measures").[78] In April 2024, the MOF and the Cyberspace Administration of China (CAC) jointly issued a rule on the issue of data security for accounting firms that carry out audit services for certain clients, including Chinese companies seeking overseas listings.[79]

Two important points can be made here. First, Circulars 29 and 44 share a similar if not the same objective, namely, safeguarding confidential information and state secrets that are generated in the process of overseas listings of Chinese companies. Technically, Circular 44 seems to reinforce the regulatory standards of Circular 29 and can be seen as "regulation version 2.0" of the subject matter. Second, access to audit documents, particularly audit working papers, seems to have received special attention from Chinese authorities, as evidenced by the specific laws and regulations noted above. Indeed, China has also issued a large number of laws and regulations for the general issues of data protection and privacy, including the three basic laws in this area (the Cybersecurity Law, the Data Security Law, the Personal Information Protection Law)[80] and a string of rules issued by relevant regulators such as the CAC.[81] Further, apart from the laws and rules discussed

[78] Kuaijishi Shiwusuo Shenji DangAn Guanli Banfa (会计师事务所审计档案管理办法) [The Measures for the Management of Auditing Archives of Accounting Firms] (issued January 11, 2016 and effective July 1, 2016).

[79] Kuaijishi Shiwusuo Shuju Anquan Guanli Zanxing Banfa (会计师事务所数据安全管理暂行办法) [Interim Measures for the Administration of Data Security for Accounting Firms] (issued by the Ministry of Finance and the Cyberspace Administration of China on April 15, 2024, effective October 1, 2024), art. 2.

[80] Zhonghua Renming Gongheguo Wangluo Anquan Fa (中华人民共和国网络安全法) [Cybersecurity Law of the People's Republic of China] (promulgated November 7, 2016 and effective June 1, 2017); Zhonghua Renming Gongheguo Shuju Anquan Fa (中华人民共和国数据安全法) [Data Security Law of the People's Republic of China] (promulgated June 10, 2021 and effective September 1, 2021); Zhonghua Renming Gongheguo Geren Xinxi Baohu Fa (中华人民共和国个人信息保护法) [Personal Information Protection Law of the People's Republic of China] (promulgated August 20, 2021 and effective November 1, 2021).

[81] Shuju Chujing Anquan Pinggu Banfa (数据出境安全评估办法) [Measures for the Security Assessment of Outbound Data Transfer] issued by the Cyberspace Administration of China on July 7, 2022 effective September 1, 2022; Geren Xinxi Chujing Biaozhun Hetong Banfa (个人信息出境标准合同办法) [Measures for the Standard Contract for the Outbound Transfer of Personal Information] (issued by the Cyberspace Administration of China on February 22, 2023 effective June 1, 2023); Cujing he Guifan Shuju Kuajing Liudong Guiding (促进和规范数据跨境流动规定) [Measures on the Promotion and Standardization of Cross-border Data Flow], issued by the Cyberspace Administration of China on March 22, 2024 with immediate effect).

above, there are many other relevant laws and regulations which may come into play in the area.[82]

As the scope of information that could constitute sensitive data and state secrets is wide, complex and ambiguous, along with many sectors in China having a strong presence of the state, the possibility for a company's information to involve state secrets is not neglectable. Audit firms, therefore, need to obtain the necessary approval to minimize legal risks that may arise therein. In practice, however, there is a sizeable administrative hurdle for accounting firms to obtain the necessary clearance from "competent authorities." To start with, it is not clear which governmental departments are the competent authorities. The issue can be exacerbated by the fact that depending on the specific information concerned, multiple competent authorities may be involved, such as the MOFCOM, the CSRC, the CAC, the NAAC, the Ministry of State Security and the National Administration of State Secrets Protection. An extra layer of complicity may arise as to how those authorities may coordinate among themselves. Further, there are unanswered questions as to how to make an application for approval from the competent authorities and how the application will be assessed by the competent authorities.

7.4 US–China Disputes over Access to Chinese Audit Documents

7.4.1 SEC's Action against Audit Firms Working for Chinese Companies

Since the 2010s, the PCAOB has started to step up its efforts to regulate audit firms working for China Concept Stocks as a series of auditing scandals involving them began to emerge. For instance, Ernst & Young (EY) was named in two class-action lawsuits over its audit work for a

[82] For example, Zhonghua Renmin Gongheguo Dang'an Fa (中华人民共和国档案法) [Archives Law of the People's Republic of China] (promulgated by the Standing Comm. National People's Congress, September 5, 1987, revised June 20, 2020 effective January 1, 2021); Kuaiji Dang'an Guanli Banfa (会计档案管理办法) [Accounting Archives Management Measures] (promulgated by the Ministry of Finance, Bureau of State Archives, December 11, 2015 effective January 1, 2016); Zhonghua Renmin Gongheguo Baoshou Guojia Mimi Fa Shishi Tiaoli (中华人民共和国保守国家秘密法实施条例) [The Regulation on the Implementation of the Law of the People's Republic of China on Guarding State Secrets] (promulgated by the State Council, January 17, 2014 effective March 1, 2014).

Chinese company named Sino-Forest,[83] and KPMG was implicated in the audit scandal of China Forestry.[84] In response, the PCAOB became more serious about the regulation of the relevant auditing firms, which had never been inspected at that time. As mentioned above, under the Sarbanes–Oxley Act, a foreign accounting firm registered with the PCAOB is also obliged to produce its audit working papers for inspection upon request.[85] However, when the PCAOB requested the production of audit working papers, the relevant auditing firms all refused to comply on the grounds that doing so would violate Chinese law, particularly the law governing the protection of state secrets, which may restrict foreign access to relevant financial records and documents relating to Chinese companies.[86]

The refusal of the audit firms to provide relevant documents seriously affected the ability of the US regulators to regulate US-listed Chinese companies, and thus, a series of lawsuits were brought over access to audit documents. For instance, the first such lawsuit targeted Deloitte's member firm in China, which was the auditor for Longtop Financial Technologies.[87] Deloitte signed off six audit reports until a research firm in 2011 alleged that the company's profit margin was unreasonably high. Deloitte then discovered that the company forged the entire bank balance and resigned from acting as the auditor. Deloitte refused the PCAOB's request to provide relevant documentation, arguing that if it were to comply with the PCAOB's request, it would violate Chinese law and attract legal liabilities in China.[88] The SEC then sued Deloitte in May 2012. In the same year, the SEC requested relevant documents from all the other Big Four firms in its investigations into nine more US-listed Chinese companies. The accounting firms all refused to cooperate,

[83] Sino-Forest was a private company and not a SOE, despite its name containing "Sino." In its books it had forests that did not actually exist. Eventually Sino-Forest would bankrupt in 2012, with damages awarded to plaintiff in civil lawsuits for up to US$7.6 billion. Ernst & Young would have to pay up to $125 million to settle.

[84] China Forestry had its turnover overstated by at least 92 percent, and its plantation assets overstated by at least 87 percent. China Forestry was a private company incorporated in the Cayman Islands.

[85] Section 106(1) of the Sarbanes–Oxley Act, 15 USC 7216.

[86] *See* Section 7.2.5.

[87] Longtop was a Chinese software company and was listed on the NYSE from 2007. Its profit and bank balance were forged with some help from the bank's staff. The fraud was only discovered following repeated challenges and a physical visit to the bank by Deloitte.

[88] Paul Gillis, *The Big Four and the Development of the Accounting Profession in China* (Emerald, 2014), p. 150.

following Deloitte's argument in their own challenges. Then, all the Big Four audit firms were sued for their refusal to provide audit documents.[89]

While these cases were ongoing, the US and China regulators had been in constant negotiation. The CSRC had long criticized the attempts of the US side to "take actions on a unilateral basis," expressing its strong opposition to any inspection of Chinese firms without a bilateral agreement.[90] The CSRC stated that the oversight of Chinese accounting firms should fully rely upon the work of the CSRC itself and that cross-border inspection must abide by the principles of respecting mutual sovereignty and cooperating as equals. In July 2012, the SEC Chairman Mary Schapiro visited Beijing to discuss the problem of access to audit documents.[91] Then, in November 2012, a CSRC delegation went to Washington for further discussion. It was not until shortly before the scheduled public hearing of the Longtop case that the CSRC informed the SEC that relevant audit documents would be allowed to be handed over.[92] In the end, all the accounting firms provided relevant documents to the SEC.

7.4.2 The 2013 China–US MoU

The aforementioned lawsuits and the eventual settlement set the stage for the US and Chinese regulators to come to an agreement. Following heated disputes and court actions, authorities in the US and China reached an agreement in 2013. This was the result of a long series of high-level bilateral discussions during a period of an overall good relationship between the US and China.[93] The issue was raised as early as 2009 when the two countries established a bilateral Strategic and Economic Dialogue during the Obama and Hu Jintao presidency.[94] In the first Dialogue meeting, the issue of PCAOB's inspections was already included on the agenda. Then, in the third round of meetings

89 SEC Order dated December 3, 2012, www.sec.gov/litigation/admin/2012/34-68335.pdf.

90 CSRC, "Re: Public Company Accounting Oversight Board; Notice of Filing of Proposed Amendment to Board Rules Relating to Inspection" (File No. PCAOB-2008-06), May 15, 2009, www.sec.gov/comments/pcaob-2008-06/pcaob200806-1.pdf.

91 "Chinese vice premier meets SEC chair," *Xinhua*, July 3, 2012.

92 Sarah N. Lynch, "SEC, Deloitte resolve dispute over Longtop audit work papers," *Reuters*, January 28, 2014.

93 Paul Gillis, *The Big Four and the Development of the Accounting Profession in China* (Emerald, 2014), p. 157.

94 Ibid.

in 2011, both sides agreed to make joint efforts to accelerate reaching an agreement on the issue.[95] In the same year, the Sino-US Symposium on Audit Oversight was held in Beijing.

On May 10, 2013 the PCAOB, the CSRC and the Chinese Ministry of Finance signed a Memorandum of Understanding on Enforcement Cooperation ("2013 China–US MoU"), establishing a cooperative framework for requesting and receiving assistance from each other in carrying out audit investigation and enforcement, including obtaining audit documents.[96] The MoU defines investigations narrowly as inquiries into the actions or omissions of audit firms only, excluding investigations on issues arising from the companies they audited.[97] The assistance for such investigations is to provide "information and documents held in the files of the Requested Party," and such information may include "documents sufficient to identify all audit review or other professional services" and "audit working papers or other documents held by audit firms."[98] The PCAOB can request financial records in relation to an investigation and may pass those documents to the SEC after Chinese regulators approve that doing so does not violate their local laws. Information received through the MOU may be used solely to conduct administrative enforcement proceedings, including the imposition of sanctions on audit firms based in China.[99] Under the MoU, a request can be denied on the following four grounds: (1) where providing documents is contrary to a party's domestic law; (2) where the request is not made in accordance with the MoU; (3) where the request is against public interest or essential national interest; and (4) where the request lacks sufficient specificity.[100]

The signing of the MoU seems to represent a significant breakthrough in the cooperation of securities regulators between the two jurisdictions. However, many difficulties were encountered in the actual implementation of the MoU to provide access to relevant audit documents.[101] As of

[95] Department of State, "Remarks at the Opening Session of the U.S.–China Strategic and Economic Dialogue," May 9, 2011, 2009-2017.state.gov/secretary/20092013clinton/rm/2011/05/162881.htm.

[96] PCAOB, "PCAOB Enters into Enforcement Cooperation Agreement with Chinese Regulators," May 24, 2013, pcaobus.org/News/Releases/Pages/05202013_ChinaMOU.aspx.

[97] 2013 China–US MoU, art. II.

[98] Ibid.

[99] 2013 China–US MoU, art. VII.

[100] 2013 China–US MoU, art. III (b)(i)–(iv).

[101] PCAOB, "PCAOB Enters into Enforcement Cooperation Agreement with Chinese Regulators," pcaobus.org/News/Releases/Pages/05202013_ChinaMOU.aspx.

April 2020, there were only four instances of the CSRC assisting the US regulators with access, as well as one joint inspection of an audit firm.[102] It is unclear how many requests were made over the same period, but the PCAOB was clearly dissatisfied. In a subsequent policy paper, the PCAOB stated that it could not gain access to the audit work and practices of accounting firms in the PRC, as well as audit firms in Hong Kong whose clients had operations in the PRC.[103] According to the PCAOB, "since signing the MoU in 2013, Chinese cooperation has not been sufficient for the PCAOB to obtain timely access to relevant documents and testimony necessary to carry out our mission . . . nor have consultations undertaken through the MoU resulted in improvements."[104] Later rounds of dialogue also failed to further advance the cooperation.[105]

7.4.3 The 2020 HFCAA

In 2020, there occurred again some serious accounting frauds perpetuated by Chinese companies, with one of the most high-profile cases involving a company named Luckin Coffee. Since early 2020, rumors in the market had pointed to the company's fraudulent financials. When the company announced that its internal audit confirmed the allegations of fabricated sales figures, US investors suffered a great loss as its share value dived in one day from US$26.2 to US$6.4.[106] The auditor of Luckin Coffee was an associated firm of EY in China. Although the firm was registered with the PCAOB, it was not subject to inspection.

[102] CSRC, Press Release, April 27, 2020, www.csrc.gov.cn/pub/newsite/zjhxwfb/xwdd/202004/t20200427_374552.html.

[103] SEC, "Statement on the Vital Role of Audit Quality and Regulatory Access to Audit and Other Information Internationally: Discussion of Current Information Access Challenges with Respect to U.S.-listed Companies with Significant Operations in China," December 7, 2018, www.sec.gov/news/public-statement/statement-vital-role-audit-quality-and-regulatory-access-audit-and-other.

[104] PCAOB, "PCAOB Enters into Enforcement Cooperation Agreement with Chinese Regulators," pcaobus.org/news-events/news-releases/news-release-detail/pcaob-enters-into-enforcement-cooperation-agreement-with-chinese-regulators_430.

[105] Department of the Treasury, "2016 U.S.–China Strategic and Economic Dialogue Joint U.S.–China Fact Sheet – Economic Track," July 6, 2016, www.treasury.gov/press-center/press-releases/Pages/jl0484.aspx.

[106] Jennifer Wang, "China's Luckin Coffee Founder Is $1 Billion Poorer after Company Announces Fraud Investigation," *Forbes*, April 30, 2020.

The SEC quickly made a strongly worded statement criticizing the quality of financial information and disclosure from China.[107] In response, the CSRC stated in a press conference that they have always taken a positive attitude toward cross-border regulatory cooperation and supported overseas securities regulators to investigate and deal with financial frauds committed by overseas-listed Chinese companies.[108] The CSRC cited an example of cooperation in 2016–2017, where the Chinese regulator assisted its US counterpart in the inspection of three US-listed companies. Yet, in any case, by early 2020 the US regulators became more disappointed with the implementation of the 2013 MoU.

The US Senate followed up on the issue and passed the "Holding Foreign Companies Accountable Act" (HFCAA) by unanimous consent in May 2020.[109] On December 2, 2020 the US House of Representatives also passed the HFCAA. Again, this passing was in a unanimous vote, which indicates bipartisan support and broad consensus on a hardline stance against Chinese companies. Finally, on December 18, 2020 then US President Donald Trump signed the bill into a formal law. In brief, if a US-listed foreign company retains an audit firm located in a foreign jurisdiction which cannot be inspected or investigated by the PCAOB because of a position taken by one or more authorities in the foreign jurisdiction, it will be subject to heightened regulation of disclosure, and if the situation persists for three years, it will be forcibly delisted. While the HFCAA purports to apply to all US-listed foreign companies, the HFCAA mainly targets companies from the PRC.

7.5 Hong Kong–Mainland China Disputes over Access to Audit Documents

7.5.1 A Case Study: SFC v. Ernest Young

Similar to the litigations initiated by the SEC over the issue concerning access to audit working papers of Chinese companies, Hong Kong's

107 SEC, "Emerging Market Investments Entail Significant Disclosure, Financial Reporting and Other Risks; Remedies are Limited," April 21, 2020, www.sec.gov/news/public-statement/emerging-market-investments-disclosure-reporting.

108 CSRC, press release dated April 27, 2020, www.csrc.gov.cn/pub/newsite/zjhxwfb/xwdd/202004/t20200427_374552.html.

109 S.945 – 116th Congress (2019–2020). The US House of Representatives also included provisions, which are substantially similar to the Holding Foreign Companies Accountable Act, in the National Defence Authorization Act.

securities regulator, namely, the Securities and Futures Commission (SFC), started to bring suit against audit firms in the early 2010s, with a prominent example being the case of *SFC v. Ernst & Young*[110]. There, when investigating an allegedly fraudulent listing application of a Chinese company, the SFC asked for access to relevant audit documents from Ernest & Young (EY), which provided audit services for the company.

Under Section 183 of Hong Kong's Securities and Futures Ordinance (SFO),[111] when the SFC has reasonable cause to believe that a party has in their possession any record or document which contains information relevant to an investigation, the party must produce to the SFC any specified record or document. Furthermore, failure to comply with this section without reasonable excuse constitutes a criminal offense.[112]

In 2010, while the listing application of the company was still pending, EY resigned as its reporting accountant and auditor, stating that there were inconsistencies in its accounting records. The SFC followed up with an investigation and asked EY to provide relevant audit documents. However, EY refused on the grounds that doing so may violate relevant PRC laws, such as the law on state secrets. Then, the SFC brought a case under s183 of the SFO in 2012, seeking an order to compel EY to produce the audit documents. In the trial, EY made two main arguments: first, it does not own the documents as they belong to its mainland joint venture firm, namely, Ernst & Young Hua Ming LLP (EYHM); second, the documents contained state secrets and thus were not allowed to be produced in Hong Kong. The court responded to the first argument, holding that EY had an enforceable right under the PRC laws of agency of entrustment to require the documents from EYHM. As for the second argument, the court held that EY failed to prove the existence of state secrets in the requested documents and that if prior approval was required under the PRC law before the audit working papers could be sent to Hong Kong, EY had the burden to make the necessary applications for approval. It is worth noting that this case is special in the sense that somehow, EY had the documents already transferred to its Hong Kong office from the beginning. Hence, it became extremely difficult for EY to sustain its argument that the

110 HCMP 1818/2012.

111 Cap. 571 Securities and Futures Ordinance (SFO).

112 SFO, s. 184(1)(a).

documents contained state secrets and thus could not be transferred out of the PRC without prior approval. In the end, the court ordered EY to produce the relevant audit documents.[113]

7.5.2 *Audit Oversight in Hong Kong and Its Cooperation with the Mainland*

The *SFC v. Ernst & Young* case alarmed the Chinese regulators, as it may have the effect of empowering a foreign court to determine the existence of state secrets in audit documents and then ordering the production of them overseas. This means that the Chinese regulators could be sidestepped in the process. Hence, on May 26, 2015, the Ministry of Finance issued a regulation to reiterate that the relevant documents involved in the auditing of Chinese companies, particularly audit working papers, may be subject to claims of state secrecy under Chinese law and cannot be taken out of the PRC without the relevant authorities' prior consent.[114] This regulation was issued just several days after the EY case, showing a sense of emergency and urgency to plug the possible loophole on the part of Chinese regulators.

Further, the PRC regulators started to have serious negotiations with Hong Kong regulators about regulatory cooperation on the issue. In May 2019, the PRC Ministry of Finance and Hong Kong's newly reformed Financial Reporting Council (FRC) signed a Memorandum of Understanding (2019 FRC MoU).[115] Under the MoU, as Hong Kong's auditor regulator, the FRC can request the Ministry of Finance for assistance to obtain access to audit working papers stored on the Mainland in order to conduct its inspections and investigations in relation to the accounting profession. Two months later, a similar agreement for securities regulatory cooperation was signed by the SFC, the CSRC and the Ministry of Finance (2019 SFC MoU).[116]

[113] *SFC v. Ernst & Young* (a firm), HCMP 1818/2012.

[114] Kuaijishi Shiwusuo Congshi Zhongguo Neidi Qiye Jingwai Shangshi Shenji Yewu Zanxing Guiding (会计师事务所从事中国内地企业境外上市审计业务暂行规定) [Interim Provisions on Accounting Firms' Provision of Auditing Services for the Overseas Listing of Enterprises in Chinese Mainland] (issued by the Ministry of Finance on May 26, 2015 effective from July 1, 2015).

[115] FRC, "Press Release," May 22, 2019, www.afrc.org.hk/media/qmkcj0t5/2019__press-release_final_eng.pdf.

[116] Tri-partite Memorandum of Understanding on Cooperation, signed by the SFC, the CSRC and the Ministry of Finance on July 3, 2019.

Under this agreement, the SFC can also request the Mainland authorities to assist in providing audit working papers in the course of its securities enforcement action.

The FRC was established in December 2006 and came into full operation in 2007, but at that time its mandate was limited to initiating investigations after noncompliance or misconduct had occurred. It was not until October 2019 that the FRC was transformed into the full-fledged independent auditor regulator of Hong Kong, vested with direct powers of inspection, investigation, recognition of overseas auditors of listed entities and discipline concerning auditors of public interest entities. It also has the responsibility of overseeing the performance of the Hong Kong Institute of Certified Public Accountants (HKICPA) of their functions in relation to auditors of listed entities, including registration, setting of standards on professional ethics, auditing and assurance and setting of continuing professional development requirements. On October 22, 2021 the FRC was transformed again to become the independent regulatory body for the accounting profession, renamed the Accounting and Financial Reporting Council (AFRC), with expanded statutory functions, including, among others: the issuance of practising certificates to certified public accountants; inspection, investigation and discipline work of the accounting profession; overseeing the HKICPA's performance in its various statutory professional functions; and conducting policy research and publishing guidelines to promote the quality of financial reporting, audit quality and corporate governance.[117]

7.6 Recent Developments and Future Prospects

7.6.1 The 2022 China–US Agreement

As the HFCAA has a three-year transitional period clause, it was everyone's guess at the time of its passage as to how the regulators of China and the US would move and what might happen eventually.[118] The HFCAA requires the PCAOB to determine whether it is unable to inspect or investigate completely registered public accounting firms located in a foreign jurisdiction because of a position taken by one or more

[117] The official website of the Accounting and Financial Reporting Council, www.afrc.org.hk/.

[118] Robin Hui Huang, "The US–China Audit Oversight Dispute: Causes, Solutions, and Implications for Hong Kong" (2021) 54(1) *The International Lawyer* 151.

authorities in the foreign jurisdiction. After the PCAOB makes such a determination, the SEC should take certain actions with respect to covered issuers that retain firms subject to a PCAOB determination. Specifically, a listed company needs to disclose whether it employs a foreign accounting firm that the PCAOB is unable to inspect or investigate and also report to the SEC whether it is owned or controlled by a foreign government.[119] Based on the above information, the SEC may decide to put such companies on a list as Identified Issuers, and if a company remains on the list for three years, the SEC can prohibit its stock from trading on any national exchange or over-the-counter markets.[120] Further, in its annual reports, the company is required to disclose some additional information, such as the percentage of shares owned by government entities, whether government entities have a controlling financial interest, the names of each official of the Chinese Communist Party who is a member of the board and whether the articles of incorporation contain any charter of the Chinese Communist Party.[121]

On December 16, 2021 the PCAOB released a determination report that it was unable to inspect or investigate completely registered public accounting firms headquartered in the PRC and Hong Kong.[122] Then, on March 8, 2022 the SEC followed up to set out the first list of five issuers identified under the HFCAA.[123] This puts more pressure on Chinese companies and regulators as it suggested a real possibility of delisting from the US. Indeed, many US-listed Chinese companies, such as Alibaba and NetEase, pursued secondary listings in Hong Kong as a hedge against the potential risk of delisting from the US.

Since then, the situation has started to change significantly, with increasing signs of Chinese regulators seeking ways to defuse the crisis. On August 26, 2022 the CSRC and Ministry of Finance signed a Statement of Protocol (SOP) Agreement with the PCAOB regarding cooperation in the oversight of PCAOB-registered public accounting firms in China and Hong Kong ("2022 China–US Agreement"). The announcement of the agreement seemed to have reassured the financial world: the Nasdaq Golden Dragon China Index surged on the news, and so did the Hong Kong Hang Seng Index. However, the full content of the

[119] Holding Foreign Companies Accountable Act, Section 2(2).
[120] Holding Foreign Companies Accountable Act, Section 2(3).
[121] Holding Foreign Companies Accountable Act, Article 3.
[122] PCAOB, "2021 HFCAA Determination Report" (December 16, 2021).
[123] https://www.sec.gov/hfcaa.

agreement has never been publicly disclosed. The CSRC, the SEC and the PCAOB just made their own press statements separately, and the Ministry of Finance, despite being a signatory, did not even make a statement.

According to the statements, there are three common points about the regulatory cooperation matter: First, all the regulators agree to be cooperative to solve the issue of access to audit documents of US-listed Chinese companies; second, there is a need to protect sensitive data that may be contained in audit documents; third, audit documents will be transported to Hong Kong for inspection by the US regulators.

In September 2022, PCAOB inspectors went to Hong Kong to inspect relevant audit documents with the assistance of Chinese regulators, and on December 15, 2022 the PCAOB announced that it secured unprecedented, complete access to inspect and investigate audit firms located in the PRC.[124] The PCAOB selected two firms for inspection, namely, KPMG Huazhen LLP in mainland China and PricewaterhouseCoopers in Hong Kong, and inspected a total of eight engagements between the two firms, including large state-owned enterprises and issuers in sensitive industries.[125] On November 23, 2023 for the first time, the PCAOB imposed substantial penalties on China-based audit firms.[126]

Overall, this is a historic and positive development. It shows that the 2022 China–US Agreement could be and has been implemented effectively. For the first time in history, the two sides have successfully solved the audit oversight dispute. As a result, the specter of delisting faced by US-listed Chinese companies has been dispelled, at least for the time being.

7.6.2 Lingering Concerns

As discussed above, the 2022 China–US Agreement has achieved some initial success, representing a win-win situation for both the US and China. Specifically, the two sides have managed to strike a deal and to date, the agreement has been running reasonably well. However, as the

124 PCAOB, "2022 HCFAA Determination Report" (December 15, 2022).

125 PCAOB, "PCAOB Secures Complete Access to Inspect, Investigate Chinese Firms for First Time in History," December 15, 2022 available at https://pcaobus.org/news-events/news-releases/news-release-detail/pcaob-secures-complete-access-to-inspect-investigate-chinese-firms-for-first-time-in-history.

126 See PCAOB, FACT SHEET: PCAOB Imposes Historic Sanctions on China-Based Audit Firms (November 30, 2023).

SEC noted about the signing of the agreement, "while this is a step forward, it is just a step in a process."[127] Indeed, although the 2022 China–US Agreement has had a good beginning, it does not mean that it will solve the audit oversight dispute once and for all.

The regulatory agreements, including the 2022 China–US Agreement and the two Mainland–HK MoUs, have limited utility in the sense that they can only solve the issue of access to audit documents of Chinese companies in enforcement actions taken by foreign regulators and not private litigation brought by investors or other private parties. Under the regulatory agreements, foreign regulators can directly gain access to audit documents with the assistance of the Chinese authorities, and apparently, private parties do not have this green lane and will face far more difficulties in dealing with the issue. This presents an important issue, as it can arise in many types of private litigation, including securities litigation for misstatement, shareholder disputes over corporate governance and dividend payment and corporate insolvency cases.

Further, there are concerns over whether and how the 2022 China–US Agreement will continue to function smoothly, particularly due to the changing China–US relations. It seems that from the very beginning, the two sides have had some important disagreements about the 2022 Agreement. This is intuitively reflected in the fact that the 2022 China–US Agreement has never been made public. Further, there are noticeable differences between the statements made by the two sides in relation to the nature and content of the agreement.[128] Indeed, some commentators have argued that China might renege on the 2022 China–US Agreement and PCAOB inspections might not continue indefinitely.[129]

It is clear that geopolitics represents an important source of divergence between the interests of the Chinese authorities and their US counterparts, potentially undermining their cooperation and coordination under the 2022 China–US Agreement. However, this does not necessarily mean that the agreement will definitely be torn up in the foreseeable future.

[127] SEC, "Fact Sheet: PCAOB Agreement with China on Audit Inspections and Investigations," available at https://www.sec.gov/files/china-sop-fact-sheet.pdf.

[128] For a more detailed discussion, see Robin Hui Huang, "The Past and Future of the China–US Audit Oversight Dispute: A Geopolitical Perspective," *Journal of International Economic Law* (forthcoming).

[129] Jesse M. Fried and Tamar Groswald Ozery, "The Holding Foreign Companies Accountable (HFCA) Act: A Critique" (2024) 14(2) *Harvard Business Law Review* 257, 271.

Although the contradictions and potential conflicts between China and the US are increasingly manifest, the relationship is more likely to be characterized by a state of "fight but not break."[130] In this arrangement, while both sides maintain a posture of strategic competition, they simultaneously avert an all-out confrontation by sustaining a delicate balance and engaging in necessary cooperation. Hence, despite geopolitical tension between China and the US, there will remain opportunities for them to maintain regulatory cooperation on audits of US-listed Chinese companies.

[130] For a more detailed discussion, see Robin Hui Huang, "The Past and Future of the China–US Audit Oversight Dispute: A Geopolitical Perspective," *Journal of International Economic Law* (forthcoming).

8

Regulating Securities Misconduct across Borders

The Mainland China–Hong Kong Case

8.1 Introduction

With the increasing globalization of the capital markets, there has been a heightened need for effective regulatory cooperation between jurisdictions to facilitate detecting, investigating and prosecuting cross-border securities misconduct such as insider trading and market manipulation.[1] A useful case study in this regard is the regulatory cooperation between Mainland China and Hong Kong, owing to the accelerated process of market integration and transformation.[2]

As investment and securities trading persists across the globe, it follows that market misconduct activities that disrupt normal market order and reap illegal profits from law-abiding investors, garnering the likes of insider trading, price rigging, market manipulation and so on will increase as well.[3] While the internationalization of securities listing and trading enhances the liquidity of global markets and provides investors with wider choices, cross-border market misconduct activities simultaneously pose new and increasingly complex challenges for securities regulators around the world.[4] There is a wide consensus among governments, regulators and international bodies that enforcement and collaboration are needed to regulate cross-border securities law contravention.[5] Inadequate regulation of such cross-border misconduct will give rise to

[1] US Securities and Exchange Commission, "International Cooperation in Securities Law Enforcement" (2004), pp. 1, 2, www.sec.gov/about/offices/oia/oia_enforce/intercoop.pdf.

[2] *See* Section 8.3.1.

[3] *See generally* Donald C. Langevoort, "Cross-Border Insider Trading" (2001) 8 *Journal of Financial Crime* 254.

[4] Ibid., pp. 255–261.

[5] Frank O. Kwabi, Agyenim Boateng and Emmanuel Adegbite, "International Equity Portfolio Investment and Enforcement of Insider Trading Laws: A Cross-Country Analysis" (2019) 53 *Review of Quantitative Finance and Accounting*, 327, 327–338.

market performance issues.[6] Studies show that effective cooperation between jurisdictions is greatly beneficial to the integrity and performance of their markets, resulting in higher earning quality,[7] as well as an increased volume of international portfolio investment for these jurisdictions.[8] On the flip side, a hindrance to cross-border securities law enforcement brings adverse effects on market integrity and performance – it is shown that abnormal trading in shares is especially abundant before the announcement of cross-border corporate deals, as compared to domestic ones.[9]

The internationalization of securities listing and trading takes place on both the issuer's side and the investor's side.[10] Securities issuers increasingly seek to raise capital internationally, as companies themselves are now able to list, cross-list or have their shares otherwise traded in foreign markets.[11] Investors diversify their portfolios across geographic regions by trading and holding an increasing proportion of securities issued by foreign companies.[12] The marketplaces for trading these instruments can then also easily traverse borders as the advancement of market linkages and information technology greatly facilitate trading.[13] In terms of trading volume, cross-border listing and trading activities are especially prominent for the highly globalized US market, trading within the EU as well as trading between the Mainland China and Hong Kong markets.[14]

6 Roger Silvers, "The Effects of Cross-Border Cooperation on Disclosure Enforcement, Earnings Attributes, and Transparency" (2021) 40 *Journal of Accounting and Public Policy*, 1, 3.

7 Ibid., p. 2.

8 *See* Kwabi, above note 5, pp. 328–329.

9 Guo Lixiong and Zhang Xueting, "Do Cross-Border Mergers and Acquisitions Import More Aggressive Insider Trading?" (2019) (unpublished draft), 4, papers.ssrn.com/sol3/papers.cfm?abstract_id=3281446.

10 *See generally* US Securities and Exchange Commission, "Internalization," www.sec.gov/answers/internalization.htm.

11 Narjess Boubakri, Jean-Claude Cosset and Anis Samet, "International Cross-Listings and Subsequent Security-Market Choices: Evidence from ADRs" (2013) 48 *Financial Review*, 311, 312.

12 Srinidhi Kanuri and Robert W. McLeod, "Does It Pay to Diversify? U.S. vs. International ETFs" (2015) 24 *Financial Services Review*, 249, 250.

13 Timofey Chuykov, Arda Emirdag, Brett Matlosz and Ailin Sarybekova, "How Has the Development of Financial Technology Affected Trading?" (2024) *OxJournal*, www.oxjournal.org/how-has-the-development-of-financial-technology-affected-trading/#:~:text=AI%20algorithms%20can%20process%20huge,securities%20at%20the%20optimal%20times.

14 Qian Sun, Wilson H. S. Tong and Xin Zhang, "How Cross-Listings from an Emerging Economy Affect the Host Market?" (2013) 37 *Journal of Banking & Finance*, 2229, 2229.

The defining characteristic of a cross-border market misconduct case is that there can be multiple nationalities at different loci.[15] First, it is the nationality of the offender, that is, the inside trader or tipper.[16] Second, it is the nationality of the issuer whose shares are involved.[17] Third, it is the location of the information, where evidence on the case can be obtained, as well as the location of the market where the trading occurred.[18] Also relevant may be the nationality of investors who were harmed by the acts of market misconduct.[19] In an increasingly fragmented global investment market, these locations can often be found across multiple national borders.[20] For instance, a case may involve a US national obtaining insider information about a potential M&A deal of a Chinese company, which then acts on the information by trading on the Hong Kong market.[21] This was the case in the *Tiger Asia* case which was prosecuted by regulators both in the USA and in Hong Kong.[22]

Different regulators from various jurisdictions face a similar problem of dealing with the enforcement of securities law against cross-border personnel and activities.[23] While market offenders travel around the world in their respective trades, market misconduct behavior is similar and persistent across time, asset type and jurisdictions.[24] A core set of behaviors recurs over time and can be grouped into seven broad clusters.[25] This includes insider dealing, price manipulation, circular trading, misrepresentation, influencing reference price, collusion in information disclosure and improper order handling.[26] These patterns of market

[15] *See* Langevoort, above note 3, p. 255.
[16] Ibid.
[17] Ibid.
[18] Ibid.
[19] Ibid., pp. 255–257.
[20] Ibid.
[21] *See generally* David Smyth, "*SFC v. Tiger Asia* – 'Round 2'" (2013) *Hong Kong Lawyer*, www.hk-lawyer.org/content/sfc-v-tiger-asia-%E2%80%93-round-2.
[22] Ibid.
[23] Roger Silvers, "Cross-Border Cooperation between Securities Regulators" (2020) 69 *Journal of Accounting and Economics*, 1, 2, www.sciencedirect.com/science/article/pii/S0165410120300033.
[24] *See* FICC Markets Standard Board, "Behavioural Cluster Analysis: Misconduct Pattern in Financial Markets" (2018) 1, 3, fmsb.com/wp-content/uploads/2018/10/FMSB_BCA_Book_Final.pdf. In order to review the behavioral pattern and cause of market misconduct, the FICC Markets Standards Board recently concluded an extensive horizontal study on 390 cases of market misconduct across twenty-six jurisdictions.
[25] Ibid., pp. 10–11.
[26] Ibid., p. 10.

misconduct tend to adapt to new technologies and market structures and are now increasingly prevalent across borders.[27]

Bringing about effective cross-border market regulation – and thereby curbing disruption of market misconduct – is therefore a highly important policy issue for securities regulators and investors around the world.[28] This chapter will analyze the issues in law enforcement related to cross-border market misconduct, as well as the legal and institutional arrangement of a cross-border regulatory regime. In particular, as a case study, this chapter will focus on the experience of China's and Hong Kong's markets in dealing with the issues faced by both jurisdictions when conducting cross-border investigations and enforcement. Regulatory cooperation between the two jurisdictions is highly relevant in the analysis of global responses to cross-border market misconduct activities for several reasons. First, there has been an increasingly strong connection between the two markets in the form of Stock-Connect and Bond-Connect programs.[29] Second, as a specific example of in-depth mutual regulatory assistance, the two jurisdictions have entered into a series of bilateral agreements on regulatory cooperation.[30] Third, the experience of Chinese and Hong Kong regulators also bears significance on further market linkages that will be seen increasingly across major markets, for instance, the Shanghai–London Stock Connect which was launched in 2019.[31]

8.2 Background

8.2.1 Regulatory Goals

An effective regulatory regime would have two limbs. First, there would be enforcement in actual cases of misconduct, including case detection,

[27] Ibid., p. 9.

[28] *See generally* International Organization of Securities Commissions (IOSCO), "Credible Deterrence in the Enforcement of Securities Regulation," www.iosco.org/library/pubdocs/pdf/IOSCOPD758.pdf.

[29] *See generally* Connect Hub, HKEX, www.hkex.com.hk/Mutual-Market/Connect-Hub?sc_lang=en#:~:text=Bond%20Connect%20launched%20in%202017,the%20end%20of%20the%20year.

[30] Technical Committee of the International Organization of Securities Commissions (IOSCO), "Principles Regarding Cross-Border Supervisory Cooperation: Final Report," May 2010, p. 7, www.iosco.org/library/pubdocs/pdf/IOSCOPD322.pdf.

[31] London Stock Exchange, "London Stock Exchange Group Today Welcomes Huatai Securities," June 18, 2019, *News and Insights*, p. 1, www.londonstockexchange.com/discover/news-and-insights/london-stock-exchange-group-today-welcomes-huatai-securities.

investigation and prosecution.[32] Yet, while exposing market misconduct and pursuing subsequent prosecution is the most visible work of a securities regulator, they only form part of successful market regulation.[33] Second, the enforcement can create and maintain a credible level of deterrence against market misconduct.[34] The overarching policy goal is to create a market environment with certainty and credibility in enforcement, and thus deter potential offenders from committing offenses.[35] When damage is prevented *ex ante*, the policy objectives of maintaining market order and protecting investors' interests are best served.[36] This deterrence requires successful sanctioning of any detected cases in the first limb, but it goes beyond case numbers and prosecution of specific acts.[37] Proper consideration is required on a range of other legal and institutional factors. It relies on the infrastructure and public knowledge of a sufficient cross-border enforcement and cooperation regime, in order to signal to potential offenders the risk and consequence of them being exposed and prosecuted.[38]

If there is oversight of cross-border market misconduct, either in terms of enforcement or in terms of deterrence, a regulatory gap is left open.[39] Potential offenders may then try to engage in regulatory arbitrage – that is, evading regulations of one place, and seeking illegal gains by picking locations where such a gap exists.[40] The International Organization of Securities Commissions (IOSCO) has identified a number of factors that contribute to credible deterrence including legal certainty, the capacity to obtain information, agency cooperation, resolute enforcement action, strong sanction, public understanding and good regulatory governance.[41] All these factors tie into the expectations of the persons who are contemplating committing market misconduct, such as whether the misconduct is expected to be detected, whether that detection would be rigorously investigated, prosecuted against and punished for and how severe the

[32] Masamichi Yamamoto, "International Enforcement Cooperation in Cases of Cross-Border Market Misconduct in view of Regulatory Gaps and Overlaps" (2020) 21 *Oregon Review of International Law* 39, 45–62.

[33] Ibid., p. 44.

[34] Ibid., p. 62.

[35] *See generally* IOSCO, above note 28, p. 6.

[36] Ibid.

[37] Ibid., p. 7.

[38] *See* Yamamoto, above note 32, p. 73.

[39] Ibid., p. 46.

[40] Ibid., p. 47.

[41] IOSCO, above note 28, pp. 10–53.

consequences would be.[42] In a cross-border setting, these factors have added layers of complexity because more than one regulator and jurisdiction are involved.[43]

8.2.2 *Detection and Investigation*

As connections between markets multiply and investors are presented with a wider choice of asset classes and trading channels, the need for cross-border market surveillance strongly increases.[44] Detection must be done in a timely manner in order to facilitate enforcement.[45] Access to multiple streams of information in domestic and foreign exchanges, ideally in real-time, can enhance regulators' abilities to detect abnormal trading, especially in a cross-border setting.[46] A good example of cross-border surveillance is the Transaction Reporting Exchange Mechanism (TREM), set up by the European Securities and Markets Authority to facilitate the aggregation and exchange of transaction data among regulators within the EU.[47] The public is also an important source of information leading to case detection, and a well-rounded detection regime will include effective mechanisms to receive tips and complaints from the public.[48]

While the trend of cross-border trading and the attendant market misconduct is on the rise, the number of prosecuted cross-border cases nonetheless represents a small fraction of all market misconduct prosecutions.[49] There can be several explanations for this lesser number of reported cases: first, there are smaller portions of offenders taking the

[42] Ibid., pp. 8–9.
[43] Ibid., p. 45.
[44] *See generally* Emerging Markets Committee of the International Organization of Securities Commissions (IOSCO), "Approaches to Market Surveillance in Emerging Markets" (2009), www.iosco.org/library/pubdocs/pdf/ioscopd313.pdf.
[45] *See* Jane Austin, *Insider Trading and Market Manipulation: Investigating and Prosecuting across Borders* (Edward Elgar, 2017), p. 148.
[46] IOSCO, above note 28, p. 45.
[47] *See* Council Directive 2014/65 of May 15, 2014 on markets in financial instruments and amending Directive 2002/92/EC and Directive 2011/61/EU, OJ 2014 No. L173, June 12, 2014, p. 157.
[48] International Organization of Securities Commissions (IOSCO), "Credible Deterrence in the Enforcement of Securities Regulation," p. 17, www.iosco.org/library/pubdocs/pdf/IOSCOPD758.pdf.
[49] Gail. E. Henderson, "Insider Trading and Market Manipulation: Investigating and Prosecuting across Borders" (Book Review) (2018) 34 *Banking & Finance Law Review*, 71, 72.

international route; second, the complexity of cross-border market misconduct may have caused a lower detection rate; third, the difficulties involved in successfully prosecuting a cross-border case dissuade regulators to pursue such cases, even if abnormal trading is detected.[50] If the latter two explanations are reasonably true to some extent, much has yet to be done to improve case detection and enforcement cooperation between regulators.[51]

When an incident of cross-border market misconduct is detected, there is next the problem of ascertaining the case jurisdiction of that offense.[52] A national regulator can potentially claim jurisdiction if any of the locations or nationalities involved falls within its jurisdiction.[53] As a result, multiple regulators may be able to claim jurisdiction in a case involving two or more locations.[54] As such, securities regulators often have regulatory interests that extend beyond their borders.[55] As the benefit of spending regulatory resources becomes diffused across multiple jurisdictions, there can potentially be a "free rider" problem for regulators.[56] Most often regulators take the approach of looking at the site of the transaction and will intervene only if the trade occurred within its border.[57] This is sensible as this serves to maintain the integrity of a regulator's domestic market.[58] But problems arise as trading can now easily occur in foreign locations, and the listing of shares to a particular stock exchange is becoming less of the geographical attribute of a company.[59] In practice, it is often not a straightforward exercise to determine which regulator should enforce its jurisdiction when multiple jurisdictions are involved simultaneously.[60] This gives rise to uncertainty, or worse, lack of oversight on cross-border market misconduct.[61] The decision to exercise jurisdiction carries further relevance than the prosecution process faced by the defendant.[62] For instance, depending on the venue

[50] Ibid., pp. 71–77.
[51] Ibid., p. 77.
[52] *See* Langevoort, above note 3, p. 255.
[53] Ibid.
[54] Ibid., pp. 254–263.
[55] Ibid., pp. 254–255.
[56] Ibid., p. 259.
[57] Ibid., p. 258.
[58] Ibid.
[59] Ibid., pp. 254–263.
[60] Ibid.
[61] Ibid., p. 255.
[62] Ibid.

of the trial, there may be different treatment for people who are eligible for civil rights of action pertaining to a particular case.[63]

Another relevant consideration is the issue of giving credit to the performance of a regulator.[64] Caseload numbers and the handling of high-profile cases are important for a regulator's goodwill and record.[65] These numbers can be used as a form of assessment metric for the agency's budgeting and as performance indicators for its personnel.[66] Meanwhile, landmark cases are also often important when promulgating a regulator's policy objective and determination within its local market.[67] Although it cannot be ascertained, these factors may inherently affect a regulator's decision to take up or give up a case. The decision process is internal to the regulators and is not visible, except for the result. Thus, it is unclear if regulators discuss among themselves or have a set of underlying rules.

8.2.3 *The Role of IOSCO*

A regulator who claims jurisdiction over a case then needs to initiate an investigation to obtain the information it requires for a successful prosecution.[68] In a cross-border case, the information may be located in overseas jurisdictions, and international assistance from overseas regulators is needed.[69] The primary form of international enforcement cooperation is through the Multilateral Memorandum of Understanding Concerning Consultation and Cooperation and the Exchange of Information (MMoU), which was created in 2002 by the IOSCO and has since become the global standard for enforcement cooperation with 124 signatories.[70] The MMoU gives regulators around the world a mutual understanding in terms of how they should consult, cooperate and exchange information with one another for securities enforcement purposes.[71] As evidence of its effectiveness, joining the MMoU regime

63 Ibid.
64 *See* Yamamoto, above note 32, p. 64.
65 *See* Langevoort, above note 3, pp. 256–260.
66 Ibid.
67 Ibid., p. 256.
68 *See generally* IOSCO, "Investigating and Prosecuting Market Manipulation," May 2000, www.iosco.org/library/pubdocs/pdf/IOSCOPD103.pdf.
69 Ibid.
70 *See* Silvers, above note 6, pp. 5–6.
71 Ibid., pp. 2–5.

has been associated with increased cross-border enforcement and enhanced market liquidity.[72]

But the MMoU has its limitations.[73] To the extent that global standards are not translated into legislation in a local jurisdiction, the MMoU is not binding on a particular regulator as it is not based on enforceable treaty obligations.[74] Further, it specifically omits cooperation in instances of criminal prosecution, as such inclusion would complicate the adoption of the multilateral agreement itself.[75] The MMoU has the feature of being task-oriented and does not emphasize wider enforcement cooperation.[76] The agreement is designed to facilitate specific evidence collection and exchange, which may not be useful for sharing less tangible information, such as strategic information concerning market situations.[77] Also, it is only concerned with information sharing, but not joint investigation and enforcement.[78]

The IOSCO's MMoU has brought about a level of global convergence in regulations adopting similar types of market governance.[79] Yet, there often exist discrepancies and conflicts with respect to the substantive law regulating market misconduct, the procedure of prosecution, the legal liabilities to be imposed, the severity of sanction, the availability of remedies and so on.[80] These discrepancies make cross-border enforcement far more complicated and less effective as compared to purely domestic enforcement.[81] To reduce the effect of regulatory arbitrage, the scope and definition of market misconduct offenses need to be refined and harmonized between jurisdictions.[82] Some of these differences can be harmonized by implementing rule changes, but it is not without difficulties due to the distinct legal traditions in jurisdictions around the world.[83]

72 Ibid., pp. 3–5.
73 *See* IOSCO, above note 30, p. 15.
74 Ibid., p. 46.
75 Ibid., p. 51.
76 Ibid., p. 5.
77 Ibid., p. 35.
78 Ibid., p. 47.
79 David Bach and Abraham Newman, "Transgovernmental Networks and Domestic Policy Convergence: Evidence from Insider Trading Regulation" (2010) 64 *International Organization*, 505–506.
80 Ibid., p. 522.
81 Ibid., pp. 509–510.
82 Ibid., pp. 506–507.
83 Ibid., p. 508.

Over the years, the IOSCO has taken a more active and expanded role in setting standards and recommendations for cross-border regulatory cooperation, especially following the 2008 global financial crisis.[84] The original MMoU was revised in 2012, followed by the setting up of a task force in 2013.[85] Since 2018, an enhanced version of the MMoU has been put in place, which is neatly named the "Enhanced Memorandum of Understanding Concerning Consultation and Cooperation and the Exchange of Information" (EMMoU).[86] The EMMoU addresses some weaknesses of the original agreement.[87] For example, while criminal prosecution is precluded from the scope of the MMoU, the new memorandum specifically includes criminal prosecution under one of the permissible uses of the information exchanged.[88]

The EMMoU provides its signatories with greater power in enforcement assistance, including enabling them to share audit work papers, compel physical attendance for testimony, freeze assets, obtain phone and internet service records and more.[89] According to the IOSCO, all signatories to the original MMoU are expected to eventually migrate to the EMMoU.[90] Yet, this increased scope and power in the EMMoU also makes it harder to be widely adopted – at present only ten countries' regulators have signed the agreement.[91] Short of wide adoption of the EMMoU, and with the benefit of maintaining market integrity and fostering cooperation, the IOSCO encourages member regulators to enter into bilateral agreements with deeper commitments to share oversight responsibility and take joint enforcement action.[92]

[84] *See generally* Austin, above note 45.

[85] *See* International Organization of Securities Commissions (IOSCO), "2013 List of Non-signatories to the MMoU," p. 2, www.iosco.org/v2/about/?subSection=mmou&subSection1=2013_list.

[86] *See* International Organization of Securities Commissions (IOSCO), "Text of the EEMoU" (2016), p. 1, www.iosco.org/about/pdf/Text-of-the-EMMoU.pdf.

[87] Ibid.

[88] Ibid., pp. 3–4.

[89] *See* International Organization of Securities Commissions (IOSCO), "Enhanced MMoU Flyer," p. 1, www.iosco.org/about/pdf/Enhanced%20MMoU%20Flyer.pdf.

[90] *See generally* International Organization of Securities Commissions (IOSCO), "EMMoU Concerning Consultation and Cooperation and the Exchange of Information," www.iosco.org/v2/about/?subSection=emmou.

[91] *See generally* International Organization of Securities Commissions (IOSCO), "Signatories to EMMoU," www.iosco.org/v2/about/?subSection=emmou&subSection1=signatories. Hong Kong is one of the signatories as an independent jurisdiction within China, while Mainland China itself is not a signatory.

[92] *See* Bach and Newman, above note 79, p. 519.

Adding to the omission of criminal proceedings from the MMoU, in many jurisdictions, there are also protections from criminal prosecution.[93] This protection in itself also results in wide discrepancies between different jurisdictions. For example, in the United Kingdom, it is explicitly provided that information obtained by securities regulators under certain circumstances cannot be used in criminal proceedings.[94] Australia further provides for self-incrimination privileges to be extended to civil penalty proceedings.[95] Even where information is nevertheless exchanged between regulators, such protection might render the criminal prosecution unsuccessful in court if it is challenged.[96] Such protection from criminal prosecution may impede the sharing of evidence and information among regulators, especially for regulators in places where there is less distinction between a civil or criminal sanction.[97]

8.3 The Mainland–Hong-Kong Case: Market and Regulation

8.3.1 Market Integration and Transformation

The securities markets in Hong Kong and Mainland China are deeply intertwined and increasingly integrated.[98] On the Hong Kong Stock Exchange (HKEX), the term "Mainland China enterprises" is used to refer to companies listed in Hong Kong but based in Mainland China.[99] Depending on the domicile and the type of controlling shareholders, Mainland China enterprises can be divided into three categories, including H-shares, Red Chip companies and Mainland private enterprises.[100] First,

[93] *See Text of the EEMoU*, at art. 2(1)(g)(ii).

[94] Financial Services and Markets Act 2000, c. 8, § 174(2) (UK), www.legislation.gov.uk/ukpga/2000/8/section/174.

[95] Uniform Evidence Act 1995, § 128 (Wales), classic.austlii.edu.au/au/legis/nsw/consol_act/ea199580/s128.html.

[96] *See*, for example, *United States v. Allen*, 864 F.3d 63 (2d Cir. 2017).

[97] Masamichi Yamamoto, "Information Exchange between Securities Regulators in Parallel Proceedings against Cross-border Market Misconduct" (2019) 28 *Michigan State International Law Review*, 33, 111–112.

[98] *See generally* Robin Hui Huang, "'Yiguoliangzhi' Beijingxia De Xianggang Yu Neidi Zhengquan Jianguan Hezuo Tizhi: Lishiyanbian Yu Qianjingzhanwang" ("一国两制"背景下的香港与内地证券监管合作体制：历史演变与前景展望) [The Prospect and Evolution of the Securities Regulatory Cooperative Regime between Hong Kong and Mainland China under the "One Country, Two Systems" Arrangement] (2017) 5 *Bijiaofa Yanjiu (比较法研究) [Journal of Comparative Law]*, 12.

[99] Ibid., p. 13.

[100] *See* Robin Hui Huang, *Securities and Capital Markets Law in China* (Oxford University Press, 2014), pp. 10–12.

H-shares are shares issued by a company domiciled/registered in the Mainland, the par value of which is denominated in Renminbi, and which are subscribed for and traded in Hong Kong dollars.[101] Second, "Red-chip Stock" companies are companies domiciled/registered in an overseas jurisdiction such as the Cayman Islands, which have more than 50 percent of total business incomes from Mainland China and which meet one of the following two criteria about controlling shareholders: (1) the company has at least 30 percent shareholding held in aggregate directly by Mainland China entities, and/or through companies which are controlled by Mainland China entities; or (2) the company has below 30 percent but 20 percent or above shareholding held in aggregate directly by Mainland China entities, and/or through companies which are controlled by Mainland China entities, and there is a strong influential presence, on a judgmental basis, on the company's board of directors.[102] Importantly, "Mainland China entities" are narrowly defined to mean state-owned organizations and entities controlled by China's state, provincial or municipal authorities. If the controlling shareholders of the companies are Chinese private entities which are outside the scope of "Mainland China entities," they would fall into the third category of "Mainland private enterprises,"[103] which is sometimes referred to as "P-chip Stock" in practice. In more recent years, Red-chip Companies and Mainland China entities have been collectively referred to as Non-H-share Mainland enterprises.[104]

The above three types of Mainland China enterprises collectively make up the majority of the Hong Kong securities market, in terms of the number of listed companies, the amount of market capitalization and the value of turnover.[105] As of the end of November 2024, there were a total of 2,624 companies listed on the HKEX, 56.1 percent of which (1,472) were Mainland China enterprises, including 358 H-shares and 1,114 Non-H-share Mainland enterprises.[106] Further, Mainland China

[101] HK Exchanges & Clearing Ltd. (HKEX), *HKEX Factbook 2019*, p. 247, www.hkex.com.hk/-/media/HKEX-Market/Market-Data/Statistics/Consolidated-Reports/HKEX-Fact-Book/HKEX-Fact-Book-2019/FB_2019.pdf.

[102] HKEX, *Fact Book 2021*, p. 353, www.hkex.com.hk/-/media/HKEX-market/market-data/statistics/consolidated-reports/HKEX-fact-book/HKEX-fact-book-2021/fb_2021.pdf.

[103] Ibid., p. 1.

[104] HKEX, *Overview of the listed market*, www.hkex.com.hk/Global/Exchange/FAQ/Getting-Started/Overview-of-the-listed-market?sc_lang=en#collapse-3.

[105] *See* HKEX, above note 101, p. 1.

[106] HKEX, *HKEX Monthly Market Highlight*, www.hkex.com.hk/Market-Data/Statistics/Consolidated-Reports/HKEX-Monthly-Market-Highlights?sc_lang=en&select={B874D9B6-E6B3-44CC-AC36-B566A6363CCD}.

enterprises accounted for 79.3 percent of the total market capitalization and 90.55 percent of the total turnover value.[107]

The risk factor of cross-border market misconduct is thus compounded by the fact that the business operations of Chinese companies listed in Hong Kong occur mostly within the Mainland, and not Hong Kong where the stock exchange and the government regulator are situated.[108] It is also worth noting that the same company can cross-list both in the Mainland market as A-Share and in the Hong Kong market as H-Share, a model which has become increasingly common in recent years, particularly for large companies.[109]

Next, there are newly added avenues of cross-border securities trading.[110] The launch of the Shanghai–Hong Kong Stock Connect in November 2014 provided new channels through which investors in China and Hong Kong can directly trade stocks listed on each other's market.[111] This has been followed a similar stock connect program between Shenzhen and Hong Kong, namely the Shenzhen–Hong Kong Stock Connect in 2016.[112] These Connect programs provide a two-way traffic of securities trading.[113] In the northbound direction, a Hong Kong-based investor can place an order in Hong Kong through a Hong Kong intermediary.[114] The order will be placed onto the Mainland markets and will be denominated and transacted in Renminbi.[115] In a southbound direction, a Mainland-based investor will order through either a Shanghai or Shenzhen intermediary, with the trade being denominated in Hong Kong dollars and cleared in Renminbi.[116] The Connect programs provide an easier and more direct way for overseas investors to access the Chinese capital market, as compared with the

107 Ibid.

108 *See* Huang, above note 98, p. 32.

109 Ibid.

110 HKEX, "HKEX Connect Story" (October 2022), pp. 1, 2, www.hkex.com.hk/-/media/HKEX-Market/Mutual-Market/Stock-Connect/Reference-Materials/Resources/HKEX-Connect-Story.pdf.

111 Ibid.

112 Ibid.

113 HKEX, "HKEX Information Book for Investors Stock Connect," September 23, 2024, pp. 1, 6, www.hkex.com.hk/-/media/HKEX-Market/Mutual-Market/Stock-Connect/Getting-Started/Information-Booklet-and-FAQ/Information-Book-for-Investors/Investor_Book_En.pdf.

114 Ibid., p. 5.

115 Ibid.

116 Ibid., p. 15.

traditional route of the Qualified Foreign Institutional Investor (QFII) and Renminbi Qualified Foreign Institutional Investor (RQFII) programs.[117]

> Since the launch of the [above two Stock Connect programs], total Stock Connect turnover has continued to hit new records, with strong participation from both Mainland and international investors ... As of September 2024, [which marked the Stock Connect's 10th anniversary,] the market capitalisation of securities portfolios held in Hong Kong by Mainland Chinese investors through Stock Connect was over HK$3.3 trillion, more than 200 times that at the end of 2014.[118]

Northbound and Southbound Stock Connect average daily turnover (ADT) reached RMB 136.3 billion and HK$43.9 billion respectively in the first ten months of 2024, accounting for 7.3 percent and 17.2 percent of the total turnover of the Mainland China and Hong Kong markets.[119] Besides enhancing liquidity, the implementation of the Shanghai–Hong Kong Connect brings about beneficial changes in corporate behavior, such as Chinese companies improving information disclosure to attract foreign investment.[120] Due to the success of the Stock Connect programs, the Connect programme has gradually "expanded into other asset classes, [such as the Mainland–Hong Kong] Bond Connect in 2017, ETF Connect in 2022, and Swap Connect in 2023."[121]

The deep linkage of issuers and investors across the two markets gives rise to particularly heightened stakes for cooperation between regulators.[122] The closeness of social connection and personnel travel between the two places further adds to the risk factors of any cross-border market misconduct behavior.[123] In summary, there are ample cross-border

[117] HKEX, above note 110, p. 2. The QFII program, launched since 2002, is the mechanism through which licensed foreign institutional investors can invest in the onshore A-shares market of China. The RQFII program was launched in 2011 and is a similar institutional investment mechanism that is relevant for offshore Renminbi flowing back into the Chinese market. The QFIIs and RQFIIs are subject to various requirements in relation to qualification, registration and the scope of investment. Before September 10, 2019 there were also quota limitations on the volume of investment.

[118] HKEX, "HKEX Celebrates 10th Anniversary of Connect Programme," November 2024, www.hkex.com.hk/News/News-Release/2024/241118news?sc_lang=en.

[119] Ibid.

[120] Aaron S. Yoon, "Credibility of Disclosures in Weak Enforcement Institutions: Evidence from Shanghai–Hong Kong Connect" (2018) working paper, available at zicklin.baruch.cuny.edu/wp-content/uploads/sites/10/2018/02/AaronYoon_Paper.pdf.

[121] *See* HKEX, above note 118.

[122] *See* Yamamoto, above note 97, p. 36.

[123] Ibid., p. 91.

activities and linkages in terms of capital investment, listing, corporate operation, cross-market trading and personnel movement.[124] Possible scenarios of cross-border market misconduct are as follows: The perpetrator may be a person situated in either Hong Kong or Mainland China; the company whose shares are involved may be listed on the Hong Kong market, the Chinese market or both; for insider trading, the information involved may be generated in either jurisdiction; for other types of market misconduct, the location involved may be in either jurisdiction or both, for instance, when a group of traders simultaneously manipulate a particular share listed on both markets.[125] The new channel of cross-border trade through the Stock Connect is also a potential avenue for market misconduct.[126] The convenience of trading shares listed on one market through another allows for a potential offender to pick which jurisdiction to trade in.[127] This has already been seen in the first insider dealing case through the Stock Connect in 2016.[128]

8.3.2 *Framework for Regulatory Cooperation*

Despite the handover of Hong Kong to China, the cooperation and coordination between regulators of the two jurisdictions should not be taken for granted.[129] The Chinese government constantly encourages the rapid development of its own onshore financial markets, particularly that of Shanghai and Shenzhen.[130] Due to the uniqueness of Hong Kong's history and economic system, Hong Kong's economy has been viewed as independent and "foreign" to China since the handover.[131] Hong Kong is a city with a special self-governing status within China due to its British colonial background.[132] Its market economy has developed over a long period of time, and its common law system has much in parallel with English Law.[133] When Hong Kong was handed over to China in 1997, the city already had a world-leading securities market, whereas the Chinese market was still in its early

[124] *See* Yoon, above note 120, p. 4.
[125] *See* Yamamoto, above note 97, p. 92.
[126] *See* Huang, above note 98, pp. 30–31.
[127] Ibid., p. 31.
[128] *See generally* Announcement No. 20 (promulgated by China Securities Regulatory Commission, October 26, 2017), The People's Bank of China (December 17, 2017) at 1.
[129] *See* Huang, above note 98, p. 12.
[130] Ibid., p. 29.
[131] Ibid., p. 16.
[132] Ibid.
[133] Ibid., p. 18.

transitioning stage at the time.[134] All of Hong Kong's economic infrastructure and common law system have been kept in place constitutionally since then, under the "One Country-Two Systems" arrangement.[135]

This constitutional arrangement effectively puts the Chinese securities market and the Hong Kong securities market under two legal jurisdictions and the oversight of two securities regulators.[136] The former is regulated by the China Securities Regulatory Commission (CSRC), and the latter by Hong Kong's Securities and Futures Commission (SFC).[137] The SFC participates in international regulatory conventions, such as the IOSCO, in its own right.[138] Therefore, it is more appropriate to view the regulators and exchange owners of the two sides as approaching each other on the basis of dealing as foreign entities, with both cooperation and competition in mind.[139]

Regarding agreements relevant to investigatory assistance, there are four sets of regulatory agreements in place between China and Hong Kong.[140] The mutual trust between the Chinese and Hong Kong governments and their respective regulators enables deep cooperation initiatives.[141] This stems from the long-term relationship between the CSRC and SFC, with the SFC being one of the earliest overseas regulators to connect with CSRC and assist with the development of the Chinese stock market.[142] The first agreement is the Memorandum of Regulatory Cooperation entered early in 1993.[143] Then, in 2003, Hong Kong became a signatory of the IOSCO MMoU, with China also joining in 2007.[144]

[134] Ibid., p. 16.

[135] Basic Law of the Hong Kong Special Administrative Region (Xianggang Jiben Fa), arts. 1–11, www.basiclaw.gov.hk/en/basiclaw/chapter1.html.

[136] *See* Huang, above note 98, p. 14.

[137] Ibid., p. 14.

[138] Ibid., p. 15.

[139] Ibid., p. 13.

[140] *See generally* Securities and Futures Commission (SFC), "Cooperative Arrangements with the CSRC and Mainland Exchanges" (March 10, 2020), www.sfc.hk/en/About-the-SFC/Regulatory-collaboration/Mainland-China/Cooperative-arrangements-with-the-CSRC-and-Mainland-exchanges.

[141] *See* Huang, above note 98, p. 22.

[142] Ibid., p. 13.

[143] *See generally* Securities and Futures Commission (SFC), "CSRC Regulatory Cooperation Memorandum," June 1993, www.sfc.hk/en/About-the-SFC/Regulatory-collaboration/Mainland-China/Cooperative-arrangements-with-the-CSRC-and-Mainland-exchanges.

[144] International Organization of Securities Commissions (IOSCO), "Signatories to Appendix A and Appendix B List," 1, 4–6, www.iosco.org/v2/about/?subSection=mmou&subSection1=signatories.

Because both Hong Kong and China are signatories, the MMoU is one of the legal avenues for information exchange between regulators of the two sides.[145] The third agreement is the Strengthening of Regulatory and Enforcement Cooperation under the Mutual Access between the Mainland and Hong Kong Stock Markets ("Stock Connect MoU") signed in 2016 after the opening of the Shanghai–Hong Kong Stock Connect.[146] The fourth one is especially related to enforcement cooperation concerning stock futures.[147]

The Stock Connect MoU created an in-depth cooperative framework between the CSRC and SFC, which is especially needed because of its extra market linkage.[148] There is first the element of active notification, where the regulators would immediately alert one another about any information concerning suspected misconduct in the other's market once it is identified.[149] Each would notify the other when it commences a cross-border investigation.[150] There is then the element of assistance.[151] The parties agree to actively facilitate, provide support and coordinate with each other in respect of the use of information.[152] Furthermore, there is a mechanism for joint investigation.[153] In respect of significant and urgent cases relating to both jurisdictions or where the suspects, witnesses or evidence are located in both jurisdictions, the two agencies might commence a joint investigation.[154] Once a joint investigation is commenced, a joint task force will be set up to tackle the case.[155] Hence, under the various agreements and the Stock Connect MoU, there are two routes to investigate cross-border market misconduct, namely, seeking investigatory assistance or conducting a joint investigation.[156] The existence of this joint investigation

[145] *See generally* CSRC and SFC, "Memorandum of Understanding between the CSRC and the SFC on Strengthening of Regulation and Enforcement Cooperation under the Mutual Access between the Mainland and Hong Kong Stock Market," February 17, 2023 [hereinafter Stock Connect MoU], www.sfc.hk/-/media/EN/files/ER/MOU/ENF_MOU_Eng_2016.pdf.

[146] Ibid.

[147] *See generally* SFC, above note 140.

[148] Stock Connect MoU, art. 1.

[149] Ibid., art. 3.

[150] Ibid., art. 4.

[151] Ibid., art. 5.

[152] Ibid., art. 7.

[153] Ibid., art. 6.

[154] Stock Connect MoU, art. 6.

[155] Ibid.

[156] *See generally* ibid. at arts. 6–7.

mechanism takes the potential cooperation between the two much deeper than the scope of the IOSCO MMoU.[157]

8.3.3 Two Case Studies

Two landmark cases, one civil and one criminal, serve to illustrate cross-border market misconduct and the ensuing enforcement actions between Mainland China and Hong Kong.[158]

The first cross-border administrative sanction case involving Stock Connect was pursued two years after its launch and led to a constitutional challenge against the use of cross-border evidence.[159] In the *Tang Hanbo* case, the CSRC investigated Tang, a Chinese private speculator, for alleged price manipulation in the Mainland market in relation to shares of Zhejiang China Commodities City Group and four other companies.[160] Tang and his two accomplices manipulated stock prices over a period of around five months by self-dealing and artificially creating a fake price hike.[161] Tang and his team deliberately came to Hong Kong to evade regulatory oversight.[162] The trades were executed through the northbound Stock Connect channel using multiple accounts, while Tang and his team stayed at Tang's Hong Kong home and hotels.[163] Concurrently, the Hong Kong SFC commenced an investigation into Tang concerning the disclosure of interest issues.[164] The SFC obtained a search warrant before a magistrate court in respect of the disclosure matter and seized several notebook computers.[165] On the next day of the search, the CSRC also took simultaneous action on the Mainland to control Tang's accomplices.[166] The computers were later transferred to CSRC for their market manipulation investigation.[167]

157 Ibid.
158 *See generally Tang Hanbo v. The Securities and Futures Commission* (2016) 1 H.K.L.R.D. 272.
159 Ibid., pp. 1–3.
160 Ibid., p. 4.
161 Ibid.
162 Onc Lawyers, "Join Forces: SFC Co-operated with CSRC to Sanction against Manipulative Trading," May 31, 2017, pp. 1, 4, www.onc.hk/en_US/publication/join-forces-sfc-co-operated-with-csrc-to-sanction-against-manipulative-trading.
163 *Tang Hanbo*, 1 H.K.L.R.D. 272, p. 11.
164 Ibid., p. 4.
165 Ibid., pp. 6–7.
166 Ibid., p. 8.
167 Ibid., p. 9.

Tang launched a judicial review challenge in the Hong Kong courts, alleging that the search warrant had been obtained illegally because it was requested based on an unrelated disclosure of interest, and thus the evidence in the case was also transferred illegally.[168] In essence, Tang hoped that the procedural deficiencies that existed within the enforcement of cooperation between the CSRC and SFC would favor him in court.[169] The court instead put the uncertainty to rest, ruling that the regulators had legally followed the protocol in their cooperation, and there was no hidden motive in obtaining the search warrant.[170] Even if the evidence collected by the SFC was not for a particular case, transferring any information to the CSRC in fulfilling assistance requests is within the power and mandate of the SFC based on the MMoU and Stock Connect MoU.[171] This case clarified and significantly strengthened the position of enforcement cooperation between regulators on both sides. The CSRC administrative sanction was finally handed down in March 2017,[172] with Tang receiving a heavy fine of RMB 90 million plus the confiscation of a sum equal to his calculated illegal gains of RMB 240 million.

The first criminal sanction relating to the Shanghai–Hong Kong Stock Connect came in 2019.[173] The defendants in the case again utilized the new channel to trade across borders.[174] The defendant, Sang Renzhao, was an investment banker at UBS Securities based in Shanghai.[175] In May 2017, Sang participated in the advising of the Chinese shipping giant COSCO's plan to take over OOCL, a Hong Kong carrier.[176] He immediately purchased shares of COSCO on the Mainland market using a third-party account and sold them all when the takeover

[168] Ibid., p. 2.

[169] *See generally Tang Hanbo*, 1 H.K.L.R.D. 272.

[170] Ibid., p. 18.

[171] Ibid.

[172] Clifford Chance, "China Regulator Levies Huge Fine for Market Manipulation" (March 2017), www.cliffordchance.com/content/dam/cliffordchance/briefings/2017/03/china-regulator-levies-huge-fine-for-market-manipulation.pdf.

[173] PKU Law, "Shanghai Publicly Sentenced a Securities Crime Case Involving the 'Shanghai–Hong Kong Stock Connect'", June 20, 2019 [hereinafter *Sang Case*], pkulaw.cn/case/pal_a3ecfd5d734f711d577294ad3ee2c4c4f45e4a93740f2852bdfb.html?match=Exact.

[174] Ibid.

[175] Ibid.

[176] Ibid.

announcement was made public.[177] At the same time, Sang leaked the information to the second defendant, Chen, who then traded through thirty-six different accounts in the Hong Kong market on a much larger scale through the Stock Connect channel.[178] The illegal profit he made amounted to RMB 125 million, from which Sang was paid RMB five million.[179] Separately, Sang also tipped off his university classmate, Wang, who traded on both the Mainland and Hong Kong market: first on the Mainland market for shares of the acquirer company to reap a profit of RMB 320,000, and then on the Hong Kong market for shares of the target company, returning a RMB 1.4 million surplus.[180]

The series of insider trading was not detected by regulators but was rather exposed by Sang's girlfriend on an internet posting as their relationship turned sour.[181] Regulators quickly followed up on the tip and unearthed the trades above.[182] Throughout the investigation and the court trial, both Sang and Chen denied their guilt and did not return the illegal gains.[183] At sentencing, the court stated that their market misconduct acts were particularly serious, and both were sentenced to nine years imprisonment.[184] Sang was also fined RMB 12 million and Chen RMB 240 million.[185] Further, the two were ordered to return the illegal gains of RMB 5.13 million and RMB 125 million.[186] The third defendant, Wang, admitted his wrongdoing, was given a suspended sentence, and was fined of RMB 1.7 million.[187] Unlike the Tang case above, this case was investigated entirely by Chinese agencies.[188] The fact that the market misconduct in this case involves both the Chinese and Hong Kong markets raises questions about the decision as to which regulator should exercise jurisdiction and its implication on the investigation,

177 Ibid.
178 Ibid., pp. 1–2.
179 Ibid., p. 2.
180 Ibid.
181 *See generally* Joanne Chiu and Zhou Wei, "Former UBS Banker in China Convicted in Cross-Border Insider Trading Case" (2019) *Wall Street Journal*, www.wsj.com/articles/former-ubs-banker-in-china-convicted-in-cross-border-insider-trading-case-11561111660.
182 *Sang Case*, above note 173, p. 2.
183 Chiu and Wei, above note 181, p. 1.
184 *Sang Case*, above note 173, p. 2.
185 Ibid.
186 Chiu and Wei, above note 181, p. 1.
187 *See generally* ibid.
188 *See generally* ibid.

sanction and remedy.[189] These questions, along with other issues, will be explored in Section 8.4.[190]

8.4 Discrepancies in Substantive Rules

8.4.1 Misconduct Definition

The regulation of market misconduct is generally similar between the two jurisdictions but with some differences.[191] These differences should not affect the overall and general operations against market misconduct, except in specific cases where conflict may arise.[192] These discrepancies in law may lead to "regulatory arbitrage," such that potential perpetrators of market misconduct will choose a jurisdiction where there is less chance of prosecution or less severe consequences if convicted.[193] Some of these differences stem from the distinct legal systems of the two places.[194] The Securities Law of China was first passed in 1998, with a recent substantial amendment in 2019.[195] There are considerable additions in the regulation on insider trading, market misconduct and marked increases in the punishment for contravention.[196] There is an added explicit expansion of the jurisdiction of the regulatory authority in overseas listings and trading.[197] Altogether there are newly expanded powers and scope of regulation for Chinese authorities.[198] At the same time, the Chinese legal regime is usually couched in broad terms, leaving details to be fleshed out later via administrative rules and regulations.[199] Hong Kong's Securities and Futures Ordinance (SFO) has a longer

[189] *See generally* above note 173.

[190] *See generally* Zhonghua Renmin Gongheguo Zhengquan Fa (中华人民共和国证券法) [Securities Law of the People's Republic of China] (promulgated by NPC Financial and Economic Affairs Committee, December 29, 1998 effective July 1, 1999) [hereinafter Chinese Securities Law]; Zhengquan ji Qihuo Tiaoli (证券及期货条例) [Securities & Futures Ordinance (Cap. 571)] (promulgated by SFC, March 2002, effective April 1, 2003) [hereinafter SFO].

[191] *See generally* ibid.

[192] *See generally* ibid.

[193] *See generally* ibid.

[194] *See generally* Chinese Securities Law.

[195] *See* ibid., art. 191.

[196] *See* ibid., art. 2(3).

[197] *See generally* ibid.

[198] *See generally* ibid.

[199] *See generally* ibid.

history of revision,[200] and it was also modeled after the relevant laws of other major common law jurisdictions, notably Australia and the UK. Its provisions are much longer and more specific; as such, some legal differences may arise between Hong Kong and the Mainland, as Hong Kong law provides for more specific rules applicable to different circumstances.[201]

Potential legal conflict between the two jurisdictions concerns the scope and definition of market misconduct activities.[202] Hong Kong's regulation of insider trading provides for specific statutory defenses to insider dealing in nine circumstances, including where the insiders conduct trades among themselves.[203] It also contains a general exempting provision if it can be proven that the purpose of any trade "is not for securing or increasing a profit or avoiding or reducing a loss by using inside information."[204] Another example of the exemption from insider dealing prohibition is where one deals in the listed securities for the sole purpose of acquiring shares required to be qualified as a director of a corporation.[205] Some of these exemptions may find parallels in the judicial interpretation of the Chinese Securities Law issued by the Supreme People's Court,[206] but most exemptions are unclear whether they apply in the Mainland. In a cross-market trading scenario, it remains unclear, for example, whether some Hong Kong exemptions are applicable for a person trading Hong Kong stock on the Mainland

200 *See generally* SFO; *see also* Wangwei Lin, "A Destined Intermediary? The Role of Hong Kong in Shaping the Regulatory Framework of China's Securities Market" (2012) 33 *Company Lawyer*, 145–151.

201 *See generally* Reed Smith LLP., "Hong Kong Regulatory Update: SFC Proposes Substantial Enhancements to Statutory Enforcement Powers" (2022), www.reedsmith.com/en/perspectives/2022/06/hong-kong-regulatory-update-sfc-proposes-substantial-enhancements; Zuigao Renmin Fayun, Zuigao Remin Jianchayuan Guanyu Banli Neimu Jiaoyi, Xielu Neimu Xingxi Xingshi Anjian Juti Yingyong Falv Rugan Wenti de Jieshi (最高人民法院、最高人民检察院关于办理内幕交易、泄露内幕信息刑事案件具体应用法律若干问题的解释) [Interpretation of the Supreme People's Court and the Supreme People's Procuratorate on Several Issues Concerning the Specific Application of Law in the Handling of Criminal Cases of Engaging in Insider Trading or Leaking Insider Information] (promulgated by the Supreme People's Court Gazette & the Supreme People's Procuratorate Communique, March 29, 2012) at art. 4 (China) [hereinafter Chinese Securities Law Interpretation]; *see also* SFO, art. 271.

202 *See generally* ibid.

203 SFO, art. 271.

204 Ibid., art. 271(3).

205 Ibid., art. 273(1).

206 Chinese Securities Law Interpretation, above note 201, art. 4.

or vice versa.[207] Similar situations of discrepancies between exemptions can be found in the regulation of market manipulation,[208] price rigging[209] and false trading.[210]

Another potential discrepancy is the geographic reach of the securities laws.[211] This is relevant and should be ascertained if regulators from either side have jurisdiction over a particular case.[212] The Chinese Securities Law specifies its extraterritorial jurisdiction, stating that where the offering and trading of securities outside China "disrupt[s] the order of the domestic market" and "infringe[s] upon the lawful rights and interests" of Chinese investors, the perpetrator of such market misconduct will fall within the jurisdiction of Chinese law.[213] Being China's formal message in asserting her extraterritorial jurisdiction, this article was newly inserted under the 2019 amendment.[214] It is written in a general manner and encompasses all types of market misconduct found in the law. Given that the amendment to the Chinese Securities Law only came into force on March 1, 2020 it remains to be seen how it will operate to regulate market misconduct outside its jurisdiction.[215] There may be difficulties in reaching foreign traders, and although the most likely overseas market the Chinese authorities could exert jurisdiction over seems to be that of Hong Kong, it would overlap with Hong Kong's regulator, as well as be subsumed into the existing cooperation agreements of the two sides.[216] Therefore, an application of China's new extraterritorial jurisdiction may not be observed until test cases arise in the future.[217]

As for Hong Kong's SFO, most of its provisions on market misconduct do not provide for jurisdiction over overseas parties and misconduct.[218] For instance, the offense of insider dealing is concerned only with shares

[207] *See generally* ibid.; SFO, above note 190.
[208] SFO, art. 278.
[209] Ibid., art. 275.
[210] Ibid., art. 274.
[211] *See generally* Chinese Securities Law, art. 2(3).
[212] *See generally* Chinese Securities Law.
[213] Ibid., art. 2(3).
[214] Ibid.
[215] Ibid., art. 226.
[216] *See generally* ibid.
[217] *See* Weining Zou, Yisong Li and Jiapeng Li, "An Analysis of the Application of the Long-Arm Jurisdiction Clause under PRC Securities Law," May 5, 2020, www.junhe.com/legal-updates/1189?locale=en.
[218] *See generally* SFO, above note 190.

listed on the Stock Exchange of Hong Kong.[219] As cross-border trading is now highly convenient, this raises uncertainty as to whether the statutes provide Hong Kong's regulator with jurisdiction over a particular cross-border case,[220] for example, if the perpetrator plans and executes trades within Hong Kong but through foreign markets concerning foreign securities.[221] The SFC has sought to extend its jurisdiction by relying on a general catch-all provision in the SFO.[222] The relevant wording of the catch-all provision does not mention geographical reach but simply provides that "a person shall not . . . engage in any act, practice or course of business which is fraudulent or deceptive."[223] In *Securities and Futures Commission v. Young Bik Fung*,[224] during a secondment to a bank in Hong Kong, a lawyer who had access to classified information came to knowledge about a proposal to take over a bank in Taiwan. The defendant and his three relatives then gathered a large sum to acquire shares in the Taiwanese bank, which was listed on the Taiwan Stock Exchange.[225] In court, it was challenged whether the SFC had the jurisdiction to prosecute this cross-border insider trade.[226]

The Hong Kong court held that if the fact pattern of market misconduct is seen to have a sufficient connection to Hong Kong, then a court *may* apply common law principles and extend its jurisdiction in specific cases, and it did so in this case.[227] The Court of Appeal first confirmed that this provision has no extraterritorial jurisdiction per se.[228] The court went on to apply a common law test to determine whether a crime can be put under Hong Kong's jurisdiction based on its substantial element.[229] Where a criminal act has been committed, the common law test asks whether a "substantial measure of the activities constituting [the] crime" took place within the local jurisdiction.[230] If so, local jurisdiction is

219 Ibid., art. 291.
220 Ibid.
221 Ibid.
222 Ibid., art. 300.
223 Ibid.
224 *See Securities and Futures Commission v. Young Bik Fung* [2017] H.K.C.A. 108, CACV 33/2016, (C.A. November 9, 2017) (Legal Reference System).
225 Ibid., para. 2.
226 Ibid., para. 50.
227 Ibid., para. 51.
228 Ibid., para. 50.
229 *See Young Bik Fung*, CACV 33/2016 (citing *HKSAR v. Krieger* [2014] 3 H.K.L.R.D. 404, aff'd, *HKSAR v. Wong Tak Keung* [2015] 18 H.K.C.F.A.R. 62).
230 *Young Bik Fung*, CACV 33/2016, para. 51.

applicable.[231] In the *Young Bik Fung* case, although the company, the exchange where the stock was traded and the account used were all located overseas, the court ruled that the acts of gathering the funds in Hong Kong, including borrowing and liquidating other assets, already constituted a "substantial part" of the trade, and thus local jurisdiction could apply.[232] When we compare this legal position on jurisdiction with that of the Chinese Securities Law's stated extraterritorial jurisdiction, there is a clear disparity in terms of the legal certainty of jurisdiction.[233] Although the SFC's jurisdiction was recently supported by the court in the abovementioned case, as compared with Chinese law, it remains highly case-sensitive and subject to legal challenge.[234]

8.4.2 *Misconduct Liability*

There is a wide gap in terms of the severity of sanctions between Mainland China and Hong Kong, and the enforcement outcome of a case may differ based on where it is pursued.[235] This includes the severity of the sentencing, civil sanctions and civil remedies available to any investors.[236] On top of any fine imposed, the extent of civil liability that may be realistically claimed in court will form part of a person's consideration when they contemplate committing an offense.[237] Therefore, it is an integral part of the deterrence against market misconduct.[238] Comparatively speaking, a case sentenced in Hong Kong may face a lighter punishment.[239] The maximum sentence in a criminal prosecution is ten years imprisonment and a HKD 10 million fine.[240] The court also has the power to order a convicted person to pay a sum not more than the gain or potential loss evaded from the market misconduct.[241] This sanction applies to all types of market abuse defined under the SFO, including insider dealing, false trading, price rigging, disclosure of false

231 Ibid., para. 52.
232 Ibid., paras. 61, 64, 68.
233 *See generally* Yamamoto, above note 32.
234 Ibid.
235 Ibid., p. 69.
236 *See generally* Langevoort, above note 3.
237 Ibid.
238 *See generally* Yamamoto, above note 32.
239 SFO, art. 303(1)(a).
240 Ibid., art. 303(2)(d).
241 Ibid.

or misleading information and market manipulation, resulting in these types of market misconduct being sentenced similarly based on the maximum penalty.[242]

Under the Mainland's criminal code, the level of punishment for the different types of market misconduct is provided separately.[243] The offense of insider trading attaches a higher level of penalty, with the perpetrator liable to a maximum of ten years imprisonment, and a fine of two to a maximum of five times the illegal gains.[244] For the offense of disseminating false information to disrupt the market, the maximum fine is RMB 100,000.[245] For the offense of market manipulation, the maximum fine is not specified.[246] Empirically, the fine issued is often in specific multiples of the illegal gains, depending on the severity of the case, and is most often issued at two times the illegal gains.[247] In some judgments from the Mainland Courts, the sum of illegal gains is to be separately confiscated on top of the fines, while some were not so stated.[248]

Setting a fine as multiples of the presumed illegal gains has the benefit of not having to determine the exact amount of illegal gains, which could be a difficult task in some cases. However, this method of fine setting may give rise to a considerably higher fine than that of Hong Kong. For example, in the *Sang* case, after being sentenced to nine years imprisonment the defendant was fined RMB 240 million,[249] which is twenty-four times the maximum fine in Hong Kong.[250] Another subtle factor that may be at play in sentencing is the relative severity attached to a particular monetary sum. Taking the disparity of price and income level

242 Ibid., arts. 303(1), 291, 295, 296, 298, 299.

243 Zhonghua Renmin Gongheguo Xingfa (中华人民共和国刑法) [Criminal Law of the People's Republic of China] (promulgated by National People's Congress, March 14, 1997 effective October 1, 1997), art. 180, CLI.1.17010(EN) (Lawinfochina) [hereinafter Chinese Criminal Law].

244 Ibid.

245 Ibid., art. 181.

246 Ibid., art. 182.

247 Robin Hui Huang, "Enforcement of Chinese Insider Trading Law: An Empirical and Comparative Perspective" (2021) 68 *American Journal of Comparative Law*, 517, 530, 557.

248 Ibid., pp. 526–527.

249 *See* above note 173.

250 SFO, art. 303(1)(a).

into consideration, an equal numerical amount could be felt as heftier in Mainland China.[251]

As for the availability of civil compensation, it is a changing and developing regime for both Mainland China and Hong Kong. In the Chinese Securities Law, there are provisions stating the right to claim compensation from parties dealing with insider information.[252] Similar rights of action to claim compensation caused by market manipulation are also provided.[253] In practice, however, it is not easy to obtain compensation in court due to the lack of details in the bringing and hearing of cases of insider trading and market manipulation.[254] To be sure, a private right of action could be theoretically based on the existing law of contract or the tort regime; however, due to the special nature of insider trading, such as the impersonality and anonymity of exchange transactions, it is extremely difficult, if not impossible, to assert insiders' liability on these conventional grounds.[255] The Supreme People's Court of China issued a circular in 2003 to provide more detailed rules on the hearing of securities civil cases, but it only applied to cases against securities misrepresentation, and excluded other types of securities fraud such as insider trading.[256] Overall, the Chinese civil compensation regime is in a state of flux, and sizable uncertainty lies in the actual handling of these claims by different courts.[257]

The first civil compensation case concerning insider trading came before the court in September 2008, arising out of an administrative

[251] Note the above discussion serves as an illustration of the disparity of punishment across the China–Hong Kong border, but a more complete picture requires further empirical research to also consider the frequency of enforcement, the totality of sanction on each defendant, and so on. Meanwhile, such disparity may be seen in any different jurisdictions, even for jurisdictions with similar legal systems and income levels, *See* Lev Bromberg, George Gillian and Ian Ramsay, "Financial Market Manipulation and Insider Trading: An International Study of Enforcement Approaches" (2017) 8 *Journal of Business Law* 652.

[252] Chinese Securities Law, art. 53.

[253] Ibid., art. 55.

[254] Robin Hui Huang, "Compensation for Insider Trading: Who Should Be Eligible Claimants?" (2006) 20 *Australian Journal of Corporate Law*, 1, 2.

[255] Ibid., pp. 16, 23–24.

[256] Robin Hui Huang, "Private Enforcement of Securities Law in China: A Ten-Year Retrospective and Empirical Assessment" (2013) 61 *American Journal of Comparative Law*, 757, 760–761.

[257] Ibid.

sanction.[258] But it was seen as not properly pursued and was thus withdrawn.[259] Investors had to wait until 2015 to witness the first successful compensation claim.[260] In that case, in a series of 507 claims each assessed by the court over three years of litigation, 354 of them were, in the end, approved by the court.[261] The inside trader finally paid up to RMB 40 million in damages.[262] This case was hailed as a pioneering test case and sparked heated discussion concerning the proper legal criteria for investor compensation.[263] For example, in regard to the method of ascertaining loss, one provision in a previous Chinese Securities Law's amendment draft circulated in 2015 purported to set the loss caused by insider trading as the "difference between the price for which an investor bought or sold the shares, and the average market price within a 10 days after the disclosure of the insider information."[264] This blunt proposal was later dropped in the final amendment and the current method of calculation is still not specified.[265] Within the geography of China, there is also a disparity in the likelihood of obtaining investor compensation, as empirical observations suggest it is more likely to receive civil compensation in courts of more economically advanced provinces.[266]

Another important new development for the Chinese civil compensation regime is a class action lawsuit system specifically set up for investor protection.[267] The Supreme People's Court of China has launched this class action lawsuit system by issuing further provisions

[258] Jin Sheng, "Private Securities Litigation in China: Passive People's Courts and Weak Investor Protection" (2015) 26 *Bond Law Review*, 94, 131.

[259] Ibid.

[260] Huang, above note 247, p. 531.

[261] Chen Nanshan, "The First Instance Appeal of Everbright Securities' Erroneous Order Case Was Rejected and the Two Plaintiffs Were Ordered to Pay 33,800 Yuan" *First Financial APP*, February 16, 2016, www.yicai.com/news/4750149.html.

[262] Ibid.

[263] Research Group of the No. 2 Intermediate Court of Shanghai Municipality, "Zhengquan Shichang Neimu Jiaoyi Minshi Peichang Zeren Wenti Yanjiu" (证券市场内幕交易民事赔偿责任问题研究) [On Issues Related to Civil Liability of Insider Trading in Securities Market] (2016) 18 *Zhengquan Fayuan (证券法苑) [Securities Law Forum]*, 394–415.

[264] Draft Amendments on the Securities Law of the People's Republic of China (April 20, 2015), art. 92, npcobserver.com/wp-content/uploads/2019/04/securities-law-draft-revision.pdf.

[265] Chinese Securities Law, art. 53.

[266] Li Huang, "Local Protection in Chinese Securities Litigation: A 20-Year Empirical Study of Securities Cases in China" (2019) 49 *Hong Kong Law Journal*, 1089, 1120.

[267] Chinese Securities Law, art. 65.

in 2020.[268] Investors who have sustained losses may start an "Ordinary Representative Litigation" in a private lawsuit,[269] or join a "Special Representative Litigation" initiated by an investor protection agency.[270] Participation in this class action scheme seems to be convenient and is expected to significantly lower the cost burden of individual investors.[271] Given the newness of the system, its actual effects are still waiting to be observed.

In Hong Kong, class action lawsuits are not available, and the steep legal cost makes it hard for individual investors to seek civil compensation against losses arising from market misconduct.[272] However, there is another channel of civil compensation through litigation by the SFC.[273] In 2013, the SFC utilized a general order provision under the SFO to seek compensation from a defendant for an insider trading lawsuit for the first time.[274] The provision allows the SFC to petition the court to issue various orders designed to remedy and prevent the recurrence of breach.[275] Where a person has contravened a provision of the SFO, the court may direct a party to take steps at the court's discretion, "including steps to restore the parties to any transaction to the position in which they were before the transaction was entered into."[276] The Court of Final Appeal affirmed the use of this provision as a free-standing remedy to compensate up to more than 1,800 investors who incurred losses due to insider trading.[277] The compensation is calculated by the difference

268 Zuigao Renmin Fayuan Guanyu Zhengquan Jiufen Daibiao Ren Susong Ruogan Wenti De Guiding (最高人民法院关于证券纠纷代表人诉讼若干问题的规定) [Provisions of the Supreme People's Court on Several Issues Concerning Representative Actions Arising from Securities Disputes] (promulgated by the Judicial Comm. Sup. People's Ct., July 30, 2020 effective July 31, 2020) [hereinafter Chinese Class Action Rules].

269 Ibid. art. 1; Chinese Securities Law, art. 95, paras. 1–2.

270 Chinese Class Action Rules, art. 1; Chinese Securities Law, art. 95, para. 3.

271 *See generally* Chinese Class Action Rules.

272 Paul Kwan and Mandy Pang, "Class and Group Actions Laws and Regulations 2025: Hong Kong," in Annabelle Saunders (ed.), *Class and Group Actions Laws and Regulations 2025* (International Comparative Legal Guides, 2024), iclg.com/practice-areas/class-and-group-actions-laws-and-regulations/hong-kong?.

273 SFO, art. 305(1).

274 Padma Venkat, "Hong Kong *Tiger Asia Case*: Are Insider Traders Losing Their Stripes?" (May 9, 2013) *CFA Institute*, blogs.cfainstitute.org/marketintegrity/2013/05/09/hong-kong-tiger-asia-case-are-insider-traders-losing-their-stripes/.

275 SFO, art. 213.

276 Ibid., art. 213(2)(b).

277 Charltons, "SFC's Power to Seek Compensation for Investors" (2015), www.charltonslaw.com/hong-kong-law/sfc-powers-to-seek-compensation-for-investors/.

between the actual price of the underlying stocks sold by the insider, and the value of those shares taking into account the insider information as assessed by expert evidence.[278]

While this approach taken by the SFC seems expedient for individual investors in Hong Kong, it also means that the availability of compensation is dependent upon positive action in seeking compensation by the regulator, compared with the method in Mainland China of claiming through private lawsuit or collective lawsuit after an official sanction is made.[279] It is not known whether the SFC has sought another compensation order to date.[280] Taken together, the generally lower level of fine and sentencing length, plus the lesser availability of civil remedy, at least in theory, means a comparatively lower sanctioning strength for Hong Kong as compared to China.[281]

8.5 Challenges to Legal Enforcement

8.5.1 Difficulties with Information Exchange

Against the background of the closely connected markets of Hong Kong and the Mainland, an important step for case detection is to achieve cross-border and cross-market surveillance.[282] A holistic scope of market surveillance would ideally include cross-market, cross-border and cross-asset surveillance.[283] Cooperative efforts for regulators in Mainland China and Hong Kong regarding regular joint-detection have yet to be established.[284] Under various agreements, regulators of both sides have agreed to communicate if and when cross-border market misconduct is

[278] Ibid.

[279] The Chinese regime for securities private litigation has long had a prerequisite requirement that the bringing of securities private litigation requires a prior penalty decision from the regulator or a criminal judgment. *See* Robin Hui Huang, "Private Enforcement of Securities Law in China: A Ten-Year Retrospective and Empirical Assessment" (2013) 61 *American Journal of Comparative Law*, 757, 762. In July 2020, the SPC reiterated the requirement for the newly introduced "special representative litigation," *See* Chinese Class Action Rules, art. 5.

[280] *See* Charltons, above note 277.

[281] Ibid.

[282] *See* IMF, "People's Republic of China–Hong Kong Special Administrative Region: Financial Sector Assessment Program-Technical Note-Regulation and Supervision of Secondary Markets" (June 15, 2021) *IMF Country Reports No. 21/115*, 4–9.

[283] Ibid.

[284] Press Release, "New Measures to Deepen Financial Cooperation between Hong Kong and the Mainland" (June 13, 2025) (on file with Hong Kong Monetary Authority).

detected and investigated by either side.[285] In 2018, the CSRC disclosed a total of around twenty alerts from Hong Kong and twelve instances of investigation assistance requests made by the CSRC.[286] But the primary focus of the MOUs lies in case handling, and there is little guidance as to the issue of detection.[287] The MOUs mainly facilitate the request and exchange of information for investigation after the market misconduct has been detected, instead of being a regular or day-to-day information exchange, as is required by cross-market surveillance.[288]

One barrier to cross-market surveillance is the consolidation of market data across different markets.[289] The market data of Hong Kong, Shanghai and Shenzhen markets are not consolidated into a single system for easy monitoring.[290] Regulators in the United States faced this issue with its multiple decentralized domestic markets, and the failure to effectively monitor them has been attributed as one of the main reasons for some major market crashes, especially the 2008 global financial crisis.[291] In response, the SEC required all US exchanges to adopt common standards and centralize data, that is, the consolidated audit trail which began its implementation in 2017.[292]

A crucial requirement for cross-market and cross-border monitoring is to have common reporting standards across jurisdictions.[293] For instance, in the Mainland market, each market participant can directly hold shares, whereas in Hong Kong, a large portion of trading and holding are on a nominated basis, that is, conducted by trading brokers

285 Stock Connect MoU, above note 145.

286 China Securities Regulatory Commission, *Annual Report* (2018), 74, www.csrc.gov.cn/csrc_en/c102063/c1372574/1372574/files/P020191021577549600990.pdf.

287 China Securities Regulatory Commission, "SFC and CSRC Enter Into a MoU on Regulatory Cooperation" (February 16, 2023), www.csrc.gov.cn/csrc_en/c102030/c7125023/content.shtml.

288 Ibid.

289 HKEX, "HKEX, SSE and SZSE Announce Plans to Adjust Market Data Dissemination for Southbound," April 12, 2024, www.hkex.com.hk/News/Market-Communications/2024/2404122news?sc_lang=en&utm.

290 Ibid.

291 Sean Ross, "Major Regulations Following the 2008 Financial Crisis," *Investopedia* www.investopedia.com/ask/answers/063015/what-are-major-laws-acts-regulating-financial-institutions-were-created-response-2008-financial.asp.

292 17 C.F.R. § 242.613 (2024).

293 Yan Laws, "Trust and Nominee Holding of Shares in Hong Kong Companies: Law and Practice," www.cnhklawyer.com/en/trust-and-nominee-holding-of-shares-in-hong-kong-companies-law-and-practice/.

on behalf of the actual owner.[294] In particular, to resolve monitoring issues in this regard, new cooperative measures are being put in place.[295] Regulators are trying to ride the wave of the development of Regulatory Technology (RegTech) to improve regulatory efficacy.[296] For example, the Mainland securities markets have adopted a system where "all orders must bear the respective securities account numbers linked to the corresponding investors, which will be further carried to the clearing end."[297] This allows for more efficient market surveillance and enables quicker response.[298] This however did not exist in Hong Kong.[299] Hence in 2018, a Northbound Investor ID Model was implemented for the Stock Connect, so that every Hong Kong investor trading in the Mainland-bound direction now has a unique ID number that can be traced in real time.[300] The southbound identification was later announced in October 2019,[301] whereby the Investor ID of the Mainland investors trading through the channel would be sent over to SFC. This common reporting standard initiative is expected to facilitate cross-border abnormal trading detection and enforcement actions.[302]

It could be hard to tell whether or not, and why, a case is handled one way and not another. In the Tang case, the illegal gains involved amounted to RMB 40 million, but Tang was never criminally charged for cross-market misconduct.[303] In a later case, Tang himself was criminally charged in a separate market misconduct offense that

294 Ibid.

295 Ibid.

296 Roslyn Doktor, Robb Henzi and Landry Signé, "What is RegTech and What Does It Mean for Policymakers?" (June 21, 2022) *World Economic Forum*, www.weforum.org/stories/2022/06/what-is-regtech-and-what-does-it-mean-for-policymakers/.

297 HKEX, "Northbound Investor ID Model: FAQ" (October 15, 2018), para. 2, www.hkex.com.hk/-/media/HKEX-Market/Mutual-Market/Stock-Connect/Reference-Materials/Northbound-Investor-ID-Model/NB-Investor-ID-FAQ-Eng.pdf.

298 Ibid.

299 Ibid.

300 HKEX, "Northbound Investor ID Model," www.hkex.com.hk/Mutual-Market/Stock-Connect/Reference-Materials/Northbound-Investor-ID-Model.

301 Securities and Futures Commission of Hong Kong, "Launch of investor identification for southbound trading under Stock Connect," December 20, 2019, apps.sfc.hk/edistributionWeb/gateway/EN/news-and-announcements/news/doc?refNo=19PR121.

302 Ibid.

303 Ma Jingyu (马婧妤), "Shouzong Kuajing Caozong An Zao Dingge Chufa" (首宗跨境操纵案遭顶格处罚 情节堪比《窃听风云》) [The First Cross-Border Manipulation Case Was Punished. The Circumstances Are Comparable to "Eavesdropping"] *Shanghai Zhengquan Bao (上海证券报) Shanghai Securities News*, March 3, 2017, www.cs.com.cn/xwzx/201703/t20170313_5203995.html.

occurred domestically in Shanghai and was sentenced to three years and six months imprisonment.[304] The illegal gains in this later case were at a much lower figure of RMB 24 million,[305] thus it is unclear why the former case was not prosecuted as a criminal case despite the much larger sum involved. One possible reason could be the cross-border nature of the first case, creating certain hindrances to the availability of evidence vis-à-vis different enforcement agencies.[306] The SFO provides that the SFC cannot transfer information collected via powers under section 179 or section 183 (to compel a person to provide evidence) for use in criminal prosecution if a person claims he might be criminally charged by a foreign regulator.[307] In a cross-border setting, this may bring about some uncertainty in information exchange and enforcement.[308]

8.5.2 *Differences in the Regulatory Architecture*

First, in terms of the main regulator, both Mainland China and Hong Kong adopted a sector-based structure of financial regulation, with the CSRC and the SFC being the main securities regulators in both regions, respectively.[309] But there are significant differences in the institutional environments in which the two securities regulators operate.[310] For instance, the CSRC does not enjoy the same measure of independence as the SFC and is subject to more serious issues of resource constraints and regulatory capture.[311] As will be discussed below, the institutions for

304 Zuigao Renmin Fayuan Fabu 7 Jian Renmin Fayuan Yifa Chengzhi Zhengquan Qihuo Fanzui Dianxing Anli (最高人民法院发布7件人民法院依法惩处证券、期货犯罪典型案例 [现行有效]) [Interpretation on application of <Securities and Future Crimes>, CLI.3.346284] (promulgated by the Supreme People's Court Gazette, September 24, 2020 effective September 24, 2020) lawinfochina.com/display.aspx?id=34213&lib=law.

305 Ibid.

306 *See generally* Ma Jingyu, above note 303.

307 SFO, art. 186(6).

308 *See AA v. The Securities and Futures Commission*, [2019] 41 H.K.C. 246 (C.F.I.) (In early 2016, a Hong Kong investor filed with the Hong Kong High Court for a judicial review, alleging that the Hong Kong regulator unconstitutionally provided self-incriminatory evidence to the Japanese regulator for use in administrative proceedings.)

309 Robin Hui Huang and Dirk Schoenmaker (eds.), *Institutional Structure of Financial Regulation* (Routledge, 2015), pp. 232–233.

310 Ibid.

311 For a more detailed discussion, *see* Robin Hui Huang, *Securities and Capital Markets Law in China* (Oxford University Press, 2014), pp. 35–40.

law enforcement are also different, and apart from the two main regulators, other actors may also play a role in the regulatory landscape.[312] These differences may have an impact on the willingness and ability of the securities regulators on either side to cooperate.

Hong Kong has some special institutions for securities law enforcement, which are not present in Mainland China.[313] For certain types of market misconduct such as insider trading and market manipulation, the SFO lays down a dual system of regulation, namely, a civil penalty route and a criminal prosecution route.[314] Under the civil penalty route, the case will be brought by the SFC before the Market Misconduct Tribunal (MMT), which is an independent body established under the SFO.[315] Each panel of the MMT when hearing a case is chaired by a judge or former judge of the High Court assisted by two lay members who are usually prominent members of the business and professional community in Hong Kong.[316] All decisions are determined by the majority of the panel members, but questions of law are determined by the chairman alone.[317] The MMT applies civil procedures, including the civil standard of proof,[318] but can impose a range of orders which are not remedial but punitive in nature.[319] In respect of criminal prosecutions, the SFC can prosecute summary offenses under the SFO in its name before the Magistrates' Court but must refer more serious and indictable offenses to the Department of Justice for prosecution.[320]

In line with the principle against "double jeopardy," the SFC can only choose to employ either the civil or criminal route, but not both.[321] Once a civil or criminal proceeding is commenced, it cannot be withdrawn to initiate proceedings through the alternative route.[322] Hence, choosing a route has enforcement implications for the SFC, and the

312 Ibid., p. 35.
313 Huang and Schoenmaker, above note 309, pp. 202–210.
314 SFO, art. 252, 253.
315 SFO, art. 251.
316 Ibid.
317 SFO, Schedule 9, art. 24.
318 SFO, art. 252.
319 SFO, art. 253.
320 Department of Justice of the HKSAR and Securities and Futures Commission, "Memorandum of Understanding between the Department of Justice of the HKSAR and the Securities and Futures Commission," March 4, 2016, www.doj.gov.hk/en/community_engagement/press/pdf/memorandum_e.pdf.
321 SFO, art. 283.
322 Ibid.

calculus of such a choice can be quite complex. If the market misconduct is less serious and/or the evidence is not sufficiently strong for a criminal prosecution, the SFC may choose the civil penalty route.[323] But there is also the risk that the SFC may shirk its responsibility by choosing the easy way of handling the case, namely, the civil route, even if the misconduct is very serious and/or the evidence is sufficiently strong.[324] To avoid this issue, the SFC must obtain the consent of the Secretary for Justice to institute the MMT proceedings.[325] According to empirical research, from 2003 to 2015, there were twelve cases concluded via the civil penalty route and twelve criminal cases during the same period, suggesting that the two routes had been used in a generally balanced and appropriate manner.[326]

While the SFC can choose to investigate and pursue securities law offenses in a criminal prosecution with the Department of Justice's consent, a criminal case may at the same time also fall under the functions of the Hong Kong Police.[327] SFC and the Hong Kong Police signed a MoU to set out their cooperation and relationship in such cases.[328] Whether it is the SFC or the police that should be responsible for a case is determined by asking which agency is in a better position to handle the case, and whether it would be duplicative for the other agency to conduct a parallel investigation.[329] It is also possible to set up a joint task force to commence a joint investigation.[330] In terms of assistance, because the SFC does not have the power of arrest if the SFC has obtained an arrest warrant from a magistrate, it may request the police for help in its execution.[331] The SFC may also request the police for

323 SFO, art. 252.

324 Ibid.

325 SFO, art. 252A.

326 Robin Hui Huang, "Xianggang Zhengquan Shichang Shidang Xingwei Shencaichu Zhidu Jiqi Qishi" (香港证券市场失当行为审裁处制度及其启示) [The Hong Kong Market Misconduct Tribunal and Its Inspiration for Mainland China] (2018) 1 *Touzizhe* 投资者 *[Investors]*, 184. (75 percent of the cases were related to insider trading.)

327 Securities and Futures Commission and Hong Kong Police of the HKSAR, "Memorandum of Understanding between the Hong Kong Police of the HKSAR and the Securities and Futures Commission," August 25, 2017, www.sfc.hk/web/files/ER/MOU/MoU_SFC-%20HKP_25%20Aug%202017.pdf.

328 Ibid.

329 Ibid., pp. 2–3.

330 Ibid., p. 3.

331 Ibid., pp. 4–5.

assistance to conduct searches under a search warrant if there is a threat to the safety of SFC personnel.[332] In practice, however, due to the relative independence of the two agencies, the two agencies have little communication with each other in the conduct of securities cases.[333]

In turn, for Mainland China, the division of responsibility in investigating a securities law crime is more clear-cut between the securities regulators and the police. While cases of administrative punishment are handled by the CSRC, if it is determined that a case of market misconduct is of a particularly serious nature, the case will be referred to the police department for investigation and where appropriate, further referred to the procuratorate for criminal prosecution.[334] The guidance for handling a criminal case of market misconduct can be found in its 2011 Notice.[335] Where a case is "significant, complicated or difficult," the CSRC may request reference opinions, and assistance in arrests from the police or transfer the case altogether to the police.[336] Upon investigation of a criminal case, if it is found that the acts do not constitute a crime and the procuratorate decides not to prosecute the matter shall then be transferred back to the CSRC for administrative sanctions.[337] In a cross-border enforcement setting, if a case is handled as a criminal case, it is unclear whether the SFC has direct cooperation mechanisms with China's police department, or if it is to be handled through the CSRC.[338] Under the agreements between Mainland and Hong Kong regulators, the transfer of information onward to other agencies is not specifically mentioned, although one side can ask for the consent of the other if

332 SFC, "SFC statement on Police investigation Concerning Next Digital shares," September 11, 2020, www.sfc.hk/en/News-and-announcements/Policy-statements-and-announcements/SFC-statement-on-Police-investigation-concerning-Next-Digital-shares.

333 Ibid.

334 Zuigao Renmin Fayuan, Zuigao Renmin Jianchayuan, Gonganbu, Zhongguo Zhengjianhui Guanyu Banli Zhengquan Qihuo Weifa Fanzui Anjian Gongzuo Ruogan Wenti de Yijian (最高人民法院、最高人民检察院、公安部、中国证监会关于办理证券期货违法犯罪案件工作若干问题的意见) [Opinions of the Supreme People's Court, the Supreme People's Procuratorate, the Ministry of Public Security, and the China Securities Regulatory Commission on Several Issues Concerning <The Work of the Handling of Cases of Securities and Futures-Related Violations and Crimes>, Judicial Interpretation No. 30] (promulgated by Supreme People's Court, April 27, 2011 effective August 30, 2012), www.spp.gov.cn/spp/flfg/gfwj/201208/t20120830_2441.shtml.

335 Ibid.

336 Ibid.

337 Ibid.

338 Ibid.

the information is to be used for purposes other than that originally stated in a request.[339]

One important implication for the institutional structure is that the investigative powers given to agencies across borders are different. These differences in power accorded by the law of both places affect the investigative power of agencies of both sides and are again a source of regulatory arbitrage. The CSRC and the SFC have similar powers to enter premises, seize records and so on, except the SFC is required to obtain a magistrate's warrant before exercising these powers.[340] On top of that, the CSRC has the power to restrict a suspected person from leaving the territory and to restrict further dealing in securities by the person.[341] On the other hand, the SFC is given a wide power of compelling information from persons under investigation, which is not present for their Chinese counterparts.[342]

Section 183 of the SFO allows the SFC to require a person to produce any record or document that may be relevant to an investigation, to give an explanation in respect of any record, to attend a meeting with an investigator at a time and place required by the SFC and to give the investigator "all assistance."[343] The main point about this compelling power is that if one fails to comply with a Section 183 request, it would constitute a criminal offense in itself.[344] In a recent investigation, the SFC issued a Section 183 Notice not only requiring a person to produce specific emails in an email account but also to provide the login names and passwords to email accounts and other digital devices seized.[345] This far-reaching notice was challenged in a judicial review for being disproportionate, but the Hong Kong court upheld this overarching power of the SFC.[346]

339 CSRC and SFC, "Memorandum of Understanding between the CSRC and the SFC on Strengthening of Regulatory and Enforcement Cooperation under Shanghai–Hong Kong Stock Connect," October 17, 2014, www.sfc.hk/web/files/ER/MOU/ENF_MOU_October2014.pdf.

340 SFO, art. 191; Chinese Securities Law, art. 170.

341 Chinese Securities Law, art. 170.

342 SFO, art. 191.

343 SFO, art. 183(1)(d); *see also* SFO, art. 179 (provides for similar investigating power on a listed company).

344 SFO, art. 184(1).

345 *Cheung Ka Ho Cyril v. Securities and Futures Commission* [2020] H.K.C. 270 (C.F.I).

346 Ibid.

8.5.3 *Lack of Extradition Arrangements*

Further, effective cross-border enforcement entails the transfer of the accused between jurisdictions in suitable cases.[347] In between overseas jurisdictions and between Hong Kong and other jurisdictions, extradition is possible and is the usual practice.[348] But as of now, there is no extradition arrangement between Hong Kong and the Mainland despite their geographical proximity.[349] This is perhaps not a small deficiency in the enforcement cooperation between the two jurisdictions. Without an arrangement to transfer an accused person, the focus of regulators could be restricted only to offenders who are physically present within their respective jurisdictions.[350] In at least two cases, the SFC has failed to put an insider trading offender onto the court because the accused reportedly fled back to Mainland China.[351] The accused in one case, Pan Caihong,[352] was a Mainland lawyer and frequently travelled to Hong Kong. It was alleged that she sold shares in a company after she became aware of negative inside information about the company.[353] She failed to attend a hearing at the court and a warrant was issued by the court for her arrest.[354] In another case, a finance manager of a listed company subsidiary was suspected of insider dealing.[355] Similarly, she did not appear for the hearing and left Hong Kong.[356] An arrest warrant was issued for her in 2016.[357] In both cases the SFC could not take further action across borders and the arrest warrants could not be enforced.[358]

347 SFC, "Arrest warrant for Mainland lawyer issued in insider dealing case," June 23, 2011, apps.sfc.hk/edistributionWeb/gateway/EN/news-and-announcements/news/doc?refNo=11PR74.

348 Jeff Li, "Hong Kong–China Extradition Plans," *BBC*, December 13, 2019, www.bbc.com/news/world-asia-china-47810723.

349 Ibid.

350 Huang and Schoenmaker, above note 309, pp. 202–210, 232–233.

351 For example, ibid.; Tang Xian (唐嫻), SFC, October 2, 2018, www.sfc.hk/en/Regulatory-functions/Enforcement/Have-you-seen-these-people/People-subject-to-arrest-warrants/Tang-Xian.

352 SFC, above note 347.

353 Ibid.

354 Ibid.

355 Tang Xian, above note 351.

356 Ibid.

357 SFC, "People subject to arrest warrants," April 1, 2021, www.sfc.hk/en/Regulatory-functions/Enforcement/Have-you-seen-these-people/People-subject-to-arrest-warrants.

358 Ibid.; Tang Xian, above note 351.

The first effort at legislative change was in mid-2019 when the Hong Kong government proposed a bill to amend the existing law on extradition.[359] The current law in Hong Kong provides for the mechanism of wanted person transfer, but it explicitly states that it is not applicable to any arrangement between Hong Kong and Mainland China.[360] The amendment sought to change that and allow extradition to the Mainland.[361] At the same time, however, it was strongly viewed that the extradition bar is an important safeguard of Hong Kong's unique judicial system, and the bill soon drew widespread social and international attention until it was finally retracted due to an unfavorable response.[362] But even in the early stages of the legislative process, in order to smoothen its acceptability in the Legislative Council, a number of commercial crimes were already removed from the bill after intense lobbying from the business sector.[363] When the bill finally reached the legislative body, it excluded crimes related to taxes, securities and futures trading, intellectual property and company law offenses.[364] In this form, even if the bill was passed, it would not have assisted with extradition regarding market misconduct enforcement.[365] Two observations may be made from this episode. First, the preferable legal regime for the business sector is overwhelmingly the Hong Kong legal system.[366] Second, the government agreed with the business sector in this regard and did not rush to change the current law on extradition regarding crimes of a

[359] The Fugitive Offenders and Mutual Legal Assistance in Criminal Matters Legislation (Amendment) Ordinance 2019 (Fugitive Offenders Ordinance), www.legco.gov.hk/yr18-19/english/bills/b201903291.pdf.

[360] Fugitive Offenders Ordinance (1999) Cap. 503, art. 2(1)(a).

[361] Fugitive Offenders Ordinance, above note 359.

[362] SCMP Reporters, "Hong Kong Leader Carrie Lam Announces Formal Withdrawal of the Extradition Bill and Sets Up a Platform to Look into Key Causes of Protest Crisis," *South China Morning Post*, September 4, 2019, www.scmp.com/news/hong-kong/politics/article/3025641/hong-kong-leader-carrie-lam-announce-formal-withdrawal.

[363] Alvin Lum, "Hong Kong–Mainland China Extradition Plan to be Watered Down by Exempting 9 Economic Crimes, under Intense Pressure from Business Community; Officials Back Down on Contentious Proposal to Send Suspects across the Border after Business Chambers Voice Concern," *South China Morning Post*, March 26, 2019, www.scmp.com/news/hong-kong/law-and-crime/article/3003320/hong-kong-mainland-china-extradition-plan-be-watered.

[364] Ibid.

[365] Ibid., p. 2.

[366] *See* Holmes Chan, "Explainer: Hong Kong's Five Demands – withdrawal of the extradition bill," *Hong Kong Free Press*, December 23, 2019, hongkongfp.com/2019/12/23/explainer-hong-kongs-five-demands-withdrawal-extradition-bill/.

commercial nature.[367] As such, the lack of cross-border transfer of market misconduct offenders may not be resolved soon.[368]

8.6 Suggestions and Implications

8.6.1 General Observations

The above sections assessed the status of cooperation between regulators in Mainland China and Hong Kong and examined the factors affecting the effectiveness and legal certainty of cross-border enforcement. It should first be noted that the overall assessment concludes that good infrastructure for cross-border enforcement cooperation is in place. There is a deep level of cooperation between the two regulators: the CSRC and SFC.[369] Seeing as most of the world's regulators cooperate on the basis of the IOSCO MMoU, the bilateral engagement between China and Hong Kong is much more comprehensive.[370] On top of the large volume of cross-border trade between the two places, this engagement is made possible due to the close political ties of the two governments.[371]

Besides the information exchange mechanism, the MoU between China and Hong Kong provides for the added mechanism of joint investigation, which is encouraged by the IOSCO, but is not present in the multilateral MMoU.[372] In the case of information exchange and investigative assistance, the bilateral Stock Connect MoU does not rule out cooperation between the two sides in regard to criminal prosecution, which is omitted in the IOSCO MMoU.[373] Although cooperation is being pushed forward by the EMMoU, it has received little interest as of

[367] Ibid.
[368] Ibid.
[369] *See* "Memorandum of Understanding between the CSRC and the SFC," above note 339, p. 1.
[370] Ibid.
[371] Hong Kong Monetary Authority, "Hong Kong: The Global Offshore Renminbi Business Hub" (2016), 2, www.hkma.gov.hk/media/eng/doc/key-functions/monetary-stability/rmb-business-in-hong-kong/hkma-rmb-booklet.pdf?utm.
[372] ONC Lawyers, "Court endorsing SFC's power to collect evidence to assist CSRC" (2017), www.onc.hk/en_US/publication/court-endorsing-sfc-s-power-to-collect-evidence-to-assist-csrc?page=81.
[373] *See generally* "Memorandum of Understanding between the CSRC and the SFC," above note 339.

now.[374] Because the process of uptake in such a large-scale multilateral agreement is gradual and slow, bilateral arrangements such as the one between China and Hong Kong serve an important function, especially for jurisdictions with close connections and lower risks of market misconduct activities.[375]

The above analysis also reveals some weaknesses that call for further adjustment to create and maintain a high level of credible deterrence. While the enforcement cooperation framework provides for a joint operation mechanism, to date there has yet been an instance where a joint operation has been undertaken since the Shanghai–Hong Kong Stock Connect came into operation.[376] The prosecuted cases up until this point were still collaborated by the two sides but only through the usual information exchange mechanism.[377] It was not that there were no instances where joint investigation was possible as some previous cases could have been investigated jointly.[378] Under the Stock Connect MoU, it states that a joint investigation may be commenced in respect of a "significant and urgent case [. . .] relating to both jurisdictions, or where any of the suspects, witnesses or evidence are located in both jurisdictions . . ."[379]

In the Tang case, the SFC and CSRC could have opted for the joint investigation route instead of the investigatory assistance route.[380] The relevant case facts are: Tang conducted the trade physically in Hong Kong; the trade was done through the Hong Kong market; and the evidence of the trade was found on Tang's computer in Hong Kong.[381] Hence, it would seem that there were ample grounds that conform with the requirement under the Stock Connect MoU for a joint

374 *See* IOSCO, "Enhanced Multilateral Memorandum of Understanding Concerning Consultation and Cooperation and the Exchange of Information" (EMMoU), www.iosco.org/v2/about/?subsection=emmou (showing the relatively small number of signatories to the EMMoU).

375 "Memorandum of Understanding between the CSRC and the SFC," above note 339, p. 1.

376 Clifford Chance, "Shanghai–Hong Kong Stock Connect: CSRC and SFC Jointly Tackle Market Manipulation" (2016), p. 1, www.cliffordchance.com/content/dam/cliffordchance/briefings/2016/11/shanghaihong-kong-stock-connect-csrc-and-sfc-jointly-tackle-market-manipulation.pdf.

377 Ibid.

378 Ibid., pp. 1–2.

379 "Memorandum of Understanding between the CSRC and the SFC," above note 339, p. 3.

380 *Tang Hanbo v. The Securities and Futures Commission* [2017] 1 H.K.L.R.D. 272, (272, 277), (C.F.I.).

381 Ibid., pp. 272–273.

investigation.[382] This was mentioned in the trial as Tang complained that the SFC and CSRC had conducted a de facto joint investigation on market manipulation but fell short of carrying out a formal one.[383] If it was a joint investigation, the constitutional challenge episode – where Tang complained about procedural irregularity – could have been spared.[384] In fact, given the sufficient connection to both jurisdictions provided by trades through the Stock Connect channel, every case that trades through this channel would likely come under the simultaneous jurisdiction of both regulators.[385] For now, it remains to be seen when the two agencies will undertake a formal joint investigation. A possible reason for the lack of such a joint investigation could be that the two sides are waiting for a perfect first case to set a good precedent. It could also be that a joint operation, while agreed in principle, is nonetheless difficult to conduct in practice, not least in part due to the many legal and operational differences between the two jurisdictions.[386]

8.6.2 *Specific Proposals*

Some legal discrepancies concern the scope of offense and their exemptions.[387] Given the close connection of listing and trade between the two jurisdictions, discrepancies in the law may give rise to confusion and uncertainty for any cross-border enforcement action.[388] The disparity in the availability of civil remedies may also create fairness issues between investors across borders.[389] Both of these can be resolved in future amendments (and/or judicial interpretation by the Mainland) if the laws of both sides can be harmonized.[390] The European Union has provided a good example in this regard: it has issued the first Market Abuse Directive (MAD) in 2003[391] and the second Market Abuse Directive

382 Ibid., pp. 277–278.
383 Ibid., p. 281.
384 Ibid., pp. 283–284.
385 "Memorandum of Understanding between the CSRC and the SFC," above note 339, p. 1.
386 *Tang Hanbo*, 1 H.K.L.R.D. 272, (282).
387 Ibid., 283.
388 "Memorandum of Understanding between the CSRC and the SFC," above note 339, p. 1.
389 Ibid., p. 3.
390 Ibid.
391 Directive 2003/6/EC of the European Parliament and of the Council of January 28, 2003 on Insider Dealing and Market Manipulation (Market Abuse), OJ 2003 No. L96, April 12, 2003, p. 16.

(MAD II) in 2014,[392] to develop consistent definitions of market misconduct as well as consistent penalties for such misconduct among the Member States.

It is certain that inherent differences, such as the discrepancies in the scale of fines and sentencing, would be harder to harmonize.[393] Even if their laws were harmonized into the same or similar wording, inherent differences in their legal system would still differentiate the enforcement outcome across the two places.[394] The criminal sentencing practice in the Hong Kong courts is rooted in the common law court system, giving the judge wide discretion in deciding the length of imprisonment for a specific defendant, after taking into account a series of personal circumstances.[395] Furthermore, a conventional discount of one-third of the prison term will be readily applied if a defendant pleads guilty to a crime before the trial begins in a Hong Kong court.[396] The same customary discount is not available in a Mainland court, and the extent of leniency upon a guilty plea depends on each judge.[397] These differences stemming from the court system itself are not easy to reconcile through the harmonization of securities law.

A longer-term solution to these sanctioning discrepancies across borders is perhaps to establish a common regulatory and sanctioning agency, but this would be an ambitious goal. Short of a unified agency, some part of the sanctioning regime could be harmonized to a certain extent, especially in regard to administrative sanction as it is civil in nature and does not involve the criminal prosecution regime or court sentencing regime.[398] For instance, the EU Common Market has often tried to tend toward harmonizing various aspects of their financial

[392] *See*, Directive 2014/57/EU of the Parliament and of the Council of April 16, 2014 on Criminal Sanctions for Market Abuse (Market Abuse Directive), OJ 2014 No. L173, June 12, 2014, p. 173.

[393] IMF, above note 282.

[394] Ibid., pp. 4–5.

[395] Grenville Cross, “Traditional Approach to Prison Sentences Should be Preferable,” *China Daily*, February 21, 2024, www.chinadailyhk.com/hk/article/377304.

[396] *Hong Kong v. Ngo Van Nam* [2016] 5 H.K.L.R.D. 1, 35 (H.C.).

[397] *See* Xin He, “Plea Leniency and Prosecution Centredness in China’s Criminal Process” (2023) 254 *China Quarterly*, 448, 460–462.

[Guiding Opinions on the Application of the Leniency System for Admitting Guilt and Accepting Punishment], effective from November 10, 2019 promulgated by the Supreme People’s Court, the Supreme People’s Procuratorate, the Ministry of Public Security, the Ministry of State Security, et al.

[398] *See generally* “Opinions of the Supreme People’s Court,” above note 334.

regulations, including the sanction regime for financial misconduct.[399] While acknowledging the autonomy of each EU Member State to determine their sanctioning scale and method, the EU Council passed directives to set guidelines for various levels of maximum fines imposed on insider trading, market manipulation and so on.[400] These guidelines and recommendations for harmonization cannot be made without first conducting in-depth studies and dialogues into the sanctioning practices of all the jurisdictions involved, which is also one initial preparatory step that regulators and policy researchers in Mainland China and Hong Kong should embark on.

The absence of an extradition arrangement is another critical shortfall for establishing a credible cross-border enforcement regime between Mainland China and Hong Kong, and this factor could also be a subtle reason why some cases are pursued in one jurisdiction and not the other.[401] Presently, once a perpetrator crosses borders, there is no legal and practical way of apprehending a suspect, no matter how serious a case is or how strong the evidence is on hand.[402] This problem is significant, especially for Hong Kong as it is a tiny financial city, and crossing the Mainland and Hong Kong borders is very convenient.[403] Most residents of both sides can easily cross the border with minimal visa requirements and the daily volume of mutual personnel traffic is enormous.[404] Without extradition, one way to enforce securities law is for either side to exercise extra-territorial jurisdiction and to prosecute a case in each jurisdiction's courts.[405] But this is not an adequate solution, as there is great uncertainty about such a method of case handling, and it will not be suitable for every case.[406] An optimal solution would be for Mainland China and Hong Kong to agree on some form of extradition.[407] Given the political backlash

399 Commission Regulation 596/2014 of the European Parliament and of the Council of April 16, 2014 on Market Abuse (Market Abuse Regulation) and Repealing Directive 2003/6/EC of the European Parliament and of the Council and Commission Directives 2003/124/EC, 2003/125/EC and 2004/72/EC, OJ 2014 No. L173, June 12, 2014, pp. 1, 13.

400 Ibid., pp. 47–49.

401 *See* Chan, above note 366.

402 Ibid.

403 Ibid.

404 "Hong Kong's Mainland-Bound Tourism Undermines Local Retail," *Economist Intelligence Unit*, January 15, 2024, www.eiu.com/n/hong-kong-mainland-bound-tourism-undermines-local-retail/.

405 *See* Chan, above note 366.

406 Ibid.

407 For example, Alvin Lum, above note 363, p. 2.

as mentioned previously, the two regulators of the two sides could push for a more limited kind of extradition, for example, one that requires proper judicial safeguards and applies only to a limited number of specific market misconduct offenses.

A rapidly developing innovation in the regulatory effort is the use of information technology to aid market surveillance and monitoring, termed RegTech.[408] In essence, RegTech utilizes technologically advanced tools such as big data analytics, cloud computing and machine learning.[409] There are important advantages of utilizing RegTech in market surveillance.[410] For instance, it is generally more reliable and capable of identifying more complex behavioral patterns and detecting cases of misconduct.[411] The securities regulators in China and Hong Kong have started to explore ways of using RegTech in relation to cross-border enforcement, but more needs to be done.[412] First, as RegTech is based on big data analysis, its efficacy would be undermined where data is hard to come by.[413] It is thus important for the two sides to improve the mechanism for data sharing and exchange, and even consider establishing a common data center.[414] Second, there is a need for more investment and development in the field of RegTech.[415] Indeed, despite the importance of RegTech, it has largely remained a fancy concept, seeing quite limited use in practice.[416] As cross-border securities transactions involve highly complex legal issues, it calls for specialized rather than general RegTech and thus requires close collaboration between technical and legal experts as a development strategy.[417]

Lastly, looking beyond the bilateral setting between China and Hong Kong, it should be noted that between a global convention such as the IOSCO MMoU that includes most of the world's securities regulators, and a small-scale model of bilateral cooperation as detailed in

408 Financial Industry Regulatory Authority, "Technology-Based Innovations for Regulatory Compliance ('RegTech') in the Securities Industry," September 2018, p. 2.
409 Ibid.
410 Ibid., p. 3.
411 Ibid., p. 4.
412 Hong Kong Monetary Authority and KPMG, "Transforming Risk Management and Compliance: Harnessing the Power of Regtech" (2018), pp. 18–19, www.finra.org/sites/default/files/2018_RegTech_Report.pdf.
413 Financial Industry Regulatory Authority, above note 408, p. 4.
414 Ibid., p. 9.
415 Ibid., p. 2.
416 Ibid., p. 3.
417 Hong Kong Monetary Authority and KPMG, above note 412, pp. 18–19.

Section 8.3.2, there can be other types of multijurisdictional groups.[418] Canada's regulator has been coordinating response to market fraud by the US and Canada, through their Cross-Border Market Fraud Initiative (CPMFI).[419] The initiative seeks to use innovative, coordinated and timely actions to detect and deter penny stock abuses.[420] The German regulator BaFin also joined the Initiative in 2019, creating a transatlantic task force.[421] Such functional grouping may allow regulators to coordinate on specific issues without casting the net too wide so that more in-depth cooperation remains on the table.[422] Moving forward from a bilateral setting between China and Hong Kong, the two regulators can build on the existing cooperative framework and explore the possibility of enlarging this framework to other relevant markets, for example, Singapore or London.[423]

8.7 Conclusion

Due to the increasing integration of securities markets at regional and international levels, there is a pressing need to examine the regulatory arrangements for cross-border securities misconduct.[424] This requires regulators to have well-functioning infrastructure for information exchange and enforcement cooperation and ideally harmonized legal rules and sanctioning practices in order to minimize regulatory arbitrage.[425]

A case in point is the interaction of the securities markets in Mainland China and Hong Kong.[426] The two markets are highly connected in terms of capital and personnel movement, corporate activities as well as securities listing and trading through various connected channels.[427] At the same time, the regulators of the two jurisdictions act

418 Ibid., p. 26.

419 *See*, Canadian Securities Commission, "Evolving Securities Enforcement for a Digital World" (2018/2019) *FY2018/19 Enforcement Report*, pp. 6, 13, www.securities-administrators.ca/uploadedFiles/General/pdfs/CSA-Enforcement-Report_FINAL201819.pdf.

420 Ibid., pp. 10, 13.

421 Ibid., p. 13.

422 Ibid.

423 Hong Kong Monetary Authority and KPMG, above note 412, pp. 62–64.

424 Ibid., p. 54.

425 Ibid.

426 Ibid.

427 Ibid.

independently and their legal system differs distinctively.[428] The CSRC and SFC have signed a number of bilateral agreements for regulatory cooperation, ranging from information exchange to mutual assistance in prosecution.[429] Nevertheless, due to various reasons, these cooperative arrangements have not been as effective as expected in practice.[430]

Significant discrepancies exist in relation to the scope of offenses, the severity of punishment, the power of agencies and the institutional structure of regulation.[431] This has the effect of weakening the certainty and effectiveness of enforcement action with respect to cross-border market misconduct.[432] Efforts should be made to minimize these discrepancies by harmonizing the substantive rules on the definition of, and the liability for, market misconduct. It will also be useful for the regulators on both sides to jointly issue guidelines on specific issues relating to cross-border regulatory cooperation. In the long term, it is worth exploring the possibility of setting up a unified monitoring, investigating and sanctioning regime. While the Mainland–Hong Kong case has its distinctive features, it exhibits some issues of general application and thus can contribute to the international discourse on the regulation of cross-border securities misconduct.

[428] *See* "Memorandum of Understanding between the CSRC and the SFC," above note 339, p. 3.
[429] Ibid., p. 1.
[430] *See generally* Chance, above note 376.
[431] *See generally* Huang and Schoenmaker, above note 309.
[432] *See generally* Yamamoto, above note 32.

9

China's Recognition and Enforcement of Foreign Securities Judgments

9.1 Introduction

Over the past decades, Chinese companies have been actively seeking overseas listings, notably in the US and Hong Kong. As the number of overseas-listed Chinese companies grows, the occurrence of market misconduct also increases. Amid the rising number of scandals from Chinese issuers listed overseas, there is an acute question of whether there is adequate oversight and investor protection against these Chinese issuers. The oversight system of the US market depends significantly on private enforcement actions against corporate wrongdoings, namely, civil litigation brought by aggrieved investors, such as securities class actions.[1] A successful regime of private securities litigation (PSL) depends on both substantive rules and enforcement mechanisms. In the context of cross-border securities transactions, there is an additional layer of complexity in the recognition and enforcement of foreign judgments.[2]

For foreign securities judgments against Chinese issuers, there is an important problem with judgment recognition and enforcement in China. As is often the case for these companies listed overseas, their main assets, business and senior management usually reside outside of the listing place. If a judgment is held against a Chinese issuer in a foreign court, it may not be effective unless it is recognized and enforced by a Chinese court. Therefore, it is important to critically examine China's recognition and enforcement of foreign securities judgments and explore ways to deal with the issues associated with it.

[1] Maria Glover, "The Structural Role of Private Enforcement Mechanism in Public Law" (2011) 53 *William & Mary Law Review* 1153.

[2] In practice, the US securities class actions are usually concluded with settlement rather than judgment. As settlement requires court approval, it is treated largely in the same way as judgment when it comes to recognition and enforcement by a Chinese court. For brevity, the term "judgment" will thus be used to cover both judgment and settlement, unless otherwise specified. For more details on this issue, see Section 9.3.1.

This chapter proceeds as follows. Section 9.2 will first review the recent situation regarding PSL against Chinese issuers in the US. Section 9.3 will analyze the Chinese legal regime on the recognition of foreign judgments. Section 9.4 will specifically examine how Chinese courts recognize and enforce US judgments. Then, in Section 9.5, the focus will move toward the arrangements that Hong Kong and Mainland China have made for recognition and enforcement of judgments. Section 9.6 will evaluate potential solutions to the issue of recognizing and enforcing foreign securities judgments in China.

9.2 Securities Litigation against Overseas-Listed Chinese Companies

In the US, there has recently been an increasing number of PSL in the form of class action against overseas issuers, especially Chinese issuers. In 2019, a total of sixty-four securities class actions were filed against non-US issuers, and in eighteen of these filings, the defendants were Chinese issuers, increasing from fifteen in 2018.[3] Chinese companies have become the most frequently sued group of overseas issuers in the US market, which has highlighted the US–China audit oversight dispute and eventually led to the passage of the Holding Foreign Companies Accountable Act.[4]

A range of risk factors make Chinese issuers more prone to being sued. The US Securities and Exchange Commission (SEC) has noted that there are risks relating to the quality of Chinese issuers' financial reporting, the regulatory environment and the quality of corporate governance.[5] Besides, many Chinese issuers may raise capital based on innovative business models that have yet to be proven, and thus are sensitive to changes in market conditions and China's fast-evolving regulatory landscape.

[3] David H. Kistenbroker, Joni S. Jacobsen and Angela M. Liu, "Non-US Issuers Targeted in Securities Class Action Lawsuits Filed in the United States," *Harvard Law School Forum on Corporate Governance*, corpgov.law.harvard.edu/2020/03/29/non-u-s-issuers-targeted-in-securities-class-action-lawsuits-filed-in-the-united-states/; Dechert LLP, "Non-U.S. issuers targeted in securities class actions filed in the U.S.," April 1, 2019, www.dechert.com/content/dam/dechert%20files/knowledge/publication/2019/4/non-us-issuers-report-2019/NonUSIssuersReport.pdf.

[4] Robin Hui Huang, "The US–China Audit Oversight Dispute: Causes, Solutions, and Implications for Hong Kong" (2021) 54 *The International Lawyer* 179.

[5] Securities and Exchange Commission, "Disclosure Considerations for China-Based Issuers," CF Disclosure Guidance: Topic No. 10, November 23, 2020, www.sec.gov/corpfin/disclosure-considerations-china-based-issuers#_edn2.

One of the frequently alleged wrongdoings of Chinese issuers in securities class actions is the failure to disclose violations or potential violations of Chinese laws and regulations. Several recent cases illustrate this pattern. In *Theresa Gordon, et al. v. Tencent Music Entertainment Group, et al.*, the defendant, a Shenzhen-based and NYSE-listed company, failed to disclose its anti-competitive behavior.[6] Another major type of complaint relates to Chinese issuers providing false financial statements and conducting fraudulent accounting practices. This is illustrated in *Edward Lea, et al. v. TAL Education Group, et al.*[7] The defendant company was an online education and tutoring service provider headquartered in Beijing and was accused of overstating its net income in an analyst report.[8] In the more recent high-profile case of *Luckin Coffee Inc., et al.*, the company was caught for deliberately fabricating millions of dollars in sales.[9]

Plainly, the PSL against Chinese companies will be meaningful only if relevant judgments are effectively enforced. Indeed, the issue of foreign judgment recognition may lead to a smaller number of cases brought *ex ante* and lower amounts of compensation obtained *ex post*. To start with, there can be difficulties in enforcement against Chinese issuers even if a favorable judgment is handed down for foreign plaintiffs. Many Chinese issuers, especially the smaller companies listed on Nasdaq, have almost all of their assets and business operations located within China. The foreign plaintiffs and their lawyers need to consider issues of foreign judgment recognition and enforcement in Chinese courts. Consequently, the settlement amount in securities lawsuits against Chinese issuers tend to be of comparatively low value.[10] As mentioned before, overseas-listed Chinese companies usually have its senior management and most of its assets located in China. Hence, as typically stated in the disclosure documents of many Chinese issuers, "it may be difficult or impossible

6 Complaint filed by investor rights law firm, Rosen Law Firm, P.A., September 26, 2019, securities.stanford.edu/login.html?returnTo=filings-documents/1071/TMEG00_01/2019926_f01c_19CV05465.pdf.

7 Complaint filed by Glancy Prongay & Murray LLP, January 3, 2019, securities.stanford.edu/filings-documents/1066/TEG00_01/201913_r01c_18CV05480.pdf.

8 Mandate issued on December 17, 2020, securities.stanford.edu/filings-documents/1066/TEG00_01/20201217_r01x_18CV05480.pdf.

9 *In re Luckin Coffee, Inc. Securities Litigation*, Case No. 1:20-CV-01293-JPC-JLC (S.D.N.Y. 2021).

10 Geoffrey Sant, Charles M. Yablon and Stephen A. Radin et al., "Chinese Companies and US Class Actions: Securities Litigation and Product Liability" (2015) 23 *Cardozo Journal of International and Comparative Law* 738.

for investors to bring an action against us," and even if an action is successful, "the laws of China may render you unable to enforce a judgment against our assets."[11] For example, Luckin Coffee's IPO prospectus warned that "there may be difficulties in effecting service of legal process, enforcing foreign judgments or bringing actions in China against US or our management named in the prospectus based on foreign laws," and "recognition and enforcement in China of judgments of a court in any non-PRC jurisdictions to any matter not subject to a binding arbitration provision may be difficult or *impossible* [emphasis added]."[12]

The issue of recognition and enforcement of a US judgment in China is also made explicit by plaintiff counsels in securities class actions against US-listed Chinese companies. Before a settlement is reached and finalized by the court, parties must put forward reasons for their decision to settle and the sum of settlement. Upon motion by the lead plaintiff of the class, a settlement fairness hearing must be held to ascertain the fairness of the settlement. Among the reasons for settlement, there is a statement that "collecting from the judgments against the defendants, even with sufficient financial resources, was likely highly difficult as most of them reside in the People's Republic of China."[13]

In sum, there is a serious issue of having China enforce foreign securities judgments against overseas-listed Chinese companies, which in turn can seriously affect the willingness to sue and the process of legal proceedings. As most securities class action cases settle in practice, the recognition of an *actual* judgment would not be the norm. The real issue is the *prospect* of judgment enforcement, because it will impact whether and how a case may be brought, litigated and/or settled.

9.3 Chinese Regime for Recognizing and Enforcing Foreign Judgments

9.3.1 The Legislative Framework

China's regime for recognizing and enforcing foreign judgments is mainly comprised of the Chinese Civil Procedural Law

[11] Ibid., 739.

[12] Form F-1 Registration Statement of Luckin Coffee Inc., United States Securities and Exchange Commission, www.sec.gov/Archives/edgar/data/1767582/000104746919002450/a2238391zf-1.htm.

[13] Settlement notice to investors in *Re China Valves Technology* Securities Litigation, filed April 30, 2014, at 48.

(CPL)[14] and the judicial interpretation of the CPL (CPL Interpretation) issued by the Supreme People's Court (SPC).[15] In general, there are three key requirements for judgment recognition: the "legally effective" requirement, the international treaty or reciprocity requirement and the public policy defense.[16]

Specifically, upon receiving an application to recognize a foreign judgment, a Chinese court should make a decision via a three-part exercise. First, the court will review the application according to applicable international treaties that are entered into between China and the foreign jurisdiction, if any.[17] Second, where an international treaty is not applicable, the court then will consider the applicability of the principle of reciprocity to determine if there is reciprocal treatment in each other's jurisdiction. Third, if eligibility of judgment recognition is established in the first two parts, the court will then consider whether recognizing the foreign judgment would "violate the fundamental principles of the law, sovereignty, national security, or public interest of China."[18] The CPL Interpretation provides further guidance on the application for foreign judgment recognition in China. It sets out the process for making an application, such as the need to provide an original copy of the foreign judgment together with a certified translation.[19] It also stresses that where there is no applicable international treaty, and that reciprocity between the jurisdictions involved is also not found by the court, an application should be denied.[20]

A recent study examines all applications for recognizing and enforcing foreign judgments in China, finding that almost 60 percent of them

[14] Zhonghua Renmin Gongheguo Minshi Susong Fa (中华人民共和国民事诉讼法) [Civil Procedural Law of the People's Republic of China] (passed April 9, 1991 as amended in 2007, 2012, 2017 and 2021) (hereinafter "Chinese Civil Procedural Law").

[15] Zuigao Renmin Fayuan Guanyu Shiyong Zhonghua Renmin Gongheguo Minshi Susong Fa de Jieshi (最高人民法院关于适用中华人民共和国民事诉讼法的解释) [Interpretation of the Supreme People's Court on Application of the Civil Procedural Law of the People's Republic of China] (promulgated on December 18, 2014 as amended in 2020 and 2022) (hereinafter "CPL Interpretation"). Under the Chinese legal regime, SPC judicial interpretations carry the force of law.

[16] William S. Dodge and Wenliang Zhang, "Reciprocity in China–US Judgments Recognition" (2021) 53(5) *Vanderbilt Journal of Transnational Law* 1549.

[17] Chinese Civil Procedural Law, art. 289.

[18] Ibid.

[19] CPL Interpretation, art. 541.

[20] CPL Interpretation, art. 542.

failed.[21] However, most of the failed cases relate to foreign judgments obtained from jurisdictions that do not have a bilateral treaty with China – 70 percent of such cases were eventually refused by the Chinese courts on the grounds that there is a lack of reciprocity. By contrast, almost six in every ten applications succeeded if it was brought under an international treaty.

A relevant issue here is whether Chinese courts will recognize and enforce foreign court-approved settlements, given that securities class action cases are usually settled in the US. In principle, there should be little difference between judgment and court-approved settlement when it comes to judicial recognition. In China, court-approved settlement, also known as judicial mediation, has a similar legal effect to judgments, in the sense that it creates finality and res judicata, and has mandatory enforceability and coercive authority.[22] Courts in other jurisdictions such as Hong Kong and Canada have held that judicial mediation agreements in China should be enforced as Chinese judgments.[23] Under the principle of reciprocity, Chinese courts will likely treat foreign securities settlements in a similar way to judgments when dealing with the issue of recognition and enforcement. Hence, the analysis in this chapter would hold true, no matter whether the PSL against overseas-listed Chinese companies results in judgments or settlements.

9.3.2 International Cooperation Efforts

As of January 2021, China had entered into thirty-nine bilateral judicial treaties with foreign jurisdictions, thirty-five of which include a clause on mutual judgment recognition and enforcement.[24] However, the list does not include some influential common law jurisdictions such as the US,

[21] Asian Business Law Institute, "Quantitative Analysis of the Enforcement of Foreign Judgments in China," December 2020, payhip.com/b/haBy. In total there are thirty-eight applications for recognition of foreign judgments.

[22] Weixia Gu, *Dispute Resolution in China: Litigation, Arbitration, Mediation and Their Interactions* (Routledge, 2021), ch. 6; Robin Hui Huang, "Securities Dispute Mediation in China" (2016) 10(2) *Journal of Comparative Law* 185.

[23] *See*, for example, *Wei v. Mei*, No. 163 B.C.J. [2018] (ruling that the judicial mediation agreement is "conclusive and final under the Chinese law"); *Ng Yuk Keung v. Yan Xiaojie*, [2018] 6 HKC 338, [2018] HKDC 534 (stating that "the Mediation Agreement is a Court judgment/order albeit that it bears the title of a Mediation Agreement").

[24] For more details, see the official website of the Supreme People's Court of the PRC, www.court.gov.cn/shenpan-gengduo-73.html.

Canada and the United Kingdom, which are also popular jurisdictions for the overseas listing of Chinese companies.

Some recent developments may signal a greater willingness of the Chinese courts to recognize foreign judgments. In August 2018, the SPC of China and the Supreme Court of Singapore signed a Memorandum of Guidance, under which judgments obtained from both jurisdictions could be brought before their counterparts to be recognized and enforced.[25] It applies to judgments that require a person to pay a fixed or ascertainable sum of money to another in commercial cases.[26] While the memorandum has no binding legal effects, it represents a significant step in judgment recognition and enforcement between a foreign jurisdiction and China.

In 2015, the SPC issued a statement that suitable countries in the "Belt and Road Initiative" can be given preferential treatment in relation to judicial assistance.[27] Judicial assistance can be extended to these countries even if there is otherwise no evidence of reciprocity or bilateral treaties. This represents a breakthrough from the reciprocity requirement laid down by the CPL toward a more liberal treatment of certain foreign judgments. This directive from the SPC has since been relied upon in judgment recognition cases and has been cited in court commentaries.[28]

The liberal approach goes further with respect to the Association of Southeast Asian Nations (ASEAN), ten members of which are also within the scope of the Belt and Road Initiative. On June 8, 2017 the 2nd China–ASEAN Justice Forum issued a statement in the city of Nanning (Nanning Statement), affirming that:

> if two countries have not been bound by an international treaty on mutual recognition and enforcement of foreign civil or commercial judgments, both countries may, subject to their domestic laws, presume the existence

[25] China Justice Observer, "Memorandum of Guidance between the Supreme People's Court of the People's Republic of China and the Supreme Court of Singapore on Recognition and Enforcement of Money Judgments in Commercial Cases," www.chinajusticeobserver.com/p/memorandum-of-guidance-between-china-supremecourt-and-singapore-supremecourt-on-recognition-and-enforcement-of-money-judgments.

[26] Ibid., arts. 1, 7 and 8.

[27] Guanyu Renmin Fayuan Wei Yidaiyilu Jianshe Tigong Sifa Fuwu he Baozhang de Ruogan Yijian (关于人民法院为一带一路建设提供司法服务和保障的若干意见) [Opinion of the People's Court on Providing Judicial Service and Safeguard for the Belt and Road Initiative] (promulgated by the Supreme People's Court on June 16, 2015).

[28] Jie Huang, "Enforcing Foreign Monetary Judgments in China: Breakthroughs, Challenges, and Solutions in the Context of 'One Belt One Road'" (2019) 51(1) *George Washington International Law Review* 117.

> of their reciprocal relationship, when it comes to the judicial procedure of recognizing or enforcing such judgments made by courts of the other country, provided that the courts of the other country had not refused to recognize or enforce such judgments on the ground of lack of reciprocity.[29]

While the Nanning Statement is not legally binding and subject to domestic law, it is an endorsement of a more generous application of the reciprocity principle.

On July 2, 2019 the Convention on the Recognition and Enforcement of Foreign Judgments in Civil or Commercial Matters (2019 Hague Judgment Convention) was finally adopted at the Hague Conference on Private International Law. The Chinese delegation was one of the signatories to the final text. Due to various reasons, the ratification or accession process of the Convention has been slow, and it is not formally in force. If it eventually becomes widely ratified by states, it could be a potential game changer in the international practice of judgment recognition. China is also a signatory to the earlier Hague Convention of June 30, 2005 on Choice of Court Agreements (2005 Hague Choice of Court Convention), which deals with international jurisdiction and enforcement of foreign judgments in relation to disputes arising out of civil or commercial cases that involve an exclusive choice of court agreement. This Choice of Court Convention was signed by China in 2017 and has not yet been formally ratified.

In sum, China is generally supportive of bilateral and multilateral initiatives on recognition and enforcement of foreign judgments. However, the efforts are yet to cover Chinese companies' favorite destinations for overseas listing, notably the US. There is no judicial assistance treaty between China and the US, and the US is not on China's list for favorable treatments in relation to recognition and enforcement of foreign judgments. Section 9.4 will thus examine the trend of China recognizing US judgments, with particular reference to securities-related disputes.

9.4 Recognition and Enforcement of US Judgments in China

9.4.1 Cases and Recent Developments

As there is no judicial assistance agreement between the US and China, the first route of relying on an international treaty is simply not

[29] Nanning Statement of the 2nd China–ASEAN Justice Forum, June 8, 2017, para. VII, www.chinajusticeobserver.com/p/nanning-statement-of-the-2nd-china-asean-justice-forum.

applicable, and hence the recognition of US judgments in China would turn to the second route, namely, the principle of reciprocity. This hinges heavily on the individual courts' interpretation of the principle, which can be highly uncertain. Hence, there have been a very small number of cases of applying to Chinese courts for recognizing and enforcing US judgments. As of this writing, only seven relevant applications could be located, just two of which were successful.[30]

The first application for recognition of a US judgment in China was made in early 2009.[31] Following a divorce in Arizona, a foreign husband sought to enforce an order obtained from a US court. Among personal belongings and other assets, the order granted him full ownership of a flat in Beijing by paying out US$32,000 to the wife. However, the judge presiding the trial at the Changsha Intermediate People's Court refused to acknowledge the US divorce order, the reason being that there was no treaty between US and China, nor was there a reciprocal relationship. A similar case also failed to be recognized at the Hangzhou Intermediate People's Court in 2010.[32]

Back in 2009, a Chinese judgment was recognized in the US (i.e., the direct opposite of the instances above) for the very first time, which might have started to change the scene. It was a case decided in 2009 at the District Court for the Central District of California. *Hubei Gezhouba Sanlian v. Robinson Helicopter* concerned a helicopter accident in which three persons were killed in Hubei province.[33] The plaintiff sued a US helicopter manufacturer in China, but Robinson Helicopter argued that since the accident occurred in China, the matter should be under the jurisdiction of a Chinese court. The High People's Court of Hubei

[30] Our study excludes divorce cases, as they are procedural in nature and subject to more relaxed recognition standards, except those concerning enforcement of judgments on particular assets. Among the seven cases located, two of them will not be discussed in detail, because one case was finally withdrawn, namely *Senah v. Zhonghang Fushida Keji Gufen Youxian Gongsi* [Senah诉中航富士达科技股份有限公司] (Xi'an Intermediate People's Court, May 10, 2017), and the other was found to have been mistaken regarding the court's jurisdiction, namely *Matthew Yang Li v. Leifu Kangmin* [Matthew Yang Li 诉雷福康民] (Xinyang Intermediate People's Court, August 7, 2017).

[31] *Auer Douglas Hermansson v. Long Xia Lihun An* (鲍某.道格拉斯.赫曼逊与龙霞离婚案) (Changsha Intermediate People's Court, April 15, 2009).

[32] *Lin Hong v. Wang Lei* [林洪 诉 汪蕾] (Hangzhou Intermediate People's Court, July 28, 2010).

[33] *Hubei Gezhouba Sanlian Indus. Co. v. Robinson Helicopter Co.*, No. 2:06-CV-01789-FMCSSX, 2009 WL 2190197 (C.D. Cal July 2, 2009).

Province handed down a favorable judgment to the plaintiff, which was later recognized and enforced in the US.[34]

Then, in April 2017, a case tried to cite the *Robinson Helicopter* case as evidence of reciprocity in seeking judgment recognition in China.[35] This case, *Herbert Truehe et al. v. Jianxi Province Lidu Fireworks Co. Ltd.* ("Jiangxi Fireworks"), concerned a personal injury claim in which four US persons were seriously injured by fireworks produced by the defendant. The plaintiffs referred to *Robinson Helicopter* to argue for recognition of a US judgment before the court in the city of Nanchang in Jiangxi Province. However, the court rejected it, holding that no reciprocity can be found between the US and China.

The first successful case of foreign judgment recognition, *Liu v. Tao*, came in June 2017, concerning share purchases in a private company.[36] The defendant took a sum of US$125,000 but failed to execute the share transfer. A default judgment was handed down in July 2015 in favor of Liu, but the defendant had since left the US and stayed in China. Liu applied to the Wuhan Intermediate People's Court for recognition and enforcement of the US judgment. In the end, the Wuhan court accepted the evidence provided by the plaintiff on the existence of reciprocity between the US and China, which was a Chinese-language journal article discussing the *Robinson Helicopter* case as noted earlier, and thus recognized the US judgment concerned.

One year later, in 2018, a second successful recognition of a US judgment was handed down in Shanghai in the *Nalco v. Chen* case.[37] The case originated from a summary judgment against the defendant in the Federal Court of Illinois, concerning a joint venture to sell environmental equipment in China. The Chinese court recognized the US judgment on the basis of reciprocity, stating that "the U.S. courts have recognized and enforced the civil and commercial judgments made by Chinese courts for many times. Chinese courts can recognize and enforce the civil judgment of the American court involved in the case based on the principle of reciprocity."[38]

[34] Ibid.

[35] *Herbert Truehe et al. v. Jianxi Province Lidu Fireworks Co. Ltd* [赫伯特等诉江西省李渡烟花集团有限公司] (Nanchang Intermediate People's Court, April 20, 2017).

[36] *Liu Li v. Tao Li he Tong Wu* [刘利诉陶莉和童武] (Wuhan Intermediate People's Court, June 30, 2017).

[37] *Nalco v. Chen Dawei* [纳尔科诉陈大维] (Shanghai First Intermediate People's Court, September 17, 2018).

[38] *See* above note 24, p. 15.

The cases above shed light on how Chinese courts may reason in assessing the application of the recognition of a US judgment. While there is no treaty in place, if both the US and China continue to recognize each other's judgments, a positive feedback loop can be formed and the prospect of future recognition could be greatly improved.[39] On the other hand, it could be a coincidence that the *Robinson Helicopter* case was originally handed down in Hubei province, with Wuhan being its provincial capital city, and thus it could have swayed the Wuhan court to acknowledge reciprocity in its own first judgment recognition case of *Liu v. Tao*. By contrast, in the case of *Jiangxi Fireworks*, even though the same *Robinson Helicopter* case was referred to as proof of reciprocity, the court in Jiangxi Province refused to accept it. Hence, uncertainty remains as to the attitude of Chinese courts toward the recognition of US civil judgments.

Further, there are some ambiguities concerning the way the evidence of reciprocity is reviewed by the courts. In *Liu v. Tao*, the Wuhan court was satisfied with the reciprocity criteria through the production of a journal article which mentioned the *Robinson Helicopter* case. On the other hand, in the second case *Nalco v. Chen*, the Shanghai court did not point to any particular cases, but instead made a general observation that reciprocity already existed between the US and China. It is unclear how the court made this assessment and what evidential burden the applicant had to discharge.

As China is not a common law jurisdiction and does not have the rule of precedent, court judgments are not legally binding. In reality, different courts may deal with the same issue in different ways, and therefore it is not fully clear whether a US judgment can be generally recognized on the basis of reciprocity in China.[40] That said, China seems to be moving toward recognizing US judgments in recent years. Since 2016, there have been two cases in the positive, namely, *Liu v. Tao* and *Nalco v. Chen*, compared with only one in the negative, namely, *Jiangxi Fireworks*. More importantly, both *Liu v. Tao* and *Nalco v. Chen* occurred after *Jiangxi*

[39] Wenliang Zhang, "Sino-Foreign Recognition and Enforcement of Judgments: A Promising 'Follow-Suit' Model?" (2017) 16 *Chinese Journal of International Law* 515–539.

[40] Bin Sun, "The Future of Cross-Border Litigation in China: Enforcement of Foreign Commercial Judgments Based on Reciprocity" (2018) 50 *New York University Journal of International Law and Politics* 1142.

Fireworks, suggesting the more recent trend of judicial attitude leaning toward recognizing foreign judgments in China.

In summary, there have been a total of seven nonmarital cases seeking recognition of US civil and commercial judgments in China, including two successful ones. This gives a "success rate" of around 29 percent, and a recent trend of judgment recognition seems to be taking shape. It is worth noting that these cases are mainly related to divorce, contractual claims, personal injury compensation and shareholder disputes. To date, no cases have been brought to seek recognition of foreign securities judgments in China, and it is unclear whether the existing recognition cases could serve as evidence of reciprocity, a question that the following section will turn to.

9.4.2 *Challenges to Recognition of Securities Judgments*

When it comes to securities judgments, the issue of cross-border recognition and enforcement could become even more difficult. In nature, securities judgments can be seen as a type of civil and commercial judgment, and thus the next logical issue is whether foreign securities judgments should be treated differently from other types of civil or commercial judgments. Almost all jurisdictions, including China, do not have special recognition rules for securities judgments. However, securities judgments, particularly those resulting from class actions, have some special features that make them different from traditional civil judgments such as contract cases. Hence, this section will discuss the special features of US securities judgments, their impact on the issue of recognition and enforcement and the need for making special rules on their recognition and enforcement in China.

As discussed before, even where reciprocity could be found to exist between the courts of both sides, the recognition of foreign judgments will not be automatic, and the threshold of public interest and national sovereignty will still need to be met. This assessment entails broad discretion of the court, and in the case of securities class actions, a multitude of issues may lead a court to refuse foreign judgments. When a Chinese court wants to reject an application, it may tactically choose to do so on other grounds, rather than referring to public interest and national sovereignty, which may be politically sensitive.

The two US judgments that obtained recognition in China were not securities litigation against listed companies. One was about product liability, and the other concerned contractual arrangements within private companies. Even with these two successful cases of judgment recognition, it is still doubtful whether recognition will readily extend to other types of cases. Indeed, due to public interest concerns, some types of civil cases are usually excluded under bilateral treaties, such as cases of intellectual property rights which may involve public policy issues.[41] Likewise, the regime of investor protection and shareholder rights may well be viewed as a sovereign decision and thus, differ across jurisdictions. In nature, securities judgments are based on securities law which has some elements of public law.

Next, there could be a significant imbalance in the number of recognition requests for securities judgments between China and the US, potentially giving rise to public interest concerns. The recognition requests will likely be heavily one-sided with many more cases originating overseas. While there are many Chinese companies listed in the US, no foreign companies are currently allowed to be listed in the Chinese securities market. As such, if China were to enter into any bilateral agreement on recognition of securities judgments, it would effectively be one-way traffic. This problem can be exacerbated by the fact that the sum of damages in securities class action litigation is usually much larger than those in civil judgments presently recognized in China. For instance, the judgment sum in the *Robinson* case for product liability was US$6.5 million, whereas the average settlement amount for a securities class action in the US stood at around US$58 million.[42] On the other hand, the principle of reciprocity can be more difficult to apply to securities judgments than traditional civil judgments. As no foreign companies are currently listed in China, there is practically no chance for foreign courts to recognize Chinese securities judgments, thus making it virtually impossible to find reciprocity.

Further, the US securities class action has long been a subject of debate, with many people viewing it as abusive and predatory.[43] This

[41] *See*, for example, 2005 Hague Choice of Court Convention, art. 2; Memorandum of Guidance between the Supreme People's Court of the People's Republic of China and the Supreme Court of Singapore on Recognition and Enforcement of Money judgments in Commercial Cases, signed on August 31, 2018, art. 7.

[42] Laarni Bulan and Laura Simmons, "Securities Class Action Settlements: 2019 Review and Analysis," March 11, 2020, corpgov.law.harvard.edu/2020/03/11/securities-class-action-settlements-2019-review-and-analysis/.

[43] Geoffrey Sant, Charles M. Yablon and Stephen A. Radin et al., "Chinese Companies and US Class Actions: Securities Litigation and Product Liability" (2015) 23 *Cardozo Journal of International and Comparative Law* 794.

relates to the very nature of class action litigation in the US, which could conflict with legal doctrines in China. It has been pointed out that unnamed class members in an "opt out" class action could be deemed as a nonparty when seeking judgment recognition in China and may run into difficulties.[44] In the US class action, when a complaint is filed, an individual investor may or may not be registered with the litigating law firm. After a settlement is reached, eligible investors will then be notified and receive compensation. Nevertheless, the law on both sides may have been somewhat equalized with the recent introduction of the Chinese-style securities class action, also known as special representative group litigation, under the 2019 reform of securities law in China.[45] Under this new mechanism, a qualified investor protection institution can automatically represent all eligible plaintiff investors, as long as it receives authorization from fifty or more plaintiff investors to act as a representative to bring a securities civil action against market misconduct such as misstatements, unless other investors expressly opt out of the litigation.[46]

There is also uncertainty over how a Chinese court may categorize securities litigation. As mentioned before, the recognition of foreign judgments typically only encompasses commercial and civil cases, excluding cases with elements of public law. Conceptually, securities class action initiated by aggrieved investors to seek compensation are private and civil in nature. In practice, however, a large proportion of securities class action arises from, or runs concurrently with, SEC investigations. A good example is the *Luckin Coffee* case, where the securities class action was piggybacking on the SEC's investigation into the company's fraudulent activities. It then begs the question of whether China would view the follow-on litigation for compensation as purely civil in nature,

[44] Andrea Conzatti, "The Recognition of US Opt-out Class Actions in China" (2013) 44(2) *Georgetown Journal of International Law* 663.

[45] Robin Hui Huang, "Class Action in China: Challenges and Opportunities," in Brian Fitzpatrick and Randall Thomas (eds.), *The Cambridge International Handbook of Class Actions* (Cambridge University Press, 2021), pp. 350, 363–364.

[46] Zhonghua Renmin Gongheguo Zhengquan Fa (中华人民共和国证券法) [Securities Law of the People's Republic of China] (passed December 29, 1998, as amended in 2004, 2005, 2013, 2014, 2019), art. 95. The Supreme People's Court has issued a judicial interpretation on this provision. Zuigaorenminfayuan Guanyu Zhengjuan Jiufen Daibiaoren Susong Ruogan Wenti De Guiding (最高人民法院关于证券纠纷代表人诉讼若干问题的规定) [Rules of the Supreme People's Court on Relevant Issues of Securities Dispute Representative Litigation] (issued by the Supreme People's Court, effective from July 31, 2020), art. 35.

or whether it could be seen as at least partly public in nature. As far as a public sanction is concerned, China typically does not enforce such judgments and overseas-listed Chinese companies had walked away with minimal disgorgement of ill-gotten profits.[47]

The public policy issue may become more acute due to the so-called double circularity problem in transnational securities litigation.[48] As the name suggests, the problem involves two layers of circularity. The first one is the typical circularity problem in domestic securities litigation, a term traditionally used to refer to the situation where "securities litigation imposes costs on investors because of harm done to investors – without recognizing that the victim is again bearing the costs of its own injury."[49] Hence, the compensation that the plaintiff investors in the securities class action receive from the company may actually come at the expense of innocent investors who did not contribute to the securities misconduct and did not trade securities during the relevant class period. The second one may occur to cross-listed companies, which are listed in both their home markets (developing markets such as Brazil), and overseas markets (developed markets such as the US). As there are significant differences in the level of investor protection between the home and host markets, the investors in the two listing places may receive differential treatments when it comes to compensation for securities misconduct of the same company. In cross-listed Brazilian companies, for example, the US investors can receive compensation through securities class actions while the Brazilian investors in the same company cannot have the same compensation due to the lack of an effective class action regime. As discussed before, China has recently introduced the special securities representative suit which is similar to the US class action. However, as this new regime was introduced in 2019 with effect from March 2020 it remains to be seen how effective it will be in practice. Thus, the "double circularity" problem will add a further layer of complexity to the public policy considerations of the Chinese courts in recognizing US securities judgments.

[47] Jonathan Schmidt, "Inequities in Corporate and Securities Law: Disabling the Exploitative Chinese Corporation and Charting a Path to International Commercial Accountability" (2013) 14(2) *San Diego International Law Journal* 385.

[48] Erica Gorga, "The Impact of the Financial Crisis on Nonfinancial Firms: The Case of Brazilian Corporations and the 'Double Circularity' Problem in Transnational Securities Litigation" (2015) 16(1) *Theoretical Inquiries in Law* 163.

[49] John C. Coffee, Jr., "Reforming the Securities Class Action: An Essay on Deterrence and Its Implementation" (2006) 106(7) *Columbia Law Review* 1538.

In sum, while there have been some instances of Chinese courts recognizing US judgments, uncertainty remains for the recognition of US securities judgments in China.

9.5 Mainland–Hong Kong Arrangements for Judgment Recognition

This section will turn to the issue of judgment recognition and enforcement between Hong Kong and Mainland China. As it becomes increasingly important to arrange dual-listing of Chinese companies in both the US and Hong Kong, the regulation of Chinese issuers in Hong Kong is closely connected to the preceding discussion in the US–China context. For instance, while Alibaba went public on the NYSE in 2014, it sought secondary listing in Hong Kong in 2019, quoted as an "escape valve listing" by the market.[50] Over the years, Hong Kong has entered into a set of arrangements on mutual judgment recognition with Mainland China, first in 2006 and then in 2019. However, as will be discussed below, there are still many hurdles for recognition and enforcement of securities judgments.

9.5.1 The 2006 and 2019 Arrangements

The first arrangement concerning judgment recognition between China and Hong Kong was entered into in 2006 (2006 Arrangement).[51] However, in addition to usual requirements such as the finality of judgments, the 2006 Arrangement has more restrictions on its scope of applicability. First, there is a so-called commercial case restriction, that is, the 2006 Arrangement only covers judgments requiring a payment of money in business-to-business cases. It also specifically excludes certain types of contracts such as employment contracts and contracts of a

[50] "Why is Alibaba listing in Hong Kong?," *Reuters*, November 15, 2019, www.reuters.com/article/world/uk/why-is-alibaba-listing-in-hong-kong-idUSKBN1XP0JG/.

[51] Guanyu Neidi yu Xianggang Tebie Xingzhengqu Fayuan Xianghu Renke he Zhixing Dangshiren Xieyi Guanxia de Min Shang Shi Anjian Panjue de Anpai (关于内地与香港特别行政区法院相互认可和执行当事人协议管辖的民商事案件判决的安排) [2006 Arrangement on Reciprocal Recognition and Enforcement of Judgments in Civil and Commercial Matters by the Courts of the Mainland and of the Hong Kong Special Administrative Region Pursuant to Choice of Court Agreements between Parties Concerned], www.legco.gov.hk/yr06-07/chinese/bc/bc56/papers/bc560716cb2-brief-b-ec.pdf.

noncommercial nature. Second, the application of the 2006 Arrangement requires a prior written agreement on exclusive choice of court, or a specific clause on choice of court in the contract concerned. In such cases, either a Chinese court or a Hong Kong court must be clearly designated as the sole forum for resolving the relevant dispute.

In the case of PSL, there is usually no business-to-business contractual relationship between investors and listed companies, let alone any prior agreement on the choice of court. Hence, securities law cases may fall outside the scope of the 2006 Arrangement, and thus the request for a Hong Kong securities judgment to be recognized in Mainland China will likely be handled similarly as a US judgment, that is, via the principle of reciprocity.

In 2019, a new arrangement was agreed upon by Mainland China and Hong Kong to enlarge the scope of mutual judgment recognition (2019 Arrangement).[52] The 2019 Arrangement becomes effective after the two sides complete their relevant local legislation.[53] The 2019 Arrangement covers cases considered to be generally of a civil and commercial nature, and thus is much wider in scope compared to the 2006 Arrangement. However, several types of cases are still excluded from the 2019 Arrangement, including proceedings relating to administrative or regulatory matters. The Department of Justice provides a non-exhaustive list of cases as examples of excluded cases.[54] Among them are proceedings brought by the Securities and Futures Commission (SFC) under sections 214 of the Securities and Futures Ordinance (SFO).[55] This SFO provision empowers the SFC to intervene into the running of a company and seek remedies for shareholders. Further, the SFC can appeal against a decision of the Market Misconduct Tribunal under section 266 of the SFO.[56] Both examples are enforcement actions carried out by the SFC.

[52] HK Department of Justice, "Arrangement on Reciprocal Recognition and Enforcement of Judgments in Civil and Commercial Matters by the Courts of the Mainland and of the Hong Kong Special Administrative Region," www.doj.gov.hk/en/mainland_and_macao/pdf/Doc3_477379e.pdf.

[53] On January 29, 2024, the 2019 Arrangement came into force with Hong Kong passing its local law, including "Mainland Judgments in Civil and Commercial Matters (Reciprocal Enforcement) Ordinance (Cap. 645)" and "Mainland Judgments in Civil and Commercial Matters (Reciprocal Enforcement) Rules (Cap. 645 sub. leg. A)."

[54] HK Department of Justice, "Key Features of the Arrangement," footnote 1, www.doj.gov.hk/en/mainland_and_macao/pdf/Doc6_481354e.pdf.

[55] Securities and Futures Ordinance, s. 214.

[56] Securities and Futures Ordinance, s. 266.

The list of excluded cases does not include the SFO provisions on civil liability for securities misconduct, such as sections 108, 281 and 305. Hence, by way of omission, cases based on them may be regarded by the Hong Kong Department of Justice as civil in nature and could fall within the scope of the 2019 Arrangement. According to section 108 of the SFO, if a person makes any fraudulent, reckless or negligent misrepresentation that induces another person to enter into an agreement to acquire, dispose of, subscribe for or underwrite securities, the person making the misrepresentation shall be liable to pay compensation to the person who suffers pecuniary loss as a result of the misrepresentation.[57] Under sections 281 and 305 of the SFO, if a person commits market misconduct, he or she shall be liable to pay compensation by way of damages to any other person for any loss sustained as a result of the market misconduct.[58] Apart from these civil liabilities under the SFO, civil cases can also be brought under the Hong Kong Companies Ordinance, such as derivative actions[59] and unfair prejudice remedies.[60]

9.5.2 *Difficulty in Recognizing Securities Judgments*

However, under the 2019 Arrangement, PSL may still face many hurdles, including the lack of a class action regime and excessively expensive legal costs. In Hong Kong, contingency fee schemes are still illegal.[61] Further, the losing party will usually need to bear the legal costs of the winning party under the traditional "loser pays" rule. In general, Hong Kong puts high costs on investor claimants bringing civil actions against securities misconduct, and thus in practice, very few PSL cases have been brought in Hong Kong.

In theory, securities law enforcement is generally divided into public and private enforcement, which can complement and even substitute one another.[62] While the US places high value on private enforcement in the form of securities class action, Hong Kong relies heavily on the

[57] Securities and Futures Ordinance, s. 108.
[58] Securities and Futures Ordinance, s. 281, s. 305.
[59] Companies Ordinance, Cap. 622, art. 733.
[60] Companies Ordinance, Cap. 622, art. 725.
[61] Law Reform Commission of Hong Kong, "Conditional Fees Consultation Paper," 2006, www.legco.gov.hk/yr05-06/english/panels/ajls/papers/aj1024cb2-122-5e.pdf.
[62] Robin Hui Huang, "Rethinking the Relationship between Public Regulation and Private litigation: Evidence from Securities Class Action in China" (2018) 19 *Theoretical Inquiries in Law* 334.

regulators' public enforcement for investor protection, due to the limits on the private enforcement route as mentioned previously.[63] In regard to Chinese issuers listed in Hong Kong, the reliance on the SFC's public enforcement may potentially create a hurdle to judgment recognition. As noted earlier, section 214 of the SFO can be used by the SFC as a functional substitute for purely private remedies under the Companies Ordinance such as derivative suits. Further, under section 213 of the SFO, the SFC can request the court to make relevant orders to compensate the investors suffering from market misconduct.[64] In practice, the SFC has frequently used this mechanism to seek compensation for investors harmed by various forms of securities misconduct such as insider trading,[65] market manipulation[66] and misstatement.[67]

This represents a peculiar model of using public enforcement to provide private remedies in Hong Kong, which has a substitution effect on private securities litigation in Hong Kong.[68] This model is praised for its ability to "make up for the lack of private enforcement against certain types of misconduct and sometimes serve as a more effective tool to credibly commit to strong investor protection."[69] However, for cross-border securities transactions, the model may pose serious difficulties for Hong Kong securities judgments to be recognized in Mainland China. The cases brought by the SFC under the model are proceedings relating to administrative or regulatory matters in nature, and as such, will not be amenable to judgment recognition even under the 2019 Arrangement.

Hence, insofar as Chinese issuers listed in Hong Kong are concerned, PSL is not covered by the 2006 Arrangement. When the 2019 Arrangement comes into force, PSL judgment will likely be included. However, given the peculiar public enforcement model of investor protection in Hong Kong, the 2019 Arrangement may have very limited utility for recognizing securities judgments.

63 David C. Donald and Paul W. H. Cheuk, "Hong Kong's Public Enforcement Model of Investor Protection" (2017) 4(2) *Asian Journal of Law and Society* 385.

64 Securities and Futures Ordinance, Cap. 571, s. 213.

65 *SFC v. Tiger Asia Management*, FACV 10/2012, May 10, 2013, Court of Final Appeal.

66 *SFC v. Tsoi Bun*, [2014] HKEC 258.

67 *Securities and Futures Commission v. Hontex International Holdings Company Limited & Others*, August 2, 2011, Court of First Instance, HCMP 630/2010.

68 Robin Hui Huang, Hailong Li and Gavin Yao Lin, "The Anatomy of Securities Class Action in China: A Functional and Comparative Approach with the United States" (2018) 46(4) *Securities Regulation Law Journal* 372.

69 Ying Hu, "The Role of Public Enforcement in Investor Compensation: A Hong Kong Perspective" (2017) 46(3) *Common Law World Review* 216.

9.6 Proposals and Prospects

As discussed in Sections 9.4 and 9.5, it remains highly uncertain whether a foreign securities judgment would be recognized in China. While no such application has been made in practice, this uncertainty contributes to the worrying issue dubbed "Great Legal Wall of China."[70] It impacts on whether PSL would be initiated in the first place and also affects the dollar amount of the eventual compensation. This section will thus explore alternative methods to alleviate the issue.

9.6.1 PSL in Offshore Financial Centers?

Since overseas-listed Chinese issuers are typically not incorporated in China, but in offshore financial centers such as the Cayman Islands, one possible solution to the judgment enforcement issue is to litigate in these offshore financial centers. These offshore financial centers are mostly common law jurisdictions, with existing regimes for foreign judgment recognition, particularly in relation to monetary judgments.[71] Therefore, to recover assets from Chinese overseas-listed companies, one may simply choose to bring PSL in those offshore financial centers where these companies are registered. However, it may not be of much assistance to do so, because there may not be any revenue flowing into those offshore centers due to some particular arrangements adopted by the Chinese companies.

In practice, these companies usually adopt the variable interest entity (VIE) structure, which is used to circumvent Chinese regulations that restrict foreign ownership in certain industries, notably internet business. Under the VIE structure, an offshore holding company is created to make contractual arrangements with the VIEs, which are onshore Chinese companies operating the actual business. There is no direct shareholding relationship between the overseas-listed offshore holding company and the onshore Chinese companies. The offshore holding company assumes both the costs and benefits of the VIE, consolidating the VIEs' financials into its financial statement. Research suggests that less than one-fifth of US-listed Chinese issues with the VIE structure have paid or intend to pay any dividends offshore, and that "all the money made in China stays in

[70] Jesse Fried and Ehud Kamar, "China and the Rise of Law-Proof Insiders" (2022) 48 *Journal of Corporation Law*, 215.

[71] For example, in the British Virgin Islands, the Reciprocal Enforcement Act applies automatically to judgment given in the UK, as well as New South Wales of Australia.

China."[72] Hence, shareholders in these companies derive their return from the hike in stock prices, not dividends. As there can be few assets available in the offshore holding companies, the judgment enforcement issue in China could not be solved.

Another possibility is to first bring PSL in these offshore financial centers and then seek enforcement of judgments in China. As these offshore financial centers need to safeguard international transactions, they would have strong incentives to seek judicial assistance from China in enforcing judgments. However, there are currently no treaties or special arrangements between them and China. Therefore, judgments obtained from the offshore financial centers need to go through the same procedures and tests as those obtained from the US, and thus there will be a similar level of uncertainty over judgment recognition. Further, securities law in the offshore financial centers is much less sophisticated than that in the US. As such, the level of investor protection and the scope of PSL could be more limited in those jurisdictions.

9.6.2 *Using Arbitration as an Alternative?*

Another potential solution is to use arbitration, particularly in light of its increased popularity in resolving financial disputes.[73] In contrast to the system of foreign judgment recognition, arbitral awards are much more readily and widely recognized. Over 160 countries, including China, have adopted the Convention on the Recognition and Enforcement of Foreign Arbitral Awards (the New York Convention). Its wide acceptance can be explained by the parties' voluntary/contractual submission to an arbitrator to avoid the difficult issues of sovereignty or court jurisdiction in the process of judgment recognition. The CPL provides for recognition of arbitral awards in similar wordings to the provisions on judgment recognition, except there is no requirement to review on the "sovereignty, national security, and public interest" grounds.[74] Also, since the New York Convention is widely adopted, recognition of arbitral awards can go through the treaty route, which will be much more expedient and certain.

[72] Brandon Whitehill, "Buyer Beware: Chinese companies and the VIE Structure," Council of Institutional Investors, December 2017, p. 11, www.cii.org/files/publications/misc/12_07_17%20Chinese%20Companies%20and%20the%20VIE%20Structure.pdf.

[73] Robin Hui Huang and Shahla Ali, "Governing Financial Disputes in China: What Have We Learnt from the Global Financial Crisis of 2008?" (2011) 7(1) *University of Pennsylvania East Asia Law Review* 203.

[74] Chinese Civil Procedural Law, art. 290.

Further, resolving securities disputes through arbitration may have other benefits vis-à-vis court litigation.[75] The costs of arbitration tend to be lower, and thus a higher proportion of compensation money would accrue to aggrieved investors. In class action litigation, the legal costs usually represent between 25 percent and 35 percent of the litigation proceeds.[76] It would also be quicker to effectuate recovery in the case of arbitration, with the length of time being three to four times shorter than litigation.[77] Specialist arbitrators can be engaged to handle securities disputes, which are usually technical and highly complicated, whereas in court litigation, judges may not necessarily specialize in them. Hence, the US Department of Treasury encouraged the use of arbitration to resolve securities disputes.[78]

However, there is little sign of arbitration gaining widespread acceptance and traction in resolving securities disputes in the US.[79] The SEC once signaled its support for IPOs featuring a mandatory arbitration provision, but it was met with skepticism from lawyers and investor protection advocacy groups.[80] As many as twenty-nine influential professors in the US jointly wrote a letter to the SEC, arguing that mandatory arbitration may actually weaken investor protection.[81] This would limit the ability for US-listed Chinese companies to use arbitration for securities disputes and get them subsequently recognized in China. Under China's Arbitration Law which applies to both domestic and foreign-related disputes, a precondition for arbitration is that the parties have

[75] Weixia Gu, "Securities Arbitration in China: A Better Alternative to Retail Shareholder Protection?" (2013) 33(2) *Northwestern Journal of International Law & Business* 298–305.

[76] Hal S. Scott and Leslie N. Silverman, "Stockholder Adoption of Mandatory Individual Arbitration For Stock Holder Disputes" (2013) 36(3) *Harvard Journal of Law & Public Policy* 1202.

[77] Ibid., p. 1189.

[78] US Department of the Treasury, "A Financial System That Creates Economic Opportunities: Capital Markets," October 2017, pp. 33–34, home.treasury.gov/system/files/136/A-Financial-System-Capital-Markets-FINAL-FINAL.pdf.

[79] Michael S. Barr, "Mandatory Arbitration in Consumer Finance and Investor Contracts," in Robin Hui Huang and Nicholas Howson (eds.), *Enforcement of Corporate and Securities Law: China and the World* (Cambridge University Press, 2017), ch. 4.

[80] Alison Frankel, "The case against mandatory shareholder arbitration," *Reuters*, August 23, 2018.

[81] Lucian A. Bebchuk, J. Robert Brown Jr. and Samel W. Buell et al., "Re: Arbitration Provisions Threaten Market Integrity and Are Contrary to the Federal Securities Laws," October 30, 2013, law.duke.edu/sites/default/files/centers/gfmc/session_2/4_letter_to_sec_re_arbitration_bylaws-10-30-2013.pdf.

previously entered into an arbitration agreement.[82] As noted previously, however, the idea of a mandatory arbitration provision has not yet been adopted, and in practice, public investors usually do not voluntarily have prior arbitration agreements with listed companies.

A further limitation of resorting to arbitration is that arbitration agreements and arbitral awards must undergo review by local Chinese courts for enforcement. Enforcement may be refused in certain circumstances, such as when enforcement is against social and public interests.[83] This is of particular relevance to securities arbitration, because as discussed before, securities disputes may give rise to public policy issues.[84] Finally, arbitration has other weaknesses. For instance, while confidentiality is an advantage of arbitration, there is a lack of transparency and predictability. Moreover, instead of forming a class for the claim, arbitration will likely organize investor claimants in a much smaller scale and even on a personal basis. As a result, aggrieved investors may find themselves left with less bargaining power and ability to oversee the entire arbitral process.

In sum, while arbitration has great potential to resolve securities disputes, there remain some concerns over its actual utility. Arbitration may only supplement, rather than fully substitute the use of court litigation to resolve securities disputes involving overseas-listed Chinese issuers.

9.6.3 *Resolving the China–US Securities Judgment Recognition Issue*

As discussed earlier, China has recently recognized an increasing number of foreign civil and commercial judgments, made greater efforts to improve judicial assistance for the Belt and Road Initiative, and signed more bilateral treaties or arrangements.[85] This general pattern of China's positive attitude toward recognition and enforcement of foreign judgments will likely apply to PSL against overseas-listed Chinese companies, but the challenges presented by the special features of securities judgments need to be properly addressed.

82 Zhonghua Renmin Gongheguo Zhongcai Fa (中国人民共和国仲裁法) [Arbitration Law of the People's Republic of China] (promulgated by the Standing Committee of the National People's Congress, August 31, 1994 effective September 1, 1995, amended in 2009 and 2017), art. 4.

83 Ibid., art. 58.

84 *See* Section 9.4.2.

85 *See* Section 9.3.

Despite ongoing tensions with the US, China has repeatedly stated its intention to continue supporting the overseas listing of Chinese firms. In fact, with the large number of overseas-listed Chinese firms and their significance to the Chinese economy, China has a great interest in cooperating with the US in regulating them. Mutual recognition of securities judgments will also greatly benefit Chinese investors. When they invest overseas, Chinese companies listed in the US are naturally among the top choices. Moreover, enhancement to investor protection will ultimately benefit Chinese companies through the bonding effects: they would be subject to stronger regulation with better corporate governance checks and balances, thus becoming more appealing to international investors. Hence, in principle, China has incentives to deal with the issue of recognition and enforcement of foreign securities judgments.

Technically, the ideal way to enhance mutual judgment recognition is for China and the US to sign a general treaty on judicial assistance or a specific agreement on judgment recognition. Admittedly, it may be difficult to do so, particularly under the current geopolitical environment, but this is something that should be aimed for in the long term. If a bilateral treaty is too high an objective to achieve in the foreseeable future, a small but positive step forward could be taken in line with the China–Singapore arrangement discussed earlier.[86] Specifically, initiatives could first be undertaken by the top courts in the US and China in the form of a joint judicial announcement, which would send a strong message to the market that there is willingness on both sides in relation to judgment recognition and enforcement. This message is important because, as discussed earlier, securities class action lawsuits usually settle and thus it may be hard for a test case to come by to shed light on whether China would recognize a US securities judgment.[87] Without such a message, a lot of conjectures will have to be made by the market, which would lead to costs and uncertainties in securities class action lawsuits.[88]

[86] *See* Section 9.3.2.

[87] *See* Section 9.3.1.

[88] *See* Section 9.2. It is worth noting two important limitations of the suggestion for a US–China joint judicial announcement. First, unlike China's Supreme People's Court, the US Supreme Court does not issue policy guidance to lower courts outside the context of decided cases. Second, the enforcement of foreign judgments in the US is governed by state, rather than federal law, so the US Supreme Court has no authority in this area. Thanks to Professor William S. Dodge of University of California Davis School of Law for making the comments above.

There is also considerable room for China to improve its practice of judgment recognition under the principle of reciprocity. As discussed earlier, Chinese courts have started to recognize US judgments, but ambiguities remain as to the legal reasoning and evidence that may be required for applying the principle of reciprocity. Indeed, different courts in China have adopted different approaches and reached different conclusions. Apart from the lack of predictability, it is also time-consuming to rely on the principle of reciprocity for foreign judgment recognition. For instance, as an indication, the average time length is 344 days between making an application for foreign judgment recognition to a Chinese court and obtaining a final ruling on the application.[89]

Further, there is uncertainty concerning the specific types of cases that may be covered by the principle of reciprocity. As discussed before, PSL is often related to public enforcement of securities law, and thus it is unclear whether China may recognize a foreign securities judgment by reference to the prior cases of recognizing traditional civil judgments such as contract cases. Hence, it would be helpful if the SPC can issue judicial interpretations to provide more guidance on the issue of recognizing foreign judgments, including securities judgments.

Finally, China is advised to ratify the 2005 Hague Choice of Court Convention that it signed in 2017, and in the long run, consider acceding to the 2019 Hague Judgment Convention.[90] It would be ideal if both China and the US could ratify the conventions, given that the US is a top-listing destination for Chinese companies. However, even if the US refuses to do that, it would still be meaningful for China to ratify the conventions. The ratification can strongly signal China's commitment to multilateral cooperation on judicial assistance, and help enhance China's "global credibility, legitimacy and capacity in international commercial litigations."[91] This would create peer pressure on the US courts to more readily recognize Chinese judgments, and in turn, China could recognize US judgments on the basis of reciprocity. Eventually, the legitimacy and

[89] With the maximum going on for 876 days. *See* China Justice Observer, "Time and Expenses: Recognition and Enforcement of Foreign Judgments in China," www.chinajusticeobserver.com/a/time-and-expenses-recognition-and-enforcement-of-foreign-judgments-in-china.

[90] Weixia Gu, "China's Approach to Recognition and Enforcement of Foreign Civil and Commercial Judgments and International Litigation Capacity Building" (2020) 15(2) *Journal of Comparative Law* 287.

[91] Ibid., pp. 287–288.

competence of the Chinese international litigation system and the Chinese courts will be promoted, thereby making the process of recognizing and enforcing foreign judgments more efficient. In the specific context of international securities regulation, some scholars have proposed the idea of "issuer choice," under which issuers and investors can select the forum and the law for resolving securities disputes.[92] This idea can be applied to overseas-listed Chinese companies. China has recently introduced a regime for extraterritorial jurisdiction of securities law.[93] As it is couched in very general terms, there can be room for Chinese issuers to include a forum selection clause for securities claims in its articles or bylaws. In nature, the "issuer choice" idea is a private ordering mechanism and would need the support of the local courts. The Chinese courts would be more willing and able to respect the choice of the issuer and investors and accommodate the request to recognize and enforce judgments, if China were to ratify the 2005 Hague Choice of Court Convention and the 2019 Hague Judgment Convention.

9.6.4 Proposals for Hong Kong Securities Judgment Recognition

Hong Kong also serves as an offshore financial center for Chinese companies, but its role is somewhat different from the "pure" offshore centers mentioned previously such as the Cayman Islands. There is a higher chance for Chinese issuers to have some assets located in Hong Kong. As a financial center as well as a populous city, Hong Kong is a market for doing business rather than a mere listing place for many Chinese companies. Funds could be parked in Hong Kong as reserves or financial assets. Hence, it may be more practical to enforce a securities judgment against Chinese companies by targeting their assets located in Hong Kong.

Further, overseas investors could consider bringing PSL against cross-listed Chinese issuers in Hong Kong and then leveraging the relevant agreements between Hong Kong and Mainland China to seek enforcement within China where the issuer's assets are mostly located.

[92] Roberta Romano, "The Need for Competition in International Securities Regulation" (2001) 2(2) *Theoretical Inquiries in Law* 407; Wolf-Georg Ringe and Alexander Hellgardt, "The International Dimension of Issuer Liability and Choice of Law from a Transatlantic Perspective" (2011) 31(1) *Oxford Journal of Legal Studies* 50–51.

[93] Robin Hui Huang, Charles Chao Wang, Yuqi Zhou and Sunny Xiyuan Li, "Extraterritorial Jurisdiction of China's New Securities Law: Policies, Problems and Proposals" (2022) 22(2) *Journal of Corporate Law Studies* 677–708.

As discussed before, there remain significant difficulties with this route,[94] and it is thus important that Hong Kong explores ways of dealing with the issue. For instance, it could introduce a securities class action regime and lift the traditional long-standing ban on contingency fees. In order to tackle the potential effect of opening the floodgates of litigation, class actions could be limited to particular case types, such as securities compensation claims. Further, Hong Kong should push and advocate for the inclusion of judgments arising from SFC-initiated litigation into the judgment recognition arrangement between Hong Kong and Mainland China.

At the regional level, Hong Kong has long been advised to establish a comprehensive multilateral judgment recognition and enforcement framework between the Mainland, Hong Kong and Macau.[95] This suggestion can now be more feasible within the context of the Guangdong–Hong Kong–Macao Greater-Bay Area. The framework should cover a wider range of civil and commercial judgments, including securities judgments. At the international level, Hong Kong should also accede to the 2005 Hague Choice of Court Convention by seeking permission from Beijing for the Convention to be applied to Hong Kong in accordance with Article 153 of the Basic Law and, if possible, even consider joining the 2019 Hague Judgments Convention in the long run subject to the same caveat.[96]

9.7 Conclusion

In recent years, there have been a significant number of corporate scandals involving overseas-listed Chinese companies, such as the case of *Luckin Coffee* in the US. As a result, such companies have become a frequent target of PSL overseas. However, there is a risk that the plaintiff investors may end up with little redress even after winning the litigation, because overseas-listed Chinese companies usually have most of their assets located within China. If foreign judgments are unable to be recognized and enforced in China, it would affect the efficacy of

[94] *See* Section 9.5.2.

[95] Jie Huang, *Inter-regional Recognition and Enforcement of Civil and Commercial Judgment: Lessons for China from US and EU Law* (Hart, 2014), p. 186.

[96] Weixia Gu, "A Conflict of Laws Study in Hong Kong–China Judgment Regionalism: Legal Challenges and Renewed Momentum" (2020) 52(4) *Cornell International Law Journal* 637–640.

international securities regulation in compensating victims and punishing perpetrators. Hence, it is important to examine the issue of China's recognition and enforcement of foreign judgments in relation to overseas-listed Chinese companies.

China's regime for foreign judgment recognition is based upon either treaties or the principle of reciprocity. As no relevant treaty has been signed between the US and China, the principle of reciprocity becomes the main route in practice. Due to various reasons, particularly the special features of securities litigation, there is significant difficulty with the recognition of US securities judgments in China. As Chinese companies are increasingly seeking cross-listings in Hong Kong due to escalating geopolitical conflicts, the role of Hong Kong is also examined in relation to the issue of judgment recognition. While there are some judgment recognition arrangements between Hong Kong and Mainland China, significant hurdles remain in relation to securities judgments.

In a quest for solutions, this chapter investigates into the possibility of suing Chinese companies in the offshore financial centers where they are incorporated, while finding that there would be similar difficulties with judgment recognition and enforcement in China. It also examines the viability of arbitration as an alternative method of dispute resolution, arguing that arbitration may only supplement, rather than substitute, court litigation of securities disputes. Several suggestions are then made to solve the judgment recognition issue: (1) China may consider signing a bilateral treaty with the US on judgment recognition and enforcement; (2) China should clarify and provide more guidance on the principle of reciprocity; and (3) China should consider ratifying the 2005 Hague Choice of Court Convention and in the long run, even acceding to the 2019 Hague Judgment Convention. Hong Kong is also advised to expand its current judgment recognition arrangement with Mainland China to cover securities judgments, as well as joining the 2005 Hague Choice of Court Convention and when the condition is ripe, acceding to the 2019 Hague Judgment Convention, subject to Beijing's approval under the Basic Law.

10

The IPO and Listing of Foreign Companies in China

10.1 Introduction

As part of its new national strategy, China[1] has recently made great efforts to push for the internationalization of its capital markets. Historically, the Chinese securities market was established to serve domestic companies, particularly state-owned enterprises (SOEs) in its early years. As a result, it has long been closed to foreign companies.[2] As the Chinese economy continues to grow, there is a great need for China to structurally reform its capital markets, particularly in the international dimension. In December 2019, China overhauled its national securities law (2019 Securities Law), which took effect on March 1, 2020.[3] The 2019 Securities Law created the Chinese Depositary Receipt (CDR, or Cun Tuo Ping Zheng in Chinese) as a new category of security.[4] Influenced by the American Depositary Receipt (ADR) model, the CDR regime is aimed at attracting foreign companies to list in the Chinese market, especially high-tech companies that are China-based but overseas-listed.[5]

In fact, the CDR regime in the 2019 Securities Law is the product of earlier experiments.[6] In 2018, the Chinese securities regulator, the China

[1] For brevity, "China" refers to Mainland China, unless otherwise indicated.

[2] Robin Hui Huang, *Securities and Capital Markets Law in China* (Oxford University Press, 2014), pp. 9–13.

[3] *See* Order of the President of the People's Republic of China (No. 12): Securities Law of the People's Republic of China (promulgated December 29, 1998 effective July 1, 1999, amended 2004, 2005, 2013, 2014 and 2019) [hereinafter Securities Law].

[4] Ibid., art. 2.

[5] Lerong Lu and Ningyao Ye, "Chinese Depositary Receipts: What They Are, How They Work and Why This Represents a Golden Opportunity" (2018) 33 *Butterworths Journal of International Banking and Financial Law* 529.

[6] Ningyao Ye and Lerong Lu, "How to Harness a Unicorn? Demystifying China's Reform of Share Listing Rules and Chinese Depositary Receipts" (2019) 30(8) *International Company and Commercial Law Review* 454, 462.

Securities Regulatory Commission (CSRC), issued the 2018 Pilot Program Opinions.[7] This marked the first time that the Chinese government has officially opened up the Chinese capital markets to foreign companies. Although this reform is currently limited to Red-chip enterprises (*hong chou qi ye*), it marks a watershed moment in the globalization of the Chinese capital markets. Since the route of backdoor listing is not available for foreign issuers, Red-chip enterprises can only seek initial public offerings (IPO) in China under the 2018 Pilot Program Opinions.

The issuance of the 2018 Pilot Program Opinions is partly a response to the US policy changes in foreign listings, which directly affect the China Concept stock (*Zhong Gai Gu*). For a long time, the United States and Hong Kong have been the two most popular destinations for Chinese companies to tap into for overseas listings.[8] China has encouraged many SOEs, such as CNOOC and China Mobile, to be wholly or partly listed in the United States and Hong Kong.[9] However, there are instances of overseas-listed Chinese companies allegedly committed fraud, such as a recent high-profile scandal being the case of *Luckin Coffee*.[10] In 2020, as a response to the longstanding China–US audit oversight dispute, the United States passed the Holding Foreign Companies Accountable Act, under which China-based companies might be delisted from the US markets if relevant conditions could not be met by the end of a three-year deadline.[11] This made it urgent for many overseas-listed Chinese companies to seek out an alternative option. Under these circumstances, China is offering to open its capital markets to China Concept Stocks.[12]

This chapter thus aims to critically examine China's new regime for the listing of foreign companies and compare it with the models in the US and

[7] Guanyu Kaizhan Chuangxin Qiye Jingnei Faxing Gupiao huo Cuntuo Pingzheng Shidian de Ruogan Yijian (关于开展创新企业境内发行股票或存托凭证试点的若干意见) [Opinions Released on Launching Pilot Program of Issuance of Stocks or Depositary Receipts within China by Innovative Enterprises] (promulgated by the CSRC, April 12, 2018 effective April 12, 2018) [hereinafter 2018 Pilot Program Opinions].

[8] *See* Qu Feng, Shang-Jin Wei, Guiying Laura Wu and Mengying Yuan, "A Narrative on Overseas Listings by Chinese Firms" (2024) 69(5) *Singapore Economic Review* 1812.

[9] Li-Wen Lin and Curtis J. Milhaupt, "We Are the (National) Champions: Understanding the Mechanisms of State Capitalism in China" (2013) 65 *Stanford Law Review* 697, 700.

[10] Liu Yujing and Louise Moon, "Luckin Coffee's Founder Says Sorry as Nasdaq Prepares to Kick Out His Stock for Fraud, in the First Expulsion of a Chinese Company," *South China Morning Post*, May 19, 2020, www.scmp.com/business/companies/article/3085132/nasdaq-readies-delist-luckin-coffee-chinas-answer-starbucks.

[11] Robin Hui Huang, "The US–China Audit Oversight Dispute: Causes, Solutions, and Implications for Hong Kong" (2021) 54 *The International Lawyer* 151, 179.

[12] Ibid., at 171.

Hong Kong. Section 10.2 explores the legal development and market practice of the regime for the listing of foreign companies in China. Section 10.3 examines the key elements of the current regime for the listing of foreign companies in China. Section 10.4 compares the regimes for the listing of foreign companies under the US model and the Hong Kong model. Section 10.5 evaluates, based on a cross- jurisdictional comparison, the key issues of the Chinese model and predicts the future development of the Chinese regime, addressing both categories of political-economy factors and legal-regulatory factors. Section 10.6 connects this analysis to draw conclusions as to the path China should take moving forward.

10.2 Listings of Foreign Companies in China: A Background Analysis

10.2.1 Overview

Apart from the newly established Beijing Stock Exchange, China has two well- established stock exchanges, namely the Shanghai Stock Exchange and the Shenzhen Stock Exchange.[13] Initially, each of the two stock exchanges had only one Main Board, which is designed for larger and more mature companies specializing in traditional industries.[14] Later, in an effort to build a multilayered capital market, the Chinese government allowed them to set up secondary markets to cater to smaller, emerging startups in the new economy.[15] In October 2009, the Shenzhen Stock Exchange established the ChiNext Market, also known as the GEM Board (*Chuang Ye Ban*), which has proven to be a huge success in terms of the number of companies listed and trading volume.[16]

In 2019, the Shanghai Stock Exchange introduced the Science and Technology Innovation Board, abbreviated as the STAR Market (*Ke Chuang Ban*).[17] To provide a solid legal basis for the smooth functioning

[13] Arendse Huld, "China's Stock Exchange: An Introductory Guide for Foreign Investors," *China Briefing*, September 21, 2021, www.china-briefing.com/news/chinas-stock-markets-an-introductory-guide-for-foreign-investors/.

[14] Ibid.

[15] James Chen, "Shenzhen Stock Exchange (SZSE): What It Means, How It Works," *Investopedia*, June 15, 2022, www.investopedia.com/terms/s/shenzen-stock-exchange-shz-.sz.asp.

[16] Huang, *Securities and Capital Markets Law in China*, above note 2.

[17] Scott Kennedy, "Two Years In, How Does Star Market Measure," *Center for Strategic and International Studies*, January 24, 2022, www.csis.org/blogs/trustee-china-hand/two-years-how-does-star-market-measure.

of the STAR Market, the CSRC issued the 2019 STAR Registration Measures.[18] To facilitate the listing of high-tech companies, the STAR Market makes certain changes to the existing IPO regime, such as allowing the use of weighted voting rights (WVR) structures (or dual-class share structures).[19] The STAR Market also experimented with a transition from the traditional merits-review or approval system to the disclosure-based or registration system,[20] a move that was later expanded to the ChiNext Market and Main Board. It was formally recognized in the 2019 amendment of China's Securities Law.[21]

After three decades of rapid development, the Chinese stock market has become one of the world's largest capital markets. As of the end of 2020, the Shanghai Stock Exchange and the Shenzhen Stock Exchange were respectively ranked the world's fourth and seventh largest stock exchanges in terms of market value.[22] In recent years, more and more foreign companies have turned their eyes to the Chinese capital markets. To open its capital markets to foreign issuers, the CSRC issued the 2018 Pilot Program Opinions, which allows foreign issuers to get listed on the STAR Market and the ChiNext Market.[23]

[18] China Securities Regulatory Commission, Measures for the Administration of the Registration of IPO Stocks on the Science and Technology Innovation Board (March 1, 2019), www.csrcare.com/Law/LawShowEn?id=224699.

[19] The WVR regime of the STAR Market is closely modeled on that of Hong Kong. For a discussion on the introduction of the WVR structure in Hong Kong and its implications for other markets such as the STAR Market in China, see Robin Hui Huang, Wei Zhang and Siu Cheung Kelvin Lee, "The (Re)Introduction of Dual-Class Share Structures in Hong Kong: A Historical and Comparative Analysis" (2020) 20 *Journal of Corporate Law Studies* 121.

[20] Robin Hui Huang, "The Regulation of Securities Offerings in China: Reconsidering the Merit Review Element in Light of the Global Financial Crisis" (2011) 41 *Hong Kong Law Journal* 261.

[21] SECURITIES LAW, above note 3, at art. 9.

[22] Securities and Futures Commission of Hong Kong, "Market Capitalisation of the World's Top Stock Exchanges" (March 2020) www.sfc.hk/web/files/SOM/MarketStatistics/2019/a01.pdf.

[23] Accordingly, the ChiNext Registration Measures was revised in 2020. See Chuangyeban Shouci Gongkai Faxing Gupiao Zhuce Guanli Banfa Shixing (创业板首次公开发行股票注册管理办法(试行) [Measures for the Administration of Registration of IPO Stocks on the ChiNext (for Trial Implementation)] (promulgated by the CSRC, June 12, 2020 effective June 12, 2020) [hereinafter 2020 ChiNext Registration Measures]. Identical to Article 80 of the 2019 STAR Registration Measures, Article 74 of the 2020 ChiNext Registration Measures allows Red-chip Companies to apply for the listing of common stocks or CDRs on the ChiNext Market.

The Main Board had not been covered by the 2018 Pilot Program Opinions until it followed the other markets and underwent a mass-scale "registration reform" (*zhuce zhi gaige*) in 2023.[24] The listing regime of the Main Board began to embrace Red-chip Companies when the CSRC streamlined its IPO registration regime for all markets.[25] The CSRC issued the 2023 Registration Measures,[26] which incorporated the 2019 STAR Registration Measures and the 2020 ChiNext Registration Measures. This new integrated instrument applies to all IPOs of stocks on all markets within the territory of mainland China.[27] Under the registration system, the CSRC will be responsible for registering the issued stock, while the stock exchanges are responsible for reviewing the merits of the issued stock.[28] In compliance with this new regime, the Shanghai Stock Exchange issued the 2023 SSE Review Rules.[29] To streamline the rules tailored for Red-chip Companies, the CSRC has issued the Red-Chip Measures[30] and the stock exchanges revised their listing rules.[31]

24 Shouci Gongkai Faxing Gupiao Zhuce Guanli Banfa (首次公开发行股票注册管理办法) [Measures for the Administration of Registration of Initial Public Offerings of Stocks] (promulgated by the CSRC, February 17, 2023 effective February 17, 2023) [hereinafter the 2023 Registration Measures].

25 Ibid.

26 Ibid.

27 Ibid., at art. 2.

28 Ibid.

29 Shanghai Zhengquan Jiaoyisuo Gupiao Faxing Shangshi Shenhe Guize (上海证券交易所股票发行上市审核规则) [Rules of the Shanghai Stock Exchange Governing Review of the Issuance and Listing of Stocks] (promulgated by the Shanghai Stock Exchange, February 17, 2023 effective February 17, 2023) [hereinafter 2023 SSE Review Rules]. The Shenzhen Stock Exchange also issued similar rules, which will not be discussed separately.

30 Shidian Chuangxin Qiye Jingnei Faxing Gupiao huo Cuntuo Pingzheng Bing Shangshi Jianguan Gongzuo Shishi Banfa (试点创新企业境内发行股票或存托凭证并上市监管工作实施办法) [Implementation Measures for the Supervision of Domestic Issuance and Listing of Stocks or Depositary Receipts by Pilot Innovative Enterprises] (promulgated by the CSRC, June 18, 2018, amended February 17, 2023 effective June 18, 2018) [hereinafter 2023 Red-Chip Measures].

31 Shanghai Zhengquan Jiaoyisuo Gupiao Shangshi Guize (上海证券交易所股票上市规则) [Listing Rules of Shanghai Stock Exchange] (promulgated by the Shanghai Stock Exchange, February 17, 2023 effective February 17, 2023) [hereinafter 2023 SSE Main Board Listing Rules]; Shanghai Zhengquan Jiaoyisuo Kechuangban Gupiao Shangshi Guize (上海证券交易所科创板股票上市规则) [Listing Rules of Shanghai Stock Exchange STAR Market] (promulgated by the Shanghai Stock Exchange, December 31, 2020 effective December 31, 2020) [hereinafter 2020 STAR Listing Rules]; Shenzhen Zhengquan Jiaoyisuo Chuangyeban Gupiao Shangshi Guize (深圳证券交易所创业板股票上市规则) [Listing Rules of Shenzhen Stock Exchange ChiNext Market] (promulgated

10.2.2 Definition of Red-chip Company

As discussed in the preceding section, only Red-chip Companies are currently allowed to get listed on the Chinese market. Under Chinese law, the term "Red-chip Company" is broadly defined, covering any enterprise that is registered abroad but mainly engages in business activities in China.[32] Different from genuine foreign companies, Red-chip Companies have their main business or assets inside China and are actually owned or controlled by Chinese entities, including SOEs and non-SOEs.[33]

In comparison, the Hong Kong Stock Exchange's (HKEX) definition of "Red-chip Company" is much narrower with more specific details. In Hong Kong, the term "Red-chip Company" is used to refer to a China-controlled company, which has at least 30 percent shareholding held in aggregate directly or indirectly by Mainland China entities.[34] Alternatively, it must have a 20–30 percent shareholding held in aggregate directly or indirectly by Mainland China entities and there is a strong influential presence on the company's board of directors.[35] "Mainland China entities" refer to organizations controlled by China's state, provincial or municipal authorities.[36] These shares are called Red-chip Stock (*hong chou gu*) in Hong Kong.

Another relevant term is "China Concept Stock" which is more commonly used in the United States.[37] In general, there are two main ways for Chinese companies to get listed in the United States. The first is by setting up a listing vehicle in an offshore center, such as the Cayman Islands, and then get it listed in the United States.[38] The other is

by the Shenzhen Stock Exchange, February 17, 2023 effective February 17, 2023) [hereinafter 2023 ChiNext Listing Rules].

32 2018 Pilot Program Opinions, above note 7, at art. 3.

33 FTSE Russell, "Guide to Chinese Share Classes," September 2023, p. 4, www.lseg.com/content/dam/ftse-russell/en_us/documents/policy-documents/guide-to-chinese-share-classes.pdf.

34 HKEX, *Fact Book 2020*, p. 273.

35 Ibid.

36 Ibid.

37 Zhujia Yin, Luqing Shi, Yiwei Wu and Jiejin Xia, "Dual-Class Share Structures and Financial Outcomes in High-Tech Firms: Evidence from US-Listed China Concept Stocks" (2024) 22 *Journal of Chinese Economic and Business Studies* 509, 510.

38 Greg Knowles, "China's Portal to the World: Why Chinese Companies Are Using the Cayman Islands to List Overseas," *Law.com International*, May 1, 2014, www.law.com/international-edition/2014/05/01/chinas-portal-to-the-world-why-chinese-companies-are-using-the-cayman-islands-to-list-overseas/.

backdoor listing through a reverse takeover in the US stock market.[39] In short, a Chinese company can get listed by acquiring a listed shell company that is incorporated in the United States (typically Delaware or Nevada). Through the backdoor listing mechanism, the Chinese company effectively becomes listed and registered in the United States.[40] Although it is technically a US company, it is still seen as a China Concept Stock in the United States because of its direct ties to China.[41] Indeed, "China Concept Stock" is not an officially defined term and thus tends to be very broad. For instance, the US–China Economic and Security Review Commission considers a company "Chinese" if (1) it has been identified as being from China by the relevant US stock exchange or (2) it lists a PRC address as its principal executive office in filings with the SEC.[42]

From a comparative perspective, the US definition of "China Concept Stock" is very similar to the Chinese version of "Red-chip Company" to the extent that their main standard is the broad criteria of doing business or having a principal office in China. In contrast, the Hong Kong version of "Red-chip Company" is more narrowly defined than both of the US and Chinese definitions, as it references specific shareholding thresholds and the identity of the controller. Indeed, in Hong Kong, apart from Red-chip Companies, there are also a large number of Mainland private enterprises, known as "P-chip Stock," which are controlled by private entities as opposed to the Chinese government.[43] P-chip Stock would generally fall within the ambit of the Chinese version of Red-chip Company or the US concept of China Concept Stock. In practice, the Chinese concept of "Red-chip Company" could be divided into two categories, namely "big Red-chip Company" ("*da hong chou*") and "small Red-chip Company" ("*xiao hong chou*"), corresponding to what are called Red-chip Stock and P-chip Stock in Hong Kong, respectively.

[39] *See generally* Qingxiu Bu, "The Chinese Reverse Merger Companies (RMCs) Reassessed: Promising but Challenging" (2014) 12 *Journal of International Business and Law* 17.

[40] Ibid., pp. 17–18.

[41] *See*, for example, Jing Leng, "Should China Concept Stocks Be Identified as 'Chinese' or 'Foreign?'" (Yan Pan trans.) (2022) 2 *International Journal of Law, Ethics and Technology* 99 (using the same definition of "China Concept Stock").

[42] US–China Economic and Security Review Commission, "Chinese Companies Listed on Major US Stock Exchanges" (2024), p. 7, www.uscc.gov/research/chinese-companies-listed-major-us-stock-exchanges.

[43] HKEX, *Fact Book 2020*, above note 34, p. 273.

In this chapter, the term "Red-chip Companies" is used by reference to the Chinese version as stipulated under the 2018 Pilot Program Opinions unless otherwise indicated.

10.2.3 *Initial Public Offerings in China*

To enforce the pilot program, the Main Board, the STAR Market and the ChiNext Market have allowed foreign listings in the form of common stocks or CDRs. In 2019, the Securities Law recognized depositary receipts as a new form of securities.[44] The introduction of the CDR, inspired by the ADR, has created good opportunities for foreign companies to get listed in China. In theory, a foreign company can issue CDRs in China through two channels.

First, a Red-chip Company can issue CDRs under the channel of the 2018 Pilot Program Opinions. On June 6, 2018, the CSRC officially issued the Measures for the Administration of Offering and Trading of Depositary Receipts (CDR Measures),[45] which stipulated the institutional foundations for issuing CDRs. The 2018 CDR Measures defined CDRs as "securities issued by the depositary and offered based on overseas securities within China and representing the rights and interests of overseas underlying securities."[46] CDR issuers shall perform the same obligations as those applicable to the issuer of ordinary shares.[47] Nevertheless, their corporate governance shall be governed by the company law regimes of the overseas jurisdictions where they are registered.[48] The CDR issuer shall guarantee that the assets income and other rights that are actually enjoyed by CDR holders are equivalent to the rights of overseas underlying securities holders.[49]

Second, a foreign company can issue CDRs in China under the Shanghai–London Stock Connect (*hu lun tong*) channel. On June 17, 2019, the CSRC and the Financial Conduct Authority of the United Kingdom issued a joint announcement approving the Shanghai Stock

44 SECURITIES LAW, above note 3, at art. 2.

45 Cuntuo Pingzheng Faxing yu Jiaoyi Guanli Banfa Shixing (存托凭证发行与交易管理办法(试行) [Measures for the Administration of Offering and Trading of Depositary Receipts (for Trial Implementation)] (promulgated by the CSRC, June 6, 2018 effective June 6, 2018) [hereinafter 2018 CDR Measures].

46 Ibid., at art. 2.

47 Ibid.

48 Ibid., at art. 3.

49 Ibid., at art. 35.

Exchange and the London Stock Exchange's launching of the Shanghai–London Stock Connect.[50] To date, nevertheless, there has been no case of CDR listing through this channel.[51]

10.2.4 *Backdoor Listing in China*

Like many other markets, the Chinese stock market allows for so-called backdoor listing, whereby a company can get listed through a reverse takeover of a listed shell company.[52] The Measures for Regulating Takeovers of Listed Companies (Takeover Measures)[53] provide detailed rules on reverse takeovers by domestic entities. However, it is practically impossible for foreign entities to use the backdoor listing mechanism in the Chinese stock market due to further layers of special regulations.

Since 2002, foreign financial institutions that qualify as Qualified Foreign Institutional Investors have been only allowed to purchase limited percentages of shares in Chinese listed companies.[54] In 2006, the Ministry of Commerce and five other Chinese governmental agencies jointly promulgated the Provisions on the Takeover of Domestic Enterprises by Foreign Investors (2006 Foreign M&A Provisions),[55] which streamlines China's foreign M&A regime. Takeovers of listed

[50] *See* Shanghai Stock Exchange, www.sse.com.cn/assortment/stock/slsc/home/.

[51] Ibid.

[52] Erik P. M. Vermeulen, "High-Tech Companies and the Decision to 'Go Public': Are Backdoor Listings (Still) an Alternative to 'Front-Door' Initial Public Offerings" (2015) 4 *Penn State Journal of Law and International Affairs* 421, 422–424; Ziyi Tang and Baili Ke, "Caixin Explains: Why the Backdoor to China's Stock Markets Is So Attractive," *Caixin Global*, January 17, 2019, www.caixinglobal.com/2019-01-17/caixin-explains-why-the-back-door-to-chinas-stock-markets-is-so-attractive-101371176.html.

[53] Shangshi Gongsi Shougou Guanli Banfa (上市公司收购管理办法) [Measures for Regulating Takeovers of Listed Companies] (promulgated by the CSRC, September 28, 2002 effective December 1, 2002, amended in 2006, 2008, 2012, 2014 and 2020) [hereinafter Takeover Measures]; *see* also Robin Hui Huang, "China's Takeover Law: A Comparative Analysis and Proposals for Reform" (2005) 30 *Delaware Journal of Corporate Law* 145 (discussing China's takeover law); Robin Hui Huang and Charles Chao Wang, "The Mandatory Bid Rule Under China's Takeover Law: A Comparative and Empirical Perspective" (2020) 53 *The International Lawyer* 195.

[54] *See* Robin Hui Huang, "China's New Regulation on Foreign M&A: Green Light or Red Flag" (2007) 30 *UNSW Law Journal* 802, 806–807.

[55] *See* Guanyu Waiguo Touzizhe Binggou Jingnei Qiye de Guiding (关于外国投资者并购境内企业的规定) [Provisions on the Takeover of Domestic Enterprises by Foreign Investors] (promulgated by the Ministry of Commerce, State-owned Assets Supervision and Administration Commission of the State Council, State Administration of Taxation, State Administration for Industry and Commerce, China Securities Regulatory

companies by foreigners require approval from the Chinese government.[56] There are also other relevant regulations on foreign M&As in China, such as the Measures for the Administration of Strategic Investment in Listed Companies by Foreign Investors[57] and the Provisions on Issues concerning the Implementation of the Administrative Measures for Securities Investment Made in China by Qualified Foreign Institutional Investors.[58]

In general, where a single foreign investor holds the shares of a Chinese listed company through a Qualified Foreign Institutional Investor, its shareholding shall not exceed 10 percent, and the total proportion of shares held by all foreign investors in a single listed company shall not exceed 30 percent.[59] Under the Chinese takeover law, however, 30 percent is the legal benchmark for gaining corporate control of a listed company in China.[60] Thus, it is impractical for foreigners to conduct backdoor listings through reverse takeovers. For the sake of completeness, this chapter briefly mentions the route of backdoor listing in China, but the focus will be on the IPO method of listing, which is currently the only possible avenue for foreign companies to get listed in the Chinese stock markets.

10.2.5 Market Data

What follows is our attempt to collect all the cases involving the listing of Red-chip Companies in the Chinese capital markets. As of May 2023, there had been no cases of foreign listings in the Main Board and

Commission and State Administration of Foreign Exchange, August 8, 2006, revised June 22, 2009 effective September 8, 2006).

56 Ibid., at art. 6.

57 Waiguo Touzizhe Dui Shangshi Gongsi Zhanlüe Touzi Guanli Banfa (外国投资者对上市公司战略投资管理办法) [Measures for the Administration of Strategic Investment in Listed Companies by Foreign Investors] (promulgated by the Ministry of Commerce, China Securities Regulatory Commission, State Administration of Taxation, State Administration for Industry and Commerce and State Administration of Foreign Exchange, December 31, 2005, revised October 28, 2015 effective January 31, 2006).

58 Guanyu Shishi Hege Jingwai Jigou Touzizhe Jingnei Zhengquan Touzi Guanli Banfa (关于实施〈合格境外机构投资者境内证券投资管理办法〉有关问题的规定) [Provisions on Issues Concerning the Implementation of the Administrative Measures for Securities Investment Made in China by Qualified Foreign Institutional Investors] (promulgated by the CSRC, July 27, 2012 effective July 27, 2012).

59 Ibid., at art. 9.

60 Takeover Measures, above note 53, at art. 84.

ChiNext Market,[61] probably because these markets have only been open to foreign companies for a very short period of time. Nevertheless, STAR Market has witnessed twelve listing applications by Red-chip Companies, among which six have registered and taken effect. Compared with domestic issuers, Red-chip Companies' securities issuance has great potential for growth.

We have compiled the relevant data on these companies from the official website of the Shanghai Stock Exchange, which is shown in Table 10.1.

In 2019, Ninebot Limited became the first CDR-issuing company.[62] Half of the applicant companies belong to the electronic equipment manufacturing industry, which complies with the strategic positioning of STAR Market.[63] The majority of the companies are registered in the Cayman Islands. Many Red-chip Companies seek a cross-listing, as they had already been listed on other exchanges before they applied to be cross-listed in China. All these overseas-listed companies have been primarily listed on the HKEX, and one has been cross-listed both on Nasdaq and the HKEX. Over half of the Red-chip Companies have chosen to issue common stocks instead of CDRs. Four companies have adopted variable interest entity (VIE) structures and three of them have a WVR structure.

10.3 The Listing Regime for Foreign Companies in China: Key Elements

Under the 2018 Pilot Program Opinions, only Red-chip Companies are allowed to issue common stocks or CDRs.[64] In general, the listing of foreign companies receives national treatment. They are largely subject to the same substantive and procedural rules applicable to domestic Chinese companies. Due to the special nature of listings of foreign companies, there are certain rules designed specifically for them, such as the higher financial threshold. These special rules will be discussed in detail in the following section.

[61] Shanghai Stock Exchange, Project Dynamics, www.sse.com.cn/listing/renewal/ipo/; Shenzhen Stock Exchange, List of Stocks, www.szse.cn/market/product/stock/list/.

[62] Shanghai Stock Exchange, No. 9 Co., Ltd., listing.sse.com.cn/renewal/xmxq/index.shtml?auditId=103&anchor_type=0.

[63] Tian Xuan, "STAR Market Plays Significant Role in Accelerating Tech Innovation of Chinese Companies," July 31, 2024, www.globaltimes.cn/page/202407/1317104.shtml.

[64] *See* 2018 Pilot Program Opinions, above note 7.

Table 10.1 *Securities listings of Red-chip Companies*[a]

Application date	Status	Company name & securities category	Industry	Domicile	Cross- listing venue	VIE	WVR
Apr. 17, 2019	Success	Ninebot Ltd. (CDR)	Electronic equipment manufacturing	Cayman Islands	No	Yes	Yes
June 26, 2019	Success	China Resources Microelectronics Ltd. (common stock)	Electronic equipment manufacturing	Cayman Islands	No	No	No
June 1, 2020	Success	Semiconductor Manufacturing International Corp. (common stock)	Electronic equipment manufacturing	Cayman Islands	HKEX	No	No
July 7, 2020	Success	GalaxyCore Inc. (common stock)	Electronic equipment manufacturing	Cayman Islands	No	No	No
Sept. 1, 2020	Terminated	Geely Automobile Holdings Ltd. (common stock)	Automobile manufacturing	Cayman Islands	HKEX	No	No
Nov. 4, 2020	Terminated	Yitu Ltd. (CDR)	Information technology	Cayman Islands	No	Yes	Yes

Jan. 29, 2021	Success	BeiGene Ltd. (common stock)	Pharmaceutical manufacturing	Cayman Islands	NASDAQ/ HKEX	No	No
Mar. 12, 2021	In Process	Megvii Technology Ltd. (CDR)	Information technology	Cayman Islands	No	Yes	Yes
June 29, 2021	Terminated	Minth Group Ltd. (common stock)	Automobile manufacturing	Cayman Islands	HKEX	No	No
Sept. 13, 2021	Success	InnoCare Pharma Ltd. (common stock)	Pharmaceutical manufacturing	Cayman Islands	HKEX	No	No
Oct. 8, 2021	Terminated	Lenovo Group Ltd. (CDR)	Electronic equipment manufacturing	Hong Kong	HKEX	Yes	No
Nov. 4, 2022	In process	Huahong Semiconductor Co. Ltd. (common stock)	Electronic equipment manufacturing	Hong Kong	HKEX	No	No

[a] Ibid.

10.3.1 Issuer Categories

10.3.1.1 The Pilot Program

At the current pilot stage, only Red-chip Companies are allowed to get listed in the Chinese capital markets.[65] Since the route of backdoor listing is not available to foreign issuers, Red-chip Companies can only issue common stocks and CDRs, and then get listed as a single-market listing or as cross-listing companies.[66] The major channel is the pilot program, which was pillared by the 2018 Pilot Program Opinions and the 2023 Red-Chip Measures.[67] Red-chip Companies should be in line with the Chinese national strategy of development, hold core technologies and enjoy a high level of market recognition.[68] The industries in which the Red-chip enterprises operate include the internet, big data, cloud computing, artificial intelligence, software and integrated circuits, high-end equipment manufacturing, biomedicine and other high-tech industries and strategic emerging industries.[69] To promote high-tech industry growth, the government has gradually expanded the scope of the pilot program.[70]

In March 2020, the CSRC issued the Innovation Guidelines.[71] It provides a set of quantitative criteria for determining whether a company could be recognized as an innovative enterprise. First, in the most recent three years, its research and development (R&D) investment shall account for over 5 percent of business income or exceed 60 million

[65] Gao Wei and Xiao Yi, "Initial Public Offerings Laws and Regulations 2024 – China," *Global Legal Insights* (2024), www.globallegalinsights.com/practice-areas/initial-public-offerings-laws-and-regulations/china/.

[66] Ibid.

[67] 2018 Pilot Program Opinions, above note 7, at art. 2.

[68] Robert Atkinson, "China Is Rapidly Becoming a Leading Innovator in Advanced Industries," *Information Technology and Innovation Foundation*, September 16, 2024, itif.org/publications/2024/09/16/china-is-rapidly-becoming-a-leading-innovator-in-advanced-industries/.

[69] 2018 Pilot Program Opinions, above note 7, at art. 3; 2023 Red-Chip Measures, above note 30, at art. 6.

[70] China Securities Regulatory Commission, Announcement on Expanding the Pilot Scope of Red-Chip Enterprises for Domestic Listing (September 17, 2021) www.csrc.gov.cn/csrc/c101802/c1496491/content.shtml.

[71] Kechuang Shuxing Pingjia Zhiyin Shixing (科创属性评价指引(试行)) [Guidelines for the Evaluation of Science and Technology Innovation Attributes (for Trial Implementation)] (promulgated by the CSRC, March 20, 2020, amended April 16, 2021 effective March 20, 2020) [hereinafter Innovation Guidelines].

yuan.[72] Second, the proportion of R&D personnel in that year shall not be less than 10 percent of all employees.[73] Third, it shall have over five patents for invention, which generate the main business income for the company.[74] Fourth, the compound growth rate of its business income in the most recent three years shall reach 20 percent, or its business income in the most recent year shall reach 30 million yuan.[75]

10.3.1.2 The Stock Connect Program

In addition to the route of 2018 Pilot Program Opinions, foreign companies can also issue CDRs in China under special arrangements between China and foreign countries. Currently, the Shanghai–London Stock Connect program includes two business directions: eastbound and westbound.[76] Eastbound business refers to the issuance of CDRs on the Main Board of the Shanghai Stock Exchange by qualified London Stock Exchange-listed companies.[77] Westbound business refers to the issuance of global depositary receipts (GDR) on the Main Board of London Stock Exchange by Chinese companies listed in the Shanghai Stock Exchange.[78]

On June 20, 2019, Huatai Securities Co., Ltd. issued the first GDR under the Shanghai–London Stock Connect program and got listed on the London Stock Exchange.[79] The success of the Shanghai–London Stock Connect program marked a milestone in the internationalization process of China's capital markets. By March 8, 2021, four Chinese- listed companies from the Shanghai Stock Exchange had issued GDRs in the London Stock Exchange, including SDIC Power Holdings Co., Ltd, China Yangtze Power Co., Ltd, China Pacific Insurance (Group) Co., Ltd. and Huatai Securities Co., Ltd.[80] However, there have been no

[72] Ibid., at art. 1.
[73] Ibid.
[74] Ibid.
[75] Ibid.
[76] Ningyao Ye and Lerong Lu, "Building a Eurasian Capital Market: Understanding the Operating Mechanism and Legal Framework of Shanghai–London Stock Connect" (2020) 35 *Journal of International Banking Law and Regulation* 67.
[77] Ibid.
[78] Shanghai–London Stock Connect, Official Website of the Shanghai Stock Exchange, www.sse.com.cn/assortment/stock/slsc/home.
[79] Lucie Holloway and Nandeep Roopray, "Shanghai–London Stock Connect Welcomes Its First Issuer: Huatai Securities," *London Stock Exchange Group*, June 17, 2019, www.lseg.com/en/media-centre/press-releases/2019/shanghai-london-stock-connect-welcomes-its-first-issuer-huatai-securities.
[80] Shanghai–London Stock Connect, above note 79.

London Stock Exchange-listed companies issuing CDRs in China under the Shanghai–London Stock Connect program.[81] As this Stock Connect channel is not actively used in practice, this study will only focus on the Pilot Program channel.

10.3.2 Issuer Qualifications

10.3.2.1 Financial Thresholds

To get listed in China, foreign companies must satisfy certain financial conditions. There are different financial thresholds, depending on whether the Red-chip Company is already listed overseas or is yet to do so.

The first type is overseas-listed Red-chip Companies.[82] The market value of an ordinary overseas-listed Red-chip Company must be no less than 200 billion yuan.[83] The market value can be scaled down to 20 billion yuan if the company is a high-tech company.[84] It must have independently developed internationally leading technology, strong technological innovation capabilities and a relatively advantageous position in the industry competition.[85]

The second type is non-listed Red-chip Companies. An ordinary non-listed Red-chip Company should have an operating revenue of over 3 billion yuan and an estimated value of over 20 billion yuan in the latest year.[86] High-tech, non-listed Red-chip Companies are subject to lower requirements. The estimated market value can be scaled down to 5 billion yuan or 10 billion yuan.[87] If the company has satisfied an operating revenue of over 1 billion yuan, among other criteria, the estimated market value requirement can be waived.[88]

Although non-listed Red-chip Companies are subject to relatively lower thresholds than overseas-listed Red-chip Companies, the

[81] Ibid.
[82] Gao Wei and Xiao Yi, above note 66.
[83] 2018 Pilot Program Opinions, above note 7, at art. 3; 2023 Red-Chip Measures, above note 30, at art. 7.
[84] CSRC, Announcement on Relevant Arrangements for Innovation Pilot Red-chip Enterprises to Go Public in China (April 30, 2020), www.gov.cn/zhengce/zhengceku/2020-05/07/content_5509578.htm.
[85] 2023 SSE Main Board Listing Rules, above note 31, at art. 3.1.4.
[86] 2018 Pilot Program Opinions, above note 7, at art. 3; 2023 Red-Chip Measures, above note 30, at art. 8.
[87] 2023 SSE Main Board Listing Rules, above note 31, at art. 3.1.5.
[88] 2023 Red-Chip Measures, above note 30, at art. 8.

requirements in general are still much higher than those imposed on domestic issuers (with the exception of only a few high-tech companies).[89] Table 10.2 summarizes the major financial thresholds for these different categories of issuers.

As a result, Red-chip Companies may prefer to change their domicile back to China to get listed more efficiently with lower costs. As a domestic issuer, the company will no longer be subject to the 2018 Pilot Program Opinions.[90] This brings about two advantages: (1) the financial requirements for domestic issuers are usually much lower than those imposed on Red-chip Companies; (2) according to our interviews with insiders of some of China's top securities companies and law firms, the listing process for a domestic issuer is much simpler than that for a Red-chip Company in practice.[91]

10.3.2.2 Other Requirements

The 2023 Registration Measures provide other listing requirements applicable to both foreign issuers and domestic issuers. Further, the 2018 CDR Measures set out conditions of CDR issuance, which are similar to those for common stock issuance.[92]

First, there are organizational requirements. The issuer must have conducted business operations for three or more consecutive years.[93] For a Red-chip Company, the corporate form may be subject to the legal provisions of its place of registration. It must have a sound and well-functioning organizational structure as well as relevant institutions and personnel.[94]

Second, there are accounting requirements. The financial statements must fairly reflect the financial status, operating results and cash flow of the issuer in all important aspects.[95] An auditing report with an unqualified opinion shall be issued by a certified public accountant.[96] An internal

89 2023 SSE Main Board Listing Rules, above note 31, at art. 3.1.2; 2020 STAR Listing Rules, above note 31, at art. 2.1.2; 2023 ChiNext Listing Rules, above note 31, at art. 2.1.2.

90 See above Section 10.3.

91 Interview with a Senior Officer of a Top Securities Firm, April 10, 2023, Shanghai [hereinafter Shanghai Securities Firm Officer Interview]; Interview with a Partner of a Leading Law Firm, March 8, 2023, Beijing [hereinafter Beijing Law Firm Partner Interview].

92 2018 CDR Measures, above note 45, at art. 5.

93 2023 Registration Measures, above note 24, at art. 10.

94 Ibid.

95 Ibid.

96 2023 Registration Measures, above note 24, at art. 11.

Table 10.2 *IPO financial thresholds for Red-chip Companies and domestic companies*

Categories of issuer		Market value (yuan)	Operating revenue of latest year (yuan)	Estimated market value (yuan)
Overseas-listed Red-Chip Company	Ordinary Overseas-listed Red-Chip Company	200 billion	N/A	N/A
	High-tech Overseas-listed Red-Chip Company	20 billion	N/A	N/A
Non-listed Red-Chip Company	Ordinary Non-listed Red-Chip Company	N/A	3 billion	20 billion
	High-tech Non-listed Red-Chip Company (1)	N/A	N/A	10 billion
	High-tech Non-listed Red-Chip Company (2)	N/A	500 million	5 billion
	High-tech Non-listed Red-Chip Company (3)	N/A	1 billion	N/A
Domestic issuer	Main Board	N/A	600 million to 800 million	5 billion to 8 billion
	STAR Market	N/A	100 million to 300 million	1 billion to 4 billion
	ChiNext Market	N/A	100 million to 300 million	1 billion to 5 billion

Note: Table 10.2 created by author.

control authentication report with an unqualified conclusion in the last three years shall be issued by a certified public accountant.[97]

Third, the issuer's business must be fully established and capable of operating independently and continuously.[98] The relevant business requirements include:

(1) the issuer has complete assets and maintains independent operations with respect to its business activities, personnel, finance and organization; moreover, there must be no horizontal competition that may have materially adverse effects on the issuer or bring about any unfair affiliated transactions;
(2) the issuer's principal business, control rights, management team and core technicians must be stable; and
(3) there must be no significant disputes concerning the ownership of key assets, core technologies, trademarks or intellectual property.[99]

Last, the issuer's production and business operation shall comply with laws and regulations as well as state industry policies.[100] In the previous three years, the issuer and its controlling shareholder and actual controller must not have any criminal records.[101] No director, supervisor or senior executive should have received any penalties imposed by the CSRC or be under any official investigation.[102]

10.3.3 Offering Procedures

The listing of CDRs is governed by the same procedural rules as the listing of common stocks.[103] Chinese law only regulates the public issuance of CDRs, while the issuance of the underlying securities of CDRs by the foreign company is essentially subject to the company law of the jurisdiction where the company is registered.[104] In practice, Red-chip Companies are often registered in the Cayman Islands, and thus the issuance of underlying securities is governed by the Cayman Islands'

[97] Ibid.
[98] Ibid.
[99] 2023 Registration Measures, above note 24, at art. 12.
[100] Ibid.
[101] 2023 Registration Measures, above note 24, at art. 13.
[102] Ibid.
[103] 2018 Pilot Program Opinions, above note 7.
[104] Prospectus of Ninebot Limited, *Star Market*, May 1, 2023, static.sse.com.cn/stock/information/c/202009/7ffb311d2ef648b28966c4812d1a77f1.pdf.

company law.[105] Hence, we will only discuss the Chinese rules on the issuance of CDRs below.

To begin with, the board of directors of the foreign issuer shall make a resolution on the specific plan for the offering.[106] Then the board must submit the resolution to the shareholders' meeting for approval.[107] The foreign issuer shall produce listing application documents and submit them to the Shanghai Stock Exchange.[108] After receiving the application, the exchange shall raise inquiries with the issuer and make a decision on whether to approve the application based on the inquiry process.[109] If the exchange approves the application, it shall transfer the materials to the CSRC for registration. Otherwise, it shall simply reject the application.[110] The examination opinion shall be formed within a specified time period from the date when registration application documents are accepted.[111] The CSRC shall, within twenty working days, decide whether to approve the registration.[112] The decision of the CSRC shall be effective for one year.[113] Where the exchange or the CSRC rejects the application, the issuer may not file a new application until six months thereafter.[114]

Although the procedures of CDR issuance are similar to those of common stock issuance, there are some notable differences in terms of information disclosure. For instance, the CDR issuer must disclose the main differences between the company law at the place of overseas registration and Chinese company law and address the impact of such differences on investor protection.[115] Further, the CDR issuer and other information disclosure obligors shall ensure that the information disclosed in overseas markets is disclosed in China at the same time.[116]

105 *See* Wang Hanqi, "Implications of Cayman's Economic Substance Laws on Red-chip structure," *Law Asia: China Business Law Journal*, May 14, 2019, law.asia/implications-caymans-economic-substance-law-Red-chip-structures/.
106 2023 Registration Measures, above note 24, at art.14.
107 Ibid.
108 Ibid, at art. 16.
109 Ibid., at art. 19.
110 Ibid., at art. 20.
111 Ibid., at art. 21.
112 Ibid., at art. 24.
113 Ibid., at art. 25.
114 Ibid., at art. 28.
115 2018 CDR Measures, above note 45, at art. 17.
116 Ibid., at art. 22.

10.3.4 *Special Issues*

10.3.4.1 Variable Interest Entity Structure

Red-chip Companies usually adopt a variable interest entity (VIE) structure, also known as an agreement-based control structure, under which Red-chip Companies obtain actual control of Chinese domestic businesses through agreement. The VIE structure helps circumvent restrictions that China imposes on foreign equity ownership in sensitive industries.[117] It is comprised of a series of contractual arrangements that enable relevant parties to the contracts to obtain control over counterparty companies without having to directly own shares in the latter.[118]

Although the 2018 Pilot Program Opinions allow overseas-listed Chinese companies to return to Chinese capital markets as foreign issuers, Red-chip Companies from sensitive and non-sensitive industries often adopt different strategies. On one hand, Red-chip Companies from sensitive industries must keep the VIE structure. In 2020, China passed the Foreign Investment Law,[119] which sets forward foreign investment restrictions via a "negative list."[120] The foreign company status of Red-chip Companies can only be maintained via a VIE structure. On the other hand, Red-chip Companies from non-sensitive industries often dismantle the VIE structure in practice. After dismantling the VIE structure, a Red-chip Company can remain a foreign-registered company that controls the domestic operating entity through a shareholding relationship.

In practice, as shown earlier, most, if not all, companies have dismantled the VIE structure when getting listed in China.[121] According to our interviews with investment bankers in some of China's top securities

[117] *See* Li Guo, "Chinese Style VIEs: Continuing to Sneak Under Smog" (2014) 47 *Cornell International Law Journal* 569 (providing a fuller discussion of the VIE structure); Shen Wei, "Will the Door Open Wider in the Aftermath of Alibaba?: Placing (or Misplacing) Foreign Investment in a Chinese Public Law Frame" (2012) 42 *Hong Kong Law Journal* 561.

[118] Li Guo, above note 118, at 569.

[119] Zhonghua Renmin Gongheguo Waishang Touzi Fa (中华人民共和国外商投资法) [Foreign Investment Law of the People's Republic of China] (promulgated by the National People's Congress, March 15, 2019 effective January 1, 2020) [hereinafter Foreign Investment Law].

[120] *See* ibid. at art. 4 (defining "negative list" as a special administrative measure issued by the State Council for access of foreign investment into specific fields as imposed by the state, which accords national treatment to foreign investment outside of the list).

[121] *See* Section 10.2.5.

companies and law firms,[122] there are several possible reasons, which are summarized below.

First, Red-chip Companies from non-sensitive industries are often encouraged by the exchange to dismantle their VIE structures before they can get listed in China, as the VIE structure is too complicated for the regulator to look through.[123] The 2018 Pilot Program Opinions provide a convenient channel for them to get listed in China without changing their foreign domicile (so that they do not incur the cost of scrapping the Red-chip structure), and the VIE structure can be dealt with separately.[124]

Second, for a Red-chip Company from non-sensitive industries, the financial benefit of dismantling the VIE structure seems to outweigh the cost. According to our interviews, the cost of dismantling the VIE structure is about 30 to 40 million yuan (US$4.36 to US$5.81 million), which is not a huge cost for most Red-chip Companies.[125] More importantly, in practice, the listing process for companies with the VIE structure is much more cumbersome than that for non-VIE companies due to the complex legal issues surrounding the VIE structure.

Finally, the ambiguous status of the VIE structure has long been a controversial issue that needs to be handled with care. The regulator does not want to send an unequivocal message to the market that the VIE structure is now legal by allowing Red-chip Companies to keep the VIE structure in their listings on the Chinese securities market. Hence, the regulator allows the retention of the VIE structure on a case-by-case basis and will give the green light only when there is a great need to attract Red-chip Companies that are genuinely high-tech, strategically important and highly recognized in the market.

10.3.4.2 Weighted Voting Rights Structure

Under the weighted voting rights (WVR) structure, the number of voting rights carried by each special voting share is greater than that carried by each ordinary share.[126] If overseas-listed Chinese companies have WVR arrangements, they must adequately disclose relevant information on

[122] Shanghai Securities Firm Officer Interview, above note 92; Beijing Law Firm Partner Interview, above note 92.
[123] Ibid.
[124] Ibid.
[125] Ibid. (CNY to USD exchange rate as of March/April 2023).
[126] 2023 SSE Main Board Listing Rules, above note 31, at art. 15.1.

their risk factors and corporate governance in a prominent position in their prospectus.[127] Various measures to protect investors should also be implemented.[128] An issuer with the WVR structure shall meet at least one of the following listing criteria: (1) the expected market value is not less than 20 billion yuan, and the net profit for the last year is positive; or (2) the expected market value is not less than 10 billion yuan, the net profit for the last year is positive, and the operating revenue for the last year is not less than 1 billion yuan.[129]

The 2018 CDR Measures provide more detailed rules on the WVR structure, as the CDR regime is focused on attracting foreign high-tech companies.[130] Where the CDR issuer has special arrangements in relation to shareholders' voting rights and corporate control, it shall disclose relevant information in conspicuous positions on the prospectus and periodical reports and explain the various measures adopted to protect investors.[131]

10.3.4.3 Valuation Adjustment Mechanism

In practice, some Red-chip Companies have issued preferred securities to institutional investors, such as private equity (PEs) and venture capital (VCs), under the so-called valuation adjustment mechanism (VAM), also known as the Gambling Agreement (*Dui Du Xie Yi*).[132] The preferred securities can be either shares or convertible bonds, and the holders of such securities can ask the company or its controlling shareholder to redeem them on various conditions, such as when the company fails to get listed or meet certain financial criteria.[133] Red-chip Companies and their investors are required to undertake that they will not exercise redemption rights during the process of the listing application and will terminate all redemption rights before getting listed.[134]

127 2023 Registration Measures, above note 24, at art. 43.
128 2018 Pilot Program Opinions, above note 7, at art. 5.
129 2023 SSE Main Board Listing Rules, above note 31, at art. 3.1.6.
130 2018 CDR Measures, above note 45.
131 Ibid., at arts. 17 and 19.
132 Yuanke Yin, Zhenning Tang, Jiaxing Zhao and Xi Zhao, "Research on Gambling Agreement in Private Equity Financing" (2023) 154 *SHS Web of Conferences* 1.
133 Ibid.
134 Shanghai Stock Exchange, Notice on Matters Related to Red-chip Enterprises Applying for Issuance and Listing on the STAR Market, english.sse.com.cn/news/newsrelease/c/5121243.shtml.

10.4 International Experiences: The United States and Hong Kong

10.4.1 Overview

To get listed in the United States, foreign issuers must comply with the Securities Act of 1933 and the Securities Exchange Act of 1934, in addition to satisfying the listing requirements of each stock exchange. Generally, there are two channels through which foreign companies can get listed in the United States: IPO and backdoor listing (also known as a reverse merger). As previously discussed, IPO remains the only viable pathway for foreign companies seeking listing status in China, and thus this section will focus on the issuance of shares through IPO for foreign companies in the United States. Foreign issuers may utilize two listing vehicles: ADRs and common stock.[135] Foreign issuers that qualify as FPIs can enjoy certain regulatory accommodations not available to US domestic issuers.

In Hong Kong, foreign issuers may issue common stocks via primary listing or secondary listing.[136] A primary listing can take the form of a single-market listing on the HKEX or a dual-primary listing on both the HKEX and a foreign stock exchange.[137] A dual-primary listing is a kind of cross-listing that is subject to the full regulatory requirements in both Hong Kong and the relevant foreign jurisdiction.[138]

Conversely, a secondary listing in Hong Kong is an approach where the foreign company has its principal listing place in a foreign jurisdiction before getting cross-listed in Hong Kong.[139] As a secondary listing jurisdiction, Hong Kong can place some reliance on the regulatory efforts of the principal listing jurisdiction, thus applying a decreased level of regulation on the foreign company second-listed in Hong Kong.[140]

135 *See* Securities and Exchange Commission, Marketplace Rules, www.sec.gov/files/rules/other/nasdaqllcf1a4_5/nasdaqllcamendrules4000.pdf.

136 HKEX, Understanding the Requirements and Risks Relating to Overseas Issuers, www.hkex.com.hk/Listing/Rules-and-Guidance/Listing-of-Overseas-Companies/Understanding-the-Risks-of-Investing-in-Overseas-Issuers?sc_lang=en.

137 Ibid.

138 Ibid.

139 Ibid.

140 Ibid.

10.4.2 The United States

10.4.2.1 Listing of American Depositary Receipts

In general, the United States only allows domestically registered companies to issue shares and get listed on US stock exchanges.[141] Foreign companies can issue American Depositary Receipts (ADRs) instead.[142] An ADR is a negotiable certificate that indicates the ownership of American Depositary Shares (ADS).[143] Guaranty Trust Co., the predecessor of J.P. Morgan, pioneered the ADR concept. In 1927, it created the first ADR, enabling US investors to buy shares of the famous British retailer Selfridges.[144] Before that, American investors who wanted to purchase shares of a non-US listed company could only do so on foreign exchanges. This method would encounter many difficulties, such as currency-exchange issues as well as regulatory differences between US exchanges and foreign exchanges.[145] In contrast, ADRs are traded in US dollar and are cleared through US settlement systems, allowing ADR holders to avoid transactions in foreign currencies.[146]

10.4.2.2 Listing of Common Stocks

A foreign company may also list common stocks directly on US exchanges without employing ADRs if it is registered in Canada or other jurisdictions joining the United States' Multi-Jurisdictional Disclosure System (MJDS).[147] The SEC has adopted a MJDS for Canadian issuers since 1991, under which eligible Canadian issuers are allowed to conduct securities offerings and listings in US capital markets by use of documents prepared under Canadian requirements.[148]

The MJDS system has certain advantages, such as streamlined registration statements, limited SEC review and simplified continuous

141 NYSE, IPO GUIDE, www.nyse.com/publicdocs/nyse/listing/nyse_ipo_guide.pdf.
142 Corporate Finance Institute, "American Depositary Shares (ADS)," corporatefinanceinstitute.com/resources/knowledge/trading-investing/american-depositary-shares-ads/.
143 Ibid.
144 Ibid.
145 Ibid.
146 SEC, "Accessing the US Capital Markets: A Brief Overview for Foreign Private Issuers," www.sec.gov/divisions/corpfin/internatl/foreign-private-issuers-overview.shtml.
147 SEC, "Topic 16 – Multijurisdictional Disclosure System," www.sec.gov/corpfin/cf-manual/topic-16.
148 Ibid.

reporting.[149] However, most jurisdictions do not have an MJDS arrangement with the United States, and thus companies from these jurisdictions cannot directly issue common stocks in the United States. Further, ADRs are usually more attractive to foreign issuers due to the less stringent disclosure duties.[150] Hence, ADRs have become the common vehicle for foreign companies to seek listings in the United States. In practice, the majority of foreign companies listed on US stock exchanges have chosen to issue ADRs instead of common stocks.[151] This also holds true for Chinese companies.[152]

10.4.2.3 Preferential Treatment for Foreign Private Issuers

A foreign issuer can enjoy preferential regulatory treatments when issuing ADRs or common stocks if it qualifies as a so-called Foreign Private Issuer (FPI).[153] By definition, an FPI is an enterprise incorporated under the laws of a foreign country.[154] According to Rule 405 of Regulation C under the Securities Act and Rule 3b-4 under the Exchange Act, a foreign company qualifies as an FPI if it satisfies either of the following two tests: (1) the relative degree of its US share ownership (shareholding test); or (2) the level of its US business contacts (business contacts test).[155]

Under the first test, namely, the shareholding test, a foreign company qualifies as an FPI if 50 percent or less of its outstanding voting securities are held by US residents.[156] Foreign companies must look through the record ownership of brokers or nominees holding securities for their customers' accounts.[157]

If a foreign company cannot meet the first test, it may try the second test, under which it can qualify as an FPI if it falls into any of the following circumstances: (1) the majority of its executive officers or directors are not

149 SEC, "FAQ about the US–Canadian Multijurisdictional Disclosure System," media2.mofo.com/documents/faqs-multijurisdictional-disclosure-system.pdf.

150 *See* Mark Saunders, "American Depository Receipts: An Introduction to US Capital Markets for Foreign Companies" (1993) 17 *Fordham International Law Journal* 48.

151 NYSE, above note 142.

152 *See* US–China Economic and Security Review Commission, "Chinese Companies Listed on Major US Stock Exchanges" (2024).

153 SEC, "Accessing the U.S. Capital Market: A Brief Overview for Foreign Private Issuers," www.sec.gov/divisions/corpfin/internatl/foreign-private-issuers-overview.shtml.

154 17 C.F.R. § 230.405 (2024) (defining FPI).

155 Ibid., at §§ 230.405, 230.3b-4.

156 17 C.F.R. § 240.3b-4 (2024).

157 Ibid., at §§ 230.405, 230.3b-4.

US citizens or residents; (2) less than 50 percent of the issuer's tangible and intangible assets are located in the United States; or (3) the issuer's business is not administered principally in the United States.[158]

To attract foreign companies to get listed in the United States, less stringent regulatory requirements have been applied to foreign companies that are recognized as FPIs. For example, the NYSE allows FPIs to choose between the Alternate Listing Standards for FPIs or the domestic listing criteria. Under the Alternate Listing Standards, a foreign issuer needs to meet a relatively lower level of requirements regarding distribution, size and price, as well as financial standards.[159] Under the federal securities law, foreign issuers have historically been subject to different requirements on registration and disclosure from US domestic issuers.[160] The main aspects are outlined below.

First, FPIs benefit from relaxed securities registration requirements. Rule 12g3-2(b) of the Securities Exchange Act provides an automatic exemption from registration requirements under Section 12(g),[161] given that the FPI meets all the following conditions:

(1) it is not required to file reports under Sections 13(a) or 15(d) of the Exchange Act;
(2) it maintains a listing of securities on one or two non-US exchanges (Primary Trading Market) that comprise more than 55 percent of its worldwide trading volume;
(3) it publishes material items of information on its website, in the English language, that
    (a) it has made public pursuant to the laws of the country of its incorporation;
    (b) it has filed with the principal stock exchange in its Primary Trading Market; or
    (c) it has distributed to its security holders.[162]

Second, the requirements of continuous information disclosure are also relaxed for FPIs. An FPI does not have to abide by the standard disclosure rules applied to domestic issuers. For example, there is no

[158] Ibid.
[159] NYSE, Listed Company Manual § 103.00.
[160] Roberta S. Karmel and Mary S. Head, "Barriers to Foreign Issuer Entry into US Markets" (1993) 24 *Law and Policy in International Business* 1207.
[161] 17 C.F.R. § 240.12g3-2(b) (2024).
[162] Ibid.

requirement to file quarterly or current reports, and the annual reports do not need to be as detailed as those filed by a domestic issuer.[163]

Third, there are special accounting standards for FPIs. The SEC has adopted rules specific to FPIs that recognize international and home jurisdiction accounting standards.[164] For example, FPIs may present financial statements pursuant to US generally accepted accounting principles (GAAP) or home country accounting standards.[165]

Lastly, FPIs can also receive preferential treatment on corporate governance issues. For example, they are not obligated to appoint a majority of directors that meet independence requirements or establish a compensation committee of independent directors.[166] There is no requirement of shareholder approval for FPIs before issuing more than 20 percent of stock in a private placement or an acquisition.[167]

10.4.3 Hong Kong

In general, the Listing Rules of HKEX apply equally to domestic and foreign issuers. For foreign issuers, however, there are additional or special requirements contained in Chapter 19.[168] Chapter 19 applies to non-HK issuers seeking either a primary or a secondary listing on HKEX.[169]

10.4.3.1 Recognized Jurisdictions and Acceptable Jurisdictions

The HKEX divides foreign jurisdictions into two categories, namely, Recognized Jurisdictions and Acceptable Jurisdictions. Companies registered in these two categories are eligible for listing in the HKEX. Foreign companies from Recognized Jurisdictions and Accepted Jurisdictions receive similar national treatment.[170]

163 17 C.F.R. § 240.13a-1 (2024); NYSE, Listed Company Manual § 203.03; *see* also Jesse M. Fried and Ehud Kamar, "China and the Rise of Law-Proof Insiders" (2023) 48 *Journal of Corporate Law* 217.

164 SEC, above note 154.

165 Ibid.

166 Ibid.

167 NYSE, Listed Company Manual § 303A.00; NASDAQ, Listing Center Rulebook §§ 5615 (a)(3), 5635.

168 HKEX, HKEX Main Board Listing Rules ch. 19.01 (2025).

169 Ibid., at ch. 19.02.

170 *See* HKEX, "Consultation Paper: Listing Regime for Overseas Issuers" (March 2021), www.hkex.com.hk/-/media/HKEX-Market/News/Market-Consultations/2016-Present/

First, in addition to Hong Kong, the Listing Rules list three foreign jurisdictions, namely, China, the Cayman Islands and Bermuda, as Recognized Jurisdictions.[171] For China-based issuers, they need to comply with an additional layer of regulation, namely, Chapter 19A, due to special issues such as distinctive features of Chinese corporate governance and various restrictions on foreign exchange.[172]

Second, the SFC and the HKEX jointly issued the Joint Policy Statement Regarding the Listing of Overseas Companies in 2007 (2007 JPS), which was revised in 2013 and 2018.[173] The JPS sets out guidance for relevant foreign companies seeking to list on the HKEX. It aims to ensure Hong Kong remains an attractive listing venue for foreign companies by reducing unnecessary regulatory burden and preserving high standards of regulation, enforcement and corporate governance. To date, the HKEX has approved twenty-five foreign jurisdictions as Acceptable Jurisdictions, including developed economies such as Australia, England and Wales, Germany, Japan and Singapore, as well as developing economies such as Brazil, India and Russia.[174]

10.4.3.2 Primary Listing of Common Stocks

When foreign companies from Recognized Jurisdictions and Accepted Jurisdictions seek a primary listing in Hong Kong, they receive national treatment and are subject to the full regulatory requirements of Hong Kong securities laws. Unless otherwise provided, the HKEX Main Board Listing Rules are applicable to foreign companies in the same way to Hong Kong companies.

The primary listing of common stocks must be in the public interest, and the overseas issuer must be incorporated in a jurisdiction where the

March-2021-Listing-Regime/Consultation-Paper/cp202103.pdf (explaining that in addition to common rules applicable to all foreign issuers, there are specific rules applicable to Acceptable Jurisdictions). The HKEX has published a Country Guide for each Acceptable Jurisdiction to provide guidance for foreign issuers incorporated in that jurisdiction, which shows the criteria HKEX considers when applying the Listing Rules to such issuers. Published in 2021, the HKEX consultation paper proposed removing all distinctions between Recognized Jurisdictions and Acceptable Jurisdictions in the future.

171 HKEX, Joint Policy Statement Regarding the Listing of Overseas Companies (2018), para. 3.

172 HKEX, Main Board Listing Rules, above note 169.

173 HKEX, Joint Policy Statement, above note 172, at para. 7.

174 HKEX, List of Acceptable Overseas Jurisdictions, www.hkex.com.hk/Listing/Rules-and-Guidance/Listing-of-Overseas-Companies/List-of-Acceptable-Overseas-Jurisdictions?sc_lang=en.

standards of shareholder protection are at least equivalent to those provided in Hong Kong. This is a mandatory requirement under the Listing Rules.[175] If this is not possible, foreign companies can achieve equivalent standards by varying their constitutional documents to provide as such.[176]

10.4.3.3 Secondary Listing of Common Stocks

The secondary listing regime is provided by the HKEX Main Board Listing Rules.[177] The disclosure requirements are usually less stringent for secondary listings. The overseas issuer must appoint, and maintain the appointment of, a person authorized to accept service of process and notices on its behalf in Hong Kong.[178]

A foreign company seeking a secondary listing on the Hong Kong Stock Exchange must possess a substantial market capitalization and demonstrate a consistent record of regulatory compliance within its primary listing jurisdiction. Additionally, the issuer is required to have its "center of gravity" located outside of the Greater China region.[179] Chapter 19C of the HKEX Main Board Listing Rules enumerates some of the factors that determines the center of gravity, such as where the issuer is incorporated and the issuer's history.[180] There are currently two routes whereby secondary listing can be effected on the HKEX, which can substantially reduce the compliance costs of qualified issuers from qualified exchanges or qualified jurisdictions.[181]

The first route is the traditional secondary listing method via Chapter 19. Foreign issuers which do not have a center of gravity in Greater China can seek a secondary listing under Section 5 of the JPS.[182] The JPS mechanism applies to secondary listings as well as primary listings. As discussed before, the HKEX publishes a Country Guide for each of the twenty-five Acceptable Jurisdictions.[183] For example, the JPS

[175] HKEX, Main Board Listing Rules, above note 169, at ch. 19.05.
[176] Ibid.
[177] Ibid., at chs. 19 and 19C.
[178] Ibid., at ch. 19.30.
[179] HKEX, Joint Policy Statement, above note 172, at para. 14.
[180] HKEX, Main Board Listing Rules, above note 169, at ch. 19C.
[181] HKEX, "Secondary Listings in Hong Kong," www.hkex.com.hk/Listing/Rules-and-Guidance/Listing-of-Overseas-Companies/Secondary-Listings-in-Hong-Kong?sc_lang=en.
[182] HKEX, Joint Policy Statement, above note 172, at para. 5.
[183] HKEX, Consultation Paper, above note 171.

in England and Wales applies to both primary and secondary listing applicants.[184]

The second route is the new secondary listing method via Chapter 19C. Before 2018, the HKEX only accepted secondary listings from overseas-listed entities which had a center of gravity beyond Greater China.[185] In 2018, the HKEX added Chapter 19C to facilitate the listing of companies from emerging and innovative sectors.[186] An issuer primarily listed on a Qualifying Exchange (including the NYSE, NASDAQ and the Main Market of the London Stock Exchange) is regarded as a "Qualifying Issuer" for a potential secondary listing.[187] Regardless of whether they have a center of gravity in Greater China, Qualifying Issuers can seek a secondary listing under Chapter 19C.[188]

Traditional and new secondary listings are subject to some common requirements. For instance, the secondary listing must be in the public interest, and the foreign issuer's primary listing must be on an exchange where the standards of shareholder protection are at least equivalent to those provided in Hong Kong.[189] However, the 2007 JPS has more stringent shareholder protection standards than those applied to Qualifying Issuers under Chapter 19C. A Qualifying Issuer under Chapter 19C must demonstrate that it is "both eligible and suitable for listing."[190] Shareholder protection rules in the WVR structure are not applicable to Qualifying Issuers.[191]

10.4.3.4 Hong Kong Depositary Receipts

The HKEX has introduced a regime for Hong Kong Depositary Receipts (HDRs) on its Main Board since July 1, 2008.[192] The listing requirements

[184] HKEX, "Country Guide: England and Wales" (20 December 2013, updated January 2022), www.hkex.com.hk/-/media/HKEX-Market/Listing/Rules-and-Guidance/Other-Resources/Listing-of-Overseas-Companies/A-List-of-Acceptable-Overseas-Jurisdictions/cg_englandwales.pdf?la=en.

[185] ACCLIME, "Secondary Listings in Hong Kong," hongkong.acclime.com/insights/secondary-listings- hong-kong/.

[186] *See* HKEX, "Research Report: Reform and Breakthrough of Hong Kong's Listing Regime" (September 2019).

[187] HKEX, Secondary Listings, above note 182.

[188] HKEX, Main Board Listing Rules, above note 169, at ch. 19C.

[189] Ibid. at ch. 19.30.

[190] Ibid. at ch. 19.05.

[191] Ibid.

[192] HKEX, HKEX's Framework for Depositary Receipts (HDRs) (December 31, 2024), www.hkex.com.hk/-/media/HKEX-Market/Listing/Rules-and-Guidance/Archive/Frequently-Asked-Questions/clean/FAQ_6.pdf.

for HDR issuers are generally the same as those for stock issuers in relation to the admission, listing process and continuing obligations under Chapter 8.[193] However, HDR issuers also have to comply with more requirements set out in Chapter 19B. These requirements are mainly related to the contents of the deposit agreement and other depositary receipt-specific matters.[194] For example, the listing conditions of HDRs include: (1) the HDRs must be freely transferable and (2) the securities that the HDRs represent must be fully paid and free from all liens and any restrictions on the right of transfer to the depositary.[195]

10.4.4 Summary

As the top two listing destinations for overseas-listed Chinese companies, the United States and Hong Kong have developed distinct regulatory models for the listing of foreign companies. On one hand, the US model and the Hong Kong model share some common features. First, as international financial centers, both are open to the listings of foreign companies at all levels of their capital markets. In addition to common stocks, they both allow foreign companies to issue depositary receipts. Second, both models have designed parallel channels for foreign companies from different jurisdictions. Hong Kong differentiates between Recognized Jurisdictions and Accepted Jurisdictions, while the United States differentiates between MJDS jurisdictions and non-MJDS jurisdictions. Third, both grant preferential treatments to attract foreign companies in the form of relaxed regulatory requirements. To offer flexibility to high-tech startups, both models accommodate and permit special arrangements, such as the WVR structure.

On the other hand, there are some important differences between the two models. First, the Hong Kong model differentiates between primary listing and secondary listing. A foreign issuer can have the benefit of relaxation or exemption of some regulatory requirements only in the case of secondary listing. By contrast, the US model does not have the concept of secondary listing as a condition for special regulatory treatments. In the United States, foreign issuers are subject to a lower level of regulatory requirements than domestic issuers, as long as they qualify as an FPI, no matter whether they have a primary listing elsewhere.

193 HKEX, Main Board Listing Rules, above note 169, at ch. 8.
194 HKEX, Framework for Depositary Receipts, above note 193.
195 HKEX, Main Board Listing Rules, above note 169, at ch. 19B.09.

Historically, the FPI regime was initially designed for cross-listings of foreign companies and has later been gradually expanded to apply to foreign companies that are listed solely in the United States. As the status of FPI brings the benefits of relaxed regulatory requirements, most foreign companies have chosen to qualify as an FPI.[196]

Second, the Hong Kong model attaches more importance to the issuance of common stocks by foreign companies. In Hong Kong, a foreign issuer has the freedom to choose between issuing common stocks or HDRs, regardless of whether they are from a Recognized Jurisdiction or an Accepted Jurisdiction. A vast majority of foreign companies choose to issue common stocks in Hong Kong because it is easier and cheaper to issue common stocks than HDRs. To date, there has been only one case of HDR issuance, namely, Fast Retailing Co., Ltd., a Japanese company that issued HDRs in 2014.[197] In comparison, the US model centers on the issuance of depositary receipts by foreign companies. As noted previously, foreign issuers cannot issue common stocks in the United States if their home jurisdictions do not have a MJDS arrangement with the United States.[198]

10.5 Improvement Suggestions and Development Prospects

10.5.1 Improving China's Listing Regime for Foreign Companies

10.5.1.1 Overview

As Table 10.3 shows, the Chinese regulatory model for the listing of foreign companies has both similarities and differences with the United States and Hong Kong models. In particular, the Chinese model has two distinctive features. The first feature is the absence of preferential treatment for foreign companies. The second feature is the underuse of depositary receipts, which will be further discussed in Section 10.5.2.3. In China, there are no preferential treatments in the form of relaxed regulatory requirements for foreign companies seeking to get listed in China. Moreover, the financial requirements for the listing of Red-chip Companies are much higher than those for domestic issuers. As

[196] Stoxray, "What is A Foreign Private Issuer?" stoxray.com/academy/what-is-a-foreign-private-issuer.

[197] HKEX, List of Depositary Receipts, www.hkex.com.hk/Listing/Rules-and-Guidance/Listing-of-Overseas-Companies/Depositary-Receipt-Framework/List-of-Depositary-Receipts?sc_lang=en.

[198] *See* Section 10.4.2.2.

Table 10.3 *A comparison of the regimes for listing by foreign companies in China, the United States and Hong Kong*

Jurisdiction	Applicable scope	Preferential treatment	Secondary listing	Common stock	Depositary receipt
China	Red-chip Companies	No	No	Yes	Yes (CDR)
United States	Foreign companies registered in MJDS and non-MJDS jurisdictions	Yes (FPI)	No	Yes (only for MJDS issuers)	Yes (ADR)
Hong Kong	Foreign companies registered in recognized and accepted jurisdictions	Yes (secondary listing)	Yes	Yes	Yes (HDR)

discussed above, it is much more complicated for Red-chip Companies to get listed in China than their domestic peers.[199] This issue, if not addressed properly, would impede the listing of foreign companies in China and ultimately interrupt the internationalization process of Chinese capital markets.

10.5.1.2 Suggestions on the Granting of Preferential Treatment

Compared with the US model, the Hong Kong model is more suitable for China to learn from. In general, China should establish an effective secondary listing regime to grant preferential treatment in order to attract foreign companies to its capital markets. Hong Kong grants preferential treatment to certain foreign issuers, depending on whether their listings in Hong Kong are secondary listings. The rationale is that if a foreign issuer is primarily listed in another jurisdiction and is subjected to a regulatory level comparable to that in Hong Kong, the HKEX can free ride on the regulatory efforts of the jurisdiction of primary listing. In fact, the special treatment for secondary listing is also justified on the grounds that if secondary listing were to be subject to the full panoply of regulatory requirements, there would be an issue of double regulation for foreign issuers. In practice, the secondary-listing regime of Hong Kong has proven to be very effective in attracting foreign issuers. There has recently been a string of Chinese high-tech companies, such as JD.com, Baidu and NetEase, that have chosen to undertake secondary listings in Hong Kong.[200]

The US model is not well-suited to China. As discussed above, most foreign issuers in the United States have somehow found a way to qualify as FPIs so as to enjoy preferential treatment.[201] Historically, as with Hong Kong, the United States designed the FPI regime for cross-listings to avoid double regulation. But the FPI regime has been later expanded to foreign issuers that are solely listed in the United States. As a result, the FPI regime has serious loopholes in practice. The recent wave of scandals involving China Concept Stocks has brought the issue into the limelight. For various reasons, the China Concept Stocks are not regulated as

[199] *See* Sections 10.2 and 10.3.

[200] Grady McGregor, "Gaming Giant NetEase Soars in Hong Kong IPO as Chinese Firms Seek US Alternative," *Fortune*, June 11, 2020, fortune.com/2020/06/11/netease-ipo-hong-kong.

[201] *See* Section 10.4.2.3.

rigorously as US domestic firms are under US corporate and securities law.[202] Further, as they are registered and listed overseas, they generally do not come under the regulation of China either. Hence, these companies have been described as "law proof," and the current FPI regime has been criticized as a historical mistake.[203] It is submitted that China should avoid making that very same mistake.

10.5.1.3 Suggestions on the Promotion of Chinese Depositary Receipts

The second important feature of China's listing regime for foreign companies is the underuse of depositary receipts. It appears that many foreign issuers have chosen to issue common stocks in China, which is similar to the case in Hong Kong. In the US market, foreign companies have to issue ADRs because most jurisdictions do not have a MJDS treaty with the United States to issue common stocks. Further, CDRs and HDRs are not as popular as ADRs due to the complexity and costs of their issuance. China has transplanted its depositary receipt regime from the United States, mainly due to the tremendous influence of the US capital markets and the great success of its ADR regulation.

To date, Xiaomi Group is the only company that has ever applied to issue CDRs on the Main Board of the Shanghai Stock Exchange.[204] In the end, however, Xiaomi decided to withdraw its CDR issuance application.[205] It is not fully clear as to the exact reasons behind Xiaomi's application and subsequent withdrawal, but anecdotal evidence suggests that the withdrawal may be attributed to economic considerations. For example, Xiaomi's CDR issuance price, if CDRs were in fact issued, would be set at a level lower than its Hong Kong share price.[206]

It remains to be seen whether the CDR issuance will be a success. As discussed earlier, there have been several companies that made applications for issuing CDRs.[207] It seems that Red-chip Companies prefer to issue common stocks over CDRs. This may be explained by the following

202 Fried and Kamar, above note 164.

203 Ibid.

204 CSRC, Xiaomi Jituan Gongkai Faxing Cuntuo Pingzheng Zhaogu Shuoming Shu (小米集团公开发行存托凭证招股说明书) [Xiaomi Group's Prospectus for Public Issuance of Depositary Receipts], June 14, 2018, www.csrc.gov.cn/pub/zjhpublic/G00306202/201806/t20180614_339903.htm.

205 Ibid.

206 Ibid.

207 *See* Section 10.2.5.

factors. First, the financial costs for CDR issuance may be higher than those for common stock issuance. The deal structure for issuing CDRs is generally more complicated, thus increasing issuance costs. Compared with common stocks, issuing CDRs requires the prior issuance of underlying securities in accordance with the company law regime of the jurisdiction of registration, most notably the Cayman Islands. Moreover, in creating CDRs from underlying securities, there are extra service fees that need to be paid to the depositary agent bank. For example, the CDR service fee paid by Ninebot to its agent bank is 0.01 yuan per share.[208] Second, CDRs are issued by foreign companies, and thus are exposed to special risks inherent in foreign investment.[209] Under the pilot program, CDRs can only be traded in the Chinese securities market and are generally not allowed to be converted into their underlying securities issued overseas, unless otherwise stipulated by the CSRC.[210] Finally, according to our interviews, as the CDR is still alien to most Chinese investors, Red-chip Companies are concerned that it may be harder to attract Chinese investors to participate in the offering of CDRs than that of common stocks.

Notwithstanding the drawbacks, CDRs provide an important channel for foreign companies to seek listings on the Chinese markets. China should learn from the US ADR experience to further improve its CDR regulation.

First, China should allow investors to purchase and exchange depositary receipts with underlying shares in a more flexible and convenient way. Although well-resourced investors may prefer to buy and hold foreign shares directly, retail investors and smaller institutions usually do not wish to do so. This is because direct holding of foreign shares involves complicated issues such as share registration, tax reclaims, currency conversion and possibly investor registration in the corresponding foreign jurisdiction. In the United States, these onerous procedures are handled by the depositary of ADRs. Accordingly, the use of ADRs

208 Ninebot Limited, "Prospectus for Public Offering of Depositary Receipts (Registration Draft)," at p. 60, static.sse.com.cn/stock/information/c/202009/7ffb311d2ef648b28966c4812d1a77f1.pdf.

209 Fidelity, "Understanding American Depositary Receipts (ADRs)," www.fidelity.com/learning-center/investment-products/stocks/understanding-american-depositary-receipts.

210 China Securities Depository and Clearing Corporation Limited, Cuntuo Pingzheng Dengji Jiesuan Yewu (存托凭证登记结算业务投资者问答) [Answering Investors' Questions on CDR Registration and Settlement Business], www.cs.ecitic.com/newsite/tzzjy/cxqyzq/bmgzyywgz/zgjs/201807/P020180702706411518659.pdf.

may enable an issuer to reach a larger investor base than would be possible in the case of common stocks.

Second, China can introduce more types of depositary receipts for foreign issuers to choose from. There are many types of ADRs available in the United States, which shows the ADR's inclusiveness and international attraction. For instance, the ADRs can be "sponsored" or "unsponsored."[211] The ADRs can be broadly categorized into three "levels," depending on the extent to which the foreign company has access to the US market.[212] Level 1 ADR establishes a securities market presence in the United States but may not be used to raise capital.[213] It is the only type of ADR that may be unsponsored and may be traded only on the over-the-counter market. Thus, it has the least stringent regulatory requirements and is typically highly speculative. Level 2 ADR is traded on a national securities exchange but may not be used to raise capital.[214] Level 3 ADR may be used to raise capital and traded on a national securities exchange.[215] China should also establish a restricted program to encourage the issuance of CDRs to institutional investors only. For instance, foreign companies may issue ADRs under SEC Rule 144A in a private placement to qualified institutional buyers (QIBs).[216] Further, foreign companies may issue offshore ADRs under SEC Regulation S to offshore, non-US residents that are not registered with any US securities regulation authority.[217]

10.5.2 The Way Forward and Factors to Consider

10.5.2.1 The Experiment with Red-Chip Companies

China's regime for the listing of foreign companies is currently limited to Red-chip Companies that are registered overseas but are owned and

[211] *See* SEC, "Investor Bulletin: American Depositary Receipts" (August 2012), www.sec.gov/investor/alerts/adr-bulletin.pdf (explaining that sponsored ADRs are those in which the non-US company enters into an agreement directly with the US depository bank to arrange for recordkeeping and other services. An unsponsored ADR is set up without the cooperation of the non-US company and may be initiated by a broker dealer wishing to establish a US trading market. The former can be listed on major exchanges, while the latter can be traded on the over-the-counter market).

[212] Ibid.

[213] Ibid.

[214] Ibid.

[215] Ibid.

[216] Ibid.

[217] *See* J. Michael Pinegar and Ravi Ravichandran, "Raising Capital in Emerging Markets with Restricted Global Depositary Receipts" (2010) 16 *Journal of Corporate Finance* 622.

controlled by Chinese entities.[218] Genuine foreign companies, namely, companies that are really owned or controlled by foreigners, cannot get listed in China for the time being. This is typical of China's gradualist approach to economic reform, which has proven to be very successful. The regulatory reform of the Chinese capital markets is no exception.[219]

Back in 2011, to build Shanghai as an international financial center, the Shanghai Stock Exchange made a serious effort to establish the so-called International Board (*Guo Ji Ban*).[220] Many multinational companies, including HSBC Holdings and Bank of East Asia, have expressed interest.[221] However, this effort did not come to fruition due to many reasons.[222] For instance, there were grave concerns that the International Board might divert the funds away from the Main Board and therefore exert an adverse impact on the stability of these particular capital markets. Besides, the plan also faced some long-standing institutional obstacles, such as stringent rules on capital control and the lack of free convertibility of the Chinese currency. The Chinese government learned a lesson from this failed effort and thus adopted a gradualist approach to establishing the listing regime for foreign companies.

As the name suggests, the 2018 Pilot Program Opinions is essentially an experiment, and if it goes well, the reform will likely expand to genuine foreign companies. The interesting question, however, is why Red-chip Companies were chosen for experimentation. Several possible reasons contribute to this.

First, the experiment with Red-chip Companies reflects China's national strategy to encourage the development of high-tech industry. Many Red-chip Companies are high-tech companies or the so-called new economy companies, such as Alibaba, Tencent and Xiaomi.

218 Grace Yan and Rong Yan, "Hong Kong Listing: Setting Up Red-Chip Structures" *China Business Law Journal*, June 23, 2021, law.asia/hong-kong-listing-setting-up-red-chip-structures/.

219 *See* Huang, *Securities and Capital Markets Law in China*, above note 2.

220 Tencent Finance and Economics, "Shangjiaosuo Guojiban Tuichu Tiaojian Yi Jiben Chengshu" (上交所：国际版推出条件已基本成熟) [Shanghai Stock Exchange: The Conditions for Launching the International Board Are Basically Mature], May 16, 2011, finance.qq.com/a/20110516/004666.htm.

221 Ibid.

222 "Shangjiaosuo Guojiban NianneiNanyi Tuichu" (上交所国际版年内难以推出) [The International Board of the Shanghai Stock Exchange is Difficult to be Launched within This Year], *China Daily*, May 8, 2009, www.chinadaily.com.cn/zgzx/2009-05/08/content_7755139.htm.

Second, Red-chip Companies are within the reach of Chinese regulators, as their major businesses, core personnel and material assets are mainly located in China. The market professionals they hire for the securities offering process, such as auditors and lawyers, are obligated to make all relevant materials accessible to the regulators. In contrast, US regulators face the problem of the "Great Legal Wall" in regulating China Concept Stocks.[223] For instance, despite many rounds of negotiation and some arrangements, US regulators have long complained that they are denied access to relevant materials such as audit working papers.[224]

Third, the experiment with Red-chip Companies conforms with China's national security interests. The 2020 Foreign Investment Law requires the government to designate forbidden or restricted foreign investment items on the negative list to protect key industries in China.[225] Compared with genuine foreign companies, Red-chip Companies can hardly pose a national security threat to China.

Last but not least, there is a practical need to provide Red-chip Companies with an option of getting listed back in China. In 2020, the United States passed the Holding Foreign Companies Accountable Act, under which China Concept Stocks may be delisted if US regulators continue to be denied access to their audit work papers.[226] In light of such risks, an increasing number of China Concept Stocks have decided to seek listings in China.

In the long run it could be expected that China's listing regime for foreign companies will be extended from Red-chip Companies to all foreign companies. Today, it is still hard to predict whether, and if so, how China will successfully go through this process, as it will depend on a variety of factors, which may be broadly divided into two categories, namely, political-economy and legal-regulatory factors. These two categories of factors will be discussed, in turn, in Sections 10.5.2.2 and 10.5.2.3 below.

223 *See* Huang, The US–China Audit Oversight Dispute, above note 11.

224 *See* ibid.

225 Foreign Investment Law, above note 120, at art. 4; *see* also Robin Hui Huang, "The Regulation of Foreign Investment in Post-WTO China: A Political Economy Analysis" (2009) 23 *Columbia Journal of Asian Law* 185. (providing a more detailed discussion of this issue); Yuwen Li and Cheng Bian, "A New Dimension of Foreign Investment Law in China: Evolution and Impacts of the National Security Review System" (2016) 24 *Asia Pacific Law Review* 149.

226 *See* Huang, "The US–China Audit Oversight Dispute," above note 11.

10.5.2.2 Political-Economy Factors

To put the discussion in perspective, we will first examine the broader political-economy context in which the reform is carried out.

First, listing in China has some unique advantages which may appeal to foreign companies, such as raising the company's profile and facilitating product marketing in a fast-growing economy.[227] Besides, foreign companies are eager to be cross-listed in China due to the high level of valuation in the Chinese capital markets.[228] According to the market segmentation thesis, when stocks are cross-listed, stocks in advanced markets can enjoy higher valuation than those in emerging markets.[229] For instance, the price of ADRs usually carry premiums over the price of shares issued in an emerging market.[230] However, China does not seem to follow this general pattern. An empirical study conducted by the People's Bank of China shows that from 2002 to 2020, the China-listed shares have an average premium of around 30 percent over the ADRs issued by the same group of companies and around 34 percent over their shares listed in Hong Kong.[231] Lower cost of capital and greater liquidity (or higher speculation) of the Chinese market can partly explain the premiums of China-listed shares.[232]

Moreover, the fast-changing global geopolitical pattern could bring about a deep change in the world's economy and thus create new opportunities in the global supply chain. Specifically, China's recent Belt and Road Initiative (BRI) would not only promote the export and global adoption of Chinese capital and technology but also help with the growth of small- and medium-sized enterprises (SMEs) in emerging economies within the scope of BRI. Eventually, these BRI-based foreign companies may wish to get listed and raise funds on China's stock market.

227 Donald Clarke, "The Bonding Effect in Chinese Cross-Listed Companies: Is It Real?" in Robin Hui Huang and Nicholas Calcina Howson (eds.), *Enforcement of Corporate and Securities Law: China and the World* (Cambridge University Press, 2017), pp. 88, 94.

228 *See* Vihang R. Errunza and Darius P. Miller, "Market Segmentation and the Cost of Capital in International Equity Markets" (2000) 35 *Journal of Financial and Quantitative Analysis* 577.

229 Ibid., at 589.

230 Matthieu Stigler, Ajay Shah and Ila Patnaik, *Understanding the ADR Premium under Market Segmentation* (National Institute of Public Finance and Policy, 2010).

231 Xuechun Zhang, Ruihui Xu and Xue Liu, "AH and A-ADR Premiums," *The People's Bank of China Working Paper Series No. 2020/9*, November 2, 2020, admin.fangchan.com/uploadfile/uploadfile/annex/2/2414/5fb4b2346f6c5.pdf.

232 *See* Guo Lin and Tang Liang, "Cost of Capital and Liquidity of Cross-Listed Chinese Companies" (2008) 1 *Journal of Knowledge Globalization* 1, 1–18.

But on the other hand, there are also factors that may restrict the expansion of China's listing of foreign companies. One important reason is that going public in the United States has many advantages for a foreign company, including ready access to the world's largest equity market, diversification of shareholder base and enhanced corporate visibility in the United States.[233] However attractive it maybe to tap into the world's second-largest economy, China's immature capital market may not be the first choice for many genuine foreign companies.

Besides, China–US political and economic tensions will inevitably influence foreign companies' willingness to get listed in China. Since the trade war, China's economy has exerted a gradual trend of decoupling with the global economy. This new circumstance may discourage genuine foreign companies to seek a single-market listing in China. In 2020, China unveiled a "dual circulation" strategy to sever its dependence on overseas markets in the fourteenth Five-Year Plan (2021–2025).[234] The idea of internal circulation, namely, the domestic cycle of production, distribution and consumption, was brought on by a deepening rift with the United States. The tensions between China and the United States have exposed China's vulnerability as it relies heavily on US high-tech products in supply chains.[235] The new trend leads to uncertainties for foreign issuers.

Also worthy of notice is that, under China's current stringent regime for capital control, foreign companies may have difficulties transferring money across borders after raising funds within China. Capital controls in China are used for many purposes, such as preventing undesired capital flight, controlling the exchange rate and managing the size of foreign exchange reserves.[236] In recent years, China's policymakers have been very concerned about possible capital flight spurred by the Sino-US trade war and diplomatic tensions.[237] In 2017, China used tough capital

[233] NYSE, IPO Guide, above note 142.

[234] Kevin Yao, "What we know about China's 'dual circulation' economic strategy," *Reuters*, September 16, 2020, www.reuters.com/article/china-economy-transformation-explainer-idUSKBN2600B5.

[235] Ibid.

[236] Karen Yeung, "China 'Stuck' as Rigid Controls on Capital Outflows Becoming Harder to Peel Back," *South China Morning Post*, August 26, 2020, www.scmp.com/economy/china-economy/article/3098814/china-stuck-rigid-controls-capital-outflows-becoming-harder.

[237] Samuel Shen and Andrew Galbraith, "China constricts capital outflows with eye on Yuan stability," *Reuters*, October 11, 2018, www.reuters.com/article/us-china-markets-soft-landing-analysis-idUSKCN1ML1SW.

controls to put the brakes on outbound deals.[238] On the other hand, capital controls can be used in the opposite direction. In 2021, as bubble risk pressure rose due to aggressive stimulus policies in the United States, China eased its capital control to allow more domestic investment abroad.[239] Either way, capital control may bring about uncertainties to foreign issuers. Although this maybe a long process, the Chinese government should consider gradually relaxing its stringent capital control to allow free flow of capital, so that foreign issuers are more willing to get listed in China.

Therefore, it could be predicted that many genuine foreign companies might prefer to cross-list in the Chinese market, rather than become solely listed in China, and may cautiously conduct a cost–benefit analysis before making informed investment decisions.

10.5.2.3 Legal and Regulatory Factors

Under the legal bonding theory, foreign companies choose to get cross-listed in the United States because they can enjoy higher valuation and lower costs of capital by bonding themselves to tougher securities regulation in the United States.[240] This theory highlights the important role of the investor protection law and market regulation in attracting foreign issuers.

Over the years, China has gradually established a legal framework for investor protection both under company law and securities law. Drawing on overseas experiences, China has built up a modern system of corporate governance, including the imposition of fiduciary duties on directors and senior management[241] and the institution of independent

[238] Maggie Zhang, "China's Tough Capital Controls Put the Brakes on Outbound Deals," *South China Morning Post*, April 5, 2017, www.scmp.com/business/global-economy/article/2085109/chinas-tough-capital-controls-put-brakes-outbound-deals.

[239] Karen Yeung, "China's Strict Capital Controls May Be Eased to Allow Investment Abroad as Bubble Risks Grow," *South China Morning Post*, March 4, 2021, https://www.scmp.com/economy/china-economy/article/3124029/chinas-strict-capital-controls-may-be-eased-allow-investment.

[240] *See* John C. Coffee Jr., "Racing Towards the Top: The Impact of Cross-Listing and Stock Market Competition on International Corporate Governance" (2002) 102 *Columbian Law Review* 1757.

[241] Rebecca Lee, "Fiduciary Duty without Equity: 'Fiduciary Duties' of Directors under the Revised Company Law of the PRC" (2007) 47 *Virginia Journal of International Law* 898; Guangdong Xu, Tianshu Zhou, Zeng Bin and Shi Jin, "Directors' Duties in China" (2013) 14 *European Business Organization Law Review* 57.

directors.[242] There is also a full panoply of shareholder remedies. In addition to various forms of direct suits, such as shareholder inspection rights,[243] appraisal remedy[244] and oppression remedy,[245] Chinese investors can also bring directive actions to sue directors, senior management and controlling shareholders who misbehave, thereby causing harm to their companies.[246]

Chinese securities law has also made great achievements both in terms of substantive rules and enforcement mechanisms.[247] China has set up a relatively robust financial regulatory architecture, continuously improved the rules on securities offerings and listings and set out detailed rules on various forms of market misconduct, including insider trading,[248] market manipulation[249] and misstatements.[250] On the other hand, enforcement strategies of securities law have traditionally been divided into two broad categories, namely, public enforcement and private enforcement. In general, public enforcement is initiated by a state official such as a regulator or a prosecutor, while private enforcement is by a private party in the form of civil actions for compensation or rescission. China has long relied more on public enforcement to combat market misconduct, such as insider trading,[251] but has paid increasing attention to private enforcement. The Chinese regime for private securities litigation performs a similar function to the US securities class action to the extent that it can aggregate multiple suits arising from the same securities

242 Donald C. Clarke, "The Independent Director in Chinese Corporate Governance" (2006) 31 *Delaware Journal of Corporate Law* 126.

243 Robin Hui Huang and Randall Thomas, "The Law and Practice of Shareholder Inspection Rights: A Comparative Analysis of China and the US" (2020) 53 *Vanderbilt Journal of Transnational Law* 907.

244 Zhonghua Renmin Gongheguo Gongsi Fa (中华人民共和国公司法) [Company Law of the PRC] (promulgated by the National People's Congress, December 29, 1993, effective July 1, 1994, amended in 1999, 2004, 2005, 2013 and 2018), arts. 74 and 142.

245 Colin Hawes, Alex K. L. Lau and Angus Young, "The Chinese 'Oppression' Remedy: Creative Interpretations of Company Law by Chinese Courts" (2015) 63 *American Journal of Comparative Law* 559.

246 Robin Hui Huang, "Shareholder Derivative Litigation in China: Empirical Findings and Comparative Analysis" (2012) 27 *Banking and Finance Law Review* 619.

247 *See* Huang, *Securities and Capital Markets Law in China*, above note 2.

248 SECURITIES LAW, above note 3, at arts. 50–53.

249 Ibid., at art. 55.

250 Ibid., at arts. 19 and 78.

251 *See*, e.g., Robin Hui Huang, "Enforcement of Chinese Insider Trading Law: An Empirical and Comparative Perspective" (2021) 68(3) *American Journal of Comparative Law* 517.

misconduct, such as prospectus misstatements.[252] In the recent 2019 reform of the securities law, China introduced a so-called special representative suit, which represents an interesting innovation by combining the Chinese-style and US-style class action.[253] Apart from court litigation, investors can also seek remedies through alternative dispute resolution mechanisms such as arbitration and mediation.

However, despite all these impressive achievements, China still lags behind many advanced markets, such as the United States and Hong Kong, in terms of the effectiveness of the legal and regulatory regime for corporate governance and investor protection. From the legal bonding perspective, it is more likely for China to attract foreign companies from other emerging economies, particularly those involved in the Belt and Road Initiative. China still has a long way to go in addressing legal and institutional problems in order to make itself more attractive to high-quality foreign companies from developed economies. For instance, there is a great need to enhance the independence and capacity of relevant regulators, such as the CSRC,[254] as well as the courts, which have long been subject to the issue of local protectionism.

Finally, under the reputational bonding theory, a variant of the legal bonding theory, China should improve its reputational mechanism in regulating the market and protecting investors. According to the reputational bonding theory, cross-listed companies can use disclosure requirements and the scrutiny of market analysts to build up reputational assets.[255] An effective reputational mechanism will help channel resources to companies with a good law-abiding record.[256] The establishment of such a mechanism will depend on several factors, such as

[252] *See*, for example, Xin Tang (汤欣) and Zhuozhuo Li (李卓卓), "Xin Xiu Xujia Chenshu Minshi Peichang Sifa Jieshi Pingxi" (新修虚假陈述民事赔偿司法解释评析) [Comments on the New Judicial Interpretation on Civil Compensation for Securities Misstatement] (2022) 3 *Falv Shiyong (法律适用) [Journal of Law Application]* 61–72.

[253] *See*, for example, Fa Chen, "The Chinese-Style Securities Class Action Mechanism for Investor Protection: Context, Content, Comparison and Consequence" (2022) 30 *Asia Pacific Law Review* 287; Robin Hui Huang, "Class Action in China: Opportunities and Challenges," in Brian Fitzpatrick and Randall Thomas (eds.), *Cambridge International Handbook of Class Actions* (Cambridge University Press, 2021), pp. 350–365.

[254] *See* Robin Hui Huang, "Institutional Structure of Financial Regulation in China: Lessons from the Global Financial Crisis" (2010) 10 *Journal of Corporate Law Studies* 219.

[255] Jordan Siegel, "Can Foreign Firms Bond Themselves Effectively by Renting US Securities Laws?" (2005) 75 *Journal of Financial Economics* 319.

[256] Ibid.

independence of analysts, sophistication of investors and freedom of expression.

10.6 Conclusion

Under China's current pilot program, only Red-chip Companies are allowed to get listed in the Chinese capital markets. This pilot program has several important features in relation to issuer classes, issuer qualifications and the use of special arrangements such as variable interest entity structures, weighted voting rights and valuation adjustment mechanism. In general, the listing of foreign companies is afforded national treatment, meaning they are generally subject to the same substantive and procedural listing requirements as domestic issuers. However, the financial requirements imposed on foreign companies are currently more stringent than those for domestic entities. To examine the rationale behind this disparity and to explore how Red-chip Companies may leverage the program in practice, we collected relevant market data on Red-chip Companies that have applied for listing in China and conducted interviews with insiders of leading securities firms and law firms in the country.

This study further evaluated the Chinese regulatory framework by comparing it with those in the United States and Hong Kong, both of which are international financial centers and preferred destinations for Chinese companies seeking overseas listings. While the Chinese model of regulating foreign listings has both similarities and differences with the United States and Hong Kong, a comparative analysis suggests that China would benefit from aligning more closely with the Hong Kong model. Specifically, preferential treatment should be extended only to firms that are cross-listed in China, rather than broadly applied to all foreign issuers. In order to improve the utility of CDRs, China should adopt elements from the US system of ADRs, particularly by allowing investors greater flexibility in purchasing and exchanging depositary receipts with underlying shares. Moreover, diversifying the structure of CDRs could better accommodate the varied needs of different categories of foreign issuers.

The current pilot program reflects the gradualist approach China has long adopted to its economic reform. In the long term, it is anticipated that the program will be extended from Red-chip Companies to genuine foreign companies. The selection of Red-chip Companies for experimentation is well justified within its framework. However, it is hard to predict whether, and if so, how China will successfully go through this process, as it will depend on a variety of factors, which may be broadly divided into two categories, namely, political-economy as well as legal-regulatory factors. One thing is clear: for China to succeed in attracting foreign issuers, it must continue to strengthen the legal and institutional foundations of its capital markets.

11

Conclusion

In the past few decades, many Chinese companies have chosen to list overseas, particularly in the US and Hong Kong. Under the legal bonding theory, when a company cross-lists in a foreign market, it effectively bonds itself to the more robust regulation of the listing place, which may help enhance its corporate governance and business performance. The overseas listing of Chinese companies offers a good case study due to the disparity between China's regulatory regime and those in the listing places. However, existing empirical research shows ambiguous or, at best, weak effects of legal bonding. This calls for a closer examination of how to interpret these available empirical results and why the legal bonding is not as strong as expected. Three factors can be identified to help explain the empirical anomaly. First, technical or methodological issues, such as selecting the research period and case samples, may contribute to the lower-than-expected bonding effect, as China has been continuously improving its regulatory regime, and the bonding effects tend to be stronger in the early years. Second, the bonding effects may also be affected by political-economy considerations of relevant stakeholders involved in the overseas listing process of Chinese companies. In more recent years, the rise of geopolitics has increasingly impacted the pattern of international financial regulation. Third, and most importantly, some specific regulatory issues may have seriously hindered the functioning of the legal bonding mechanism in various ways. This has important implications for the understanding and evaluation of the relevant Chinese law and policy in the area.

Since the early 1990s, in line with the gradualist approach China has adopted to reforming its economy and society at large, China has made continuous efforts to build and strengthen its regulatory regime for overseas listing of domestic enterprises. In the process, China has also considered the political-economy environment in which it operates. While China continues to welcome foreign investment and facilitate overseas listing of Chinese companies, it has put more emphasis on national security issues, such as foreign investment security, cyber security and data security. The comprehensive filing regime for all overseas-listed Chinese companies that the CSRC introduced in 2023 is a very important development and has far-reaching implications. It marks a new stage in the Chinese regulatory regime for the overseas listing of Chinese companies. It has unified the supervision of direct and indirect overseas listings of Chinese companies and strengthened information disclosure. This move has been widely regarded as a positive step, as it improves transparency of overseas listing activities, enhances certainty in regulatory compliance and facilitates cross-border regulatory coordination. However, there can be significant challenges in the implementation of the new regime.

Further, with the increasing internationalization of its securities market, China has recently introduced Article 2(4) of the 2019 Securities Law in order to deal with the important issue of extraterritorial jurisdiction over cross-border securities transactions. While it represents an important development, the provision is couched in very broad terms, bringing uncertainties and difficulties to its application in practice. This book proposes a phased reform agenda for improvement: In the short run, the effect test under Article 2(4) should be clarified with more guidance; in the long run, China should go beyond the effect test to consider other relevant tests such as the conduct test and the transactional test. The recent high-profile case of *Luckin Coffee* is carefully studied to show the factors that China may consider in applying Article 2(4), including the test of national interests, the principle of international comity and the issue of judicial recourse constraints.

Another overarching issue of China's regulatory regime for overseas-listed Chinese companies is the national security review of foreign investment, as the overseas listing of domestic companies will necessarily introduce foreign investors and thus give rise to foreign investment issues. Hence, this book critically examines China's national security review regime of foreign investment and compares it with that of the United States. Over the years, China has gradually established a comprehensive legal framework for national security review of foreign investment. Recent efforts were made to refine the public enforcement mechanism of the review in tandem with a new "pre-establishment national treatment plus negative list" system under the 2020 Foreign Investment Law. The United States also enacted the Foreign Investment Risk Review Modernization Act of 2018 to enhance its national security review regime. By analyzing the laws and practices of

China and the United States, this book finds that the national security review regimes of the two jurisdictions have functional convergences despite some formal divergences caused by diverse political-economy landscapes. Their functional convergences are highlighted by China's local practices, such as the de facto national security screening in the name of anti-monopoly review. There are many factors affecting China's national security review regime for foreign investment, including the ongoing (and escalating) US–China competition (or conflict) at the international level and the evolution of state or party capitalism at the domestic level.

The book then looks into some specific issues of China's regulatory regime for overseas listings of Chinese companies. To start with, the legality of the structure of a variable interest entity (VIE) has long been a subject of contention since it was first used by Chinese companies to get listed overseas in the early 2000s. The VIE structure allows foreign investors to participate in overseas-listed Chinese companies through contractual control rather than a shareholding relationship, thus bypassing relevant restrictions on foreign investment in China. This book argues that China adopts a policy of strategic ambiguity about the legality of the VIE structure so as to balance the need to protect national security and the need to facilitate overseas listings of Chinese companies. There are institutional reasons behind this policy, including interest group politics of regulatory agencies and the rent-seeking activities of regulatory officials. The policy of strategic ambiguity will likely continue in the foreseeable future, and so will the uncertainty over the legality of the VIE structure. However, the level of uncertainty is not as high as perceived by some commentators arguing that there is no law or no legal protection for investors in the VIE market.

Audit oversight is a significant issue in the context of a company conducting listings across borders. In practice, the auditing of overseas-listed companies is usually undertaken by local accounting firms, raising the issue of whether the regulators of the host market can reach the local accounting firms and relevant documents in their possession, particularly audit working papers. Specifically, there may be a conflict between the power of the host market's regulator to access audit documents and the need of the home jurisdiction to protect sensitive information in the documents. Indeed, until recently, this legal conflict has long been a serious dispute between the Chinese securities regulators and their counterparts in the US and Hong Kong. Under the "one country, two systems" framework, Hong Kong regulators and Mainland China regulators successfully entered into several agreements for regulatory cooperation in 2019. In comparison, the China–US audit dispute presents a much more difficult issue. Only after the US Congress intervened to pass the Holding Foreign Companies Accountable Act in 2020 could the US regulators finally reach an agreement with the Chinese regulators in 2022. This is a good start, but given the China–US geopolitical tensions, it remains to be seen whether the China–US 2022 Agreement will be implemented effectively as expected in the future.

As the capital market becomes increasingly globalized, there has been a heightened need for more effective regulatory cooperation between jurisdictions to facilitate detecting, investigating and prosecuting cross-border securities misconduct such as insider trading and market manipulation. A useful case study in this regard is the regulatory cooperation between Mainland China and Hong Kong, owing to the accelerated process of market integration and transformation. This book provides a comprehensive and critical examination of the way in which Mainland China and Hong Kong coordinate and cooperate to regulate cross-border securities market abuse, and based on the examination, make suggestions and draw implications. While the Mainland–Hong Kong cooperation has produced good achievements, there remain many important issues which can be broadly divided into two categories: substantive rules on the definitions of market misconduct and penalties for such misconduct; enforcement mechanisms in relation to information exchange, regulatory architecture and extradition arrangement. This book suggests that the substantive rules be harmonized and the enforcement mechanisms be unified to the extent possible and that the International Organization of Securities Commissions (IOSCO) can play a more significant role in setting standards and coordinating enforcement for securities regulation across borders.

The enforcement issue can go deeper. In general, overseas-listed Chinese companies are subject to the securities regulation of listing places and can be sued thereunder against their securities misconduct. As overseas-listed Chinese companies usually have their main assets located in China, it is important that Chinese courts recognize and enforce foreign securities judgments. However, there are many difficulties in this area, which undermine the efficacy of the regulation of cross-border securities transactions. In the quest for solutions, this book assesses the possibility of suing Chinese companies in the offshore financial centers where they are incorporated, finding that there would be similar issues with judgment enforcement in China. It also examines the viability of using arbitration as an alternative, arguing that arbitration may only supplement rather than substitute court litigation for resolving securities disputes. China should consider signing a bilateral treaty with the US, clarifying the principle of reciprocity, and ratifying the 2005 Hague Choice of Court Convention and even the 2019 Hague Judgment Convention. Hong Kong is also advised to expand its current judgment recognition arrangement with Mainland China to cover securities judgments and join the relevant international conventions.

Finally, cross-border listings should be understood as two-way traffic, including outbound listings (domestic companies going overseas) and inbound listings (foreign companies coming to China). Indeed, the issue of inbound listings is critical to the efforts of China to internationalize its capital market. This book thus examines how China has tried to develop and regulate the initial public offering and listing of foreign companies in its domestic market. Since 2018, China has launched a pilot program to allow the listing of "Red-chip Companies," which are established by Chinese people in offshore financial centers and are technically foreign companies. The Chinese regime for regulating foreign listings has similarities and differences with those in the US and Hong Kong, both of which have developed capital markets and are top destinations for Chinese companies to get listed overseas. This book suggests that China should follow the Hong Kong model to grant preferential treatment only to those cross-listed in China and also learn from the US experience with American Depositary Receipts to enhance the utility of Chinese Depository Receipts. At a more fundamental level, the 2018 pilot program reflects the gradualist approach that China has long adopted to conduct its economic reform, and in the long run, it will likely be expanded to cover more foreign companies. The prospect of China successfully achieving this goal will depend on a variety of factors, including political-economy factors and legal-regulatory factors. To this end, China needs to further improve the legal and institutional infrastructure of its securities markets.

These research findings will not only contribute to the existing literature on China's regulatory regime for overseas listings of domestic companies but also provide comparative insights for other jurisdictions that may face similar issues. They also have important practical implications for policymakers, regulators, judges, market institutions and participants both inside and outside China. For each of these audiences, the book has offered suggestions and words of caution.

Going forward, there is an area for further research: the impact of the rise of geopolitics on China's regulation of cross-border listings, including outbound listings of Chinese companies and inbound listings of foreign companies. In general, as geopolitical competition or conflict intensifies, states possess both the incentives and tools to ramp up their use of cross-border finance to advance their objectives. Driven largely by security concerns, states may erect new barriers to cross-border listings. Specifically, how will the regulators of both the home jurisdiction, namely, China, and the host jurisdictions, notably the US, respond to the rise of geopolitics? Whether, and if so, how will they adapt substantive rules and enforcement strategies? Beyond the regulators, how will other public actors and self-regulatory organizations such as stock exchanges respond? Will judges play a greater role in providing some outside oversight of national security issues? To what extent will the rise of geopolitics weaken international regulatory cooperation on cross-border listings? How will companies, investors, market intermediaries and other private actors respond to the rise of geopolitics? Will they restructure their activities, adopt new contractual provisions or otherwise adapt?

In sum, China's regulatory regime for cross-border listings is in significant flux, and the rise of geopolitics is set to have far-reaching implications. There are a variety of questions, both normative and empirical, on which research remains limited. This is a challenging area of study and requires a multidisciplinary approach, and thus, I hope that more scholars will weigh in from different disciplines and different jurisdictions. This book aims to begin a conversation and spark public debate in this area, serving as a starting point for further research.

INDEX

Printed by Integrated Books International,
United States of America